TRAIL GUIDE
TO LEARNING

Paths of Progress

Volume Two

DEBBIE STRAYER & LINDA FOWLER

Trail Guide to Learning: Paths of Progress - Volume 2

by Debbie Strayer and Linda Fowler

"A Day in the Life..." section contributed by Ashley Wiggers.

Published by Geography Matters, Inc.

2 Volume Set ISBN: 978-1-931397-69-8

Library of Congress Control Number: 2011924038

Printed in the United States of America

Geography Matters, Inc.
800.426.4650
www.geomatters.com

Dedication

We dedicate this book to all those who have bravely chosen to follow the path that the Lord laid before them, in spite of the time, sacrifice and faith it took to do so.

~Debbie Strayer

This book is lovingly dedicated to my mom, Edith, and mom-in-law, Laura, who continually amaze and inspire me…and to all the other moms out there whose hearts are anchored in their families. Bless you!

~Linda Fowler

Acknowledgements

Debbie~

To my husband Greg - Building families is a lot like building nations. You obediently followed the Lord's leading to find His path for us, diligently built and strengthened us to serve Him and each other, and creatively solved problems and encouraged each of us in our unique gifts and talents. Your love and example have inspired us all. Thank you for giving us these gifts, my love.

To my children - You are such blessings to me, and the reason that all of these works exist. I have learned, and continue to learn so much from each of you, especially during the precious time we spent together homeschooling. I am grateful that you know me and love me anyway, counting it as one of God's great blessings in my life. Ashley, thank you for taking up pen as well. How amazing to see my "pathway dream" fulfilled.

To my friend and co-author Linda - Our first book was an amazing jump into a fast moving, yet God-ordained, river. Our second book reflected His goodness and blessing, even as our vision grew larger. Our third book once again shows God's goodness, strength, and creativity. Thank you for taking this journey with me. Oh, the treasures we will have to offer our grandchildren!

To my family at Geography Matters - Thank you so much for partnering with me in this quest to bring Ruth's principles to life. Your wisdom and skill continue to make new and beautiful works appear that were once only dreams. May God richly bless you all for your perseverance, faith, and kindness towards me.

Linda~

Thank you, thank you, thank you to my amazing husband, Coke, for your unfailing support of this great adventure—evidenced daily by an uncanny ability to offer just the right encouragement and, maybe more importantly, to eat take-out with a smile. How incredibly blessed I am!

Shout-outs also to my unique and quirky kids, both those birthed and those grafted (through marriage)—Caleb, Cathryn, Betsy, Matt, Tracy, and Travis—for being so wonderfully individual and creative, and for giving me a tiny measure of understanding. How I wish we could've walked the Paths together!

To you of the Wiggers clan—Cindy, Josh, Alex, Ashley, and Libby—I'm so grateful. Your dedication and creative genius have attached wings to this project and prepared it to fly far beyond our hopes. Thank you so much for embracing the dream!

And you Debbie, my dear friend and cohort, are truly one of the most genuine and gifted people I know. I can't thank you enough for rescuing me from the aimlessness of my empty nest and inviting me to share the journey. It has been challenging, hilarious, stressful, humbling, euphoric, and a gigantic blessing. Even though it's not enough, thank you!

May the Lord bless and protect you all as you come and go, may He give you peace, and lavish His grace on all your efforts!

Table of Contents

Preface

Overview of the *Trail Guide to Learning Series* xi

Introduction to the *Trail Guide to Learning* Series

Why did we write the *Trail Guide to Learning* Series? xiii

What should you know about the third level
of the *Trail Guide to Learning* Series? xiv

Notes to make using the curriculum easier xiv

How will your school week look with the third level
of the *Trail Guide to Learning* Series? xv

Who can use this curriculum? xv

How can you adjust this curriculum to
accommodate middle school students? xvi

Lesson Contents xvii

   Copywork & Dictation xvii

   Reader xviii

   Read-Aloud & Discussion, Narration & Reflective Writing.... xviii

   Word Study xix

   Geography, Science, History & Economics xx

   Writing, Editing & Spelling xxi

   Music, Doing & Art... xxii

   Independent Reading & Record Keeping xxii

Student Notebook.. xxiii

Supportive Resources... xxiv

   Assessments xxiv

   Light for the Trail Bible Curriculum xxiv

   Lapbooks xxiv

   Parent Planner.. xxv

   Student Planner xxv

   Middle School Supplement xxv

Required Resource List.. xxvi

Optional Supportive Resources xxvi

Cultivating Greatness Unit

Lesson 1 1

Lesson 2 21

Lesson 3 39

Lesson 4 57

Lesson 5 77

Lesson 6 97

Success Takes Flight Unit

Lesson 1 111

Lesson 2 129

Lesson 3 149

Lesson 4 167

Lesson 5 187

Lesson 6 205

Reach for the Stars Unit

Lesson 1 217

Lesson 2 237

Lesson 3 253

Lesson 4 267

Lesson 5 283

Lesson 6 299

Appendix C

Lesson At A Glance

Cultivating Greatness 315

Success Takes Flight...321

Reach for the Stars...327

Skills Chart

Cultivating Greatness 333

Success Takes Flight...336

Reach for the Stars...338

Challenge Spelling List **340**

Presentation Feedback Sheet **342**

Conference Summary **342**

Game Answer Key

    Cultivating Greatness 344

    Success Takes Flight...347

    Reach for the Stars..350

Appendix D

Word Search **357**

Word Scramble **360**

Crossword **363**

Instructions

    Game Instructions..366

    Question Quest Game Board 369

    Claymation Istructions 370

Bingo

    Cultivating Greatness 375

    Success Takes Flight...383

    Reach for the Stars..391

Preface

Overview of the *Trail Guide to Learning* Series

What is the big picture of the *Trail Guide to Learning* Series, and why is it important to know? Just like the themes of this book, the answer to this question puts the pieces together in a way that you can use them. The two themes of this book are tools for thinking and the way systems and people work together. How does this information fit with the big picture of the series?

The first level, *Paths of Exploration*, shows the role that explorers played in the opening of America. It also models the way thoughts begin. When you begin thinking about something, you may only have questions. When the explorers came to our land, they had more questions than answers. Then they began exploring and discovered much new information, just as you do when you start to think about a question. They opened the way for the rest of us to follow by showing us how to ask questions. They observed their surroundings and recorded what they saw, which in turn brought up new questions as well as new understanding. For the explorers, as well as us, there were always questions to ask and answer, but the beginning of skilled observation, recording, and learning was set and a path blazed for those who would come next.

The second level, *Paths of Settlement*, introduces those who did come next, the builders and settlers. These citizens and leaders came to pursue the dream of freedom and began to build homes, communities, towns, and states that would give that opportunity to all who followed. Men and women devoted their lives to providing the structure of good government, good citizenship, and good examples for others to follow, so that they too could receive the blessings of freedom. As with our learning process, certain standards help us understand what works and what to do next. This level shows the laws of government and science that provide order to our thinking and the way we live. As they brought into being the rule of law that would govern us and secure the opportunity for freedom, our Founders knew that these laws would be tested with the struggles that all groups of people, both small and large, have to face.

The third level, *Paths of Progress*, talks about those who came along to help solve the many problems and difficulties we encountered, as people and as a nation. The focus in this level is on the scientists and inventors who devoted their time, understanding, and hopes to finding answers for the struggles and boundaries we faced. The nature of these determined people teach us much about the thinking process and how to share answers that others can understand. Inventors and scientists work together, building on each other's work to further the help that they give to others. The various topics studied in this level show the problem-solving process, the resulting improvements, and the way systems, such as systems in the body, work together to create success for the whole.

As the third level in the *Trail Guide to Learning* Series, *Paths of Progress* completes the process of preparation for the next step of thinking and learning we will explore in our next Path when we look at Ancient and World History. At the middle school level, students are ready in their maturity and thinking ability to look at civilizations of ancient history and compare them to their understanding of what a good citizen, government, and nation look like. Now they have a standard by which to compare other nations, events, and leaders effectively and to see principles in action.

Introduction to the
Trail Guide to Learning Series

Why did we write the *Trail Guide to Learning* Series?

- We wanted to create curriculum that was easy to use, yet able to lead students to develop higher thinking skills.

- We wanted the things learned to come from real books, discussion, and a variety of activities so that students would enjoy the process.

- We wanted information from different subject areas taught together in relationship to geography, as it occurs in real life.

- We wanted students to become better communicators by learning and practicing language skills along with what they were learning, instead of through separate drill and practice. That way their drawing, writing, and speaking would be a natural response to their thinking and learning.

- We wanted this book itself to be more than just a teacher's guide. We wrote it as a source of information for your student and a teacher's education course for you, giving you bite-sized and timely explanations of what we suggest you do, and why.

- Lastly, we wanted to provide a way to support your family's worldview.

It has taken years of labor and a team of workers, but we are excited to have met these goals in the third of the series, *Paths of Progress*.

It is important for you to know who helped produce this level, because that helps explain why it is different from other curricula, and why you can have confidence when using it. The team of people who designed, wrote, read, edited, and supported this effort is impressive. It includes veteran home educators Greg and Debbie Strayer, Coke and Linda Fowler, Josh and Cindy Wiggers, as well as young adults who were home educated, Ashley (Strayer) and Alex Wiggers. Renowned home education author, Dr. Ruth Beechick, remains Debbie's mentor and continues to influence her thoughts and works through personal input. We also highly value the assistance of the families who are using the first two levels of the *Trail Guide to Learning* Series, *Paths of Exploration* and *Paths of Settlement*, with their children and continue to give us helpful feedback.

Why does all this matter? As we say in our Steps for Thinking, "The key to understanding the actions of others is to understand their thoughts." If you know what our goals were, you will have a good starting point to use this curriculum to fit your own goals for your students. Now, look at the parts of the book and see how easy it is to make your goals a reality.

What should you know about the third level of the *Trail Guide to Learning* Series?

New in this Level: You will find several **new** sources of encouragement and information in *Paths of Progress*. *Thinking Skills Reminders* are placed throughout the text, helping you connect assignments and activities to the thinking skills they require.

Notes to make using the curriculum easier:

- Support is just a click away! Our Yahoo user group gives you an opportunity to be a part of the community of those who are traveling the Trail! Post questions, share experiences, and read the thoughts of others who are using our materials with their families. You can find the group at:
  http://tech.groups.yahoo.com/group/LearningSeries

- Because various editions of the same book often have different page numbers, the reading assignments in *Paths of Progress* include the first words of each passage. You may find it helpful to mark reading assignments ahead of time so that the flow of your school is not interrupted with finding beginning and ending points.

- A standard materials list is included below. Most lessons require the use of these items:

crayons, markers, or colored pencils	highlighters
scissors, glue, tape	index cards
dictionary, thesaurus	CD player
Student Notebook	

  Included at the beginning of each lesson is a list of books and anything else needed for that lesson that is not part of the standard materials list.

- This curriculum continues to direct students to use research as an important part of gaining information. We believe parents are the best supervisors of their children's use of computers. Since online resources may be the source of information, we expect students to follow their parents' guidelines whenever they use the computer. Webpage descriptions can be misleading, and information locations can change, so we encourage parents to maintain supervision of all student computer use.

How would your school week look with the third level of the *Trail Guide to Learning* Series?

Paths of Progress consists of six units:

- **Great Leaps**
- **Perseverance Pays Off**
- **Success Takes Flight**
- **Making Connections**
- **Cultivating Greatness**
- **Reach for the Stars**

The first three are found in Volume 1, and the second three in Volume 2.

- Each unit contains six lessons with five parts and is designed to take about a week—but you retain the freedom to make the curriculum's schedule fit the needs of your students.

- Because of this, even though one Part can take one day, this curriculum is your servant, not your master.

- Flexibility is built in, since every Lesson 6 completes the assignments for the unit and provides a time of review and assessment.

- In addition, large parts of the lessons in Unit 6, Reach for the Stars, are devoted to review of the other units studied throughout the year. This review is an important part of making learning permanent.

Who can use this curriculum?

This curriculum targets grades 5, 6, and 7, but can be easily adapted for 4th grade abilities by reducing reading assignments, increasing the amount the teacher reads aloud, and substituting oral responses for written work. Younger students can easily fit into the activities, discussions, and presentations. Lapbooks are available that coordinate with many parts of the lessons. These are a great way to include younger students in curriculum lessons while they have their own age appropriate activities to complete. The tactile and visual reinforcements of the graphic organizers used can increase learning and retention for many students. Older students may also take the opportunity to "be the teacher" to younger siblings through the use of the lapbook activities. (See more about lapbooks in the Supportive Resources section of this introduction.)

In most assignments, the recommended activity levels are noted with icons: ✿✿ for the lowest, ✿ for higher, and ✿ for highest. **If there is no icon present, the activity is to be completed by all levels.** Before beginning a lesson, look at the Materials List in Part 1 to be sure you have the books and other items needed to complete the activities, in addition to the list of supplies used regularly. Also, most Part 5s contain additional resources and suggestions for **Enrichment Activities**. Enrichment Activities are available for your older students (8th grade and up) who are completing the curriculum with you, or for younger students who complete the lessons quickly or who just enjoy learning on a more in-depth level.

Grade level markings for assignments throughout the curriculum represent:

- ✿✿ 5th grade
- ✿ 6th grade
- ✿ 7th grade

Enrichment Activities:

- 8th grade and up
- Advanced students
- All students wanting to learn more

How can you adjust this curriculum to accommodate middle school students?

The upper level reading, thinking, presentation, and discussion activities are appropriate for this age. The Enrichment Activities provide an opportunity for more in-depth study, which is the best way to extend learning to a deeper level. Assign additional literature to read from the Enrichment Activities section, and then follow the format in the language skills sections (choose a passage to write from dictation, define unknown vocabulary, identify usage and mechanics activities in the literature read, etc.) In writing, extend the activities to include greater length, or greater frequency. In the science and history activities, ask your middle school students to learn more about the topics to share with you or other students. Challenge them to vary their presentation styles to include multi-media presentations, plays, games, etc. This is a perfect time to increase responsibility for learning and sharing what they know.

Middle School Supplements are available for each level of the *Trail Guide to Learning* Series to provide more challenging assignments for older students, while maintaining the focus on similar content for multi-age teaching. These are available as digital downloads from Geography Matters.

A typical lesson should begin with an introduction of the **Steps for Thinking**. These are the big ideas demonstrated through the reading, discussion, and other activities of the lesson. Explain each step to your children and talk with them about any questions or ideas they have about it. You will revisit the **Steps for Thinking** at the end of the lesson, so don't require your students to understand them thoroughly at the beginning. By the end of the lesson, they will have more experience with the concepts and be able to discuss them more thoroughly.

Answers to the questions asked in the text and the Student Notebook are located either on the last page of each lesson or in one of that volume's appendices. In Volume 1, Appendix A contains teacher aides. These include At A Glance guides for each unit in the volume, skills and topics lists, answer keys, and Challenge Spelling lists. These spelling lists are comprised of words from the literature selections and make an excellent resource when you feel your students are ready for increased difficulty in their spelling practice. Appendix B includes charts and references helpful to the lessons and instructions for various games and activities assigned in the text. In Volume 2, Appendices C and D correspond to the same descriptions.

The **Student Resource CD**, which accompanies the text, contains Student Notebook pages for all three levels, game components, and other resources helpful in completing various activities. In addition, there is a section for the teacher that includes record-keeping and instructional tools from Appendices A and C.

Lesson Contents

Here is an in-depth description of each section in a typical lesson and how to use it. After you read this and begin using the curriculum, you will find many margin notes in the text to remind you of the important points contained here.

A. Copywork & Dictation

Copywork & Dictation provides a consistent method for students to see, hear, and write language correctly. It is the first step in learning language skills. Start your student with copying the passage. After copying, he should match what he has written word for word to the text and correct anything that is not the same. This level is appropriate for many fourth and fifth graders throughout the year. It may also be appropriate for older students, and needs to continue for as long as your student seems sufficiently challenged. From time to time, you may want to attempt a bit of dictation by asking your child to choose a sentence himself to write from dictation. Allow him to choose a sentence or passage that he has already worked with, to build confidence. Don't worry, this isn't cheating. Your goal is to build the ability to read and write language, and *teaching* means providing the support needed to be successful. Assessment should come later.

If your student is a sixth or seventh grader, evaluate his level when he has copied the passages a few times and decide whether this activity seems too easy for him. If so, try dictating, or speaking, the first few words of a sentence slowly and ask your student to write down what he hears. If he can write down at least a portion of the words correctly, then he is ready for dictation. The ability to write from dictation is a skill that must learned. It may be difficult at first, so give your student the help he needs. Allow him to become familiar with the sentence, or sentences, you dictate at first. You may even want to let him choose the sentence. After he is very successful at writing from dictation using this method, gradually start adding a few words of your choice. Remember that success is your goal, not quickly moving to more difficult dictation passages. Going through the process too quickly, without allowing your student the time to become successful and confident, may create resistance toward this type of language learning.

Another common problem, especially for younger students, is the struggle with handwriting. Before beginning the Copywork & Dictation process, decide whether manuscript or cursive handwriting is more easily used by your student. If handwriting is very frustrating and difficult for him, try different writing tools and surfaces. If he continues to experience difficulty, it is perfectly acceptable to allow your child to type the passages. The goal is for your student to see the words, hear the words, and write the words. Remember that it is more important for him to learn the spelling mechanics and reading skills that result from dictation and copying than it is to handwrite the passage.

B. Reader

The natural method of learning continues in this section, the **Reader** assignments. These assignments occur in real literature, and there are several reasons why this is important. Real literature is more interesting. The language used is more natural. A willingness to read builds as your student experiences the success of reading a real book.

Struggling readers are to read their assignments aloud. The purpose for this is to build reading fluency. Fluency, or the ability to read something effortlessly, is also an important part of comprehension. If a student can read a passage aloud with expression, correct phrasing, and attention to punctuation, it is much more likely that he will also understand the meaning of the passage. To practice fluency at all levels, use passages that your student can read without constant decoding. In other words, start with a few sentences that seem easy for the student to read. Often, you can have him choose the passages for fluency practice, and sometimes you can select them in order to gauge his growth. To do this, find a passage that is a sentence or two longer than the last one he read, or one that contains structures requiring attention to punctuation, such as dialogue. Real books are perfect for this fluency practice. Artificial fluency practice is unnecessary when literature provides such an abundant source of reading materials.

Each reader is coordinated with the unit and provides a ready-made history or science lesson. The lives of real people become linked to places and events. In turn, this connection brings character and convictions to light, as well as great adventures and drama. From the wellspring of literature, examples of mechanics and word usage come, as well as phonics principles, spelling patterns, and vocabulary.

Every student is to read or listen to **all** literature selections for the unit. Reading or hearing the various perspectives adds richness to the stories and depth to the understanding of the events and circumstances of the times. Critical thinking skills build as the related stories allow students to compare and contrast to find similarities and differences. An artist's illustrations contribute to learning about context clues, and the divisions of chapters and paragraphs help students recognize important main ideas and details that support the bigger ideas. All of these lessons come naturally from real books.

C. Read-Aloud & Discussion, Narration & Reflective Writing

Most parents agree that it is good to read aloud to young children to develop pre-reading skills. However, the benefits don't stop there. Reading aloud to children of all ages is one of the easiest, most enjoyable, and effective ways to share ideas and begin thoughtful conversations. Since your child does not have to worry about decoding during read-aloud time, he can focus totally on the meaning of what he is hearing. This allows him the opportunity to think about the ideas and information being presented and to formulate his own thoughts. It prepares your child to respond to what he has heard through discussion, retelling, or reflective writing.

Read-Aloud: As you read aloud, you also model fluency, expression, and comprehension. When your voice reflects punctuation, your child can see its purpose and the way it makes the passage more understandable. As he listens and sometimes follows along with his eyes, your child sees the language and hears it read correctly, which provides an excellent example for his reading. Because of this, Read-Aloud assignments are an important part of each lesson.

Narration and Discussion: Read-Aloud assignments also provide the basis for student responses. As they listen, it is natural for them to respond by speaking, which is a good first step toward meaningful discussion. In the give-and-take of discussion, you can listen to your children's understanding of the passage, ask questions, and share your thoughts. All of these combine to expand their thinking on the topic. It also lends itself to the natural memory practice of narration, or retelling. As students become familiar with the process of retelling, their ability to recall main ideas and details develops. Narration can take many forms, such as predicting outcomes, asking and answering questions, as well as retelling from the point of view of a particular character. All of these activities build the ability to narrate or retell what they have heard. The last step in the process of response is writing.

Some units may include **reflective writing**, which involves responding to a passage your children have heard by writing their thoughts about it. This is one of the most complex ways for your children to respond. It is also a very concrete way to use writing to answer questions. The answers given are correct because they come from your children's thoughts and understanding of what they heard. Discussion, narration, and reflective writing are good, natural ways for a teacher to see what her students understood from what they heard.

D. Word Study

This section exists to equip your child with strategies to gain meaning from unknown or unfamiliar words. This information must be connected to other learning in order to remain with your child on a long term basis. So the best time to teach him about phonics, word usage, mechanics, vocabulary, spelling, and grammar is when he reads a word, phrase, or sentence or hears it used in a story. Study of a sound or word form is natural and makes sense to your child when he sees a need to read, understand, and use that word. Word Study activities occur in every lesson, taking advantage of the opportunities presented in the literature to connect meaning and structure for your student.

Vocabulary is a focus of this curriculum as students make and collect cards with words and meanings listed. The purpose of this activity is not memorization or dictionary skills, but understanding. By building an awareness of new or unusual words, you are teaching your student an important strategy for understanding what he has read or heard. New vocabulary words appear in the context of a lesson or story, which helps your child recognize that the way a word is used is closely connected to its meaning. This is an important reading strategy called using context clues. As your child completes the vocabulary activities in this curriculum, he sees the importance of learning and using new words as he reads, writes, discusses, and retells.

Word Building is introduced in this level, with a focus on Latin and Greek word parts and the many ways they are used today. This section builds an awareness of these word parts, an understanding of their meanings, and then uses the **Rummy Roots** game for fun practice. Students get the best of the study of word origins with a meaningful and easy-to-apply approach.

&. Geography, Science, History & Economics

The studies of Geography, Science, History, and Economics are connected. The knowledge of one area contributes to knowledge in the other areas. By considering the linkage of subjects in real life, connections occur naturally for your students. This helps them add to what they know when they encounter new information. It also helps students remember what they have learned. **Connections** are an important part of this curriculum.

Geography is the umbrella from which the other studies connect. Geography includes the study of places. If you learn about places, you learn about the impact those places have on people. If you learn about people, you learn about cultures and worldviews, and the impact those people have on places. So in the study of geography, you naturally learn about people, places, and all the ways they affect each other. All culture, history, and science connect to concepts of geography, so we study **Science** and **History** in the light of their connection to the people and places encountered by the inventors, scientists, and problem-solvers found in this level.

Science is naturally enjoyable to children when they can begin to connect its principles to their own lives. In Volume 1, students explore the building blocks of progress through the hands-on approach of *The World of Tools and Technology*. While the word *technology* does not actually describe a specific area of science, it does refer to an end-result of research and experimentation done by scientists and applied by inventors through the use of basic tools. This study is therefore a perfect connection and complement to your student's literature about inventors and scientists. Volume 2 provides an activity-based exploration of the structures and systems that make up the most astounding "machine" ever designed and created—the human body.

In addition, this curriculum encourages research and reading as a means of obtaining more information about topics of interest. Engaging students this way is often as valuable in learning science as doing activities.

History is a daily part of the curriculum through literature readings, discussions, and activities. The study of history that focuses on dates and facts alone can be dry and hard to remember. When events in history are associated through the literature, the geography, and the relevant science concepts, it connects the learning and is much more likely to be retained. Great stories and biographies help students connect to the struggles and triumphs of the times. Literature provides a basis for discussion and evaluation of the decisions made and the results that occurred. Since some of the events covered in this volume include the injustices of life and some episodes of suffering, please preview literature assignments to make sure they are appropriate for all participating students. Books read by the students, and read aloud by the teacher, provide the thread that ties the events, struggles, and decisions of the inventors, scientists, and problem-solvers together. Learning **History** could not be more natural.

Another natural connection to the study of history is the study of **Economics**. In this level, students learn the basics of economics and how they apply to the real-life situations of inventors, scientists, and their own families. The study of information from maps, graphs, and charts also gives students experience in reading and interpreting this information as it relates to economics.

F. Writing, Editing & Spelling

Learning new things should inspire a response. Since you are not limited to conventional school-type methods, you can employ an array of effective and enjoyable ways of gaining and responding to information. **Writing** is an integrated part of this curriculum. It is not a separate subject, but rather a set of skills with which to become familiar. Writing ability improves with practice and time, both of which come in the context of literature, history, science, and geography learning. Writing is best when it is a response to thinking about content learned, new ideas, or activities completed. Since writing begins with thinking, once your children engage in assigned thinking activities, the way is naturally prepared. As you use this approach, your students will begin to see themselves as writers, which is the first and most important step to becoming a writer.

Rather than relying on artificial exercises and work sheets, the **Editing** sections help build your children's awareness and recognition of punctuation, parts of speech, and correct usage in the context of their literature. Abstract grammar ideas and often-confusing rules become meaningful when illustrated and identified in this concrete way. In turn, when a concept has meaning, your student can apply it naturally in his writing.

Spelling is a skill that has several components, such as perceptual ability and memory. Some of us are naturally good at spelling, and some are not. The goal of the spelling assignments is to improve your child's ability to spell by helping him make connections to meaning, phonics, and word patterns. Memorizing a list is not as valuable to your child as increasing his ability to comfortably write words that express his understanding and opinions. The goal then, is to increase your child's ability to recognize and spell more words correctly—not just to be able to spell a new word correctly for a week or two and then forget it.

G. Music, Doing & Art

In this curriculum students will learn about many people, inventions, and innovations that have changed and advanced industry and the sciences. The **Music** sections expand that concept by demonstrating that a very similar progression has also occurred in the composition and performance of classical music. Students will learn about different periods of musical styles, some famous composers who contributed to those periods, and the development of the orchestra. In addition, since the process of **doing** something is such a powerful teacher and motivator, your child will have an opportunity to explore his own style by learning to read music and play a recorder.

New inventions very often begin with an idea, which over time may become a sketch, which eventually becomes a model, which finally becomes a design. Since clay sculpting allows almost unlimited flexibility, it is the perfect medium for students to experiment with design. In the **Art** sections, students are encouraged to practice simple techniques and then use them to express their own unique ideas. This natural process stimulates creativity and nurtures attention to detail, which in turn equips students to communicate their thoughts more effectively.

H. Independent Reading & Record Keeping

This is an important part of each student's daily schedule. It provides regular practice for word study and reading skills, as well as time for practice of thinking skills. Quiet time to consider ideas and tie new information with old is essential in building new understandings. Though you may be tempted to skip this activity to save time, please don't!

Something new in this level is a student copy of each lesson's At A Glance chart in the Student Notebook. Personally recording his accomplishments on this chart, as well as on his Reading Log, will help your child achieve a sense of responsibility and ownership for his assignments. It is also a step in developing student responsibility and independence, since these types of records are important additions to any portfolio.

Student Notebook

The Student Notebook is not only a vital part of this curriculum, but it also provides a **portfolio** of your student's work. Games, graphics, charts, and other activities assigned in the text are included in an easy, ready-to-use format for your student.

Having the Student Notebook on CD allows you to print all the pages for your child's level either before you begin a unit, or lesson by lesson. We suggest that students keep their notebooks in a three-ring bider, which allows them to add or remove pages as needed. Unit games can be printed from the CD and laminated or printed separately on card stock for greater durability. All in all, you and your students have the flexibility to adapt the notebook to your individual needs.

How can you begin to transfer the responsibility for completing assignments from yourself to your student? Reading Logs and Lesson At A Glance charts are included in the Student Notebook to facilitate this process. The student has a ready-made task list to guide and direct his efforts, and the teacher can tell at a glance what needs to be done. This checklist system encourages your student to take responsibility for his daily work and allows him to be easily accountable for assignments.

A portfolio is often the best possible written measure of student achievement. Completion of the Student Notebook creates an excellent, consecutive record of student work in reading, writing, geography, history, science, and art. The Student Notebook gives teacher, student, and evaluator a clear picture of sequential progress in each subject area, samples of student work, and examples of creative projects. It includes dates that assignments were completed, assisting with the documentation process. This helps teachers to see the amount of time spent on each unit, as well as giving your student a sense of accomplishment as he looks over the finished product.

Print the Student Notebook pages directly from the CD-ROM that came with this book. Or if you prefer, pre-printed, 3-hole punched notebooks pages are also available separately. (See Resources)

Supportive Resources

Assessments

For those who prefer not to use the portfolio method of evaluation, or who want to supplement their child's portfolio, **assessments** for each level of the first five units are available on a separate CD. The assessments for this level include both objective assessments on the content presented, as well as performance assessments in writing. Guidance is included for administering the assessments, evaluating the results, conferencing with your student, and planning for future improvements. These, coupled with your daily observations and interactive discussions and games, provide ample material upon which to base an accurate evaluation. There is no assessment for Unit 6, Reach for the Stars, since this unit is largely devoted to review of the previous five. The review activities serve as evaluation tools themselves and can be assigned point values if you choose.

Light for the Trail Bible Curriculum

This optional Bible curriculum helps your student make the most important connection of all—the one between his faith and his view of the world around him. This easy-to-use guide provides daily assignments, which include Memory Verses for the lesson, discussion topics, writing assignments, suggestions for in-depth study, and longer-term Memory Projects. These elements blend with Prayer Times, Worship Times, and Blazing the Trail (teacher sharing) to enable students to make real-life connections between the content of the curriculum and the lessons of Scripture. **New** to this supplement is a more in-depth level of Scripture study using the inductive method. This gives your children a chance to connect Scriptures and their application in both the past and present to the history and context of the passages themselves.

Lapbooks

Lapbook Activity

These resources are available to accompany each level of the *Trail Guide to Learning* Series. The lapbooks were created to build and review the concepts and content taught by the curriculum, with hands-on reinforcement. These graphic organizers can make learning memorable for all ages. If you use the lapbooks, those activities are designed to **replace** any corresponding Student Notebook assignments, particularly for younger students. They may also be beneficial to many older students who prefer a more hands-on approach to learning, or for review. Assignments that have corresponding lapbooking activities are indicated by the lapbook symbol shown on this page. Lapbooks are available printed, CD-ROM, or digital download formats.

Parent Planner

This is a new tool to help parents organize their record-keeping information. It also contains the *Teacher Connections*, which offer continuous teacher training. This wonderful resource refers teaching parents to *You Can Teach Your Child Successfully*, by Dr. Ruth Beechick. This book provides timely information that help you understand teaching strategies that work, and why.

Student Planner

This is another new tool to help your children begin to assist with the processes of record-keeping needed as you homeschool. Not only that, but it also is a source of encouragement as students see the overall plan of the curriculum for themselves as they track assignment completion and maintain reading logs. This is an easy-to-use and enjoyable way to continue the transfer of responsibility for learning from teaching parent to child.

Middle School Supplement

The Middle School Supplement enables older members of the family to learn together with their siblings, while tying subjects together in a meaningful way. It covers the same content with more challenging assignments. At the time of this printing, the supplement is available in CD-ROM and digital download format.

Required Resource List

The following materials are required for use with *Paths of Progress*. For ordering information see Resources at the back of the book.

Volume 1
Samuel F. B. Morse by John Hudson Tiner
Munford Meets Robert Fulton by Jamie Aramini
Ben and Me by Robert Lawson
The Wright Brothers by Charles Ludwig
Caddie Woodlawn by Carol Ryrie Brink
Thomas Edison by Janet and Geoff Benge
The New Way Things Work by David Macaulay
The World of Tools and Technology by Dinah Zike and Susan Simpson

Volume 2
George Washington Carver by David Collins
Strawberry Girl by Lois Lenski
The Wright Brothers by Charles Ludwig
Homer Price by Robert McCloskey
Alan Shepard by Janet and Geoff Benge
Miracles on Maple Hill by Virginia Sorensen
Human Body Basics by Libby Lim & Linda Fowler

Core (for Volumes 1 and 2)
The Story of Inventions by Frank P. Bachman
The Story of Inventions Answer Key
The Story of the Orchestra (Book & CD) by Robert Levine
Basix Recorder Method (Book & CD) by Morty Manus
Create Anything With Clay by Sherri Haab and Laura Torres
Profiles from History, Volume 3 by Ashley Wiggers
Classroom Atlas of the United States
Soprano Recorder
Rummy Roots cards
Student Notebook pages (Print from CD included with curriculum or use preprinted pages available separately.)

Optional Supportive Resources

Paths of Progress Assessments (CD-ROM)
Paths of Progress Light for the Trail Bible Curriculum (CD-ROM or digital download)
Middle School Supplement (CD-ROM or digital download)
Paths of Progress Lapbook Set Volume 1 (printed)
Paths of Progress Lapbook Set Volume 2 (printed)
Paths of Progress Lapbook, 2 Volume Set (CD-ROM or digital download)
Paths of Progress Student Notebook pages, printed and three-hole punched, available by grade level for each volume
You Can Teach Your Child Successfully by Dr. Ruth Beechick

Lesson 1, Part 1

> ### ❧ Steps for Thinking ❧
>
> 1. Understanding something new comes from asking questions and discussing the answers.
>
> 2. Relating new information to something you already know makes learning easier. Connect new information to what you already know to help it find a place in what you remember.
>
> 3. New ideas and ways of doing things are often hard for people to accept.

You may want to post the Steps for Thinking somewhere nearby for easy reference. Read these with your students, or have the students read them by themselves. Explain any concept or vocabulary that is not understood.

𝒜. Copywork & Dictation   *Language Skills*

Look carefully at your assigned passage below, and read it silently. Show your teacher any words you don't know, and practice saying them aloud. Now read the passage aloud, or ask your teacher to read it to you.

When you are finished copying or writing from dictation, compare your copy to the text and make any needed corrections.

🐾☙ Copy or write as your teacher dictates from *The Story of Inventions*, page 67, paragraph 2 ("The primary sources…").

☙ Write as your teacher dictates from *The Story of Inventions*, page 67, paragraph 2 ("The primary sources…"), and page 70, paragraph 1 ("Eli was not more than…").

ℬ. Reader   *Language Skills, History*

Strawberry Girl: page 1 (Prologue) through page 10, paragraph 4
The Story of Inventions: page 67 (Chapter 6) to the top of page 71 ("A Visit to the South")

Follow the directions below to read or listen to the assigned passage in *Strawberry Girl*.

Before you begin your assignment in *The Story of Inventions*, scan it for any words you don't know and write them on a piece of scrap paper. Read over any section titles included in the passage—and then, as you read or listen to a section, think about how it relates to its title.

When you are finished, find the Comprehension Questions at the end of Chapter 6 in *The Story of Inventions*, and use complete sentences to write the answers to Questions 1 and 2 in your Student Notebook.

❧Materials❧

- *Strawberry Girl*
- *George Washington Carver*
- *The Story of Inventions*
- *Human Body Basics*
- *The Story of the Orchestra* book & CD
- *Basix Recorder Method*
- *Create Anything With Clay*
- *Profiles from History, Volume 3*
- Recorder
- Polymer clay
- Activity (Part 1):
    Cardstock
    Brad
- Activity (Part 4)
    Rolling pin or round jar
    Table knife

ℬ. Answers to questions from *The Story of Inventions* are located in the Answer Key for that book.

🐾 Read the above assignment from *Strawberry Girl* aloud, and then follow along as someone else reads the assignment from *The Story of Inventions*.

🐾 Read the above assignment from *Strawberry Girl* silently, and then read the assignment from *The Story of Inventions* aloud.

🐾 Read the above assignments from *Strawberry Girl* and *The Story of Inventions* silently.

C. Read-Aloud & Narration
History, Language Skills, Thinking Skills

George Washington Carver: page 1 (Chapter 1) through page 6

Follow the directions below to read or listen to the above passage. Then, in your own words, tell what happened in the portion you are assigned. Try to remember as many details as possible. If necessary you may reread, or listen as your teacher rereads, the part you are to retell.

🐾 Listen carefully as your teacher reads the above assignment aloud. Choose one page to retell.

🐾 Listen carefully as your teacher reads the above assignment aloud. Choose two pages to retell.

🐾 Read the assignment aloud, and then retell the entire passage.

D. Each word in bold letters is considered a vocabulary word. It is a word that may or may not be new to your children. You can write these vocabulary words on index cards and use them for occasional review, but not for memorizing. Give your children the meaning of the words if they don't remember. Try to use the new vocabulary words during conversation, and encourage your students to do the same.

Each time your students make a vocabulary card for this unit, have them write CG (for Cultivating Greatness) in the upper left corner. This will make it possible to review vocabulary by unit at the end of the year.

D. Vocabulary
Language Skills, Thinking Skills

Gather all your Unit 3 vocabulary cards and mix them up. (These are the cards with *PPO* written in the upper left corner). Then divide them into two stacks, either by **estimating** (making your best guess) or by counting. Choose one of the piles to review in this section and set the other aside to use later in Part 3.

Begin your review by picking a card. Read the word on the front and, without looking, tell your teacher either what it means or how it was used in the story. Give yourself a point for every word you are able to use correctly—see how many points you can get!

E. Science
Thinking Skills

You've been learning about huge advances in technology, which came about through obtaining greater knowledge and creating new inventions. During the same time period, however, giant steps were also taken in understanding the most amazing and technical machine ever created—the human body.

In Volume 2 of the *Paths of Progress*, you will be guided step-by-step through *Human Body Basics*. This book introduces organs and systems that are vital to the human body, as well as the things from which they're made. To get an idea of what you'll be doing, read the Getting Started section of the *Human Body Basics* book with your

Lapbook Activity

teacher. Next, complete the reading assignment below and follow the remaining directions.

Human Body Basics, Body Basics: beginning of chapter, Atoms, & Molecules

As you read through the assigned portion, choose words that are new or unfamiliar and make vocabulary cards for them as directed. Keep your science cards separate from other vocabulary.

🌵🌵 at least three words

🐾🐾 at least four words

Read and discuss the information in the sections with your teacher and do the *Labwork 1* activity. A page for your list is provided in your Student Notebook.

When you are finished, follow the directions to complete the first *Examine This* project at the end of the chapter. The Elements Exercise is in your Student Notebook.[1]

Lapbook Activity

ℱ. Writing   *Language Skills, Thinking Skills*

Expository writing explains how to do something, usually step-by-step. Choose a science activity you completed in this lesson (or in Unit 3), and write one or two paragraphs in your Student Notebook describing how you did it. Your description should be detailed enough that anyone reading it could go through the steps and complete the same activity.

You might want to write the steps on scrap paper first, and put them in order. Then think about how you would like your paragraph(s) to read. Be sure to use words like *first, then, next,* and *finally* to connect your sentences and make the order more clear.

🌵🌵 Choose one activity.

🐾🐾 Choose two activities.

𝒢. Music   *Thinking Skills*

So far in this study, you have had opportunities to hear compositions by many major composers in a wide variety of musical styles. Each composer, his style, and the period in which he wrote music were very different from one another. Some things common to all of them, however, are the instruments used to express the compositions.

In this volume, you will study the modern orchestra sections and instruments and learn to identify some of the sounds they produce. Begin by reading pages 42 through 45 in *The Story of the Orchestra* with your teacher and discussing the information about the string section and the violin. Then listen to "Symphony No. 4" on Track

13 of your CD. Were you able to hear the *pizzicato*? How did this music make you feel?

Now listen to "Sonata for Violin and Piano in A Major" on Track 14. Retell the short story about its composition and popularity (on page 44 of the book) to your teacher or another family member. What did you enjoy or dislike about the music?

When you are finished, listen carefully to Tracks 13 and 14 again and choose your favorite. Then, draw and color a picture in your Student Notebook of the image this music brings to your mind.

H. Reading fluency is developed through having frequent silent reading opportunities that continue for the length of time suggested here. Since a primary focus of this activity is to nurture your child's enjoyment of reading, help him to choose reading materials that interest him and at a level that allows him to read with understanding by himself. You can incorporate this activity into your school day whenever it is most convenient.

H. **Independent Reading & Record Keeping**   *Thinking Skills*

Review the Lesson 1 At A Glance chart in your Student Notebook to see if all the work you've done in this part has been checked off. Also, make sure the Student Notebook pages you worked on are dated and complete.

When you are finished, choose something to read that you will enjoy. Then find a quiet, comfortable place and read for the following length of time:

🐾🖐 30 minutes   🐾 35 minutes

Be sure to write down what you read today on the Reading Log in your Student Notebook.

Lesson 1, Part 2

A. **Copywork & Dictation**   *Language Skills*

Look carefully at this lesson's Steps for Thinking and read them silently. Show your teacher any words you don't know, and practice saying them aloud. Now read the Steps aloud, or ask your teacher to read them to you.

When you are finished copying or writing from dictation, compare your copy to the text and make any needed corrections.

🐾 Copy the Steps for Thinking, and tell your teacher an example of each Step.

🖐 Write the Steps for Thinking as your teacher dictates them. Then, write one example of each Step in your Student Notebook. Be sure to use complete sentences.

❧ Write the Steps for Thinking as your teacher dictates them. Then, in your Student Notebook, write two examples of each Step. Be sure to use complete sentences.

B. Reader *Language Skills, History*

Strawberry Girl: page 10, paragraph 5 ("Birdie took the little…") through page 17, paragraph 3
The Story of Inventions: page 71 ("A Visit to the South") to page 75 ("Seeking the Reward")

Follow the directions below to read or listen to the assigned passage in *Strawberry Girl*.

Before you begin your assignment in *The Story of Inventions*, scan it for any words you don't know and write them on a piece of scrap paper. Read over any section titles included in the passage—and then, as you read or listen to a section, think about how it relates to its title.

When you are finished, find the Comprehension Questions at the end of Chapter 6 in *The Story of Inventions* and use complete sentences to write the answers to Questions 3, 4, and 5 in your Student Notebook.

❧❧ Read the above assignment from *Strawberry Girl* aloud, and then follow along as someone else reads the assignment from *The Story of Inventions*.

❧ Read the above assignment from *Strawberry Girl* silently, and then read the assignment from *The Story of Inventions* aloud.

❧ Read the above assignments from *Strawberry Girl* and *The Story of Inventions* silently.

C. Read-Aloud & Discussion *History, Language Skills, Thinking Skills*

George Washington Carver: page 7 ("Some people said…") through page 13, paragraph 1

Follow the directions below to read or listen to the above assignment. Then make up questions about the part of the story you just read or heard. Write your questions in your Student Notebook and ask your teacher to answer them. After discussing her thoughts, write down the best possible answer on the lines provided. Be sure to use complete sentences.

❧❧ Listen carefully as your teacher reads the above assignment aloud. Make up two questions.

❧ Listen carefully as your teacher reads the above assignment aloud. Make up three questions.

❧ Read the above assignment aloud, then make up four questions.

C. As you read aloud, you model fluency, expression, and comprehension. When your voice reflects punctuation, students can see its purpose and the way it makes the passage more understandable.

D. Word Building
Language Skills, Thinking Skillss

As you have learned, the English language comes from parts of many other languages. Many words you know and use often come from languages such as Greek (the language spoken in Greece) and Latin (the language spoken in Ancient Rome, but no longer used in everyday life). In this unit you will continue to learn about several word-parts and what they mean.

Today's word-part is **chrono-** or **chronos-**, which is a Greek word that means *time*.

Look up the following words in the dictionary, and write each definition in your Student Notebook. Then underline the word-part *chrono-* or *chronos-* in each word. Think and be ready to tell your teacher how each definition relates to the meaning of the Greek word.

chronology	chronometer	chronological
chronogram	chronograph	chronoscope
chronobiology	chronometric	chronometry

E. Discussion is very important in developing your child's ability to organize his thoughts. This in turn builds the ability to think and write. The goal of discussing things with your student is not just to find the answer to a particular question, but also to create a situation where thoughts are shared and considered in a detailed way. Do not rush this activity, but encourage your student to share his ideas relating to the topic or events, and any additional ideas that may come to mind. You can also share your own thoughts and questions as an example.

Lapbook Activity

E. History
Thinking Skills, Geography

Ever since the beginning of the United States, the family farm has been foundational to its character and success. Even before it became a nation, many immigrants came to this country eager to get land of their own. They longed to raise enough food for themselves and their families, free of the **shackles**, or obstacles, of working to make others successful. These family farms dotted the countryside, creating a network of frontiers, neighbors, villages, and towns throughout America. Even those who began their working lives as indentured servants in order to come to America, held out for the dream of building their own homes and becoming independent. Though the family farm has seen many changes over the years, it remains a reminder of Americans' desire to live freely.

Agriculture is the business and science of growing crops and raising livestock. Since everyone needs food to live, it is an important part of any economy. Farms are where agriculture takes place, whether they are small or large, here or in another country. As surprising as it may seem, small family farms still make up the greatest percentage of farms in America. Before the 2010 Census, or official count of the population, estimates suggested that there were over two million farms in America. A farm, for economic purposes, must sell products to others that total yearly sales of at least $1,000. If it doesn't do that, it is not considered a farm by the government. That means, in our economy, a family-run enterprise that raises crops or livestock just to feed itself is not a farm.

The vast majority of farms are small and owned by families. These small farms take up more than half of the land used for farming in America, but they do not produce most of the crops and live-stock. Though smaller in number, large farms that are usually run by businesses, not families, make up a much larger amount of the products for  sale. So even though smaller farms have more land and are greater in number, larger farms, usually non-family operations, make up a greater part of the agriculture economy. Why do you think that is?

Many of the newer practices in agriculture depend on modern technology and equipment. This technology and equipment can be very expensive and hard for small farmers to purchase. From **irrigation**, or watering systems, to **fertilizer** (used to promote plant growth) or **pesticides** (chemicals used to kill bugs that eat crops), these developments increase the amount of crops grown or livestock raised. When a greater amount of a product sells, that lowers the price of the product. Most consumers want to buy goods, such as food, at the lowest price possible. Can you think of any problems that might arise from the use of some products such as fertilizer and pesticides?

Throughout the years, farmers have done something else very important for the country. They have taken care of the land that they have farmed. Many farmers have learned how to make the soil rich and productive, use water more efficiently, or raise crops in healthier ways. You will learn much about the science of agriculture through studying great scientists like George Washington Carver. This will help you understand the importance of agriculture to your family, as consumers of food, and as residents of this country.

Where does your family get its food? Talk with your parents about why they buy your food where they do. Are there any farms in your area? Are they owned by families or by companies? Are they large or small? Are there ways to purchase food directly from farmers or gardeners, through farmer's markets or roadside stands? Is this something your parents would do? Ask them why they would or would not do this. How do you think large farms affect the ability of small farms to sell their produce?

🐾🐾 Learn more about trends in farming today, such as organic farming.

How is organically raised produce different from regular produce? Would your family purchase food that was organic? Why or why not? Tell your family what you discover.

🐾 With your parent's assistance, visit a store that sells organic produce. (Many supermarkets now have an organic section.) Use the chart in your student notebook to compare the prices of six items, such as a pound of apples, a half-gallon of milk, or a dozen eggs. Fill in the prices for foods that are non-organic and the same foods that are organic. What do you observe? What differences do you see in the descriptions of the items on their labels? Which items would you prefer and why?

F. Editing
Language Skills, Thinking Skills

In *Strawberry Girl* the use of **dialect**, or language that is particular to a certain region or group of people, paints a colorful picture of the people who lived in Florida at the beginning of the 1900s. If you are not used to listening to people who speak in a dialect, it may be hard at first to understand what they are saying. It is important to try to translate the sentences in your mind as you listen or read so that you will get the meaning of the story. This may take some practice.

Read the following sentence to your teacher and discuss its meaning:

"Shore 'nough, that do look like one of our cows, now don't it?"

It can be translated in this way:

"That surely looks like one of our cows, doesn't it?"

Choose sentences from *Strawberry Girl* that include dialect and translate them aloud for your teacher.

🐾🐾 two sentences

🐾 three sentences

🐾 four sentences

🐾🐾🐾 One of the differences between English and various dialects is that their grammar is different. **Grammar**, or the rules for speaking or writing a language, helps you know which word to choose to clearly express your thoughts. One of the most important ideas in grammar is **agreement**. In this unit, you will learn about two types of agreement.

The first type is **subject-verb agreement**. This means that the subject and verb in your sentences must agree in number. If you have a **singular** subject, or one person or thing that is the focus of your sentence, you must have a verb that goes with that one subject. Here are some examples:

Dad <u>eats</u> steak for dinner.

Mom <u>likes</u> pizza for dinner.

If you have a **plural** subject, or more than one person or thing that is the focus of your sentence, you must have a verb that goes with more than one subject. Here is an example:

Mom and *Dad* <u>eat</u> steak for dinner.

Mom and *Dad* <u>like</u> pizza for dinner.

Find sentences in your literature that show singular (one) and plural (more than one) subject-verb agreement, and write them in your Student Notebook.

🐾 one sentence showing each (singular and plural)

🐾 two sentences showing each

🐾 three sentences showing each

G. Music

Thinking Skills

Read pages 29 and 30 in the *Basix Recorder Method* to learn about key signatures and ties. Write the names of notes you're not sure of above the staffs on those pages and practice playing the melodies.

Don't forget to listen to the *Recorder Method* CD track shown on page 30 to hear a sample of that lesson and use your Finger Placement Tabs if you need to. Take the quiz and show your teacher how you did.

Be sure to spend about 20 minutes a day practicing what you have learned!

H. Independent Reading & Record Keeping

Thinking Skills

Review the Lesson 1 At A Glance chart in your Student Notebook to see if all the work you've done in this part has been checked off. Also, make sure the Student Notebook pages you worked on are dated and complete.

When you are finished, choose something to read that you will enjoy. Then find a quiet, comfortable place and read for the following length of time:

🐾 🐾 30 minutes   🐾 35 minutes

Be sure to write down what you read today on the Reading Log in your Student Notebook.

G. Personal experience helps make learning more memorable. As you encourage your child in this activity, recall any personal experiences you have had in learning something new. This could include starting a new job, practicing a difficult hobby, learning to play an instrument, and so forth. This connection between knowledge and experience can make information meaningful.

Lesson 1, Part 3

A. **Copywork & Dictation** *Language Skills*

Look carefully at your assigned passage below, and read it silently. Show your teacher any words you don't know, and practice saying them aloud. Now read the passage aloud, or ask your teacher to read it to you.

When you are finished copying or writing from dictation, compare your copy to the text and make any needed corrections.

🐾 🐾 Copy or write as your teacher dictates from *The Story of Inventions*, page 78, paragraph 1 ("Whitney's first idea…").

🐾 Write as your teacher dictates from *The Story of Inventions*, page 78, paragraphs 1 and 2 ("Whitney's first idea…").

B. **Reader** *Language Skills, History*

Strawberry Girl: page 17, paragraph 4 ("Birdie glanced…") through page 25, paragraph 1

The Story of Inventions: page 75 ("Seeking the Reward") to page 79 ("Making Rifles")

B. Every student should read or listen to all the literature selections for the unit. Reading or hearing the different perspectives adds depth to understanding the events and circumstances of the times.

Follow the directions below to read or listen to the assigned passage in *Strawberry Girl*.

Before you begin your assignment in *The Story of Inventions*, scan it for any words you don't know and write them on a piece of scrap paper. Read over any section titles included in the passage—and then, as you read or listen to a section, think about how it relates to its title.

When you are finished, find the Comprehension Questions at the end of Chapter 6 in *The Story of Inventions*, and use complete sentences to write the answers to Questions 6 and 7 in your Student Notebook.

🐾 🐾 Read the above assignment from *Strawberry Girl* aloud, and then follow along as someone else reads the assignment from *The Story of Inventions*.

🐾 Read the above assignment from *Strawberry Girl* silently, and then read the assignment from *The Story of Inventions* aloud.

🐾 Read the above assignments from *Strawberry Girl* and *The Story of Inventions* silently.

C. **Read-Aloud & Narration** *History, Language Skills, Thinking Skills*

George Washington Carver: page 13, paragraph 2 ("After Jim was gone…") through page 18

Follow the instructions below for your level. Then, in your own words, tell what happened in the story from George's point of view (or pretend you are George and tell what you think happened). Try to remember as many details as possible. Tell what you think is the most important event in the passage.

Listen carefully to the assigned passage.

Read the assigned passage aloud.

D. Vocabulary
Language Skills, Thinking Skills

In this part, finish the vocabulary review you began in Part 1.

Use the second stack of vocabulary cards (that you set aside for this part) and pick one card at a time. Read the word on the front and, without looking, tell your teacher either what it means or how it was used in the story. Give yourself a point for every word you are able to use correctly. See how many points you can get!

E. Science
Thinking Skills

Human Body Basics, Body Basics: Cells, Tissues, Organs, & Systems

As you read through the assigned sections, choose words that are new or unfamiliar and make vocabulary cards for them as directed. Keep your science cards separate from other vocabulary.

at least three words

at least four words

Read and discuss the information in the sections with your teacher, watch the *Labwork 2* video, and do the *Labwork 3* activity. Be sure your System Savvy game pieces are assembled per the directions in the Getting Started section, but don't tackle the puzzles yet.

When you are finished, look at the remaining *Examine This* projects at the end of the chapter, and:

Choose one to complete.

Complete both.

Do as much as you can, but you don't have to finish the project(s) in this part. You will have other opportunities to work on them, such as during Part 5 and in occasional Study Hall sections.

F. Writing
Language Skills, Thinking Skills

In this section, you will begin writing a **character summary**, or shortened version of the main points of what someone has said or done. Focus only on the **main events**, or changes, that have occurred in your reading so far about George Washington Carver's life, not the details. You are limited in the number of words you can use, so make sure you choose words that best describe what has taken place.

D. New vocabulary words appear in the context of a lesson or story, which helps students recognize the connection between the way a word is used and its meaning. This is an important reading strategy called using context clues.

Thinking Skills Reminder

You show what you understand by explaining how to do something or how something works.

Lapbook Activity

🐾 Use up to 50 words to write your summary.

🐾 Use up to 45 words to write your summary.

🐾 Use up to 40 words to write your summary.

G. An index card file box can be a convenient way to store your Orchestra Story cards. Alternately, a small shoe box, ziploc bag, or even rubber band may be helpful in creating a storage system that will work best for your family.

G. **Music**   *Thinking Skills*

Look back at pages 42 through 45 in *The Story of the Orchestra*.

Then, follow the directions in Appendix D to make two Orchestra Story question and answer cards about the string section, and two about the violin. Put the small letters *SI* (for string instruments) in the upper left corners of your answer cards. Do not put the small letters on the question cards—and remember to write the questions in your Student Notebook in the correct order.

For the time being, keep the Orchestra Story cards you make in this volume separate from those you made about the composers and musical periods.

H. **Independent Reading & Record Keeping**   *Thinking Skills*

Review the Lesson 1 At A Glance chart in your Student Notebook to see if all the work you've done in this part has been checked off. Also, make sure the Student Notebook pages you worked on are dated and complete.

When you are finished, choose something to read that you will enjoy. Then find a quiet, comfortable place and read for the following length of time:

🐾🐾 30 minutes   🐾 35 minutes

Be sure to write down what you read today on the Reading Log in your Student Notebook.

Lesson 1, Part 4

A. **Copywork & Dictation**   *Language Skills*

Look carefully at your assigned passage below, and read it silently. Show your teacher any words you don't know, and practice saying them aloud. Now read the passage aloud, or ask your teacher to read it to you.

When you are finished copying or writing from dictation, compare your copy to the text and make any needed corrections.

🐾 Copy or write as your teacher dictates from *Strawberry Girl*, page 7, paragraph 1 (" The old Roddenberry house…").

🐾🐾 Write as your teacher dictates from *George Washington Carver*, page 18, paragraph 3 ("Now, when you get…").

🐾 Continue writing as your teacher dictates from *George Washington Carver*, page 18, paragraph 7 ("I knew I would miss…").

B. Reader   *Language Skills, History*

Strawberry Girl: page 25, paragraph 2 ("This time Birdie…") through page 32

The Story of Inventions: page 79 ("Making Rifles") through the end of the chapter

Follow the directions below to read or listen to the assigned passage in *Strawberry Girl*.

Before you begin your assignment in *The Story of Inventions*, scan it for any words you don't know and write them on a piece of scrap paper. Read over any section titles included in the passage—and then, as you read or listen to a section, think about how it relates to its title.

When you are finished, find the Comprehension Questions at the end of Chapter 6 in *The Story of Inventions*, and use a complete sentence to write the answer to Question 8 in your Student Notebook.

🐾🐾 Read the above assignment from *Strawberry Girl* aloud, and then follow along as someone else reads the assignment from *The Story of Inventions*.

🐾 Read the above assignment from *Strawberry Girl* silently, and then read the assignment from *The Story of Inventions* aloud.

🐾 Read the above assignments from *Strawberry Girl* and *The Story of Inventions* silently.

C. Read-Aloud & Discussion   *History, Language Skills, Thinking Skills*

George Washington Carver: page 19 ("It was dark…") through page 25, paragraph 4

After reading or listening to the read-aloud assignment, talk with your teacher and try to predict what will happen in the future based on what you know of the characters and events. Write your predictions in your Student Notebook. Later you will look back and see if they were accurate. Try not to peek ahead!

🐾🐾 Listen carefully as your teacher reads the assigned passage. Write down two predictions.

🐾 Listen carefully as your teacher reads the assigned passage. Write down three predictions.

🐾 Read the assigned passage aloud; then write down at least four predictions.

B. Remember to adjust reading assignments to your children's individual needs. If they read fluently, with expression, and can retell what they have read, you may allow them to read more of the assignments silently. Occasionally ask what is happening in their story, just to get a sense of what your children are taking away from it. If a child is struggling with fluency, reading expressively, or remembering what they have read, you can increase the amount of read-aloud time.

D. Word Building

Language Skills, Thinking Skills

Earlier in this lesson you learned about the Greek word-part *chrono-* or *chronos-*. Read over the words you defined in Part 2 and tell your teacher what each one means.

Now add to your ability to use *chrono-* or *chromos-* by finding more words in the dictionary that begin with it and relate to its meaning. Write them in your Student Notebook. Be sure not to repeat any of the words you have already defined. When you are finished, pick one of your words and write a sentence that uses it correctly.

- at least three words
- at least six words
- at least nine words

E. Economics & Geography

Thinking Skills

The family farm has been a part of American life since the very beginning of the nation, but it has undergone many changes. Even though the majority of farms are family-owned enterprises today, the majority of agriculture income does not come from these farms. It comes from larger business-run enterprises. This is often due to their ability to invest in modern tools and technologies.

During early farming days the average worker cared for about 30 acres, or land equal to approximately 5,000 square yards, each. In modern times, that number has increased to over 700 acres per worker. This difference came about because of various inventions that have made farming the work of fewer people. While this change has been good for consumers, in terms of the price they pay for the food that is produced, it has been a challenge for smaller farms to keep up with the new developments in farming. If the price of food has gone down because of greater supply, then the **profit margin**, or the difference between the selling price of food and the cost of producing it, has also gone down. To get the same amount of income, a farmer would have to produce larger amounts of food. To produce larger amounts of food, he would need to use the developments that have made farming more efficient. If he is a small farmer, he is back to the same problem—the cost of purchasing tools and technologies to increase **production**, or the amount of goods and services produced.

How do small farms remain **viable**, or capable of working successfully, today? The greatest need of small farms nowadays is increased income, or the amount of money received for goods or service provided. Farm families address this problem in several ways. Currently many farmers receive **subsidies**, or grants from

Lapbook Activity

the government, to help them continue to function. These subsidies are a small percentage of the Department of Agriculture's total budget. Another way the government supports farmers in America is through a program of crop insurance. This program helps farmers purchase insurance to protect against great loss of crops or livestock. The government also supports farmers by paying them to help **conserve**, or protect, environmentally sensitive lands. Many farm families supplement the farm income by working jobs outside the farm. This is one of the most common ways farmers supplement their incomes today.

Another problem facing small farmers today is that the majority of them are older, without younger family members to take over the farm. This problem exists more now than in the past, when it was typical for businesses to pass from parents to children. Since it is more difficult nowadays to support a family by farming, children often move from the farm when they are grown to take jobs elsewhere. The difficulty of keeping up with expensive equipment and technology reduces the amount of profit available for a family to **reinvest**, or put money back into a business. For these reasons, there are fewer children willing, or able, to take on the responsibilities of the family farm. Often this inability to continue the family farm is a heartbreaking situation for the people involved.

Is the family farm worth preserving? This treasured piece of American life faces many challenges. Talk with your teacher about family farms and the challenges they face. What do you think of the help offered to farmers by the government? Can you think of ways that family farms might become more profitable? Imagine you were part of a family faced with leaving your family farm after several generations. How would you feel?

Both of the readers used in this unit highlight family farms. George Washington Carver started out his life on the Carver

What makes a person memorable? Many history books give only facts and dates, but that doesn't make historical figures seem real. Learning about their hearts—their thoughts and motives, struggles and successes, and ultimately how others remember them—makes them memorable. As teachers, it is important to communicate these things to our students and allow the lives of historical figures to make an impact on our own lives.

family farm. Though he was born a slave, he became a part of the Carver family after his mother was kidnapped. He grew up as a free man, an adopted son, helping with the work of the family farm. This introduction to plant and animal life brought George great joy and served as his first classroom.

Strawberry Girl tells the story of the Boyer family's move to the state of Florida and their fledgling years of raising produce, or fresh fruits and vegetables, and shipping it to Northern markets. The family struggled to establish and maintain their family farm in the face of a challenging climate, difficult neighbors, and changing times.

Another example of someone who benefited from life on a family farm is Sergeant Alvin York, who grew up in Tennessee. This way of life **instilled**, or established, important values in him that were tested on the stage of World War I. There, he earned his country's highest award, the Medal of Honor. Learn more about this humble hero by reading his story in *Profiles from History, Volume 3*. Following the profile, answer the discussion questions and complete the activities.

F. Spelling
Language Skills, Thinking Skills

To increase your ability to use the words you have studied in this lesson when you write, review your vocabulary and word building lists. After choosing the number of words assigned below from these lists, you and your teacher may choose words from the Challenge Spelling List in Appendix C to work on as well. You may also want to add two or three words from your own writing that you have difficulty spelling correctly. Make your spelling list on the page provided in your Student Notebook.

When you are finished, write the words you have chosen as your teacher dictates them. Then study any that you are unable to spell correctly in preparation for writing in the next lessons. Add those words to the Ongoing Spelling List in your Student Notebook. Once you can spell a word correctly in dictation, then you can cross it off. If you misspell words in your everyday writing, be sure to add them to your list. Throughout the year, you should have an ongoing list of words you are practicing.

Tips for Studying Spelling Words:

1. Read the words over. Spell each one quietly to yourself and then check to see if you were correct.

2. Use a dry-erase board or other non-permanent surface to practice writing the words. Do this quickly until you feel more confident about their spelling.

3. When the words are called out to you, practice spelling them aloud. Picture the word in your mind as you spell it.

4. Look for any meanings or letter patterns that stand out to you. Remind yourself of these patterns or meanings as you study.

5. Remember that the most important spelling skill is to develop a *sense*, when you look at your spelling of a word, that it may not be spelled correctly. It is this sense that prompts a writer to look words up in a dictionary, and repeated exposure to a word will help you remember how to spell it.

᭟ Choose eight words from the vocabulary and word building lists, and two to four Challenge Spelling words (if you and your teacher want).

᭟ Choose ten words from the vocabulary and word building lists, and three to five Challenge Spelling words (if you and your teacher want).

᭟ Choose twelve words from your vocabulary or word building lists, and four to six Challenge Spelling words (if you and your teacher want).

G. Art   *Thinking Skills*

Read about the technique described in the section titled "The Ins & Outs of Clay Weaving" on page 41 in *Create Anything With Clay*. It's not particularly easy to do, but could prove useful because of all the interesting things you can do with it.

Try it out, then form your panel into a cylinder that you can use as a pencil holder. (Remember to add a bottom to the cylinder!)

Don't forget to put any leftover clay back in its zip-lock bag.

H. Independent Reading & Record Keeping   *Thinking Skills*

Review the Lesson 1 At A Glance chart in your Student Notebook to see if all the work you've done in this part has been checked off. Also, make sure the Student Notebook pages you worked on are dated and complete.

When you are finished, choose something to read that you will enjoy. Then find a quiet, comfortable place and read for the following length of time:

᭟ ᭟ 30 minutes   ᭟ 35 minutes

Be sure to write down what you read today on the Reading Log in your Student Notebook.

Lesson 1, Part 5

This part is set aside for completion of any work left undone from the lesson and review of concepts and content. It is also a time to expand the work of the lesson with practice and games.

- Review this lesson's Steps for Thinking, found in Part 1.

- Give the Unit 3 vocabulary cards that you reviewed in this lesson to your teacher and ask her to show you their picture sides, one at a time. Tell her what the picture or clue means and then name the word written on the other side. If you can, tell what part of speech it is. Give yourself one point for correctly naming a word and one point for knowing its part of speech. Keep track of your points and see if you beat your score from Part 3!

- Listen as your teacher reads the spelling words that you studied from Part 4, especially the ones on your Ongoing Spelling List. Write each word in your Student Notebook as she dictates it. When you are finished, look at your word list and make corrections as needed. Show your teacher how you did.

- Follow the directions in the *Human Body Basics* Instructions to play both the Word Power vocabulary game and complete the System Savvy puzzles in your Student Notebook.[1] Then work on any Examine This projects you have not yet completed.

- Look back at the pages you have studied so far in the *Basix Recorder Method* and review any exercises that you would like to work on. Choose several tracks on the *Recorder Method* CD and play along with them. Use your Finger Placement Tabs if you need to, and be sure to spend at least 20 minutes practicing!

- Review the Lesson 1 At A Glance chart in your Student Notebook to see if all the work you've done in this part has been checked off. If you did an Enrichment Activity or other extra work in this lesson, be sure to write it on the lines next to the chart.

- Complete the Cultivating Greatness Word Search in your Student Notebook.[2]

Enrichment Activities

1. Learn more about the organic food industry. What qualifies a food as organic? Approximately how much money is spent on organic food every year? After you have done some research, experiment with taste testing. With your parent's permission, purchase a type of food that is organic and the same type that is not. Does the food look or taste different? Are the foods different in content or preparation? Then compare the cost of different organic and non-organic foods. (You may have done some price

Are games truly a valid part of school time? Absolutely! As your child revisits content, vocabulary, and concepts, an effective review of learning takes place. The game format makes review more inviting and, hopefully, more frequent.

Enrichment activities are suggestions for ways your child can learn more about a topic of interest, dig deeper into a subject, or gain research skills. Please feel free to use these activities as guides for your child to complete as directed, or amended to better fit his particular abilities, needs, or interests.

comparisons in Part 2E of this lesson. If so, just add one or two more items to the chart you prepared.)

When you are finished, complete this statement: I think organic foods are or are not better than regular market items. Be prepared to defend your statement with research. Share your opinion with your family.

2. If possible, talk with the owners of a family farm or produce stand. How is their business doing? What are the biggest struggles they face? How can you or your family support these smaller agricultural businesses? Compare what you learn with the information in the economics lessons. If it doesn't match up, how is it different?

3. Learn more about the role weather plays in agriculture. Are there any weather-related issues facing farmers in your area right now? (An example would be farmers in Texas who faced the extreme drought conditions of 2011. They made less profit and often had to sell stock prematurely because they couldn't provide feed for their animals.)

Additional Resources:

Sergeant York movie (1941 film with Gary Cooper, available on DVD)

Exploring the History of Medicine by John Tiner

Louis Pasteur: Founder of Modern Medicine by John Tiner

———⊗∞———

Please preview any recommended movie to ensure its content is in line with your family's values and acceptable for your children to watch.

Answers

1. Answers are in the *Human Body Basics* Answer Key.

2. Answer key is in Appendix C.

Lesson 2, Part 1

⸶ Steps for Thinking ⸶

1. You use the information you have when you make a plan and put it into action. Scientists often decide what they think will happen before trying a new plan.

2. You cannot expect a different result when doing things in the same way as before. A different result requires doing things differently.

3. Great satisfaction, or pleasure, comes from doing what you love to do, even if it is different from everyone else.

A. **Copywork & Dictation**   *Language Skills*

Look carefully at your assigned passage below, and read it silently. Show your teacher any words you don't know, and practice saying them aloud. Now read the passage aloud, or ask your teacher to read it to you.

When you are finished copying or writing from dictation, compare your copy to the text and make any needed corrections.

🐾 Copy or write as your teacher dictates from *The Story of Inventions*, page 82, paragraph 2 ("In the pleasant surroundings…").

🐾 Write as your teacher dictates from *The Story of Inventions*, page 82, paragraph 2 ("In the pleasant surroundings…"), and page 83, paragraph 1 ("The father's first thought…").

B. **Reader**   *Language Skills, History*

Strawberry Girl: page 33 ("Lessons had already…") through page 41, paragraph 1
The Story of Inventions: page 81 (Chapter 7) to page 86 ("Making His First Sewing Machine")

Follow the directions below to read or listen to the assigned passage in *Strawberry Girl*.

Before you begin your assignment in *The Story of Inventions*, scan it for any words you don't know and write them on a piece of scrap paper. Read over any section titles included in the passage—and then, as you read or listen to a section, think about how it relates to its title.

⸶ Materials ⸶

- *George Washington Carver*
- *Strawberry Girl*
- *The Story of Inventions*
- *Human Body Basics*
- *Classroom Atlas of the United States*
- *The Story of the Orchestra* book & CD
- *Basix Recorder Method*
- *Create Anything With Clay*
- Recorder
- Polymer clay
- Activity (Part 1)
    - Masking tape
    - Cooked chicken leg bone
    - Vinegar
    - Jar or other container (to hold bone)
- Activity (Part 4)
    - Rolling pin or round jar
    - Paper
    - Scissors
    - Craft glue
    - Table knife
    - Ribbon or yarn

A. The goal of copywork and dictation is for your children to become familiar with the language they hear and write. As your children become more familiar with the process, you can use a more natural delivery of dictation with fewer repetitions. Be careful to continue providing what your children need to be successful. You can let them know that as they make progress, you will add a little challenge by speaking at a more natural rate.

When you are finished, find the Comprehension Questions at the end of Chapter 7 in *The Story of Inventions*, and use a complete sentence to write the answer to Question 1 in your Student Notebook.

Read the above assignment from *Strawberry Girl* aloud, and then follow along as someone else reads the assignment from *The Story of Inventions*.

Read the above assignment from *Strawberry Girl* silently, and then read the assignment from *The Story of Inventions* aloud.

Read the above assignments from *Strawberry Girl* and *The Story of Inventions* silently.

C. Reading aloud to children of all ages is one of the easiest, most enjoyable, and effective ways to share ideas and begin thoughtful conversations.

C. Read-Aloud & Narration   *History, Language Skills, Thinking Skills*
George Washington Carver: page 25, paragraph 5 ("Other places in Neosho…") through page 30, paragraph 6

Follow the directions below to read or listen to the above passage. Then, in your own words, tell what happened in the portion you are assigned. Try to remember as many details as possible. If necessary you may reread, or listen as your teacher rereads, the part you are to retell.

Listen carefully as your teacher reads the above assignment aloud. Choose one page to retell.

Listen carefully as your teacher reads the above assignment aloud. Choose two pages to retell.

Read the above assignment aloud, and then retell the entire passage.

D. Vocabulary   *Language Skills, Thinking Skills*
Write each vocabulary word on the Vocabulary I.D. sheet in your Student Notebook. Then tell your teacher what you think each word means, based on the context in which you have read it. If you are not sure of a word's meaning, use a dictionary to look it up. You may have to remove any endings that have been added, such as an *s* or *ed*, to find that word in the dictionary. Write the definition on the Vocabulary Sheet.

Next, write the word's part of speech: noun, adjective, adverb, verb, and so forth. If you aren't sure, this can also be found in the dictionary.

reckon	palmetto	scrubby
tongue-tied	oilcloth	bayhead
knead	dummkopf	sultry
livery stable	stutter	squirm

E. Science
Thinking Skills

Human Body Basics, Musculoskeletal System: beginning of chapter & Bones

As you read through the assigned sections, choose words that are new or unfamiliar and make vocabulary cards for them as directed. Keep your science cards separate from other vocabulary.

at least three words

at least four words

Read and discuss the information in the sections with your teacher and do the *Labwork 1-4* activities. The pages you need for drawing, writing, and labeling are in your Student Notebook.

The writing part of *Labwork 4* can be used for the next section (F. Writing) assignment.

Lapbook
Activity

F. Writing
Language Skills, Thinking Skills

For this section, choose science activities you completed in this part, or in Lesson 1, Part 3, and write one or two paragraphs in your Student Notebook describing how you did each of them. Your descriptions should be detailed enough that anyone reading them could go through the steps and complete the same activities.

You might want to write the steps on scrap paper first and put them in order. Then think about how you would like your paragraph(s) to read. Be sure to use words like *first*, *then*, *next*, and *finally* to connect your sentences and make the order more clear.

Choose one activity.

Choose two activities.

G. Music
History, Thinking Skills

Continue your study of string instruments by reading pages 46 and 47 in *The Story of the Orchestra* with your teacher. Discuss the information about the viola and the cello. Then listen to part of the "Concerto for Viola and Orchestra" on Track 15 and the opening of the "William Tell Overture" on Track 16 of your CD. Were you able to **discriminate**, or tell the difference, between the instruments featured on each track? How did the music make you feel? What did you enjoy or dislike about it?

When you are finished, listen carefully to Tracks 15 and 16 again and choose your favorite. Then, draw and color a picture in your Student Notebook of the image this music brings to your mind.

G. When your children undertake the drawing activity in this section, it is not particularly important that they visualize exactly what the composer had in mind when he wrote the music. It is far more important for your students to express their personal responses to each piece. Once they have illustrated their response, they will be more likely to remember a composition.

Lapbook
Activity

H. **Independent Reading & Record Keeping**   *Thinking Skills*

Review the Lesson 2 At A Glance chart in your Student Notebook to see if all the work you've done in this part has been checked off. Also, make sure the Student Notebook pages you worked on are dated and complete.

When you are finished, choose something to read that you will enjoy. Then find a quiet, comfortable place and read for the following length of time:

      ❦❦ ✿ 30 minutes   ✿ 35 minutes

Be sure to write down what you read today on the Reading Log in your Student Notebook.

Lesson 2, Part 2

A. **Copywork & Dictation**   *Language Skills*

Look carefully at this lesson's Steps for Thinking, and read them silently. Show your teacher any words you don't know, and practice saying them aloud. Now read the Steps aloud, or ask your teacher to read them to you.

When you are finished copying or writing from dictation, compare your copy to the text and make any needed corrections.

❦❦ Copy the Steps for Thinking, and tell your teacher an example of each Step.

✿ Write the Steps for Thinking as your teacher dictates them. Then, in your Student Notebook write one example of each Step. Be sure to use complete sentences.

✿ Write the Steps for Thinking as your teacher dictates them. Then, in your Student Notebook write two examples of each Step. Be sure to use complete sentences.

B. When your child reads, make a list of any troublesome words. Look for possible patterns to the mistakes, and, before your next session, review those words. You may read them aloud, or ask your child to do so.

B. **Reader**   *Language Skills, History*

Strawberry Girl: page 41, paragraph 2 ("The church was…") through page 47

The Story of Inventions: page 86 ("Making His First Sewing Machine") to page 90 ("Offering the Machine to England")

Follow the directions below to read or listen to the assigned passage in *Strawberry Girl*.

Before you begin your assignment in *The Story of Inventions*, scan it for any words you don't know and write them on a piece of scrap paper.

Read over any section titles included in the passage—and then, as you read or listen to a section, think about how it relates to its title.

When you are finished, find the Comprehension Questions at the end of Chapter 7 in *The Story of Inventions*, and use a complete sentence to write the answer to Question 2 in your Student Notebook.

🐾 Read the above assignment from *Strawberry Girl* aloud, and then follow along as someone else reads the assignment from *The Story of Inventions*.

🐾 Read the above assignment from *Strawberry Girl* silently, and then read the assignment from *The Story of Inventions* aloud.

🐾 Read the above assignments from *Strawberry Girl* and *The Story of Inventions* silently.

C. **Read-Aloud & Discussion**   *History, Language Skills, Thinking Skills*
George Washington Carver: page 30, paragraph 7 ("Early Sunday morning…") through the top of page 36

Follow the directions below to read or listen to the above assignment. Then make up questions about the part of the story you just read or heard. Write your questions in your Student Notebook and ask your teacher to answer them. After discussing her thoughts, write down the best possible answer on the lines provided. Be sure to use complete sentences.

When you are finished, look back at the prediction or predictions you made during Lesson 1, Part 4. Were you able to predict what would happen? Be sure to mark the "Came to Pass" box for each prediction when it does happen.

🐾 Listen carefully as your teacher reads the above assignment aloud. Make up two questions.

🐾 Listen carefully as your teacher reads the above assignment aloud. Make up three questions.

🐾 Read the above assignment aloud; then make up four questions.

D. **Word Building**   *Language Skills, Thinking Skillss*
In this section you will continue learning about Greek and Latin word-parts that help to build words in the English language. Today's word-part is ***pro-***, which is a Latin word that means *before* or *for*.

Look up the following words in the dictionary and write each definition in your Student Notebook. Then underline the word-part *pro-* in each word. Think and be ready to tell your teacher how each definition relates to the meaning of the Latin word.

program	procession	proceed
🐾 proclaim	proscribe	provision
🐾 proactive	procreate	procure

E. Economics

As time passed and the East, South, and West parts of the country filled with family farms, others who yearned for opportunity or open spaces sought **refuge**, or security, in the middle of America.

The Homestead Act of 1862 paved the way for this expansion. Signed by President Lincoln, this act gave any citizen the right to claim 160 acres of surveyed government land that was not yet owned by anyone else. To show his intent to stay on the land, the person claiming it had to make improvements, such as building a home and planting crops. If he remained on the land for five years, the property became his without any cost or debt. Though this was certainly not a perfect system, it did pave the way for many to improve their lot in life. Often, people came with little in the way of equipment, money to purchase seed, or things necessary to endure the harsh winters. Others came with many dreams but little knowledge of how to farm in the harsh conditions.

Other factors added to those harsh conditions as well. Sometimes the land given to homesteaders by the government may have had a previous owner. And some landowners faced hostile Native Americans who did not seek to own or settle property permanently but wanted to continue their way of life. This way of life included hunting, fishing, or farming on land they thought could not be owned by anyone.

The settlers were also fond of building fences around their crops or livestock, which prevented wandering herds from crossing their property. This brought about conflicts with those who believed in the idea of the Open Range. This idea allowed livestock to roam freely and find pasture to graze upon, much like the herds of buffalo that previously lived in the Plains states. The invention of barbed wire in 1873 created an easier way to build fences that effectively kept livestock from trampling crops or mingling with other herds. These fences made barriers to those who wanted to move livestock freely, creating another group with whom the homesteaders had conflict.

Though some, such as George Washington Carver, tried homesteading and found the land too harsh and lonely, many remained, bearing up under the many hardships this part of the country provided. With freezing temperatures and deep snow in the winter, or drought and plains fires in the summer, this land was not for the faint of heart. To the credit of those who persevered, some family farms established back then still exist today and remain a testament to their determination. The opportunity gave homesteaders their independence. Even today, there is a modern homesteading movement, in which families live independently of outside support, growing food, maintaining livestock, and bartering with others to obtain what they need to live.

In your Student Notebook, make a list of characteristics, or qualities, that you recognize in those who live and work on family farms. Give examples from your reading or discussions. For example:

> Characteristic: hard working —The Carvers worked many hours on the farm each day.

🐾 at least five characteristics

🐾 at least six characteristics

🐾 at least seven characteristics

F. Editing   *Language Skills, Thinking Skills*

In *Strawberry Girl,* the use of dialect paints a colorful picture of the people who lived in Florida at the beginning of the 1900s. Because a dialect may be hard at first to understand, it is important to try to translate the sentences in your mind as you listen or read so that you will get the meaning of the story. This may take some practice. If you need to see an example, look back at Lesson 1 of this unit, Part 1F.

Choose sentences from *Strawberry Girl* that include dialect and translate them aloud for your teacher.

🐾 two sentences

🐾 three sentences

🐾 four sentences

🐾🐾🐾 One of the differences between English and various dialects is that their grammar is different. Grammar, or the rules for speaking or writing a language, helps you know which word to choose to clearly express your thoughts. One of the most important ideas in grammar is agreement.

In this section, continue working on subject-verb agreement. Remember, if you have a singular subject, or one person or thing that is the focus of your sentence, you must have a verb that goes with that one subject. Here are some examples:

> *Dad* eats steak for dinner.

> *Mom* likes pizza for dinner.

Teaching Tip

What helps a child remember a language lesson after it is completed? The ability to identify what was learned in the pages of a real book!

If you have a plural subject, or more than one person or thing that is the focus of your sentence, you must have a verb that goes with more than one subject. Here is an example:

Mom and *Dad* <u>eat</u> steak for dinner.

Mom and *Dad* <u>like</u> pizza for dinner.

Find sentences in your literature that show singular (one) and plural (more than one) subject-verb agreement, and write them in your Student Notebook.

one sentence showing each (singular and plural)

two sentences showing each

three sentences showing each

G. Music   *Thinking Skills*

Look over page 31 in the *Basix Recorder Method* and write the names of notes you're not sure of above the staffs on that page. Use your Finger Placement Tabs if you need to, and practice playing the melody.

Be sure to spend about 20 minutes a day practicing what you have learned!

H. Independent Reading & Record Keeping   *Thinking Skills*

Review the Lesson 2 At A Glance chart in your Student Notebook to see if all the work you've done in this part has been checked off. Also, make sure the Student Notebook pages you worked on are dated and complete.

When you are finished, choose something to read that you will enjoy. Then find a quiet, comfortable place and read for the following length of time:

30 minutes   35 minutes

Be sure to write down what you read today on the Reading Log in your Student Notebook.

Lesson 2, Part 3

A. **Copywork & Dictation**   *Language Skills*

Look carefully at your assigned passage below, and read it silently. Show your teacher any words you don't know, and practice saying them aloud. Now read the passage aloud, or ask your teacher to read it to you.

When you are finished copying or writing from dictation, compare your copy to the text and make any needed corrections.

🐾🐾 🐾 Copy or write as your teacher dictates from *The Story of Inventions*, page 92, paragraph 1 ("Before his wife left…").

🐾 Write as your teacher dictates from *The Story of Inventions*, page 92, paragraphs 1 and 2 ("Before his wife left…").

B. **Reader**   *Language Skills, History*

Strawberry Girl: page 48 ("Birdie looked from…") through page 55
The Story of Inventions: page 90 ("Offering the Machine to England") to page 93 ("Fighting for His Rights")

Follow the directions below to read or listen to the assigned passage in *Strawberry Girl*.

Before you begin your assignment in *The Story of Inventions*, scan it for any words you don't know and write them on a piece of scrap paper. Read over any section titles included in the passage—and then, as you read or listen to a section, think about how it relates to its title.

When you are finished, find the Comprehension Questions at the end of Chapter 7 in *The Story of Inventions*, and use a complete sentence to write the answer to Question 3 in your Student Notebook.

🐾🐾 Read the above assignment from *Strawberry Girl* aloud, and then follow along as someone else reads the assignment from *The Story of Inventions*.

🐾🐾 Read the above assignment from *Strawberry Girl* silently, and then read the assignment from *The Story of Inventions* aloud.

🐾 Read the above assignments from *Strawberry Girl* and *The Story of Inventions* silently.

C. **Read-Aloud & Narration**   *History, Language Skills, Thinking Skills*

George Washington Carver: page 36, paragraph 1 ("The hotel manager…") through page 40

Follow the instructions below for your level. Then, in your own words, tell what happened in the story from George's point of view. Try to remember as many details as possible. Tell what you think is the most important event in the passage.

Teaching Tip

Use the time your child spends reading aloud to encourage him to read with expression. Reading with expression shows an understanding of ideas as well as understanding of punctuation and mechanics. If your child does not read expressively, take the time to model reading with expression for him.

🐾🐾 🐾 Listen carefully to the assigned passage.

🐾 Read the assigned passage aloud.

D. Vocabulary   *Language Skills, Thinking Skills*

Show your teacher the Vocabulary I.D. sheet that you completed in Part 1 of this lesson. Ask her to review the words with you by calling them out or writing them on a dry erase board or piece of paper. Tell her what each word means or how it was used in the story and, if you can, what part of speech it is.

Give yourself one point for each correct meaning and one point for knowing the word's part of speech. Keep track of your Vocabulary I.D. points by writing them at the bottom of the sheet, and try to beat your score when you review these words again in Part 5.

E. Science   *Thinking Skills*

Human Body Basics, Musculoskeletal System: beginning of chapter & Bones

Quickly review the pages you read and discussed in Part 1 of this lesson.

Then, find the *Examine This* section at the end of this chapter and complete the first project. Use the page in your Student Notebook to record your facts.

When you are finished, complete the *Labwork 5* labeling activity in your Student Notebook.

🐾🐾 🐾 Begin work on the second project in the *Examine This* section. Do as much as you can, but you don't have to finish the project in this part. You will have other opportunities to work on it, such as during Part 5 and in occasional Study Hall sections.

F. Writing   *Language Skills, Thinking Skills*

In this section, continue writing a character summary, or shortened version of the main points of what someone has said or done. Focus only on the main events (not the details) that have occurred in your reading so far about George Washington Carver's life.

You are limited in the number of words you can use, so make sure you choose words that best describe what has taken place.

🐾🐾 Use up to 50 words to write your summary.

🐾 Use up to 45 words to write your summary.

🐾 Use up to 40 words to write your summary.

E. The Internet can be a useful tool for research, but we suggest that your child use it only with your permission and supervision, and while following your family's rules.

Lapbook Activity

G. Music
History, Thinking Skills

Look back at pages 46 and 47 in *The Story of the Orchestra*.

Then, follow the directions in Appendix D to make two Orchestra Story question and answer cards about the viola, and two about the cello. Put the small letters *SI* (for string instruments) in the upper left corners of your answer cards. Do not label the question cards—and remember to write the questions in your Student Notebook in the correct order.

Take out all the Orchestra Story cards you have made so far in this unit and separate the questions from the answers. Mix up both stacks well and then place the question card stack facedown on the table. Draw one question at a time and see if you can find its correct answer in the other stack. Remove the question and answer cards you get correct. Remember the answer keys you made in your Student Notebook.

H. Independent Reading & Record Keeping
Thinking Skills

Review the Lesson 2 At A Glance chart in your Student Notebook to see if all the work you've done in this part has been checked off. Also, make sure the Student Notebook pages you worked on are dated and complete.

When you are finished, choose something to read that you will enjoy. Then find a quiet, comfortable place and read for the following length of time:

🐾🐾 30 minutes   🐾 35 minutes

Be sure to write down what you read today on the Reading Log in your Student Notebook.

G. An index card file box can be a convenient way to store your Orchestra Story cards. Alternately, a small shoe box, ziploc bag, or even rubber band may be helpful in creating a storage system that will work best for your family.

Lapbook Activity

Connect Learning to Life:

Encouragement is a powerful thing. Be sure to recognize your child's efforts to read independently, especially if he is a reluctant reader. When I was a young person, I liked to read. I didn't realize how important it was until my father passed me one day, curled up in a chair reading, and complimented me. It was a powerful moment. I began to seek even more opportunities to read because of his encouragement. You never know the impact of just one word of recognition on your child's life, and you are showing your child how to encourage others as well.

Lesson 2, Part 4

A. **Copywork & Dictation**   *Language Skills*

Look carefully at your assigned passage below, and read it silently. Show your teacher any words you don't know, and practice saying them aloud. Now read the passage aloud, or ask your teacher to read it to you.

When you are finished copying or writing from dictation, compare your copy to the text and make any needed corrections.

🐾 Copy or write as your teacher dictates from *Strawberry Girl*, page 42, paragraph 2 ("At noonday, the preacher…").

🐾 Write as your teacher dictates from *George Washington Carver*, page 46, paragraph 2 ("But what if the snow…").

🐾 Continue writing as your teacher dictates from *George Washington Carver*, page 46, paragraph 8 ("Slowly the deep tortured feeling…").

B. **Reader**   *Language Skills, History*

Strawberry Girl: page 56 ("Soon Birdie was seated…") through page 61, paragraph 3

The Story of Inventions: page 93 ("Fighting for His Rights") through the end of the chapter

Follow the directions below to read or listen to the assigned passage in *Strawberry Girl*.

Before you begin your assignment in *The Story of Inventions*, scan it for any words you don't know and write them on a piece of scrap paper. Read over any section titles included in the passage—and then, as you read or listen to a section, think about how it relates to its title.

When you are finished, find the Comprehension Questions at the end of Chapter 7 in *The Story of Inventions*, and use complete sentences to write the answers to Questions 4 and 5 in your Student Notebook.

🐾 Read the above assignment from *Strawberry Girl* aloud, and then follow along as someone else reads the assignment from *The Story of Inventions*.

🐾 Read the above assignment from *Strawberry Girl* silently, and then read the assignment from *The Story of Inventions* aloud.

🐾 Read the above assignments from *Strawberry Girl* and *The Story of Inventions* silently.

C. Read-Aloud & Narration   *Language Skills, History, Thinking Skills*

George Washington Carver: page 41 (Chapter 6) through page 45

After reading or listening to the read-aloud assignment, talk with your teacher and try to predict what will happen in the future based on what you know of the characters and events. Write your predictions in your Student Notebook. Later you will look back and see if they were accurate. Try not to peek ahead!

Listen carefully as your teacher reads the assigned passage. Write down two predictions.

Listen carefully as your teacher reads the assigned passage. Write down three predictions.

Read the assigned passage aloud; then write down at least four predictions.

D. Word Building   *Language Skills, Thinking Skills*

Earlier in this lesson you learned about the Latin word-part *pro-*. Read over the words you defined in Part 2 and tell your teacher what each one means.

Now add to your ability to use *pro-* by finding more words in the dictionary that begin with it and relate to its meaning. Write them in your Student Notebook. Be sure not to repeat any of the words you have already defined. When you are finished, pick one of your words and write a sentence that uses it correctly.

at least three words

at least six words

at least nine words

E. History   *Thinking Skills, Geography*

The states considered the Great Plains states are a part of the Midwest section of the United States. These states were a **prime**, or main, destination for those who homesteaded. Travelers usually passed up Kansas, Nebraska, South Dakota, and North Dakota on their way to the West Coast because of the poor soil and difficult conditions. However, for many who homesteaded, the choices were limited by their lack of money. The Homestead Act allowed any citizen to obtain a **parcel**, or piece, of land.

C. Explain to your students that the value of making predictions about the stories you are reading or listening to doesn't depend on getting it right. There is great value in taking the information you have, coming up with an idea of what will take place, and then testing that idea. If you are not correct, you may learn more than if you were correct. You have gained new information about a character or event. This is **clarification,** or making something clearer. Encourage your children not to be overly concerned about always predicting correctly. Help them to welcome the opportunity to clarify their understanding.

Lapbook Activity

The small superscript numbers that appear after some of the directions in this book refer to answers found in the answer key, which is located immediately after Part 5.

Create a **profile**, or description, of what it was like in the Great Plains states. To do this, use the *Classroom Atlas of the United States* to complete this assignment. Fill out the Great Plains Profile chart in your Student Notebook. You will find the information you need in the Themes section at the front of the Atlas and in the section for the Midwest. When a map shows more than one quality for a state, such as average January temperature of 0 to 10 degrees and 20 to 30 degrees, write both as a range, like this:

1-10 degrees to 20-30 degrees

After you have completed the chart, draw some conclusions based on the data, or information, you have compiled. Answer the following questions, using your chart to help:

1. What do the climate and vegetation descriptions tell you about the kinds of plants that can grow in these states?[1]

2. What does January's average maximum temperature and average snowfall tell you about what it is like in these states in the winter?[2]

3. Which of these states would be the most difficult for people or livestock in the winter? Why?[3]

4. Which of these states would be the hardest for people or livestock in the summer?[4]

5. Look at the Total Farming Area bar graph. What are the top four states in total farming area?[5]

6. Which states have the largest number of corporate farms?[6]

7. What is the average size of the family farms in each of the Great Plains states?[7]

8. What is the average size of the corporate farms in each of the Great Plains states?[8]

9. What conclusion can you draw from this data?[9]

10. Based on the average size of the farms, which type do you think produces more profit—the average family farm or the average corporate farm?[10]

Look at the *Farming in the Midwest* Chart in your atlas. Make a list of the agricultural products for each state. What differences do you see in crops or livestock between the Great Plains states and the states further east like Wisconsin and Illinois? Make a list of the products that are produced in the Great Plains states but not in Wisconsin and Illinois. Write several sentences telling why you think this is the case.

F. Spelling

Language Skills, Thinking Skills

To increase your ability to use the words you have studied in this lesson when you write, review your vocabulary and word building lists. After choosing the number of words assigned below from these lists, you and your teacher may choose words from the Challenge Spelling List in Appendix C to work on as well. You may also want to add two or three words from your own writing that you have difficulty spelling correctly. Make your spelling list on the page provided in your Student Notebook.

When you are finished, write the words you have chosen as your teacher dictates them. Then study any that you are unable to spell correctly in preparation for writing in the next lessons. (You might want to look back at the "Tips for Studying Spelling Words" in Lesson 1, Part 4F.) Add those words to the Ongoing Spelling List in your Student Notebook (Lesson 1, Part 4). Also, don't forget to add words you misspell in your everyday writing to the list. Once you can spell a word correctly in dictation, then you can cross it off. Throughout the year, you should have an ongoing list of words you are practicing.

🐾 Choose eight words from the vocabulary and word building lists, and two to four Challenge Spelling words (if you and your teacher want).

🐾 Choose ten words from the vocabulary and word building lists, and three to five Challenge Spelling words (if you and your teacher want).

🐾 Choose twelve words from your vocabulary or word building lists, and four to six Challenge Spelling words (if you and your teacher want).

G. Art   *Thinking Skills*

The section in *Create Anything With Clay* entitled "Itty Bitty Hardback Books" shows a couple of ways you might use woven panels like the one you made in the last lesson. It also introduces some other ideas for decorating book covers.

Follow the directions on page 42 to make an accordion book. The sample has a nursery rhyme printed inside, but you can fill the pages with anything you want. Design a cover that fits your book's contents. Don't forget to put any left-over clay back in its zip-lock bag.

H. Independent Reading & Record Keeping   *Thinking Skills*

Review the Lesson 2 At A Glance chart in your Student Notebook to see if all the work you've done in this part has been checked off. Also, make sure the Student Notebook pages you worked on are dated and complete.

When you are finished, choose something to read that you will enjoy. Then find a quiet, comfortable place and read for the following length of time:

🐾 30 minutes   🐾 35 minutes

Be sure to write down what you read today on the Reading Log in your Student Notebook.

Lesson 2, Part 5

This part is set aside for completion of any work left undone from the lesson and review of concepts and content. It is also a time to expand the work of the lesson with practice and games.

- Review this lesson's Steps for Thinking, found in Part 1.

- Use the Vocabulary I.D. sheet you completed in Part 1 of this lesson to make vocabulary cards. Write each word on an index card and try to remember what it means or how it was used in the story without looking. Check the I.D. Sheet to see if you were right. Then on the back of each card, draw a picture or write a clue to help you remember what that word means. Be sure to write a small *CG* (for Cultivating Greatness) in the upper left corners.

  When you are finished, give the cards to your teacher and ask her to show you their picture sides, one at a time. Tell her what the picture or clue means, and then name the word written on the other side. If you can, tell what part of speech it is. Give yourself one point for correctly naming a word and one point for knowing its part of speech. Keep track of your points and see if you beat your score from Part 3!

- Listen as your teacher reads the spelling words that you studied from Part 4, especially the ones on your Ongoing Spelling List. Write each word in your Student Notebook as she dictates it. When you are finished, look at your word list and make corrections as needed. Show your teacher how you did.

- Follow the directions in the *Human Body Basics* Instructions to play the Word Power vocabulary game. First play with only the cards you made for the Musculoskeletal System; then combine all the cards you have made so far and see how you do.

  Complete the System Savvy puzzles in your Student Notebook.[11] When you are finished, work on any *Examine This* projects you have not yet completed.

- Look back at page 31 in the *Basix Recorder Method* and practice the song on that page. Then review any other lessons that may be giving you trouble. Be sure to spend at least 20 minutes practicing—and don't forget that you can use your Finger Placement Tabs if you need to.

- Review the Lesson 2 At A Glance chart in your Student Notebook to see if all the work you've done in this part has been checked off. If you did an Enrichment activity or other extra work in this lesson, be sure to write it on the lines next to the chart.

- Complete the Cultivating Greatness Word Scramble in your Student Notebook.[12]

Ask your children to read over the Steps for Thinking and then briefly restate each one in their own words, or give examples that they have heard or read so far. Remind them of any ideas or examples they have thought of during the past week.

Teaching Tip

Word Scrambles are a fun way to reinforce the recognition and spelling of words that are important to learn. After your children complete this Word Scramble, encourage them to make their own. Ask them to share these with each other, with friends, or with you. Remember, these activities are models for you and your children to make your own as well!

Enrichment Activities

1.　At the library or on the Internet, find out if your state is an Open Range state. Are there laws in your state that apply to the fencing of land and the responsibilities of livestock owners? Do you agree with your state's laws? Why or why not?

2.　What are the main agricultural products of your state? Are those products doing well and making profit for the agricultural businesses of your state? Compare the production of those main products for the last five years. Which year yielded the greatest produce? Which year yielded the least? What factors contributed to the highest and lowest crops?

　　Does your family buy the agricultural products of your state? Discuss this question with your family and whether or not your family is willing to support these state businesses.

3.　Have you or others in your family ever made clothes? Talk with your family members about this. If there is interest, investigate the various items of clothing that you could make for yourself. Ask someone to show you how to use a sewing machine, if one is available.

　　What are the benefits of sewing, knitting, or crocheting items of clothing? What are the drawbacks? If you have the know-how or the assistance, make an item of clothing for yourself or someone in your family. After you are finished, assess the project and decide what you learned from the experience. Would you do it again? Why or why not?

Additional Resources:

George Washington Carver: From Slave to Scientist by Janet & Geoff Benge

Simply Sewing (Kids Can Do It) by Judy Ann Sadler

Kids Inventing! A Handbook for Young Inventors by Susan Casey

Answers

1. Since there is little precipitation, a plant would not grow if it needed a lot of water.

2. The average temperature is from 2 to 50; the average snowfall is from 8 to 64 inches. Each state is cold and has snowstorms.

3. North or South Dakota; because of the lower temperatures and higher amounts of snowfall

4. probably Nebraska or Kansas; because of the higher temperatures

5. Kansas, Nebraska, North Dakota, and South Dakota

6. Nebraska and Kansas

7. the numbers in red on the bar

8. the numbers in green on the bar

9. Even though family farms hold many more millions of acres in total farming area, the average size of the corporate farms is much larger than the average size of the family farm.

10. Based on the size of the farms, it would appear that the average corporate farm would make more profit.

11. Answers are in the *Human Body Basics* Answer Key.

12. Answer key is in Appendix C.

Lesson 3, Part 1

❧ Steps for Thinking ☙

1. Learning about the way something works requires you to carefully examine, or inspect, its parts in detail.

2. Understanding an event means you have to analyze, or think about, the steps leading up to it. If you want something to happen, think about the steps that will bring that event about.

3. Sometimes when you think you know what will make something happen, you can try it out to see if it works. Always think about whether or not the things you do will hurt yourself or someone else.

A. **Copywork & Dictation**   *Language Skills*

Look carefully at your assigned passage below, and read it silently. Show your teacher any words you don't know, and practice saying them aloud. Now read the passage aloud, or ask your teacher to read it to you.

When you are finished copying or writing from dictation, compare your copy to the text and make any needed corrections.

🐾🐾👑 Copy or write as your teacher dictates from *The Story of Inventions*, page 72, paragraph 3 ("The very next day…").

👑 Write as your teacher dictates from *The Story of Inventions*, page 72, paragraph 3 ("The very next day…"), and page 73, paragraph 1 ("In Asia, the West Indies…").

B. **Reader**   *Language Skills, History*

Strawberry Girl: page 61, paragraph 4 ("The afternoon passed…") through page 71, paragraph 4

The Story of Inventions: Review page 67 (Chapter 6) to page 75 ("Seeking the Reward")

Follow the directions below to read or listen to the assigned passage in *Strawberry Girl*. When you are finished, skim each section in the review assignment from *The Story of Inventions*. Then tell your teacher examples of how the information in each section relates to its title.

ᗌ Materials ᗧ

- *George Washington Carver*
- *Strawberry Girl*
- *The Story of Inventions*
- *Human Body Basics*
- *The Story of the Orchestra* book & CD
- *Basix Recorder Method*
- *Create Anything With Clay*
- Recorder
- Polymer clay
- *Rummy Roots* Word Cards
- Activity (Part 1)
  - Clothespin
  - Timer that can clock 30-second intervals
- Activity (Part 3)
  - Uncooked chicken leg quarter
  - Sharp scissors
  - Disposable gloves (optional)
  - Wax paper
- Activity (Part 4)
  - Table knife
  - Toothpick
  - String or yarn
  - Scissors
  - Small paper punch or awl

Teaching Tip

The process of copywork and dictation gives a teacher a great deal of information. Not only does it show what your child is missing, it shows what he is getting! Reading or hearing language, and then writing it down is a multi-step process that shows understanding, processing of information and then translating that information into writing. Many times over my years as an educator, just giving a student a passage to copy or write from dictation has provided great insight into the student's ability to read, write and comprehend. Make sure to take notice of all your child does correctly when using this process, and encourage him accordingly!

🐾 Read the above assignment from *Strawberry Girl* aloud, and then give one example for each section in *The Story of Inventions*.

🐾 Read the above assignment from *Strawberry Girl*, and then give two examples for each section in *The Story of Inventions*.

🐾 Read the above assignment from *Strawberry Girl*, and then give three examples for each section in *The Story of Inventions*.

C. Read-Aloud & Narration   *History, Language Skills, Thinking Skills*
George Washington Carver: page 46 ("Carefully I planned...") through the top of page 52

Follow the directions below to read or listen to the above passage. Then, in your own words, tell what happened in the portion you are assigned. Try to remember as many details as possible. If necessary you may reread, or listen as your teacher rereads, the part you are to retell.

🐾 Listen carefully as your teacher reads the above assignment aloud. Choose one page to retell.

🐾 Listen carefully as your teacher reads the above assignment aloud. Choose two pages to retell.

🐾 Read the above assignment aloud, and then retell the entire passage.

D. Vocabulary   *Language Skills, Thinking Skills*
Write each vocabulary word on the Vocabulary I.D. sheet in your Student Notebook. Then tell your teacher what you think each word means, based on the context in which you have read it. If you are not sure of a word's meaning, look it up in a dictionary. Write the definition on the Vocabulary Sheet.

Next, write the word's part of speech: noun, adjective, adverb, verb, and so forth. If you aren't sure, this can also be found in the dictionary.

lightwood	**ceil**	**melodious**
millinery	**whimper**	**campstool**
🐾🐾 **firmament**	**tabernacle**	**disgust**
hallelujah	**jumble**	**homesteader**

E. Science   *Thinking Skills*
Human Body Basics, Musculoskeletal System: Muscles

As you read through the passage, choose words that are new or unfamiliar and make vocabulary cards for them as directed. Keep your science cards separate from other vocabulary.

🐾 at least three words

🐾 at least four words

Teaching Tip

Throughout this curriculum you will find games. Their purpose is to practice skills and review content in a fun and effective manner. Once your children become familiar with the games, they can become part of game days, family game nights, and any other time that this format fits into life. Since your children are most familiar with them, they can be leaders by helping others learn the games, rules, and the ideas behind them!

Read and discuss the information in the assigned sections with your teacher, and do the *Labwork 8-10* activities. The pages you need for these activities are in your Student Notebook.

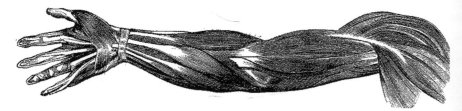

🐾🐾 Begin work on the third project in the *Examine This* section. You might want to look back at Unit 2, Lessons 3 through 5, in which you studied levers. Do as much as you can, but you don't have to finish the project in this part. You will have other opportunities to work on it, such as during Part 5 and in occasional Study Hall sections.

🐾 Extend this *Examine This* project by finding examples in the human body of all three classes of levers. Draw and label diagrams of them.

F. Writing
Language Skills, Thinking Skills

An **essay** is a type of writing that focuses on a topic and usually answers a question or tells what you think or know. Essays are not hard to write when you know how to think through them. They often start with a question or statement called a prompt. A prompt sets the stage for the essay, and usually ends with a question or direction. Here is an example of a prompt:

> You have been learning about inventors such as
>
> Eli Whitney and Elias Howe. <u>The work done by their</u>
>
> <u>inventions often took the place of many people working</u>
>
> <u>more slowly.</u> *What good and bad changes resulted from*
>
> *inventions that replaced workers?*

After you have read the prompt, think about its parts.

Part One: The first sentence tells you where the answer should come from. In this case, the answer should come from your readings about inventions and their impact on the lives of people.

Part Two: The underlined sentence gives you the context, or idea behind the question. In this case, the prompt says that the work done by their inventions often took the place of many people working more slowly.

Part Three: The sentence in italics tells what you are going to do in the essay. In this case, you are going to tell about the good and bad changes that resulted from inventions that replaced workers. You should include examples that you can find or remember from your reading. When you give an example, be sure to tell enough so your

Teaching Tip

Tell your students that when beginning to write, it is better to begin by introducing your subject rather than introducing yourself. Writing that begins by focusing on the writer, "Hi. My name is Bob, and today I am going to tell you about Robert Fulton..." makes the reader wait to get started. Students should begin writing by jumping right in with something interesting learned about the topic, such as "Being an inventor is hard work, but Robert Fulton always worked hard, even as a boy." Now your student is ready to start writing about the topic!

Lapbook Activity

reader can understand what happened and what change occurred because of the invention.

Pick an invention you have learned about in *The Story of Inventions*. Then use these questions and talk with your teacher about how you would answer the above prompt.

1. What changes, good and bad, took place for workers because of the inventions of Howe and Whitney?

2. What did each invention do and what type of worker did it replace?

3. What benefit did each invention bring to all people?

4. **Summarize**, or conclude, what you have said by telling whether or not you think the benefits brought by these inventions were greater than the changes brought about for workers.

Write a **paragraph**, or group of related sentences, that answers Questions 1 and 2 above. Then write a second paragraph that answers Question 3. End your writing with a paragraph that answers Question 4. When you are finished, ask someone to read and then retell what you have written.

🐾🐾 Follow the same instructions for a second invention you have learned about in *The Story of Inventions*.

🐾 Add one more paragraph before your conclusion that describes an invention in current times that has **displaced**, or taken the place of, many workers. Tell whether or not you think the benefits of the invention were greater than the displacement of workers. Give suggestions to help those displaced workers.

G. **Music**   *History, Thinking Skills*

Conclude your study of string instruments by reading pages 48 and 49 in *The Story of the Orchestra* with your teacher and discussing the information about the double bass and the harp. Then listen to parts of the "Carnival of Animals" on Track 17 and the "Dance of the Blessed Spirits" on Track 18 of your CD. Were you able to discriminate, or tell the difference, between the instruments featured on each track? How did the music make you feel? What did you enjoy or dislike about it?

When you are finished, listen carefully to Tracks 17 and 18 again and choose your favorite. Then, draw and color a picture in your Student Notebook of the image this music brings to your mind.

H. Independent Reading & Record Keeping *Thinking Skills*

Review the Lesson 3 At A Glance chart in your Student Notebook to see if all the work you've done in this part has been checked off. Also, make sure the Student Notebook pages you worked on are dated and complete.

When you are finished, choose something to read that you will enjoy. Then find a quiet, comfortable place and read for the following length of time:

🐾 30 minutes   🐾 35 minutes

Be sure to write down what you read today on the Reading Log in your Student Notebook.

Lesson 3, Part 2

A. Copywork & Dictation *Language Skills*

Look carefully at this lesson's Steps for Thinking, and read them silently. Show your teacher any words you don't know, and practice saying them aloud. Now read the Steps aloud, or ask your teacher to read them to you.

When you are finished copying or writing from dictation, compare your copy to the text and make any needed corrections.

🐾 Copy the Steps for Thinking, and tell your teacher an example of each Step.

🐾 Write the Steps for Thinking as your teacher dictates them. Then, in your Student Notebook write one example of each Step. Be sure to use complete sentences.

🐾 Write the Steps for Thinking as your teacher dictates them. Then, in your Student Notebook write two examples of each Step. Be sure to use complete sentences.

B. Reader *Language Skills, History*

Strawberry Girl: page 71, paragraph 5 ("At dinner Pa scolded…") through page 78
The Story of Inventions: Review page 75 ("Seeking the Reward") through the end of the chapter

Follow the directions below to read or listen to the assigned passage in *Strawberry Girl*. When you are finished, skim each section in the review assignment from *The Story of Inventions*. Then tell your teacher examples of how the information in each section relates to its title.

B. Stories help us remember the lives of real people. They help us remember the beliefs and actions that took place. It is not as important to remember details, such as dates of events, as it is to place a character in a time period. With the general time period comes context for what the character did or experienced. This, in turn, reinforces the connection to the unique qualities or events of the character's life. History, literature, and thinking skills form a great partnership.

❧ Read the above assignment from *Strawberry Girl* aloud, and then give one example for each section in *The Story of Inventions*.

❧ Read the above assignment from *Strawberry Girl*, and then give two examples for each section in *The Story of Inventions*.

❧ Read the above assignment from *Strawberry Girl*, and then give three examples for each section in *The Story of Inventions*.

C. Read-Aloud & Discussion   *History, Language Skills, Thinking Skills*

George Washington Carver: page 52, paragraph 1 ("My talk went on…") through page 57, paragraph 9

Follow the directions below to read or listen to the above assignment. Then make up questions about the part of the story you just read or heard. Write your questions in your Student Notebook and ask your teacher to answer them. After discussing her thoughts, write down the best possible answer on the lines provided. Be sure to use complete sentences.

When you are finished, look back at the prediction or predictions you made during Lesson 2, Part 4. Were you able to predict what would happen? Be sure to mark the "Came to Pass" box for each prediction when it does happen.

❧ Listen carefully as your teacher reads the above assignment aloud. Make up two questions.

❧ Listen carefully as your teacher reads the above assignment aloud. Make up three questions.

❧ Read the above assignment aloud; then make up four questions.

D. Word Building   *Language Skills, Thinking Skillss*

Review Lessons 1 and 2 by telling your teacher about the word-parts *chrono-* or *chronos-* and *pro-*. What languages do they come from? What do they mean? Read over the words that you defined in both lessons. Then follow the directions below to make up sentences for some of the words you defined, and tell them to your teacher.

When you are finished, follow the directions in Appendix D to play Word Part Concentration with some of your Rummy Roots Word Cards. From Set 1, use the cards numbered 1, 2, 3, 4, 5, 6, 7, 8, 10, 11, 12, 13, 14, 15, 16, 18, 19, 22, 25, and 28; from Set 2, use numbers 29, 30, 34, 39, 40, 41, 42, 43, 44, 45, 49, 51 and 55; and from Set 3, use numbers 52, 57, 58, 59, 73, 76 and 87.

❧ Make up sentences for at least three words you defined.

❧ Make up sentences for at least four words you defined.

❧ Make up sentences for at least five words you defined.

E. History

Thinking Skills, Geography

A Day in the Life... In this lesson, look at some very important firsts that took place between the years 1900-1920.

- In 1903, the first World Series Baseball Championship was played. The Boston Americans were the first team to win the World Series, and they are now known as the Boston Red Sox. The most winning team in World Series history is the New York Yankees. They've won 27 championships so far.

- The Boy Scouts of America organization was formed in the year 1910. Originally formed in England a few years earlier, the Boy Scouts of America, or BSA, celebrated their 100th anniversary in 2010. Today, the BSA is one of the largest organizations for youth in America.

- The Indianapolis 500 mile race, also known as the Indy 500, was first held in the year 1911. An automobile race, the Indy 500 is considered to be one of the biggest races of its kind in the world. It was billed as "The Greatest Spectacle in Racing."

- Mother's Day was first established as a national holiday in 1914. Since then, Mother's Day has become one of the biggest days for florists in America. On another note, Father's Day wasn't established as a national holiday until 1972, under President Richard Nixon.

- The United States joined World War I in 1917. This was the first war to involve so many nations and all of the major world powers. At the time it was called the Great War. The fighting began in 1914 and ended in November of 1918.

- The first radio broadcast in America took place in the year 1920. Soon after, the radio became so popular that manufacturers could not make them fast enough. Most Americans would gather around their radios in the evenings, listening to stories, news, and music.

After reading these firsts, choose one of them and learn more about it. Present what you learn to your family. Keep your presentation limited to one to three minutes in length.

When you are finished, print and cut out the Supply and Demand Vocabulary 4 game cards from your Student Resources CD. If you want, you can glue each piece onto an index card to make the cards stronger, or print them onto cardstock. Shuffle the cards, read them,

E. Charting information about the inventors studied can show differences between periods in America's progress by focusing on challenges, attitudes, and outcomes. The graphic organizer used in this lesson allows your children to compile their observations and thoughts in one place. Then, by noting the similarities and differences, they are using their thinking skills to analyze the information.

Lapbook Activity

and put them into sets of three—each word, its definition, and its example.[1]

Then follow the directions in Appendix D to play the Supply and Demand Concentration game.

F. **Editing**   *Language Skills, Thinking Skills*

In *Strawberry Girl,* the use of dialect paints a colorful picture of the people who lived in Florida at the beginning of the 1900s. Because a dialect may be hard at first to understand, it is important to try to translate the sentences in your mind as you listen or read so that you will get the meaning of the story. This may take some practice. If you need to see an example, look back at Lesson 1 of this unit, Part 1F.

Choose sentences from *Strawberry Girl* that include dialect and translate them aloud for your teacher.

🐾 two sentences

🐾 three sentences

🐾 four sentences

🐾🐾🐾 One of the differences between English and various dialects is that their grammar is different. Grammar, or the rules for speaking or writing a language, helps you know which word to choose to clearly express your thoughts. One of the most important ideas in grammar is agreement.

In this section, continue working on subject-verb agreement. Remember, if you have a singular subject, or one person or thing that is the focus of your sentence, you must have a verb that goes with that one subject. Here are some examples:

> *Dad* <u>eats</u> steak for dinner.

> *Mom* <u>likes</u> pizza for dinner.

If you have a plural subject, or more than one person or thing that is the focus of your sentence, you must have a verb that goes with more than one subject. Here is an example:

> *Mom* and *Dad* <u>eat</u> steak for dinner.

> *Mom* and *Dad* <u>like</u> pizza for dinner.

Find sentences in your literature that show singular (one) and plural (more than one) subject-verb agreement and write them in your Student Notebook.

🐾 one sentence showing each (singular and plural)

🐾 two sentences showing each

🐾 three sentences showing each

G. Music
Thinking Skills

Read and follow the directions on pages 32 and 33 in the *Basix Recorder Method* to play *high E* and learn about the *fermata*, *repeat signs*, and *1st* and *2nd endings*. Write the names of notes you're not sure of above the staffs on those pages. Then find the Finger Placement Tab in your Student Notebook and color in the circles that show which holes are covered when you play the *high E* note. When you are finished, cut out the tab and paste it on an index card.

Don't forget to listen to the *Recorder Method* CD tracks shown on those pages to hear samples of the lessons and use your Finger Placement Tabs if you need to.

Be sure to spend about 20 minutes a day practicing what you have learned!

H. Independent Reading & Record Keeping
Thinking Skills

Review the Lesson 3 At A Glance chart in your Student Notebook to see if all the work you've done in this part has been checked off. Also, make sure the Student Notebook pages you worked on are dated and complete.

When you are finished, choose something to read that you will enjoy. Then find a quiet, comfortable place and read for the following length of time:

🐾 30 minutes　　　🐾 35 minutes

Be sure to write down what you read today on the Reading Log in your Student Notebook.

—✦—

Lesson 3, Part 3

A. Copywork & Dictation
Language Skills

Look carefully at your assigned passage below, and read it silently. Show your teacher any words you don't know, and practice saying them aloud. Now read the passage aloud, or ask your teacher to read it to you.

When you are finished copying or writing from dictation, compare your copy to the text and make any needed corrections.

🐾 Copy or write as your teacher dictates from *The Story of Inventions*, page 87, paragraph 3 ("For almost a year…").

🐾 Write as your teacher dictates from *The Story of Inventions*, page 87, paragraphs 3 and 4 ("For almost a year…").

B. **Reader**   *Language Skills, History*

Strawberry Girl: page 79 (Chapter VII) through page 86, paragraph 4
The Story of Inventions: Review page 81 (Chapter 7) to page 90
("Offering the Machine to England")

Follow the directions below to read or listen to the assigned passage in *Strawberry Girl*. When you are finished, skim each section in the review assignment from *The Story of Inventions*. Then tell your teacher examples of how the information in each section relates to its title.

Read the above assignment from *Strawberry Girl* aloud, and then give one example for each section in *The Story of Inventions*.

Read the above assignment from *Strawberry Girl*, and then give two examples for each section in *The Story of Inventions*.

Read the above assignment from *Strawberry Girl*, and then give three examples for each section in *The Story of Inventions*.

C. **Read-Aloud & Narration**   *History, Language Skills, Thinking Skills*

George Washington Carver: page 57, paragraph 10 ("Moving behind the boy…") through page 63, paragraph 6

Follow the instructions below for your level. Then, in your own words, tell what happened in the story from George's point of view. Try to remember as many details as possible. Tell what you think is the most important event in the passage.

Listen carefully to the assigned passage.

Read the assigned passage aloud.

D. **Vocabulary**   *Language Skills, Thinking Skills*

Show your teacher the Vocabulary I.D. sheet that you completed in Part 1 of this lesson. Ask her to review the words with you by calling them out or writing them on a dry erase board or piece of paper. Tell her what each word means or how it was used in the story and, if you can, what part of speech it is.

Give yourself one point for each correct meaning and one point for knowing the word's part of speech. Keep track of your Vocabulary I.D. points by writing them at the bottom of the sheet, and try to beat your score when you review these words again in Part 5.

E. **Science**   *Thinking Skills*

Human Body Basics, Musculoskeletal System: Muscles

Quickly review the pages you read and discussed in Part 1 of this lesson.

Teaching Tip

Take the opportunities that occur in daily life to illustrate, and help your children understand, point of view. For example, watch or listen to a newscast together or read a newspaper or Internet article that presents an opinion about a current event. Ask your children what their point of view is on the subject, and perhaps share yours. Include as many family members as you think appropriate in the discussion. Are your points of view the same as or different from the authors of the articles or newscasts?

Lapbook Activity

Then, go to the *Examine This* section at the end of the chapter and complete the fourth project. The Lab Report is in your Student Notebook—be sure to include your drawings! (If you've forgotten how to create a Lab Report, look back at Unit 1, Lesson 1, Part 3F.)

F. Writing   *Language Skills, Thinking Skills*

Thinking Skills Reminder
Your students put previous thinking together to make something new when they modify something to make it better.

Conclusions are important because they are the last thoughts you leave with your reader. You want to make them clear and memorable. The best way to do that is to tell readers exactly what you want them to remember, and why. Give them an example of your personal connection to what you have written.

You can start a conclusion by introducing it as such:

> In conclusion, this essay has given you several of the good and bad results when an invention replaces workers. When change happens, sometimes it is hard. I know this because my uncle lost his job and had to learn how to do something new. Today he is working at a job with a future. We should all welcome change because in the end, it is better for everyone.

Another way to conclude is to tell your readers what you want them to understand from your writing and end with a question, causing them to apply your ideas to their own life.

> In conclusion, many inventions take the place of workers. This can be upsetting to people, but in the end they will be better off. More products will be made and costs will be lower. I think this makes it hard for people to support inventors because it may change the way they work. Even though it is best for everyone, people may still worry. Do you think an invention will replace you someday?

Reread the concluding paragraph you wrote in (one of) the essay(s) for Lesson 3 Part 1. **Revise**, or rewrite, your conclusion two times to reflect the two types of conclusions described in this lesson. After rewriting your conclusion, choose the one you think best fits your essay.

G. Music   *Thinking Skills*

Look back at pages 48 and 49 in *The Story of the Orchestra*.

G. Brief, spaced review is the best kind. It keeps learning fresh and it helps your child continue to connect new learning to previous knowledge. It also builds memory skills naturally.

Then, follow the directions in Appendix D to make two Orchestra Story question and answer cards about the double bass, and two about the harp. Put the small letters *SI* (for string instruments) in the upper left corners of your answer cards. Do not label the question cards—and remember to write the questions in your Student Notebook in the correct order.

Check the directions in Lesson 2, Part 3G and review the Orchestra Story cards you have made so far in this unit.

H. Independent Reading & Record Keeping   *Thinking Skills*

Review the Lesson 3 At A Glance chart in your Student Notebook to see if all the work you've done in this part has been checked off. Also, make sure the Student Notebook pages you worked on are dated and complete.

When you are finished, choose something to read that you will enjoy. Then find a quiet, comfortable place and read for the following length of time:

ᛉᛉ ✥ 30 minutes   ✥ 35 minutes

Be sure to write down what you read today on the Reading Log in your Student Notebook.

⸺⸺⸺

Lesson 3, Part 4

A. Copywork & Dictation   *Language Skills*

Look carefully at your assigned passage below, and read it silently. Show your teacher any words you don't know, and practice saying them aloud. Now read the passage aloud, or ask your teacher to read it to you.

When you are finished copying or writing from dictation, compare your copy to the text and make any needed corrections.

ᛉᛉ Copy or write as your teacher dictates from *Strawberry Girl*, page 93, paragraph 3 ("Miss Liddy hurried over…").

✥✥ Write as your teacher dictates from *George Washington Carver*, page 66, paragraph 3 ("For a moment I stopped…").

✥ Continue writing as your teacher dictates from *George Washington Carver*, page 67, paragraph 2 ("For hours I walked…").

B. Reader   *Language Skills, History*

Strawberry Girl: page 86, paragraph 5 ("Birdie took plates…") through page 94, paragraph 2
The Story of Inventions: Review page 90 ("Offering the Machine to England") through the end of the chapter

Follow the directions below to read or listen to the assigned passage in *Strawberry Girl*. When you are finished, skim each section in the review assignment from *The Story of Inventions*. Then tell your teacher examples of how the information in each section relates to its title.

Teaching Tip

Since many children are reading the assignments silently, it would be good to occasionally ask your student to tell you about what he read. You may also want him to choose his favorite part of the passage and read it aloud to you. If he finds a part that is particularly dramatic or funny, ask him to read it for you expressively. If anything happens in the story that he dislikes, ask him to make sure and tell you about it, too. These are small, natural ways to do comprehension checks.

🐾 Read the above assignment from *Strawberry Girl* aloud, and then give one example for each section in *The Story of Inventions*.

🐾 Read the above assignment from *Strawberry Girl*, and then give two examples for each section in *The Story of Inventions*.

🐾 Read the above assignment from *Strawberry Girl*, and then give three examples for each section in *The Story of Inventions*.

C. **Read-Aloud & Discussion**   *Language Skills, History, Thinking Skills*
George Washington Carver: page 63, paragraph 7 ("Eagerly the young boy…") through page 68

After reading or listening to the read-aloud assignment, talk with your teacher and try to predict what will happen in the future based on what you know of the characters and events. Write your predictions in your Student Notebook. Later, you will look back and see if they were accurate. Try not to peek ahead!

🐾 Listen carefully as your teacher reads the assigned passage. Write down two predictions.

🐾 Listen carefully as your teacher reads the assigned passage. Write down three predictions.

🐾 Read the assigned passage aloud; then write down at least four predictions.

D. **Word Building**   *Language Skills, Thinking Skills*
Continue reviewing Lessons 1 and 2 by again telling your teacher about the word-parts *chrono-* or *chronos-* and *pro-*. What languages do they come from? What do they mean? Read over the words that you defined in both lessons. Then follow the directions below to make up sentences for some of the words you defined, and tell them to your teacher.

When you are finished, follow the directions in Appendix D to play Word Part Concentration with some of your Rummy Roots Word Cards. From Set 1, use the cards numbered 1, 2, 3, 4, 5, 6, 7, 8, 10, 11, 12, 13, 14, 15, 16, 18, 19, 22, 25, and 28; from Set 2, use numbers 29, 30, 34, 39, 40, 41, 42, 43, 44, 45, 49, 51 and 55; and from Set 3, use numbers 52, 57, 58, 59, 73, 76 and 87.

🐾 Make up sentences for at least three words you defined.

🐾 Make up sentences for at least four words you defined.

🐾 Make up sentences for at least five words you defined.

Lapbook Activity

F. Educators have many different feelings about grading. For a child who struggles, grading can be very discouraging. For a child who is competitive, grading may seem like a good idea, but not if the child is overly focused on competing with others. Better to focus on personal improvement than competition with peers. Keep grading in perspective.

E. History
Thinking Skills, Geography

Think about the stories of Eli Whitney and Elias Howe you have read or listened to so far in this unit. Then complete the Invention Demand Chart 5 in your Student Notebook.

Review all the Supply and Demand Vocabulary cards you made in Units 1 and 2. Shuffle the cards, read them, and put them into sets of three— each word, its definition, and its example.

When you are finished, look over the Supply and Demand Vocabulary 4 game cards you made in Part 2 of this unit. Then follow the directions in Appendix D to play the Supply and Demand Go Fish game.

F. Spelling
Language Skills, Thinking Skills

To increase your ability to use the words you have studied in this lesson when you write, review your vocabulary and word building lists. After choosing the number of words assigned below from these lists, you and your teacher may choose words from the Challenge Spelling List in Appendix C to work on as well. You may also want to add two or three words from your own writing that you have difficulty spelling correctly. Make your spelling list on the page provided in your Student Notebook.

When you are finished, write the words you have chosen as your teacher dictates them. Then study any that you are unable to spell correctly in preparation for writing in the next lessons. (You might want to look back at the "Tips for Studying Spelling Words" in Lesson 1, Part 4F). Add those words to the Ongoing Spelling List in your Student Notebook (Lesson 1, Part 4). Also, don't forget to add words you misspell in your everyday writing to the list. Once you can spell a word correctly in dictation, then you can cross it off. Throughout the year, you should have an ongoing list of words you are practicing.

Choose eight words from the vocabulary and word building lists, and two to four Challenge Spelling words (if you and your teacher want).

Choose ten words from the vocabulary and word building lists, and three to five Challenge Spelling words (if you and your teacher want).

Choose twelve words from your vocabulary or word building lists, and four to six Challenge Spelling words (if you and your teacher want).

G. Art   *Thinking Skills*

In this section, make a small book like the diary described on page 43 in *Create Anything With Clay*. Your book doesn't have to include only blank pages though—it can contain information, a story, or a poem, if you want.

Use the cover ideas shown as inspirations to create your own special design.

Don't forget to put any left-over clay back in its zip-lock bag.

H. Independent Reading & Record Keeping   *Thinking Skills*

Review the Lesson 3 At A Glance chart in your Student Notebook to see if all the work you've done in this part has been checked off. Also, make sure the Student Notebook pages you worked on are dated and complete.

When you are finished, choose something to read that you will enjoy. Then find a quiet, comfortable place and read for the following length of time:

    🌱🌱🐾 30 minutes   🐾 35 minutes

Be sure to write down what you read today on the Reading Log in your Student Notebook.

Lesson 3, Part 5

This part is set aside for completion of any work left undone from the lesson and review of concepts and content. It is also a time to expand the work of the lesson with practice and games.

As you discuss the Steps for Thinking with your child, feel free to share the examples that have come to your mind during the lesson. Share the steps you went through in your thinking as well as your outcomes. Modeling is a very effective type of instruction, and your child will gain insight into connecting concepts and examples by hearing your thinking.

- Review this lesson's Steps for Thinking, found in Part 1.

- Use the Vocabulary I.D. sheet you completed in Part 1 of this lesson to make vocabulary cards. Write each word on an index card and try to remember what it means or how it was used in the story without looking. Check the I.D. sheet to see if you were right. Then on the back of each card, draw a picture or write a clue to help you remember what that word means. Be sure to write a small *CG* (for Cultivating Greatness) in the upper left corners.

  When you are finished, give the cards to your teacher and ask her to show you their picture sides, one at a time. Tell her what the picture or clue means, and then name the word written on the other side. If you can, tell what part of speech it is. Give yourself one point for correctly naming a word and one point for knowing its part of speech. Keep track of your points and see if you beat your score from Part 3!

- Listen as your teacher reads the spelling words that you studied from Part 4, especially the ones on your Ongoing Spelling List. Write each word in your Student Notebook as she dictates it. When you are finished, look at your word list and make corrections as needed. Show your teacher how you did.

- Follow the directions in the *Human Body Basics* Instructions to play the Word Power vocabulary game. First play with only the cards you made in the Musculoskeletal System; then combine all the cards you have made so far and see how you do.

  Complete the System Savvy puzzles in your Student Notebook.[2] When you are finished, work on any *Examine This* projects you have not yet completed.

- Look back at pages 32 and 33 in the *Basix Recorder Method* and practice those exercises. Then review any other lessons that may be giving you trouble. Choose several tracks on the *Recorder Method* CD and play along with them. Be sure to spend at least 20 minutes practicing—and don't forget that you can use your Finger Placement Tabs if you need to.

- Review the Lesson 3 At A Glance chart in your Student Notebook to see if all the work you've done in this part has been checked off. If you did an Enrichment Activity or other extra work in this lesson, be sure to write it on the lines next to the chart.

- Complete the Cultivating Greatness Crossword in your Student Notebook.[3]

Teaching Tip

Crossword puzzles, word scrambles, and other word games are great ways to increase recognition of important terms and the spelling of those words. The more frequently a child reads a word and thinks about its meaning, the more likely that child is to remember the word and use it in the future.

Enrichment Activities

1. Do you like peanuts? Look through your family's cookbooks or use the Internet to find some recipes that include peanuts. After trying several, choose your favorite and talk to your teacher about why you like it.

    *Make sure no one in your family has an allergy to nuts before attempting this activity.

2. Discuss the sports of auto racing and baseball with your family. Choose one of the sports to learn more about, such as your favorite team or driver, and where the closest competition is to your home. Depending on the season, watch part of a baseball game or car race in person, on television, or the Internet. What do you notice about the business side of the sport? Do you think a sport makes a great deal of profit for its owners and participants? Do businesses participate in the events? Tell what you think the connection is between sports and economics.

Additional Resources:

Little Britches by Ralph Moody

Booker T. Washington by Lois P. Nicholson

Answers

1. Answer key is in Appendix C.

2. Answers are in the *Human Body Basics* Answer Key.

3. Answer key is in Appendix C.

Lesson 4, Part 1

> ### ⸎ Steps for Thinking ⸎
>
> 1. Once you have tried to do something a certain way, think about how it turned out. If it didn't turn out the way you expected, make changes in what you did and try it again.
>
> 2. It is important to take the time to draw conclusions, or think about the results of what takes place around you. Not everything that is important to learn will be obvious or easy to understand.
>
> 3. The poor choices of others shouldn't stop you from doing what you believe is right.

Read over the Steps for Thinking with your children and ask what they think each one means. Discuss any unknown words or ideas. Remember, this is just an introduction. Do not be concerned if they do not show much connection to the ideas yet. Post the Steps, and refer to them throughout the week when examples arise in reading or discussion.

⸎ Materials ⸎

- *George Washington Carver*
- *Strawberry Girl*
- *The Story of Inventions*
- *Human Body Basics*
- *The Story of the Orchestra* book & CD
- *Classroom Atlas of the United States*
- *Basix Recorder Method*
- *Create Anything With Clay*
- Recorder
- Polymer clay
- Activity (Part 1)
    Timer that measures seconds
    Cardboard paper towel roll
- Activity (Part 4)
    Stiff paper
    Scissors
    Craft glue
    Toothpick
    String or yarn

A. Copywork & Dictation   *Language Skills*

Look carefully at your assigned passage below, and read it silently. Show your teacher any words you don't know, and practice saying them aloud. Now read the passage aloud, or ask your teacher to read it to you.

When you are finished copying or writing from dictation, compare your copy to the text and make any needed corrections.

🐾🌱🐾 Copy or write as your teacher dictates from *The Story of Inventions*, page 102, paragraph 2 ("This reaper…").

🐾 Write as your teacher dictates from *The Story of Inventions*, page 102, paragraph 2 ("This reaper…"), and page 103, paragraph 2 ("Although Bell's reaper…").

B. Reader   *Language Skills, History*

Strawberry Girl: page 94, paragraph 3 ("Miss Liddy bought…") through page 103
The Story of Inventions: page 99 (Chapter 8) to page 103 ("The Man Who Succeeded")

Follow the directions below to read or listen to the assigned passage in *Strawberry Girl*.

Before you begin your assignment in *The Story of Inventions*, scan it for any words you don't know and write them on a piece of scrap paper. Read over any section titles included in the passage—and then, as you read or listen to a section, think about how it relates to its title.

When you are finished, find the Comprehension Questions at the end of Chapter 8 in *The Story of Inventions*, and use complete sentences to write the answers to Questions 1 and 2 in your Student Notebook.

❦ Read the above assignment from *Strawberry Girl* aloud, and then follow along as someone else reads the assignment from *The Story of Inventions*.

❦ Read the above assignment from *Strawberry Girl* silently, and then read the assignment from *The Story of Inventions* aloud.

❦ Read the above assignments from *Strawberry Girl* and *The Story of Inventions* silently.

C. Read-Aloud & Narration   *History, Language Skills, Thinking Skills*
George Washington Carver: page 69 (Chapter 10) through page 74, paragraph 6

Follow the directions below to read or listen to the above passage. Then, in your own words, tell what happened in the portion you are assigned. Try to remember as many details as possible. If necessary you may reread, or listen as your teacher rereads, the part you are to retell.

❦ Listen carefully as your teacher reads the above assignment aloud. Choose one page to retell.

❦ Listen carefully as your teacher reads the above assignment aloud. Choose two pages to retell.

❦ Read the above assignment aloud, and then retell the entire passage.

D. Vocabulary   *Language Skills, Thinking Skills*
Write each vocabulary word on the Vocabulary I.D. sheet in your Student Notebook. Then tell your teacher what you think each word means, based on the context in which you have read it. If you are not sure of a word's meaning, look it up in a dictionary. Write the definition on the Vocabulary Sheet.

Next, write the word's part of speech: noun, adjective, adverb, verb, and so forth. If you aren't sure, this can also be found in the dictionary.

beholden	**sinkhole**	**artesian well**
scrub	**pummel**	**fodder**
❦❦ **lurch**	**dormitory**	**specimen**
barge	**botany**	**graft**

E. Science

Thinking Skills

Human Body Basics, Circulatory System: beginning of chapter, Circulation, & the Heart

As you read through the assigned pages, choose words that are new or unfamiliar and make vocabulary cards for them. Keep your science cards separate for now.

 at least three words

at least four words

Read and discuss the information in the sections with your teacher, and do the *Labwork 1-5* activities. The pages you need for writing, charting, and labeling are in your Student Notebook.

F. Writing

Language Skills, Thinking Skills

For this assignment, you will turn a section of Birdie Boyer's or Shoestring Slater's story into a play. If you would like a review of play writing, complete with examples, refer back to Unit 2, Lesson 4, Part 1F.

The purpose of a play is to tell people about a problem and how it is solved. When you write a play, you not only tell the people in it what they are to say, which is called the lines, you also tell them what they are to do, which is called the stage directions. The lines and actions tell about the problem for the characters and how it works out. Your job, as a writer and director, is to tell those who are going to put on your play several things. They are:

- the <u>setting</u>: where the play will take place

- the <u>characters</u>: who will be in the play

- the <u>lines</u>: what they are to say

- the <u>stage directions</u>: what they are to do and how to do it

The source for all your directions is a script. You will choose a section of the story of Birdie Boyer or Shoestring Slater in *Strawberry Girl* and make it into a play. It would be good to choose a section that has more than one person, and dialogue. That will make your job of writing a script easier, but if you like a section that has none, you can make up lines that you think the characters would say.

After rereading the section you chose, use the page in your Student Notebook to fill in the setting and characters needed to retell this part of the story. Obviously, when putting on a play you cannot go to the real place. You may want to pretend that things look differently, or, with your parent's permission, gather props, which are items that help make the stage look like the setting.

Thinking Skills Reminder

Students show what they understand by demonstrating, or showing, what something does.

Lapbook Activity

When creating your script, start with the name of the play, the characters, and the setting. Next, give the scene number—remember, a scene is a small division in a play that tells about a single event and moves the story forward. Just start with "Scene 1" and continue numbering until you have all the scenes you need.

So each person knows when to speak, the lines begin with a character's name, written in capital letters, followed by a colon. Since the lines in a play are speaking parts, there is no need for quotation marks.

Next come stage directions. Stage directions are put in parentheses and tell people how to move, and any other information that will help them express the lines the way you think they should be spoken.

Talk with your teacher about the resources (people, props, and space) you have to put on this play. It can be as simple or fancy as your time and family will allow. Begin to plan your play by filling out the Play Checklist in your Student Notebook.

Decide with your teacher how much effort you want to put into creating your play. It is important to know the steps to creating a play, but you can determine how much time you have to complete this project. Talk with your teacher to choose a section from *Strawberry Girl* that best fits your needs. You do not need to use all the characters or events in the literature. You can make it smaller to fit your purposes, as long as you still show what the problem is and how it is solved.

Lapbook Activity

G. **Music**   *History, Thinking Skills*

With your teacher, read pages 50 through 53 in *The Story of the Orchestra* and discuss the information about the woodwind section, the flute, and the piccolo. Then listen to parts of the "Suite No. 2 for Flute, Strings, and Basso Continuo" on Track 19 and the "Symphony No. 4" on Track 20 of your CD. Were you able to discriminate, or tell the difference, between the instruments featured on each track? How did the music make you feel? What did you enjoy or dislike about it?

When you are finished, listen carefully to Tracks 19 and 20 again and choose your favorite. Then, draw and color a picture in your Student Notebook of the image this music brings to your mind.

H. **Independent Reading & Record Keeping**   *Thinking Skills*

Review the Lesson 4 At A Glance chart in your Student Notebook to see if all the work you've done in this part has been checked off.

Also, make sure the Student Notebook pages you worked on are dated and complete.

When you are finished, choose something to read that you will enjoy. Then find a quiet, comfortable place and read for the following length of time:

☙☙ ☙ 30 minutes   ☙ 35 minutes

Be sure to write down what you read today on the Reading Log in your Student Notebook.

Lesson 4, Part 2

A. Copywork & Dictation   *Language Skills*

Look carefully at this lesson's Steps for Thinking, and read them silently. Show your teacher any words you don't know, and practice saying them aloud. Now read the Steps aloud, or ask your teacher to read them to you.

When you are finished copying or writing from dictation, compare your copy to the text and make any needed corrections.

☙☙ Copy the Steps for Thinking, and tell your teacher an example of each Step.

☙ Write the Steps for Thinking as your teacher dictates them. Then, in your Student Notebook write one example of each Step. Be sure to use complete sentences.

☙ Write the Steps for Thinking as your teacher dictates them. Then, in your Student Notebook write two examples of each Step. Be sure to use complete sentences.

B. Reader   *Language Skills, History*

Strawberry Girl: page 104 (Chapter IX) through page 112
The Story of Inventions: page 103 ("The Man Who Succeeded") to page 108 ("Carrying the Reaper to the West")

Follow the directions below to read or listen to the assigned passage in *Strawberry Girl*.

Before you begin your assignment in *The Story of Inventions*, scan it for any words you don't know and write them on a piece of scrap paper. Read over any section titles included in the passage—and then, as you read or listen to a section, think about how it relates to its title.

Teaching Tip

Teach your child how to find books that he can read independently. At your bookshelf or the library, ask your child to choose a book he has not read before. Ask him to scan through the book and choose a page to read. Ask him if there were more than five or six words that he did not know on the page. If so, tell him he may want to choose another book to read by himself. Sometimes children like looking at non-fiction books that have difficult text, but interesting pictures or illustrations. This type of book could be an occasional part of his independent reading time, but not the usual choice. The purpose of this reading time is independent practice of reading skills.

Teacher Connection

Continuous learning is an important part of education. Be sure to read the *Teacher Connection* note in your Parent Planner. Don't miss out on this important part of your homeschooling!

B. Children often think that reading silently shows more advanced reading skills. The best notion to share with your children is that understanding the story well makes you a good reader. Whether you read aloud or silently, getting the idea is the most important thing. To make sure our children didn't think of reading aloud as a lesser skill, we enjoyed reading aloud as a family throughout their schooling years, including high school.

When you are finished, find the Comprehension Questions at the end of Chapter 8 in *The Story of Inventions*, and use a complete sentence to write the answer to Question 3 in your Student Notebook.

ᵂᵞ Read the above assignment from *Strawberry Girl* aloud, and then follow along as someone else reads the assignment from *The Story of Inventions*.

ᵂ Read the above assignment from *Strawberry Girl* silently, and then read the assignment from *The Story of Inventions* aloud.

ᵂ Read the above assignments from *Strawberry Girl* and *The Story of Inventions* silently.

C. **Read-Aloud & Discussion**   *History, Language Skills, Thinking Skills*
George Washington Carver: page 74, paragraph 7 ("The words were bitter…") through page 80, paragraph 6

Follow the directions below to read or listen to the above assignment. Then make up questions about the part of the story you just read or heard. Write your questions in your Student Notebook and ask your teacher to answer them. After discussing her thoughts, write down the best possible answer on the lines provided. Be sure to use complete sentences.

When you are finished, look back at the prediction or predictions you made during Lesson 3, Part 4. Were you able to predict what would happen? Be sure to mark the "Came to Pass" box for each prediction when it does happen.

ᵂᵞ Listen carefully as your teacher reads the above assignment aloud. Make up two questions.

ᵂ Listen carefully as your teacher reads the above assignment aloud. Make up three questions.

ᵂ Read the above assignment aloud; then make up four questions.

D. **Word Building**   *Language Skills, Thinking Skillss*
In this section you will continue learning about Greek and Latin word-parts that help to build words in the English language. Today's word-part is **tele-**, which is a Greek word that means *far away*.

Look up the following words in the dictionary and write each definition in your Student Notebook. Then underline the word-part *tele-* in each word. Think and be ready to tell your teacher how each definition relates to the meaning of the Greek word.

telecast	telegraph	telescope
ᵂ ᵂ telephoto	teleconference	telemarketing
ᵂ telemeter	telethon	telecommunication

E. Economics & History   *Thinking Skills*

An important part in the development of **rural** (areas outside cities or towns) America was the general store. Often this type of store formed the core of what would eventually become a community. The general store may have started in many places as merely a trading post, or a store in a remote area where people could **barter**, or trade, products like crops or animal furs for needed supplies such as ammunition, tools, food, or medicine. Not only was the trading post a source of goods, but also a place to receive mail and catch up on news. It served as both a **functional**, or practical, place providing needed goods, and as a point of social connection for those living on the edges of civilization in frontier areas. Providing a place for bartering and serving as a center for news and social interaction continued to be features of general stores in many communities.

When more people moved into an area, other services usually became available nearby, such as a blacksmith, someone who makes or repairs things made of iron or metal, or a livery stable, where horses could be cared for, rented, or sold. This core of needed businesses often became the center of a town, attracting other businesses as the town grew in size. This was a natural growth process since it came in response to the demand for goods or services. But this process could also work in reverse. If the demand decreased for goods or services, businesses would close up and travel to locations where there were demands for what they offered.

This process of increase and decrease is still in effect today, though many times people are unwilling to allow the natural process of creating and removing businesses to occur. Sometimes **artificial support**, or man-made provision that is contrary to the principles of business, is provided rather than allowing the natural process of removing businesses for which demand has decreased. Though artificial support may keep a business running longer than it would have naturally, this type of provision usually ends up requiring long-term financial help without solving the problem.

Talk with your teacher about the natural rise and fall of businesses where you live. Can you think of a business that recently opened in your area to meet a new demand? Can you think of a business in your area that recently closed due to a lack of demand? Make a list of the businesses you think of that fall into each category. Keep track of this list and look at it again in six months to a year. Be sure to notice what has changed.

General stores have experienced the highs and lows of this natural business cycle as well, and have gone through many changes. After a general store was established in an area, it had to gauge what to carry as **merchandise**, or goods bought and sold to make a profit, based on the needs of the people. A store in the Florida frontier probably had little call for snowplows, while a store on the Great Plains would not have great demand for citrus plants. General stores also had the task of carrying a wide range of supplies for farming, tools, dry goods (such as fabric and clothing), books, medicines, and extras like toys, candy or decorations. The buying power of the customers determined the extent to which the extras were available. The establishment of specialty shops or services such as a bank, dressmaker, or restaurant depended on the size of the town and the interest and ability of the people to purchase their products.

Even today, we see the modern version of a general store, known now as a department store—which is a large store that sells many different kinds of goods in different departments. Department stores sprang from peoples' increasing desire to find everything they wanted to buy in one place, rather than going from one smaller specialty store to another. Again, as demand increased for the products they sold, the number of department stores increased. This process began around 1900.

Among the more famous of these stores is J.C. Penney. James Cash Penney had previously worked in a dry goods store in Missouri before moving to a growing mining town in Wyoming, where he established his first store in 1902. J.C. Penney has existed ever since, going through a variety of changes to accommodate customer needs. The stores were initially located in downtown areas of small towns. As populations grew towards the **suburbs**, or residential areas on the edges of towns or cities, J.C. Penney made the transition to suburban shopping malls. Adding catalog sales and, more recently, online sales, Penneys and other department stores continue to try to respond to the needs of customers.

Talk with your teacher about the department stores with which you are familiar. Using the definition of department store, make a list of the ones you visit regularly and the products that you typically purchase at these stores.

Now think about general stores. Make a list of the ways you think department stores are similar to them and ways that they are different.[1]

🌵 at least three similarities and three differences

🐾 at least four similarities and four differences

🐾 at least five similarities and five differences

🐾🐾 The nearness of customers to a general store or department store has always been a large factor in its success or failure. Using the Internet, do a search to find the department store that is closest to your home. Does your family shop at this store? Why or why not? Does your family shop at a store that is farther away? What causes your family to travel farther to shop at that store?

🐾 Talk with the members of your family about what store each one would like to see built closer to your home. Make a list of those stores. Consider sending a letter or email to encourage them to build a store closer to you. Customer feedback is important to business planning. See if they respond to your suggestion.

F. **Editing**   *Language Skills, Thinking Skills*

In *Strawberry Girl*, the use of dialect paints a colorful picture of the people who lived in Florida at the beginning of the 1900s. Because a dialect may be hard at first to understand, it is important to try to translate the sentences in your mind as you listen or read so that you will get the meaning of the story. This may take some practice. If you need to see an example, look back at Lesson 1 of this unit, Part 1F.

Choose sentences from *Strawberry Girl* that include dialect and translate them aloud for your teacher.

🌵 two sentences   🐾 three sentenences   🐾 four sentences

🌵🐾🐾 As you have learned, one of the differences between English and various dialects is that their grammar is different. Grammar helps you know which word to choose to clearly express your thoughts. One of the most important ideas in grammar is agreement.

The second type of agreement is **antecedent-pronoun agreement**. **Pronouns** are words that replace nouns or noun phrases. They are words like *you*, *them*, or *I*, and are very common in speech and writing. This means that whatever word a pronoun refers to in your sentence must agree with it in number and kind. If you have

F. Use meaning to connect grammar skills to use in writing. Show children examples of correct usage and then practice in a way that connects their own thoughts and experiences to the skill. This natural application reinforces the importance of meaning.

a singular antecedent, or word that the pronoun is about, you must have a singular pronoun. Here are some examples:

He likes to eat <u>his</u> steak.

She likes to eat <u>her</u> pizza.

If you have a plural antecedent, or more than one, you must have a plural pronoun. Here are some examples:

They like to eat <u>their</u> steaks.

We like to eat <u>our</u> pizza.

Find sentences in your literature that show singular (one) and plural (more than one) antecedent-pronoun agreement and write them in your Student Notebook.

🐾 one sentence showing each (singular and plural)

🐾 two sentences showing each

🐾 three sentences showing each

G. Music   *Thinking Skills*

Read pages 34 and 35 in the *Basix Recorder Method* to learn about the staccato dot and dotted quarter notes. Write the names of notes you're not sure of above the staffs on those pages and practice playing the melodies.

Don't forget to listen to the *Recorder Method* CD track shown on page 34 to hear a sample of that lesson and use your Finger Placement Tabs if you need to.

Be sure to spend about 20 minutes a day practicing what you have learned!

H. Independent Reading & Record Keeping   *Thinking Skills*

Review the Lesson 4 At A Glance chart in your Student Notebook to see if all the work you've done in this part has been checked off. Also, make sure the Student Notebook pages you worked on are dated and complete.

When you are finished, choose something to read that you will enjoy. Then find a quiet, comfortable place and read for the following length of time:

🐾🐾 30 minutes   🐾 35 minutes

Be sure to write down what you read today on the Reading Log in your Student Notebook.

Lesson 4, Part 3

A. **Copywork & Dictation**   *Language Skills*

Look carefully at your assigned passage below, and read it silently. Show your teacher any words you don't know, and practice saying them aloud. Now read the passage aloud, or ask your teacher to read it to you.

When you are finished copying or writing from dictation, compare your copy to the text and make any needed corrections.

🐾🐾 🐾 Copy or write as your teacher dictates from *The Story of Inventions*, page 111, paragraph 1 ("The Marsh harvester…").

🐾 Write as your teacher dictates from *The Story of Inventions*, page 111, paragraphs 1 and 2 ("The Marsh harvester…").

B. **Reader**   *Language Skills, History*

Strawberry Girl: page 113 ("There was good picking…") through page 122, paragraph 8
The Story of Inventions: page 108 ("Carrying the Reaper to the West") to page 114 ("The Worth of the Reaper")

Follow the directions below to read or listen to the assigned passage in *Strawberry Girl*.

Before you begin your assignment in *The Story of Inventions*, scan it for any words you don't know and write them on a piece of scrap paper. Read over any section titles included in the passage—and then, as you read or listen to a section, think about how it relates to its title.

When you are finished, find the Comprehension Questions at the end of Chapter 8 in *The Story of Inventions*, and use complete sentences to write the answers to Questions 4, 5, and 6 in your Student Notebook.

🐾🐾 Read the above assignment from *Strawberry Girl* aloud, and then follow along as someone else reads the assignment from *The Story of Inventions*.

🐾 Read the above assignment from *Strawberry Girl* silently, and then read the assignment from *The Story of Inventions* aloud.

🐾 Read the above assignments from *Strawberry Girl* and *The Story of Inventions* silently.

B. This part's reading assignment in *Strawberry Girl* contains the word "hell," which may be offensive to some families. Please preview page 115, paragraph 2 ("Pore thing!"….) and take whatever action you feel is appropriate.

C. Read-Aloud & Narration   *History, Language Skills, Thinking Skills*

George Washington Carver: page 80, paragraph 7 ("My invitation was like…") through page 84

Follow the instructions below for your level. Then, in your own words, tell what happened in the story from George's point of view. Try to remember as many details as possible. Tell what you think is the most important event in the passage.

Listen carefully to the assigned passage.

Read the assigned passage aloud.

D. Vocabulary   *Thinking Skills*

Show your teacher the Vocabulary I.D. sheet that you completed in Part 1 of this lesson. Ask her to review the words with you by calling them out or writing them on a dry erase board or piece of paper. Tell her what each word means or how it was used in the story and, if you can, what part of speech it is.

Give yourself one point for each correct meaning and one point for knowing the word's part of speech. Keep track of your Vocabulary I.D. points by writing them at the bottom of the sheet, and try to beat your score when you review these words again in Part 5.

E. One of the most important skills your child can gain is the ability to do research. At the beginning levels research can include searching various locations for information such as the library and the Internet with supervision. The next step is to consider the information and decide what is useful to you or relevant to the questions you are asking.

Lapbook Activity

E. Science   *Thinking Skills*

Human Body Basics, Circulatory System: Blood & Blood Vessels

As you read through the passage, choose words that are new or unfamiliar and make vocabulary cards for them. Keep your science cards separate from other vocabulary.

at least three words

at least four words

Read and discuss the information in the assigned sections with your teacher and do the *Labwork 6-7* activities. The pages you need for writing and labeling are in your Student Notebook.

When you are finished, look at the first two *Examine This* projects at the end of the chapter, and:

Choose one to complete.

Complete both.

Do as much as you can, but you don't have to finish the project(s) in this part. You will have other opportunities to work on them, such as during Part 5 and in occasional Study Hall sections.

F. Writing

Language Skills, Thinking Skills

In this section, continue writing a character summary, or shortened version of the main points of what someone has said or done. Focus only on the main events, or changes, that have occurred in your reading so far about George Washington Carver's life, not the details.

You are limited in the number of words you can use, so make sure you choose words that best describe what has taken place.

Be sure to take time to complete or review the play you began in Part 1. You may want to present your play for your family, or just share your script as part of your End of Unit Presentation.

❧❧ Use up to 50 words to write your summary.

❧ Use up to 45 words to write your summary.

❧ Use up to 40 words to write your summary.

F. Please allow extra time for your student to work on his play writing and preparations if needed.

G. Music

History, Thinking Skills

Look back at pages 50 through 53 in *The Story of the Orchestra*.

Then, follow the directions in Appendix D to make two Orchestra Story question and answer cards about the woodwind section, two about the flute, and two about the piccolo. Put the small letters *WI* (for woodwind instruments) in the upper left corners of your answer cards. Do not label the question cards—and remember to write the questions in your Student Notebook in the correct order.

Check the directions in Lesson 2, Part 3G, and review the Orchestra Story cards you have made so far in this unit.

G. An index card file box can be a convenient way to store your Orchestra Story cards. Alternately, a small shoe box, ziploc bag, or even rubber band may be helpful in creating a storage system that will work best for your family.

Lapbook Activity

H. Independent Reading & Record Keeping

Thinking Skills

Review the Lesson 4 At A Glance chart in your Student Notebook to see if all the work you've done in this part has been checked off. Also, make sure the Student Notebook pages you worked on are dated and complete.

When you are finished, choose something to read that you will enjoy. Then find a quiet, comfortable place and read for the following length of time:

❧❧ ❧ 30 minutes   ❧ 35 minutes

Be sure to write down what you read today on the Reading Log in your Student Notebook.

Lesson 4, Part 4

A. **Copywork & Dictation** *Language Skills*

Look carefully at your assigned passage below, and read it silently. Show your teacher any words you don't know, and practice saying them aloud. Now read the passage aloud, or ask your teacher to read it to you.

When you are finished copying or writing from dictation, compare your copy to the text and make any needed corrections.

🐾 Copy or write as your teacher dictates from *Strawberry Girl*, page 123, paragraph 3 ("Birdie helped Pa load…").

🐾 Write as your teacher dictates from *George Washington Carver*, page 89, paragraph 6 ("Moonlight covered the…").

🐾 Continue writing as your teacher dictates from *George Washington Carver*, page 90, paragraph 4 ("But does it ever trouble you…").

B. **Reader** *Language Skills, History*

Strawberry Girl: page 122, paragraph 9 ("Birdie had never been…") through page 131, paragraph 4
The Story of Inventions: page 114 ("The Worth of the Reaper") to the end of the chapter

Follow the directions below to read or listen to the assigned passage in *Strawberry Girl*.

Before you begin your assignment in *The Story of Inventions*, scan it for any words you don't know and write them on a piece of scrap paper. Read over any section titles included in the passage—and then, as you read or listen to a section, think about how it relates to its title.

When you are finished, find the Comprehension Questions at the end of Chapter 8 in *The Story of Inventions*, and use complete sentences to write the answers to Questions 7 and 8 in your Student Notebook.

🐾 Read the above assignment from *Strawberry Girl* aloud, and then follow along as someone else reads the assignment from *The Story of Inventions*.

🐾 Read the above assignment from *Strawberry Girl* silently, and then read the assignment from *The Story of Inventions* aloud.

🐾 Read the above assignments from *Strawberry Girl* and *The Story of Inventions* silently.

C. Encourage your children to look through their Student Notebooks at the predictions they have made about their reading. Have they improved over the course of the unit? Ask them if the process of making predictions has become easier for them and give them your observations about their progress with this skill.

C. **Read-Aloud & Discussion** *History, Language Skills, Thinking Skills*
George Washington Carver: page 85 ("'Say, maybe we should…'") through page 90, paragraph 8

After reading or listening to the read-aloud assignment, talk with your teacher and try to predict what will happen in the future based on what you know of the characters and events. Write your predictions in your Student Notebook. Later you will look back and see if they were accurate. Try not to peek ahead!

Listen carefully as your teacher reads the assigned passage. Write down two predictions.

Listen carefully as your teacher reads the assigned passage. Write down three predictions.

Read the assigned passage aloud; then write down at least four predictions.

D. Word Building   *Language Skills, Thinking Skills*

Earlier in this lesson you learned about the Greek word-part *tele-*. Read over the words you defined in Part 2, and tell your teacher what each one means.

Now add to your ability to use *tele-* by finding more words in the dictionary that begin with it and relate to its meaning. Write them in your Student Notebook. Be sure not to repeat any of the words you have already defined. When you are finished, pick one of your words and write a sentence that uses it correctly.

at least three words

at least six words

at least nine words

E. Economics & History   *Thinking Skills, History, Geography*

The ability to **stock**, or supply, goods to a store has always been one of the determiners of its success. If items needed by customers are available in a store, the store's sales will go up. This increases the store's chance of making a profit and remaining in business. If a store advertises a certain item, but then runs out of it, customers have to wait. If a customer has to wait long enough or often enough, even for a well-priced item, that customer will go elsewhere to make his purchase. A similar problem existed for trading posts and general stores.

One of the difficulties for trading posts was the limited amount of goods available due to the store's remote location. General stores were also limited in sales by what they could offer their customers. Even department stores suffer the same difficulties if demand is greater than supply. One way to solve the problem of getting **adequate**, or enough, stock is by improving the system of delivering goods to stores. The development of the railroad system in America was a great boost to the ability of stores to carry a greater variety and **quantity**, or amount, of stock. Not only could the railroad system deliver products to stores, it

E. What makes a person memorable? Many history books give only facts and dates, but that doesn't make historical figures seem real. Learning about their hearts—their thoughts and motives, struggles and successes, and ultimately how others remember them—makes them memorable. The purpose of learning about them is for their lives to make an impact on our lives.

Lapbook Activity

could also carry large amounts of raw materials to those who **manufactured**, or made, the products.

In 1825, an Englishman named George Stephenson invented the first steam **locomotive** (vehicle used to pull trains) engine. In 1826, John Stevens was doing similar work in America and is considered the father of American railroads. American railroads continued to grow and develop with the help of inventors like George Pullman, inventor of the Pullman Sleeper, a train car in which passengers could sleep while traveling. The growth of travel by railroad was important for several reasons. As more people paid to travel by train, more railroad lines were built, and the greater the expansion, or increase in size and number, of railroad systems. The more comfortable and affordable that rail travel became, the more it was used by a greater number of customers, bringing in more income for railroads.

Talk with your teacher about the benefits of railroads for businesses. What other methods were available at the time for transporting stock, raw materials, or customers to businesses? What advantages did railroads have over travel by horse and wagon or boat? Make a list of ways that businesses benefitted by this expansion of railroad service in America.

During the Civil War, railroad lines were extremely important for transporting needed ammunition, food, and supplies to troops on both sides. Because of this, building and maintaining railroads became more important than ever. If a section of train track was destroyed, supplies could not get through to the troops that needed them, so guarding and targeting railroad lines became very important. Part of the process of building railroad lines involved making accurate maps. Though mapmaking was an ancient profession, those who made maps for railroad development had to be especially careful when it came to **elevation** (height above sea level) and landforms like mountains, hills, plateaus, or plains. The greater the detail on the map, the greater the help for those planning and building railroads. Remember that railroads can be built in a variety of environments, but some things make it more difficult.

Look at the Landforms, Elevation, and Physical maps in the *Classroom Atlas of the United States*. Choose several states in which you think railroad building would be easier, and several states where you think it would be harder. Use the other theme maps in the front of your atlas to confirm that your choices are good ones based on climate, vegetation, rainfall, snowfall, and temperature. Make a list of states for each category and some reasons for your choices (from the different theme map sources).[2]

❦❦ List three states for each category, and at least three reasons for each choice.

❦ List four states for each category, and at least four reasons for each choice.

❦ List five states for each category, and at least four reasons for each choice.

F. Spelling   *Language Skills, Thinking Skills*

To increase your ability to use the words you have studied in this lesson when you write, review your vocabulary and word building lists. After choosing the number of words assigned below from these lists, you and your teacher may choose words from the Challenge Spelling List in Appendix C to work on as well. You may also want to add two or three words from your own writing that you have difficulty spelling correctly. Make your spelling list on the page provided in your Student Notebook.

When you are finished, write the words you have chosen as your teacher dictates them. Then study any that you are unable to spell correctly in preparation for writing in the next lessons. (You might want to look back at the "Tips for Studying Spelling Words" in Lesson 1, Part 4F). Add those words to the Ongoing Spelling List in your Student Notebook (Lesson 1, Part 4). Also, don't forget to add words you misspell in your everyday writing to the list. Once you can spell a word correctly in dictation, then you can cross it off. Throughout the year, you should have an ongoing list of words you are practicing.

❦❦ Choose eight words from the vocabulary and word building lists, and two to four Challenge Spelling words (if you and your teacher want).

❦ Choose ten words from the vocabulary and word building lists, and three to five Challenge Spelling words (if you and your teacher want).

❦ Choose twelve words from your vocabulary or word building lists, and four to six Challenge Spelling words (if you and your teacher want).

G. Art   *Thinking Skills*

Is any special family occasion coming up soon—like a birthday, holiday, graduation, or anniversary? If there is, think about it as you practice the techniques shown on pages 44 and 45 in *Create Anything With Clay* for creating invitations and cards.

There are a great many possibilities presented on these pages, so have fun exploring them. You never know when they might come in handy! Be sure to put any leftover clay back in its zip-lock bag.

H. **Independent Reading & Record Keeping**   *Thinking Skills*

Review the Lesson 4 At A Glance chart in your Student Notebook to see if all the work you've done in this part has been checked off. Also, make sure the Student Notebook pages you worked on are dated and complete.

When you are finished, choose something to read that you will enjoy. Then find a quiet, comfortable place and read for the following length of time:

🖐️🖐️ 30 minutes   🐾 35 minutes

Be sure to write down what you read today on the Reading Log in your Student Notebook.

Lesson 4, Part 5

This part is set aside for completion of any work left undone from the lesson and review of concepts and content. It is also a time to expand the work of the lesson with practice and games.

- Review this lesson's Steps for Thinking, found in Part 1.

- Use the Vocabulary I.D. sheet you completed in Part 1 of this lesson to make vocabulary cards. Write each word on an index card and try to remember what it means or how it was used in the story without looking. Check the I.D. Sheet to see if you were right. Then on the back of each card, draw a picture or write a clue to help you remember what that word means. Be sure to write a small *CG* (for Cultivating Greatness) in the upper left corners.

  When you are finished, give the cards to your teacher and ask her to show you their picture sides, one at a time. Tell her what the picture or clue means and then name the word written on the other side. If you can, tell what part of speech it is. Give yourself one point for correctly naming a word, and one point for knowing its part of speech. Keep track of your points and see if you beat your score from Part 3!

- Listen as your teacher reads the spelling words that you studied from Part 4, especially the ones on your Ongoing Spelling List. Write each word in your Student Notebook as she dictates it. When you are finished, look at your word list and make corrections as needed. Show your teacher how you did.

Why not just learn the meaning of a vocabulary word? Words learned individually are separate pieces of information. Words learned in the context of meaning are easier to remember and use correctly. Connecting each word to the way it was used in the story develops a more permanent link to that word in your child's mind.

Read the list of spelling words to your child. If he would rather spell them aloud than write them, it is perfectly acceptable. As you dictate each word, put small dots beside any that are misspelled. Then have your child copy them onto his Ongoing Spelling List.

- Follow the directions in the *Human Body Basics* Instructions to play the Word Power vocabulary game. First, play with only the cards you made for the Circulatory System; then combine all the cards you have made so far and see how you do.

  Complete the System Savvy puzzles in your Student Notebook.[3] When you are finished, work on any *Examine This* projects you have not yet completed.

- Look back at pages 29 through 35 in the *Basix Recorder Method* and review any exercises that may still be giving you trouble. Choose several tracks on the *Recorder Method* CD and play along with them. Be sure to spend at least 20 minutes practicing!

- Review the Lesson 4 At A Glance chart in your Student Notebook to see if all the work you've done in this part has been checked off. If you did an Enrichment activity or other extra work in this lesson, be sure to write it on the lines next to the chart.

- Complete the Cultivating Greatness Who or What Am I? in your Student Notebook.[4]

Enrichment Activities

1. Find out if there are any farms in your area that allow customers to come and harvest produce for themselves. These types of farms offer areas where you can pick your own fruits or vegetables. Talk with your family about visiting a "u-pick" site. What are the advantages to doing this? What are the disadvantages? What other methods are used to harvest crops in your area?

2. In *Strawberry Girl*, the Boyer family attended a taffy-pull. Talk with your family about making taffy and find a recipe in a cookbook or on the Internet. (If you don't care for taffy, find some other recipe for candy that your family likes to eat.) Take pictures of the event. You may want to give the candy away as gifts for holidays or birthdays.

3. Find out more about the railroads in your area. Do they offer passenger service? Are they a main source of moving cargo to businesses? Have you ever ridden on a train? If possible, find out about the cost and availability of a train ride. If you are able to ride on a train, send a postcard to a family member describing your trip.

Additional Resources:

Man of the Family by Ralph Moody

Cherry Ames, Department Store Nurse by Helen Wells

If you choose to use the assessments, remember to set aside time for that purpose when you complete this unit. You can use the results of the assessments in various ways: to determine if there is any area that needs additional study, to assign grades, or just to familiarize your child with taking assessments. Lesson 6 of each unit provides review that should help prepare your child for this activity.

Answers

1. Answers will vary, but might include the following:

    Similarities:

    - Both offer a variety of products.

    - Both are located near customers.

    - Clerks are available to assist customers and make sales at both stores.

    - Both stock items determined by customer need.

    - Either cash or bartered items exchanged for items purchased.

    Differences:

    - General stores were also centers of news and social interaction.

    - Department stores have many locations of one business; general stores usually only had one location.

    - General stores could work on a system of bartering; department stores only accept money.

    - Local products were commonly sold in general stores; items stocked in department stores are generally shipped from central locations to all stores.

    - Clerks in department stores are hired workers; clerks in general stores were often the owners of the store.

2. Answers will vary, but should include information about elevation, landforms that pose challenges to building, number of rivers to cross, climate, rain or snowfall that could delay building, or types of vegetation that would interfere with the building process.

3. Answers are in the *Human Body Basics* Answer Key.

4. Answer key is in Appendix C.

Lesson 5, Part 1

> ### ❧ Steps for Thinking ❧
>
> 1. Once you have learned to think carefully about information and decisions, you can give the best answers based on what you know. Often what you learn can help others if you share it with them.
>
> 2. Careful consideration of what you observe can lead you to new understanding. Even mistakes can be a great teacher for those willing to learn from them.
>
> 3. When people behave badly you can have the greatest impact on their behavior by not treating them the way they treated you.

❧ Materials ❧:

- *George Washington Carver*
- *Strawberry Girl*
- *The Story of Inventions*
- *Human Body Basics*
- *Classroom Atlas of the United States*
- *The Story of the Orchestra* book & CD
- *Basix Recorder Method*
- *Create Anything With Clay*
- *Profiles from History, Volume 3*
- Recorder
- Polymer clay
- Activity (Part 1)
    - Timer that measures seconds
    - 1 large round balloon
    - Rubber band
    - Plastic straw
    - Modeling clay
- Activity (Part 4)
    - Cardboard or paper mâché box
    - Table knife
    - Craft glue
    - Paintbrush

𝒜. Copywork & Dictation　　　*Language Skills*

Look carefully at your assigned passage below, and read it silently. Show your teacher any words you don't know, and practice saying them aloud. Now read the passage aloud, or ask your teacher to read it to you.

When you are finished copying or writing from dictation, compare your copy to the text and make any needed corrections.

🐾🐾🐾 Copy or write as your teacher dictates from *The Story of Inventions*, page 120, paragraph 1 ("There is scarcely…").

🐾 Write as your teacher dictates from *The Story of Inventions*, page 120, paragraphs 1 and 2 ("There is scarcely…").

ℬ. Reader　　　*Language Skills, History*

Strawberry Girl: page 131, paragraph 5 ("He stood over…") through the bottom of page 138
The Story of Inventions: page 116 (Chapter 9) to page 120 ("Preparing for Work")

Follow the directions below to read or listen to the assigned passage in *Strawberry Girl*.

Before you begin your assignment in *The Story of Inventions*, scan it for any words you don't know and write them on a piece of scrap paper. Read over any section titles included in the passage—and then, as you read or listen to a section, think about how it relates to its title.

When you are finished, find the Comprehension Questions at the end of Chapter 9 in *The Story of Inventions*, and use complete sentences to write the answers to Questions 1 and 2 in your Student Notebook.

Read the above assignment from *Strawberry Girl* aloud, and then follow along as someone else reads the assignment from *The Story of Inventions*.

Read the above assignment from *Strawberry Girl* silently, and then read the assignment from *The Story of Inventions* aloud.

Read the above assignments from *Strawberry Girl* and *The Story of Inventions* silently.

C. Talk with your children about any improvement they have made during this unit in their ability to narrate what they have read. Just like spaced review, occasional review of performance can give needed encouragement. Point out any specifics that have improved, like the ability to retell more details or the overall picture of the story. Help them see evaluation as a natural part of making progress.

C. **Read-Aloud & Narration**   *History, Language Skills, Thinking Skills*

George Washington Carver: page 90, paragraph 9 ("So that was the mystery…") through page 95

Follow the directions below to read or listen to the above passage. Then, in your own words, tell what happened in the portion you are assigned. Try to remember as many details as possible. If necessary you may reread, or listen as your teacher rereads, the part you are to retell.

Listen carefully as your teacher reads the above assignment aloud. Choose one page to retell.

Listen carefully as your teacher reads the above assignment aloud. Choose two pages to retell.

Read the above assignment aloud, and then retell the entire passage.

D. **Vocabulary**   *Language Skills, Thinking Skills*

Write each vocabulary word on the Vocabulary I.D. sheet in your Student Notebook. Then tell your teacher what you think each word means, based on the context in which you have read it. If you are not sure of a word's meaning, look it up in a dictionary. Write the definition on the Vocabulary sheet.

Next, write the word's part of speech: noun, adjective, adverb, verb, and so forth. If you aren't sure, this can also be found in the dictionary.

squatter	**doomsday**	**plaintive**
dormant	**stagnant**	**depot**
clumsily	**erosion**	**vivid**
motive	**bushel**	**tragic**

C &
Graphic
Org.

X

Inv. Look

Vocab

E. Science

Thinking Skills

Human Body Basics, Respiratory System: entire chapter

As you read through the assigned chapter, choose words that are new or unfamiliar and make vocabulary cards for them as directed. Keep your science cards separate from other vocabulary.

🐾 at least three words

🐾🐾 at least four words

Read and discuss the information in the passage with your teacher and do the *Labwork 1-3* activities. The pages you need for writing, charting, and labeling are in your Student Notebook.

When you are finished, look at the *Examine This* projects at the end of the chapter, and:

🐾 Choose one to complete.

🐾 Choose two to complete.

🐾 Complete all three.

Do as much as you can, but you don't have to finish the project(s) in this part. You will have other opportunities to work on them, such as during Part 5 and in occasional Study Hall sections.

F. Writing

Language Skills, Thinking Skills

For this section, choose science activities you have completed in this unit and write one or two paragraphs in your Student Notebook describing how you did each of them. Your descriptions should be detailed enough that anyone reading them could go through the steps and complete the same activities.

You might want to write the steps on scrap paper first and put them in order. Then think about how you would like your paragraph(s) to read. Be sure to use words like *first, then, next,* and *finally* to connect your sentences and make the order more clear.

🐾 Choose one activity.

🐾🐾 Choose two activities.

F. You may want to begin previewing ideas for the unit-end presentation with your children. This will help everyone focus on similar goals for the presentation, as well as give them time to practice and get feedback for improvement.

G. Music

History, Thinking Skills

Continue your study of woodwind instruments by reading pages 54 through 57 in *The Story of the Orchestra* with your teacher and discussing the information about the oboe, the clarinet, and the saxophone. Then listen to parts of the "Sinfonia in G Major for Two Oboes" on Track 21, the "Concerto for Clarinet and Orchestra" on Track 22, and "Bolero" on Track 23 of your CD. Were you able to discriminate between the instruments featured on each track? How did the music make you feel? What did you enjoy or dislike about it?

When you are finished, listen carefully to Tracks 21, 22, and 23 again and choose your favorite. Then, draw and color a picture in your Student Notebook of the image this music brings to your mind.

H. **Independent Reading & Record Keeping**   *Thinking Skills*
Review the Lesson 5 At A Glance chart in your Student Notebook to see if all the work you've done in this part has been checked off. Also, make sure the Student Notebook pages you worked on are dated and complete.

When you are finished, choose something to read that you will enjoy. Then find a quiet, comfortable place and read for the following length of time:

🐾🐾 🐾 30 minutes   🐾 35 minutes

Be sure to write down what you read today on the Reading Log in your Student Notebook.

Lesson 5, Part 2

A. **Copywork & Dictation**   *Language Skills*
Look carefully at this lesson's Steps for Thinking, and read them silently. Show your teacher any words you don't know, and practice saying them aloud. Now read the Steps aloud, or ask your teacher to read them to you.

When you are finished copying or writing from dictation, compare your copy to the text and make any needed corrections.

🐾🐾 Copy the Steps for Thinking, and tell your teacher an example of each Step.

🐾 Write the Steps for Thinking as your teacher dictates them. Then, in your Student Notebook write one example of each Step. Be sure to use complete sentences.

🐾 Write the Steps for Thinking as your teacher dictates them. Then, in your Student Notebook write two examples of each Step. Be sure to use complete sentences.

B. **Reader** *Language Skills, History*

Strawberry Girl: page 138, last paragraph ("A night came…") through page 145
The Story of Inventions: page 120 ("Preparing for Work") to page 128 ("His Master Invention")

Follow the directions below to read or listen to the assigned passage in *Strawberry Girl*.

Before you begin your assignment in *The Story of Inventions*, scan it for any words you don't know and write them on a piece of scrap paper. Read over any section titles included in the passage—and then, as you read or listen to a section, think about how it relates to its title.

When you are finished, find the Comprehension Questions at the end of Chapter 9 in *The Story of Inventions*, and use complete sentences to write the answers to Questions 3 and 4 in your Student Notebook.

🐾 Read the above assignment from *Strawberry Girl* aloud, and then follow along as someone else reads the assignment from *The Story of Inventions*.

🐾 Read the above assignment from *Strawberry Girl* silently, and then read the assignment from *The Story of Inventions* aloud.

🐾 Read the above assignments from *Strawberry Girl* and *The Story of Inventions* silently.

C. **Read-Aloud & Discussion** *History, Language Skills, Thinking Skills*

George Washington Carver: page 96 (Chapter 13) to the bottom of page 100

Follow the directions below to read or listen to the above assignment. Then make up questions about the part of the story you just read or heard. Write your questions in your Student Notebook and ask your teacher to answer them. After discussing her thoughts, write down the best possible answer on the lines provided. Be sure to use complete sentences.

When you are finished, look back at the prediction or predictions you made during Lesson 4, Part 4. Were you able to predict what would happen? Be sure to mark the "Came to Pass" box for each prediction when it does happen.

🐾 Listen carefully as your teacher reads the above assignment aloud. Make up two questions.

🐾 Listen carefully as your teacher reads the above assignment aloud. Make up three questions.

🐾 Read the above assignment aloud; then make up four questions.

B. Stories about famous people in history are a wonderful way to illustrate important character qualities. Children naturally enjoy the story format and more easily connect to characters and the events surrounding their lives.

Thinking Skills Reminder

Students show what they know when they recall, or retell what has been learned.

D. Word Building

Language Skills, Thinking Skillss

In this section you will continue learning about Greek and Latin word-parts that help to build words in the English language. Today's word-part is **trans-**, which is a Latin word that means *across*.

Look up the following words in the dictionary and write each definition in your Student Notebook. Then underline the word-part *trans-* in each word. Think and be ready to tell your teacher how each definition relates to the meaning of the Latin word.

Lapbook Activity

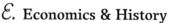

transaction	transcend	transform
transformer	transition	transference
transduce	transfigure	transcontinental

E. Economics & History

Thinking Skills, Geography

The growth of the postal service is naturally linked to the development of transportation. With each new method of transportation came a new way to deliver the mail. A variety of **post roads**, or regularly used routes to deliver mail, were used. When the country grew to the west, post roads were often routes taken by stagecoaches or horse-drawn wagons. When steamboats were invented, post roads could be waterways. Upon the development of railroads, post roads became railroad tracks. The postal service supported each new development in transportation by providing both finances for development and customers for business. As demand increased, each business prospered by the **partnership**, or mutually beneficial relationship, that developed.

New railroad routes meant new, faster ways to deliver mail and goods. It wasn't long before businessmen like Richard Sears took notice. Sears worked as a railway agent. In the late 1880s, the majority of people in America lived in rural areas, so getting goods to them often provided a challenge. Sears purchased a shipment of watches that were unwanted by the jeweler who received them. He then sold the watches to others along the rail line and made a profit. So he began a business based upon the idea of shipping products directly to customers all over America who ordered them. Sears teamed up with partner Alvah C. Roebuck in 1893 to form Sears, Roebuck, and Company. Their main customers were farmers living in the rural parts of the country.

Through the help of railroads, farmers were now able to harvest their crops, sell them to faraway buyers, and receive cash payment for them. Since they now had cash to purchase goods, they could look beyond their local general stores where they may have had to use the bartering system in the past. Now, with cash in hand and a way to receive ordered goods, farmers could purchase the things they needed from mail-order catalogs. These **catalogs**, or publications with lists of items for sale, were a source of goods with greater **inventory**, or stock, and were usually able to sell at a lower price—allowing people to save money over the prices at the general store. The Sears business thrived, and though it has gone through changes over the years that reflect the changing needs of customers, it is still in business today, over one hundred years later.

Look at the J.C. Penney and Sears catalogs on the Internet or at the actual stores. Since these are department stores, they have many types of items available. Pretend that you have $200 and you have to buy a wardrobe of clothes for cold weather, or stock a kitchen, or get the equipment you need to do a good job of taking care of the outside of your house. Look first at the J.C. Penney catalog and see how many items you could order for your money. Make a list of things you could get and their prices. Don't forget to include the shipping costs. Now make a list of the same items from the Sears catalog. Which store do you think gives you the best quality for the lowest price? Look at the websites of other stores, or go to the stores yourself, and find out if you saved money by buying your items through the catalog.

🐾🐾 Repeat this process with different items. Considering the costs of shipping, do you think you save money? Why or why not?

🐾 Explain the connection between transportation and business to your teacher. With the invention and development of the airplane, travel became even more rapid. What methods of delivering goods exist now that make doing business even easier for the customer? Look at the websites of the U. S. Postal Service, Federal Express, and United Parcel Service. What types of delivery options do they provide customers? How do you think these services have impacted businesses?

🌱🐾🐾 *A Day in the Life...* Christmas has become a most special holiday in the United States. Families gather together, children enjoy a break from school, adults get time off from work, and many houses are decorated in lights, garland, mistletoe, stockings, and a tree covered in ornaments. For many families, Christmas morning is a time of giving gifts to each other. In the afternoon, those who have labored in the kitchen are rewarded with many thanks and the enjoyment of a large family meal.

So where did all these traditions come from, and how long has Christmas been celebrated in the United States?

You'll probably be surprised to know that Christmas did not become a national holiday until the year 1870. Congress passed a bill in June of that year that was signed by President Ulysses S. Grant. Before America adopted the holiday, it was more of a festival or carnival. Over the years, it has become more of a sacred, family-centered celebration.

People put candles on their Christmas trees to decorate them before there was electricity. Families would also string pieces of popcorn and cranberries together and use them as decorations. The first year someone thought of putting electric lights on Christmas trees was 1882. Glass ornaments were mainly imported from other countries until the late 1930s, when the Corning Company began producing a line of "Shiny Brite Ornaments" made in America. Each year since then, tree ornaments, including those made by hand, have become more and more unique, extravagant, and creative. To many, decorating the tree has developed into a treasured family event.

Giving and receiving Christmas gifts has made the holiday season a major boost for the economy. Companies depend on the added seasonal income and begin planning sales early to entice shoppers. Every year the day after Thanksgiving, called Black Friday, marks the beginning of the holiday shopping season. It is called Black Friday because the many sales put retailers "in the black." This means they are making a profit. Next time you are enjoying the holiday season, remember that each gift you receive is not only a blessing for you but for the economy as well!

Talk with your family about ways that holiday celebrations connect to businesses.

F. **Editing**   *Language Skills, Thinking Skills*
In *Strawberry Girl,* the use of dialect paints a colorful picture of the people who lived in Florida at the beginning of the 1900s. Because a dialect may be hard at first to understand, it is important to try to translate the sentences in your mind as you listen or read so that you will get the meaning of the story. This may take some practice. If you need to see an example, look back at Lesson 1 Part 1F of this unit.

Choose sentences from *Strawberry Girl* that include dialect and translate them aloud for your teacher.

 two sentences   three sentences   four sentences

As you have learned, one of the differences between English and various dialects is that their grammar is different. Grammar helps you know which word to choose to clearly express your thoughts. One of the most important ideas in grammar is agreement.

In this section, continue working on antecedent-pronoun agreement. Remember that whatever word a pronoun refers to in your sentence must agree with the antecedent in number and kind. If you have a singular antecedent, or word that the pronoun is about, you must have a singular pronoun. Here are some examples:

He likes to eat <u>his</u> steak.

She likes to eat <u>her</u> pizza.

If you have a plural antecedent, or more than one, you must have a plural pronoun. Here are some examples:

They like to eat <u>their</u> steaks.

We like to eat <u>our</u> pizza.

Find sentences in your literature that show singular (one) and plural (more than one) antecedent-pronoun agreement and write them in your Student Notebook.

one sentence showing each (singular and plural)

two sentences showing each

three sentences showing each

G. Music
Thinking Skills

Read pages 36 and 37 in the *Basix Recorder Method* to learn more about dotted quarter notes and the eighth rest. Write the names of notes you're not sure of above the staffs on those pages and practice these exercises.

Don't forget to listen to the *Recorder Method* CD tracks shown on page 36 to hear samples of that lesson and use your Finger Placement Tabs if you need to.

Be sure to spend about 20 minutes a day practicing what you have learned!

H. A reading log is an important part of a portfolio. It documents sequential effort and is a satisfying way for a child to see work completion. You may also want to make a list of books read for this unit, which may include bibliographical information, such as author, publisher, and copyright date. This is an easy way to build awareness of bibliographical information.

H. **Independent Reading & Record Keeping**   *Thinking Skills*
Review the Lesson 5 At A Glance chart in your Student Notebook to see if all the work you've done in this part has been checked off. Also, make sure the Student Notebook pages you worked on are dated and complete.

When you are finished, choose something to read that you will enjoy. Then find a quiet, comfortable place and read for the following length of time:

🐾🐾 🐾 30 minutes   🐾 35 minutes

Be sure to write down what you read today on the Reading Log in your Student Notebook.

Lesson 5, Part 3

A. **Copywork & Dictation**   *Language Skills*
Look carefully at your assigned passage below, and read it silently. Show your teacher any words you don't know, and practice saying them aloud. Now read the passage aloud, or ask your teacher to read it to you.

When you are finished copying or writing from dictation, compare your copy to the text and make any needed corrections.

🐾🐾 🐾 Copy or write as your teacher dictates from *The Story of Inventions*, page 130, paragraph 1 ("The molten metal…").

🐾 Write as your teacher dictates from *The Story of Inventions*, page 130, paragraphs 1 and 2 ("The molten metal…").

B. **Reader**   *Language Skills, History*
Strawberry Girl: page 146 (Chapter XII) through page 155, paragraph 2
The Story of Inventions: page 128 ("His Master Invention") to page 133 ("Making the Process a Success")

Follow the directions below to read or listen to the assigned passage in *Strawberry Girl*.

Before you begin your assignment in *The Story of Inventions*, scan it for any words you don't know and write them on a piece of scrap paper. Read over any section titles included in the passage—then, as you read or listen to a section, think about how it relates to its title.

When you are finished, find the Comprehension Questions at the end of Chapter 9 in *The Story of Inventions*, and use complete sentences to write the answers to Questions 5 and 6 in your Student Notebook.

Read the above assignment from *Strawberry Girl* aloud, and then follow along as someone else reads the assignment from *The Story of Inventions*.

Read the above assignment from *Strawberry Girl* silently, and then read the assignment from *The Story of Inventions* aloud.

Read the above assignments from *Strawberry Girl* and *The Story of Inventions* silently.

C. Read-Aloud & Narration   *History, Language Skills, Thinking Skills*

George Washington Carver: page 100, last paragraph ("For a moment I felt…") to the bottom of page 104

Follow the instructions below for your level. Then, in your own words, tell what happened in the story from George's point of view. Try to remember as many details as possible. Tell what you think is the most important event in the passage.

Listen carefully to the assigned passage.

Read the assigned passage aloud.

D. Vocabulary   *Language Skills, Thinking Skills*

Show your teacher the Vocabulary I.D. sheet that you completed in Part 1 of this lesson. Ask her to review the words with you by calling them out or writing them on a dry erase board or piece of paper. Tell her what each word means or how it was used in the story and, if you can, what part of speech it is.

Give yourself one point for each correct meaning and one point for knowing the word's part of speech. Keep track of your Vocabulary I.D. points by writing them at the bottom of the sheet and try to beat your score when you review these words again in Part 5.

E. Science   *Thinking Skills*

Human Body Basics, Urinary System: entire chapter

As you read through the assigned chapter, choose words that are new or unfamiliar and make vocabulary cards for them as directed. Keep your science cards separate from other vocabulary.

at least three words   at least four words

Read and discuss the information in the passage with your teacher and do the *Labwork 1-4* activities. The page you need for labeling is in your Student Notebook.

C. History is easier to understand when your student learns about the lives of real people—not just the events that took place, but what was important to the person. Those who do great things, do so because of their strong beliefs and passion. The passion of others can inspire us to do great things as well!

As you and your children prepare for the end of this unit, consider using the Presentation Feedback Sheet located in Appendix C and on the Student Resource CD. If you choose to use it, be sure to review the form with your students so they know what you will be looking for as they tell about the things they have learned. Reassure them that the form is not intended for grading, but simply to help them improve their presentation skills.

Lapbook Activity

Then, go to the *Examine This* section and begin work on the project. Do as much as you can, but you don't have to finish the project in this part. You will have other opportunities to work on it, such as during Part 5 and in occasional Study Hall sections.

F. It can be difficult for some children to identify main events. When they retell a story as if they were a character in the story, it is easier to identify what may have been most important or caused the greatest change. Trying to see a situation through someone else's eyes helps children to connect with those key events that would have affected them the most.

F. **Writing**   *Language Skills, Thinking Skills*

In this section, continue writing a character summary, or shortened version of the main points of what someone has said or done. Focus only on the main events, or changes, that have occurred in your reading so far about George Washington Carver's life, not the details.

You are limited in the number of words you can use, so make sure you choose words that best describe what has taken place.

❧ Use up to 50 words to write your summary.

❧ Use up to 45 words to write your summary.

❧ Use up to 40 words to write your summary.

G. **Music**   *History, Thinking Skills*

Look back at pages 54 through 57 in *The Story of the Orchestra*.

Then, follow the directions in Appendix D to make two Orchestra Story question and answer cards about the oboe, two about the clarinet, and two about the saxophone. Put the small letters *WI* (for woodwind instruments) in the upper left corners of your answer cards. Do not label the question cards— and remember to write the questions in your Student Notebook in the correct order.

Check the directions in Lesson 2, Part 3G, and review the Orchestra Story cards you have made so far in this unit.

H. **Independent Reading & Record Keeping**   *Thinking Skills*

Review the Lesson 5 At A Glance chart in your Student Notebook to see if all the work you've done in this part has been checked off. Also, make sure the Student Notebook pages you worked on are dated and complete.

When you are finished, choose something to read that you will enjoy. Then find a quiet, comfortable place and read for the following length of time:

❧❧ 30 minutes   ❧ 35 minutes

Be sure to write down what you read today on the Reading Log in your Student Notebook.

Lesson 5, Part 4

A. **Copywork & Dictation**   *Language Skills*

Look carefully at your assigned passage below, and read it silently. Show your teacher any words you don't know, and practice saying them aloud. Now read the passage aloud, or ask your teacher to read it to you.

When you are finished copying or writing from dictation, compare your copy to the text and make any needed corrections.

🐾 Copy or write as your teacher dictates from *Strawberry Girl*, page 147, paragraph 5 ("The time had come…").

🐾 Write as your teacher dictates from *George Washington Carver*, page 107, paragraph 10 ("Behind locked doors…").

🐾 Continue writing as your teacher dictates from *George Washington Carver*, page 108, paragraph 2 ("He did just that…").

B. **Reader**   *Language Skills, History*

Strawberry Girl: page 155, paragraph 3 ("It was an impossible task…") through page 163, paragraph 7
The Story of Inventions: page 133 ("Making the Process a Success") through the end of the chapter

Follow the directions below to read or listen to the assigned passage in *Strawberry Girl*.

Before you begin your assignment in *The Story of Inventions*, scan it for any words you don't know and write them on a piece of scrap paper. Read over any section titles included in the passage—and then, as you read or listen to a section, think about how it relates to its title.

When you are finished, find the Comprehension Questions at the end of Chapter 9 in *The Story of Inventions*, and use complete sentences to write the answers to Questions 7, 8, and 9 in your Student Notebook.

🐾 Read the above assignment from *Strawberry Girl* aloud, and then follow along as someone else reads the assignment from *The Story of Inventions*.

🐾 Read the above assignment from *Strawberry Girl* silently, and then read the assignment from *The Story of Inventions* aloud.

🐾 Read the above assignments from *Strawberry Girl* and *The Story of Inventions* silently.

C. **Read-Aloud & Discussion**   *History, Language Skills, Thinking Skills*

George Washington Carver: page 104, last paragraph ("As I walked home…") through page 111, paragraph 2

After reading or listening to the read-aloud assignment, talk with your teacher and try to predict what will happen in the future, based on what you know of the characters and events. Write your predictions in your Student Notebook. Later you will look back and see if they were accurate. Try not to peek ahead!

Listen carefully as your teacher reads the assigned passage. Write down two predictions.

Listen carefully as your teacher reads the assigned passage. Write down three predictions.

Read the assigned passage aloud; then write down at least four predictions.

D. Word Building
Language Skills, Thinking Skills

Earlier in this lesson you learned about the Latin word-part *trans-*. Read over the words you defined in Part 2, and tell your teacher what each one means.

Now add to your ability to use *trans-* by finding more words in the dictionary that begin with it and relate to its meaning. Write them in your Student Notebook. Be sure not to repeat any of the words you have already defined. When you are finished, pick one of your words and write a sentence that uses it correctly.

at least three words   at least six words   at least nine words

Lapbook Activity

E. History
Thinking Skills, Geography

A Day in the Life... World War I began on July 28th, 1914 and lasted until the year 1918. Also known as the Great War and "the war to end all wars," it was the first time in history that so many countries were involved in **hostilities**, or armed conflict, with one another, hence the name World War.

The causes of World War I were many. After decades of tension in Europe, influential countries began building up their militaries, forming alliances, and preparing for conflict. The **catalyst** of, or event that set off, World War I was the **assassination**, or murder, of Archduke Franz Ferdinand, who was heir to the throne of Austria-Hungary. This led his country to declare war against the suspected culprit, Serbia. Because of alliances and treaties, other countries were required to get involved and the conflict **escalated**, or grew, into a World War. In the end, over one hundred countries participated.

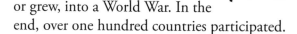

There were two main sides: the Triple Entente (later called the Allied Powers), which consisted of Britain, France, and Russia; and the Triple Alliance (later called the Central Powers) of Germany, Austria, and the Ottoman Empire. World War I was the first war to involve the use of airplanes, tanks, rapid-fire machine guns, poison gas, and the serious use of submarines. This war was also characterized by trench warfare, which was a brutal way to conduct combat. The United States joined the fight in 1917 after a German submarine sank the Lusitania, a British passenger ship. About 1,200 civilians were killed, 128 of them American. The people of the United States were outraged by this act of aggression and demanded action in return.

With the United States now involved, the Central Powers began to be pushed back. The cost in human life of this war was high, with tens of millions killed and wounded. Americans were only a fraction of those casualties. The **Armistice**, or cease-fire, was signed on November 11, 1918, ending the war. The Treaty of Versailles was then created in hopes of preventing another war. Germany, however, felt that they had been treated too harshly by the provisions of the treaty and resented their punishment. Eventually, the treaty that was meant to create peace led to another, even more **catastrophic**, World War.

Find the map entitled "World War I, 1914-1918" in your *Classroom Atlas of the United States*. Read the description, and then look at the top map. Which alliance, or group of countries working together, do you think is larger—the Allied Powers or the Central Powers? Talk with your teacher about the movement of troops shown in the bottom picture. Describe the affect of America entering the war.

Armies that fight wars **abroad**, or in other countries, must be armed and provided for by the country sending them into battle. Even though war is a terrible and painful experience for a nation and its people, some economic benefits can result for the nation. Businesses produce the particular items needed by the soldiers and bought by the nation to arm its troops. So, while the experiences of the people during a conflict are difficult, the demands of equipping and sustaining a strong army of soldiers create great economic opportunities at home.

Businesses that manufacture (make a product from raw materials) items used by soldiers—such as weapons, ammunition, vehicles to carry troops, uniforms, food that can be easily carried and eaten, medical equipment, and ways to communicate—are needed to equip the troops. Business success is dependent on customer demand, and the need for these types of goods grows greatly during any armed conflict. While they may be needed and available at home during times of peace, the demand for such things may dramatically increase during wartime.

Businesses providing the particular items needed by a nation's army may become larger or smaller, based on demand. Some companies may exist only during times of war, or may have to increase or decrease their number of employees to meet changing levels of need. Some of the manufactured items will continue to be in demand after wartime. But other things, like cannons, will not be so popular. Often, companies manufacturing war-related items have to find ways to make different products needed by the general population, in order to stay in business after a war ends.

Make a list of the items you think a nation's army would need during a time of war. Include every aspect of the army's needs that you can identify. Many items you think of may be common and needed at all times by regular citizens. But only a fighting army may need a few things on your list. Put a check next to those items that you think are particular only to the needs of an army.

F. Spelling

Language Skills, Thinking Skills

To increase your ability to use the words you have studied in this lesson when you write, review your vocabulary and word building lists. After choosing the number of words assigned below from these lists, you and your teacher may choose words from the Challenge Spelling List in Appendix C to work on as well. You may also want to add two or three words from your own writing that you have difficulty spelling correctly. Make your spelling list on the page provided in your Student Notebook.

When you are finished, write the words you have chosen as your teacher dictates them. Then study any that you are unable to spell correctly in preparation for writing in the next lessons. (You might want to look back at the "Tips for Studying Spelling Words" in Lesson 1, Part 4F). Add those words to the Ongoing Spelling List in your Student Notebook (Lesson 1, Part 4). Also, don't forget to add words you misspell in your everyday writing to the list. Once you can spell a word correctly in dictation, then you can cross it off. Throughout the year, you should have an ongoing list of words you are practicing.

- Choose eight words from the vocabulary and word building lists, and two to four Challenge Spelling words (if you and your teacher want).

- Choose ten words from the vocabulary and word building lists, and three to five Challenge Spelling words (if you and your teacher want).

- Choose twelve words from your vocabulary or word building lists, and four to six Challenge Spelling words (if you and your teacher want).

G. Art   *Thinking Skills*

Read page 46, "Little Tiny, Really Cute Covered Boxes" in *Create Anything With Clay*. Then let your imagination run wild and put your ideas to work. Have fun, and remember—these little boxes are not only useful, they also make wonderful gifts! Be sure to put left-over clay back in its zip-lock bag.

H. Independent Reading & Record Keeping   *Thinking Skills*

Review the Lesson 5 At A Glance chart in your Student Notebook to see if all the work you've done in this part has been checked off. Also, make sure the Student Notebook pages you worked on are dated and complete.

When you are finished, choose something to read that you will enjoy. Then find a quiet, comfortable place and read for the following length of time:

🌱🌱 🐾 30 minutes   🐾 35 minutes

Be sure to write down what you read today on the Reading Log in your Student Notebook.

Teaching Tip

If you have a perfectionist child who doesn't want to sculpt because his models don't come out exactly the way he wants, encourage him to think like an inventor. Many attempts create a better product!

Lesson 5, Part 5

This part is set aside for completion of any work left undone from the lesson, and review of concepts and content. It is also a time to expand the work of the lesson with a practice and games.

- Review this lesson's Steps for Thinking, found in Part 1.

- Use the Vocabulary I.D. sheet you completed in Part 1 of this lesson to make vocabulary cards. Write each word on an index card and try to remember what it means or how it was used in the story without looking. Check the I.D. sheet to see if you were right. Then on the back of each card, draw a picture or write a clue to help you remember what that word means. Be sure to write a small *CG* (for Cultivating Greatness) in the upper left corners.

  When you are finished, give the cards to your teacher and ask her to show you their picture sides, one at a time. Tell her what the picture or clue means and then name the word written on the other side. If you can, tell what part of speech it is. Give yourself one point for correctly naming a word and one point for knowing its part of speech. Keep track of your points and see if you beat your score from Part 3!

Connect Learning to Life

When you discuss the Steps for Thinking with your children, you are showing them how to connect details to ideas and concepts to examples. This is powerful modeling, so don't think the children are the only ones who can share what they have observed. When you share what you think, they see that you are still learning. This is a model for life-long learning, not just the academics of school years.

- Listen as your teacher reads the spelling words that you studied from Part 4, especially the ones on your Ongoing Spelling List. Write each word in your Student Notebook as she dictates it. When you are finished, look at your word list and make corrections as needed. Show your teacher how you did.

- Follow the directions in the *Human Body Basics* Instructions to play the Word Power vocabulary game. First, play with only the cards you made for the Urinary System; then combine all the cards you have made so far and see how you do.

  Complete the System Savvy puzzles in your Student Notebook.[1] When you are finished, work on any *Examine This* projects you have not yet completed.

- Look back at pages 29 through 37 in the *Basix Recorder Method* and review any exercises that may still be giving you trouble. Choose several tracks on the *Recorder Method* CD and play along with them. Be sure to spend at least 20 minutes practicing!

- Review the Lesson 5 At A Glance chart in your Student Notebook to see if all the work you've done in this part has been checked off. If you did an Enrichment activity or other extra work in this lesson, be sure to write it on the lines next to the chart.

- Print and cut out the Cultivating Greatness Bingo cards and clues from your Student Resources CD. Then, follow the directions in Appendix D to play the game.

Enrichment Activities

1. Weapons of warfare are much different today than they were during World War I. Research weapons of modern warfare at the library or on the Internet. What are the chief weapons used by most soldiers today? How do you think training is different today than it was in the past? After you complete your investigation, decide which military weapon you think is the most important. Share your opinion with your family. You may want to include drawings or photographs of the weapon and tell how it is used.

2. If members of your family include gift giving in their celebration of Christmas, talk with them about the guidelines they use for purchasing or making gifts. Are there ways that you can help with the planning or preparation for giving gifts? Does your family have a budget, or predetermined plan of what they are going to spend? With their advice, make a budget for your gift-giving. Will you earn the money to spend or will your family give you an allowance? How can you get the most for your money? Ask your parents for tips about wise shopping practices.

Additional Resources:

The Home Ranch by Ralph Moody

Around the World in 80 Days movie (1956 version with David Niven, available on DVD)

Please preview any recommended movie to ensure its content is in line with your family's values and acceptable for your children to watch.

Answers

1. Answers are in the *Human Body Basics* Answer Key.

Lesson 6, Part 1

A. Copywork & Dictation   *Language Skills*

Choose the number of paragraphs assigned below from Chapter 6 in *The Story of Inventions*. Look carefully at the passage you chose, and read it silently. Show your teacher any words you don't know, and practice saying them aloud. Now read the passage aloud, or ask your teacher to read it to you.

Copy, or write as your teacher dictates, the paragraph(s). When you are finished, compare your copy to the text and make any needed corrections.

🐾 one paragraph   🐾 two paragraphs   🐾 three paragraphs

B. Reader   *Language Skills, History*

Strawberry Girl: page 163, paragraph 8 ("Birdie took them tightly…") through page 171, paragraph 8
The Story of Inventions: Review Chapters 6 and 7

Follow the directions below to read or listen to the assigned passage in *Strawberry Girl*. When you are finished, skim each chapter in the review assignment from *The Story of Inventions*. Then think of some ways that the lives of Eli Whitney and Elias Howe were similar, and some ways they were different. Record your ideas on the page in your Student Notebook.

🐾 Read the above assignment from *Strawberry Girl* aloud; then think of two ways the inventors' lives were similar, and two ways they were different.

🐾 Read the above assignment from *Strawberry Girl* silently; then think of three ways the inventors' lives were similar, and three ways they were different.

🐾 Read the above assignment from *Strawberry Girl*; then think of four ways the inventors' lives were similar, and four ways they were different.

C. Read-Aloud & Narration   *History, Language Skills, Thinking Skills*

George Washington Carver: page 111, paragraph 3 ("Alone I walked…") through the top of page 117

Follow the directions below to read or listen to the above passage. Then, in your own words, tell what happened in the portion you are assigned. Try to remember as many details as possible—if necessary you may reread, or listen as your teacher rereads, the part you are to retell.

🐾 Listen carefully as your teacher reads the above assignment aloud. Choose one page to retell.

⌘Materials⌘

- *George Washington Carver*
- *Strawberry Girl*
- *The Story of Inventions*
- *Basix Recorder Method*
- *Create Anything With Clay*
- Rummy Roots cards
- Recorder
- Polymer clay
- Activity (Part 4)
    Toothpick
    Old washcloth
    Alphabet macaroni (optional)
    Rice (optional)
    String, yarn, or leather cord

🐾 Listen carefully as your teacher reads the above assignment aloud. Choose two pages to retell.

🐾 Read the above assignment aloud, and then retell the entire passage.

D. Vocabulary   *Language Skills, Thinking Skills*

Write each vocabulary word on the Vocabulary I.D. sheet in your Student Notebook. Then tell your teacher what you think each word means, based on the context in which you have read it. If you are not sure of a word's meaning, look it up in a dictionary. Write the definition on the Vocabulary Sheet.

Next, write the word's part of speech: noun, adjective, adverb, verb, and so forth. If you aren't sure, this can also be found in the dictionary.

heifer	**sass**	**ruckus**
turpentine	**calamity**	**harangue**
cultivator	**boll weevil**	**goober**
nutrition	**amino acid**	**starch**

E. Study Hall   *Thinking Skills*

This section is set aside as a Study Hall. Use it to catch up on any work that has not yet been completed in the science lessons studied in this unit. If all your science is finished, use this time to work on other assignments that are still undone.

F. Writing   *Language Skills, Thinking Skills*

In this section, complete your last character summary about George Washington Carver's life. Before you begin, look back over each of the summaries you have written in this unit.

Though you have not yet finished reading his story, write a final summary telling about the main events, or highlights, of George Washington Carver's life. Be sure that it shows what a great man he was, and the important contributions he made. This is similar to an **obituary**, or an announcement usually placed in a newspaper, telling about someone's death. A short **biography**, or story of someone's life, is often included in an obituary.

You are limited in the number of words you can use, so make sure you choose words that best describe what has taken place.

🌵🌵 Use up to 50 words to write your summary.

🐾 Use up to 45 words to write your summary.

🐾 Use up to 40 words to write your summary.

G. Music   *Thinking Skills*

Review all the Orchestra Story cards you have made in Unit 4 by matching the question cards with their correct answers.

When you are finished, follow the directions in Appendix D to make category cards for String Instruments and Woodwind Instruments, and then play Orchestra Story Question Quest with all the cards from Units 1, 2, 3, and 4.

H. Independent Reading & Record Keeping   *Thinking Skills*

Review the Lesson 6 At A Glance chart in your Student Notebook to see if all the work you've done in this part has been checked off. Also, make sure the Student Notebook pages you worked on are dated and complete.

When you are finished, choose something to read that you will enjoy. Then find a quiet, comfortable place and read for the following length of time:

🖐🖐🖐 30 minutes   🐾 35 minutes

Be sure to write down what you read today on the Reading Log in your Student Notebook.

Lesson 6, Part 2

A. Copywork & Dictation   *Language Skills*

Review your copywork or dictation assignments from Lessons 1-3 and make a list of mistakes you made more than once. Then discuss this list with your teacher. What is the main thing you need to work on to improve?

B. Reader   *Language Skills, History*

Strawberry Girl: page 171, paragraph 9 ("All that first night…") through the top of page 180
The Story of Inventions: Review Chapters 6 and 7

Follow the directions below to read or listen to the assigned passage in *Strawberry Girl*. When you are finished, skim each chapter in the review assignment from *The Story of Inventions*. Then think of some ways that the inventions of Eli Whitney and Elias Howe were similar, and some ways they were different. Record your ideas on the page in your Student Notebook.

G. Encourage your children to use their Student Notebooks to consider all that they have done in this unit and select the things they would like to share in their Unit Presentation. If your children have difficulty deciding, encourage them to share the things that were the most fun, the most interesting, and new information they learned. If there was an area of particular skill for them, be sure to include that as well. Book review cards, Steps for Thinking, and charts comparing the inventors also give a good overview of the unit's focus. They may want to make their Student Notebooks available for others to view, so now is the time to check them for neatness.

Teacher Connection

Continuous learning is an important part of education. Be sure to read the *Teacher Connection* note in your Parent Planner. Don't miss out on this important part of your homeschooling!

❅❅ Read the above assignment from *Strawberry Girl* aloud; then think of two ways Whitney's and Howe's inventions were similar, and two ways they were different.

❅ Read the above assignments from *Strawberry Girl*; then think of three ways Whitney's and Howe's inventions were similar, and three ways they were different.

❅ Read the above assignments from *Strawberry Girl*; then think of four ways Whitney's and Howe's inventions were similar, and four ways they were different.

C. **Read-Aloud & Discussion**   *History, Language Skills, Thinking Skills*
George Washington Carver: page 117, paragraph 1 ("Upon my arrival...") through the top of page 122

Follow the directions below to read or listen to the above assignment. Then make up questions about the part of the story you just read or heard. Write your questions in your Student Notebook and ask your teacher to answer them. After discussing her thoughts, write down the best possible answer on the lines provided. Be sure to use complete sentences.

When you are finished, look back at the prediction or predictions you made during Lesson 5, Part 4. Were you able to predict what would happen? Be sure to mark the "Came to Pass" box for each prediction when it does happen.

❅❅ Listen carefully as your teacher reads the above assignment aloud. Make up two questions.

❅ Listen carefully as your teacher reads the above assignment aloud. Make up three questions.

❅ Read the above assignment aloud; then make up four questions.

D. **Word Building**   *Language Skills, Thinking Skills*
Review Lessons 3 and 4 by telling your teacher about the word-parts *tele-* and *trans-*. What languages do they come from? What do they mean? Read over the words that you defined in both lessons. Then follow the directions below to make up sentences for some of the words you defined, and tell them to your teacher.

When you are finished, follow the directions in Appendix D to play Word Part Concentration with some of your Rummy Roots Word Cards. From Set 1, use the cards numbered 1, 2, 3, 4, 5, 6, 7, 8, 10, 11, 12, 13, 14, 15, 16, 18, 19, 22, 25, and 28; from Set 2, use numbers 29, 30, 34, 39, 40, 41, 42, 43, 44, 45, 49, 51, and 55; and from Set 3 use numbers 52, 57, 58, 59, 72, 73, 74, 76, and 87.

❅❅ Make up sentences for at least three words you defined.

❅ Make up sentences for at least four words you defined.

❅ Make up sentences for at least five words you defined.

E. History
Thinking Skills, Geography

Think about the stories of Cyrus McCormick and Henry Bessemer you have read or listened to in this unit. Then complete the Invention Demand Chart 6 in your Student Notebook.

Combine today's chart with Invention Demand Chart 5 from Lesson 3. Review both charts and find three things that are similar about all four inventors, and three things that are different. Make a list of these qualities on the page provided. Be sure to include this information in your presentation at the end of this lesson.

Print and cut out the Supply and Demand Vocabulary 5 game cards from your Student Resources CD. If you want, you can glue each piece onto an index card to make the cards stronger, or print them onto cardstock. Add the new cards to the ones you made in Lesson 3. Then follow the directions in Appendix D to play either the Supply and Demand Concentration or Go Fish game.[1]

F. Editing
Language Skills, Thinking Skills

Conclusions are important because they are the last thoughts you leave with your reader. You want to make them clear and memorable. The best way to do that is to tell readers exactly what you want them to remember and why. Give them an example of your personal connection to what you have written.

You can start a conclusion by introducing it as such:

> In conclusion, this essay has given you several of the good and bad results when an invention replaces workers. When change happens, sometimes it is hard. I know this because my uncle lost his job and had to learn how to do something new. Today he is working at a job with a future. We should all welcome change because in the end, it is better for everyone.

Another way to conclude is to tell your readers what you want them to understand from your writing and end with a question, causing them to apply your ideas to their own life.

> In conclusion, many inventions take the place of workers. This can be upsetting to people, but, in the end, they will be better off. More products will be made and costs will be lower. I think this makes it hard for people to support inventors because it may change the way they work. Even though it is best for everyone, people may still worry. Do you think an invention will replace you someday?

Look back over the essays you have written in *Paths of Progress*, and reread your concluding paragraphs. Choose one, and revise it by using one of the techniques described in this lesson.

G. Music   *Thinking Skills*

Scan the pages you have studied so far in the *Basix Recorder Method* and review any exercises or melodies that are difficult for you. Choose several tracks on the *Recorder Method* CD to play along with. Be sure to spend at least 20 minutes practicing!

H. Independent Reading & Record Keeping   *Thinking Skills*

Review the Lesson 6 At A Glance chart in your Student Notebook to see if all the work you've done in this part has been checked off. Also, make sure the Student Notebook pages you worked on are dated and complete.

When you are finished, choose something to read that you will enjoy. Then find a quiet, comfortable place and read for the following length of time:

   ☘ ✋ 30 minutes   ✋ 35 minutes

Be sure to write down what you read today on the Reading Log in your Student Notebook.

H. As homeschoolers, we are always looking for natural ways to transfer small pieces of responsibility for learning to our children. The reading log is a great way to pass along a small record-keeping task. At the same time, encourage your children to make their reading log something they will be proud to share with others with neat handwriting and correct spelling and punctuation of book and author names. This is also a great review of capitalization!

Lesson 6, Part 3

A. Copywork & Dictation   *Language Skills*

Choose the number of paragraphs assigned below from Chapter 8 in *The Story of Inventions*. Look carefully at the passage you chose, and read it silently. Show your teacher any words you don't know, and practice saying them aloud. Now read the passage aloud, or ask your teacher to read it to you.

Copy, or write as your teacher dictates, the paragraph(s). When you are finished, compare your copy to the text and make any needed corrections.

   ☘ one paragraph   ✋ two paragraphs   ✋ three paragraphs

B. Reader   *Language Skills, History*

Strawberry Girl: page 180, paragraph 1 ("Mrs. Boyer gave the girls…") through page 187, paragraph 3
The Story of Inventions: Review Chapters 8 and 9

Follow the directions below to read or listen to the assigned passage in *Strawberry Girl*. When you are finished, skim each chapter in the review assignment from *The Story of Inventions*. Then think of some ways that the lives of Cyrus McCormick and Henry Bessemer were similar, and some ways they were different. Record your ideas on the page in your Student Notebook.

🐾 Read the above assignment from *Strawberry Girl* aloud; then think of two ways the inventors' lives were similar, and two ways they were different.

🐾 Read the above assignments from *Strawberry Girl*; then think of three ways the inventors' lives were similar, and three ways they were different.

🐾 Read the above assignments from *Strawberry Girl* ; then think of two ways the inventors' lives were similar, and two ways they were different.

C. Read-Aloud & Narration   *History, Language Skills, Thinking Skills*

George Washington Carver: page 122, paragraph 1 ("Carefully I pulled…") through page 127

Follow the instructions below for your level. Then, in your own words, tell what happened in the story from George's point of view. Try to remember as many details as possible. Tell what you think is the most important event in the passage.

🐾 Listen carefully to the assigned passage.

🐾 Read the assigned passage aloud.

D. Vocabulary   *Language Skills, Thinking Skills*

Show your teacher the Vocabulary I.D. sheet that you completed in Part 1 of this lesson. Ask her to review the words with you by calling them out or writing them on a dry erase board or piece of paper. Tell her what each word means or how it was used in the story and, if you can, what part of speech it is.

Give yourself one point for each correct meaning and one point for knowing the word's part of speech. Keep track of your Vocabulary I.D. points by writing them at the bottom of the sheet and try to beat your score when you review these words again in Part 5.

E. Science   *Thinking Skills*

Complete the Human Body Matching game in your Student Notebook.[2] When you are finished, tell your teacher what you remember about the things named in the activity. If you need help remembering, you can look back at the pages in the unit where you learned about each thing.

F. Writing   *Language Skills, Thinking Skills*

A round character is one who has undergone great change during the course of a story. A flat character has not changed much. Mr. Slater, Shoestring's father, is a round character because he goes through some big changes in *Strawberry Girl*.

C. Encourage your children to get into character for this assignment. They can narrate, or retell, the passage using the pronoun I, stand up to look more impressive, use a deeper voice, etc. By encouraging this creativity, you are also encouraging critical thinking. What would the speaker sound like? What happened to him and how did he feel about it? This is a natural way to comprehend and express the thoughts of another person.

Lapbook Activity

Autumn - Circulatory
Nathan - Musculo skeletal
Dakota - Urinary
Addie - Skeletal
Maren - Respiratory
Jack - Digestive

Lapbook Activity

In your Student Notebook, write a short description of Mr. Slater at the beginning of the story. Include examples of things he did that show what he was like before he changed.

Then describe Mr. Slater at the end of the book. Tell what happened to cause him to change, and give examples from the story to support your opinion.

- Include at least two examples.

- Include at least three examples.

- Include at least four examples.

G. Music   *History, Thinking Skills*

Follow the directions in Appendix D to play Orchestra Story Question Quest with all the cards you have made in Units 1, 2, 3, and 4.

When you are finished, play Name That Classic with your teacher and other family members. Have someone play different tracks that you have studied in this unit from *The Story of the Orchestra* CD. Players should take turns trying to identify the instrument featured in each piece. Name the composition for an extra point!

H. Independent Reading & Record Keeping   *Thinking Skills*

Review the Lesson 6 At A Glance chart in your Student Notebook to see if all the work you've done in this part has been checked off. Also, make sure the Student Notebook pages you worked on are dated and complete.

When you are finished, choose something to read that you will enjoy. Then find a quiet, comfortable place and read for the following length of time:

- 30 minutes   35 minutes

Be sure to write down what you read today on the Reading Log in your Student Notebook.

Lesson 6, Part 4

A. Copywork & Dictation   *Language Skills*

Review your copywork or dictation assignments from Lessons 4-6, and make a list of mistakes you made more than once. Then discuss this list with your teacher. What is the main thing you need to work on to improve?

B. Reader   *Language Skills, History*

Strawberry Girl: page 187, paragraph 4 ("What you fixin'…")
through page 194
The Story of Inventions: Review Chapters 8 and 9

Lapbook Activity

Follow the directions below to read or listen to the assigned passage in *Strawberry Girl*. When you are finished, skim each chapter in the review assignment from *The Story of Inventions*. Then think of some ways that the inventions of Cyrus McCormick and Henry Bessemer were similar, and some ways they were different. Record your ideas on the page in your Student Notebook.

Read the above assignment from *Strawberry Girl* aloud; then think of two ways McCormick's and Bessemer's inventions were similar, and two ways they were different.

Read the above assignment from *Strawberry Girl* silently; then think of three ways McCormick's and Bessemer's inventions were similar, and three ways they were different.

Read the above assignments from *Strawberry Girl*; then think of four ways McCormick's and Bessemer's inventions were similar, and four ways they were different.

C. Read-Aloud & Discussion   *History, Language Skills, Thinking Skills*

George Washington Carver: page 128 ("Lonny's success led me…") through page 133

Look over all the predictions you made about the read-aloud story in this unit (Part 4, Section C of Lessons 1-5). Were most of them **accurate**, or on target? Has your ability to predict a story's events become better as you have practiced? Have you started including more details? Talk with your teacher and identify one way you have become better at making predictions. Then tell one way you need to improve in this ability.

Do you feel as though you became familiar with the **motivations** and attitudes of the book's characters? Did understanding these things help you predict the actions they would take? Talk with your teacher and think of at least one more way you can improve in your ability to predict a character's behavior and thoughts.

D. Word Building   *Language Skills, Thinking Skills*

Review Lessons 1, 2, 4, and 5 by again telling your teacher about the word-parts *chronos-* or *chonro-*, *pro-*, *tele-,* and *trans-*. What languages do they come from? What do they mean? Read over the words that you defined for these word-parts. Then follow the directions below to make up sentences for some of them, and tell them to your teacher.

Connect Learning to Life

When children immerse themselves in a story, learning about characters, setting, conflicts, history, and culture, they are given the information needed to evaluate information. One of the ways they can share the results of that evaluation is to predict what is going to happen next. This develops thinking skills that are useful in everyday life because it causes children to think ahead and consider the outcome of actions taken.

When you are finished, follow the directions in Appendix D to play Word Part Concentration with some of your Rummy Roots Word Cards. From Set 1, use the cards numbered 1, 2, 3, 4, 5, 6, 7, 8, 10, 11, 12, 13, 14, 15, 16, 18, 19, 22, 25, and 28; from Set 2, use numbers 29, 30, 34, 39, 40, 41, 42, 43, 44, 45, 49, 51 and 55; and from Set 3 use numbers 52, 57, 58, 59, 72, 73, 74, 76 and 87.

Make up a sentence for at least one word you defined using each word-part.

Make up sentences for at least two words you defined using each word-part.

Make up sentences for at least three words you defined using each word-part.

E. History
                                                      Thinking Skills, Geography

Prepare for your UNIT END PRESENTATION by completing the following activities:

Review your Supply and Demand Vocabulary cards by shuffling the deck of cards and matching each vocabulary word to its definition and example. Next, reread your Invention Demand Charts and be prepared to share that information with your family.

Review the story you read about Sergeant Alvin York in *Profiles from History, Volume 3*. Briefly tell his story to your family as part of your presentation.

Make up four questions about each of the following inventors and write them on separate index cards. Be sure to write the inventor's name in the upper left corner of his cards.

> Eli Whitney
>
> Elias Howe
>
> Cyrus McCormick
>
> Henry Bessemer

Then find a partner and follow the directions in Appendix D to play Inventors Twenty Questions.

Increase the difficulty of this game by adding cards about other inventors you have studied this year:

at least three inventors,

at least four inventors,

at least five inventors.

F. Spelling   *Language Skills, Thinking Skills*

Look at the words that are left on your Ongoing Spelling List. Practice spelling each one by covering it with your hand, spelling it silently, and then checking to see if you were correct. Do this several times until you feel comfortable spelling these words.

G. Art   *Thinking Skills*

Follow the directions on page 47, "Macaroni Letter Beads" in *Create Anything With Clay* to make beads.

If you don't have alphabet macaroni, try drawing designs or letters on the beads with a toothpick and pressing pieces of rice into the lines for the first baking. Also, you might want to make the hole through the center of your beads after you draw or press the design on top. When you are finished, thread your beads onto string or cord if you want. Be sure to put leftover clay back in its zip-lock bag.

H. Independent Reading & Record Keeping   *Thinking Skills*

Review the Lesson 6 At A Glance chart in your Student Notebook to see if all the work you've done in this part has been checked off. Also, make sure the Student Notebook pages you worked on are dated and complete.

When you are finished, choose something to read that you will enjoy. Then find a quiet, comfortable place and read for the following length of time:

Ψ Ψ ♨ 30 minutes   ♨ 35 minutes

Congratulations on completing six weeks of independent reading! Today's entry in your reading log will be the last one for this unit. Be sure to write down what you read today on the Reading Log in your Student Notebook.

Lesson 6, Part 5

This part is set aside for completion of any work left undone from the lesson and review of concepts and content. It is also a time to expand the work of the lesson with practice and games.

- Listen as your teacher reviews the Steps for Thinking from the Cultivating Greatness Unit that you have just completed. Talk about how you can apply the Steps to what you have read or discussed and see if you can think of any examples in this unit.

- Use the Vocabulary I.D. sheet you completed in Part 1 of this lesson to make vocabulary cards. Write each word on an index card and try to remember what it means or how it was used in the story without looking. Check the I.D. sheet to see if you were right. Then, on the back of each card, draw a picture or write a clue to help you remember what that word means. Be sure to write a small *CG* (for Cultivating Greatness) in the upper left corners.

  When you are finished, give the cards to your teacher and ask her to show you their picture sides, one at a time. Tell her what the picture or clue means and then name the word written on the other side. If you can, tell what part of speech it is. Give yourself one point for correctly naming a word and one point for knowing its part of speech. Keep track of your points and see if you beat your score from Part 3!

- Listen as your teacher reads the spelling words that you studied from Part 4, especially the ones on your Ongoing Spelling List. Write each word in your Student Notebook as she dictates it. When you are finished, look at your word list and make corrections as needed. Show your teacher how you did.

- Play Name-That-Classic with your teacher and other family members. Have someone play different tracks that you have studied so far from *The Story of the Orchestra* CD. Players should take turns trying to guess the names of the compositions. Award one point each time a player is correct and one bonus point each if the player can name either the composer or the instrument featured.

- Review the Lesson 6 At A Glance chart in your Student Notebook to see if all the work you've done in this part has been checked off. If you did an Enrichment Activity or other extra work in this lesson, be sure to write it on the lines next to the chart.

- Make a Unit Presentation to your family that tells about what you have learned in the Cultivating Greatness Unit. Share your Student Notebook and things you made or accomplished this unit

Culminating activities are a key part of solidifying learning. By thinking of interesting ways to present the information he or she has learned, your child's new knowledge is reinforced. Also, sharing opinions formed and skills practiced reinforces the connection between new information and past learning. Encourage your student to be the guide to the unit, acquainting others with key concepts, events, people, and activities. Allow your children to truly express their thoughts!

such your play, clay sculptures, or progress on the recorder. Don't forget to stand still and speak clearly. After your presentation, be sure to ask if anyone has questions.

- Follow the directions in Appendix D to play Cultivating Greatness Bingo.

Congratulations on completing Unit Four in *Paths of Progress*!

Answers

1. Answer Key is in Appendix C.
2. Answer Key is in Appendix C.

Lesson 1, Part 1

❧ Steps for Thinking ❧

1. Identifying a question is the first step to answering it. Put your question or idea into words. Give yourself some time to ponder, or think about, it rather than trying to answer every question immediately.

2. Consider what you already know about the problem. Talking with someone else often helps clarify, or make clear, your thoughts.

3. Learn from the work of others. Read what others have said about your question. Originality, or creativity, is not limited by understanding what others have already done.

4. The economy is directly connected to the work of scientists and inventors. The prosperity of each is dependent on the other.

A. Copywork & Dictation
Language Skills

Look carefully at your assigned passage below, and read it silently. Show your teacher any words you don't know, and practice saying them aloud. Now read the passage aloud, or ask your teacher to read it to you.

When you are finished copying or writing from dictation, compare your copy to the text and make any needed corrections.

🐾🐾🐾 Copy or write as your teacher dictates from *The Story of Inventions*, page 262, paragraph 1 ("Another pioneer of aerial…")

🐾 Write as your teacher dictates from *The Story of Inventions*, page 262, paragraphs 1 and 2 ("Another pioneer of aerial…").

B. Reader
Language Skills, History

Homer Price: page 10 (Chapter 1) to the top of page 16
The Story of Inventions: page 261 (Chapter 19) through the top of page 264

Follow the directions below to read or listen to the assigned passage in *Homer Price*.

Before you begin your assignment in *The Story of Inventions*, scan it for any words you don't know and write them on a piece of scrap

---

❧ Materials ❧

- *The Wright Brothers*
- *Homer Price*
- *The Story of Inventions*
- *The New Way Things Work*
- *Human Body Basics*
- *The Story of the Orchestra* book & CD
- *Basix Recorder Method*
- *Create Anything With Clay*
- *Classroom Atlas of the United States*
- Recorder
- Polymer clay
- Activity (Part 1):
  - Styrofoam plates
  - Marker
  - Apple wedges
  - Table knife
  - Ruler
  - Other participants
  - Paper towel roll
  - Bread or crackers
  - Water
- Activity (Part 3):
  - Newspaper
  - Masking tape
  - 1 gallon Ziploc bag
  - 1 quart Ziploc bag
  - Ruler
  - Vinegar
  - Bread
  - Plastic cloth (optional)
- Activity (Part 4G):
  - Various supplies (pages 48-49 in *Clay* book)

B. Answers to the questions from *The Story of Inventions* are located in the Answer Key for that book.

paper. Read over any section titles included in the passage—and then, as you read or listen to a section, think about how it relates to its title.

When you are finished, find the Comprehension Questions at the end of Chapter 19 in *The Story of Inventions*, and use complete sentences to write the answers to Questions 1, 2, 3, and 4 in your Student Notebook.

🐾 Read the above assignment from *Homer Price* aloud, and then follow along as someone else reads the assignment from *The Story of Inventions*.

🐾 Read the above assignment from *Homer Price* silently, and then read the assignment from *The Story of Inventions* aloud.

🐾 Read the above assignments from *Homer Price* and *The Story of Inventions* silently.

C. Read-Aloud & Narration
History, Language Skills, Thinking Skills

The Wright Brothers: Preface ("On Thursday evening…") through page 5, paragraph 5

Follow the directions below to read or listen to the above passage. Then, in your own words, tell what happened in the portion you are assigned. Try to remember as many details as possible. If necessary you may reread, or listen as your teacher rereads, the part you are to retell.

🐾 Listen carefully as your teacher reads the above assignment aloud. Choose one page to retell.

🐾 Listen carefully as your teacher reads the above assignment aloud. Choose two pages to retell.

🐾 Read the above assignment aloud, and then retell the entire passage.

D. Vocabulary
Language Skills, Thinking Skills

D. Each word in bold letters is considered a vocabulary word. It is a word that may or may not be new to your children. You can write these vocabulary words on index cards and use them for occasional review, but not for memorizing. Give your children the meaning of the words if they don't remember. Try to use the new vocabulary words during conversation, and encourage your students to do the same.

Each time your students make a vocabulary card for this unit, have them write *STF* (for Success Takes Flight) in the upper left corner. This will make it possible to review vocabulary by unit at the end of the year.

Gather all your Unit 4 vocabulary cards and mix them up. (These are the cards with *CG* written in the upper left corners). Then divide them into two stacks, either by estimating (making your best guess) or by counting. Choose one of the piles to review in this section, and set the other aside to use later in Part 3.

Begin your review by picking a card. Read the word on the front and, without looking, tell your teacher either what it means or how it was used in the story. Give yourself a point for every word you are able to use correctly. See how many points you can get!

E. Science   *Thinking Skills*

Human Body Basics, Digestive System: beginning of chapter & Digestion

As you read through the assigned pages, choose words that are new or unfamiliar and make vocabulary cards for them as directed. Keep your science cards separate from other vocabulary.

🐾 at least three words

🐾🐾 at least four words

Read and discuss the information in the passage with your teacher and do the *Labwork 1-3* activities. The pages you need for writing are in your Student Notebook.

When you are finished, look at the first two *Examine This* projects at the end of the chapter and:

🐾 Choose one to complete.

🐾🐾 Complete both.

Do as much as you can, but you don't have to finish the projects in this part. You will have other opportunities to work on them, such as during Part 5 and in occasional Study Hall sections.

F. Writing   *Language Skills, Thinking Skills*

It is always a good idea to read the things you have written aloud so you can hear how the words sound. This can help you tell if your writing really says what you want it to. Do this with the Lab Reports you wrote in Section E and make sure each one describes its experiment accurately and completely.

Revise any parts that you think could be better.

G. Music   *History, Thinking Skills*

With your teacher, read pages 58 through 61 in *The Story of the Orchestra* and discuss the information about the bassoon and the brass section. Then listen to part of the "Mother Goose Suite" on Track 25. Were you able to hear the contrabassoon? How did the music make you feel? What did you enjoy or dislike about it?

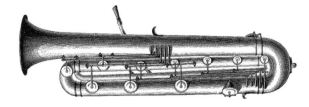

When you are finished, listen carefully to Track 25 again. Then, draw and color a picture in your Student Notebook of the image this music brings to your mind.

E. The Internet can be a useful tool for research, but we suggest that your child use it only with your permission and supervision, and while following your family's rules.

Lapbook Activity

Connect Learning to Life

Writing skills are preparation for real life, not just a school time activity. Whenever you do an activity that equips your children for life, such as learning how to write a report or directions that others can follow, point it out to them. Take time to think about the connections you see between what you are teaching your children and the way they might actually use the knowledge or skills in their daily life. Doing this regularly will help you answer that age-old question, "Will I ever use what I'm learning?"

Lapbook Activity

H. Independent Reading & Record Keeping   *Thinking Skills*

Review the Lesson 1 At A Glance chart in your Student Notebook to see if all the work you've done in this part has been checked off. Also, make sure the Student Notebook pages you worked on are dated and complete.

When you are finished, choose something to read that you will enjoy. Then find a quiet, comfortable place and read for the following length of time:

     🐾 30 minutes   🐾 35 minutes

Be sure to write down what you read today on the Reading Log in your Student Notebook.

Lesson 1, Part 2

A. Copywork & Dictation   *Language Skills*

Look carefully at the Steps for Thinking for this lesson and read them silently. Show your teacher any words you don't know, and practice saying them aloud. Then, copy or write them from dictation into your Student Notebook.

When you are finished, compare your copy to the text and make any needed corrections.

🐾 Copy the Steps for Thinking, and tell your teacher an example of each Step from your reading or your life.

🐾 Write the Steps for Thinking as your teacher dictates them. Then, in your Student Notebook write one example of each Step from your reading or your life. Be sure to use complete sentences.

🐾 Write the Steps for Thinking as your teacher dictates them. Then, in your Student Notebook write two examples of each Step from your reading or your life. Be sure to use complete sentences.

B. Reader   *Language Skills, History*

Homer Price: page 16, paragraph 1 ("Homer waited around…") through page 21, paragraph 3
The Story of Inventions: page 264, paragraph 1 ("Their next step…") through page 267

Follow the directions below to read or listen to the assigned passage in *Homer Price*.

Before you begin your assignment in *The Story of Inventions*, scan it for any words you don't know and write them on a piece of scrap paper. Read over any section titles included in the passage—and then, as you read or listen to a section, think about how it relates to its title.

When you are finished, find the Comprehension Questions at the end of Chapter 19 in *The Story of Inventions*, and use complete sentences to write the answers to Questions 5, 6, 7, and 8 in your Student Notebook.

❧ Read the above assignment from *Homer Price* aloud, and then follow along as someone else reads the assignment from *The Story of Inventions*.

❧ Read the above assignment from *Homer Price* silently, and then read the assignment from *The Story of Inventions* aloud.

❧ Read the above assignments from *Homer Price* and *The Story of Inventions* silently.

C. **Read-Aloud & Discussion**   *History, Language Skills, Thinking Skills*

The Wright Brothers: page 5, paragraph 6 ("Slowly Wilbur gathered...") through page 10

Follow the directions below to read or listen to the above assignment from *The Wright Brothers*. Then make up the assigned number of questions about the part of the story you just read or heard. Write down your questions and ask your teacher to answer them. After discussing her thoughts, write down the best possible answer in your Student Notebook. Be sure to use complete sentences.

❧ Listen carefully as your teacher reads the above assignment aloud. Make up two questions.

❧ Listen carefully as your teacher reads the above assignment aloud. Make up three questions.

❧ Read the above assignment aloud; then make up four questions.

D. **Word Building**   *Language Skills, Thinking Skillss*

As you have learned, the English language comes from parts of many other languages. Many words you know and use often come from languages such as Greek (the language spoken in Greece) and Latin (the language spoken in Ancient Rome, but no longer used in everyday life). In this unit you will continue to learn about several word-parts and what they mean. Then, in later units, you will learn how to recognize the combinations of word-parts to make new words.

Today's word-part is **micro-** or **micros-**, which is a Greek word that means *small*.

Look up the following words in the dictionary and write each definition in your Student Notebook. Then underline the word-part *micro-*

C. Since students do not have to worry about decoding during read-aloud time, they can focus totally on the meaning of what they are hearing. This allows them the opportunity to think about the ideas and information being presented, and to formulate their own thoughts.

or *micros-* in each word. Think, and be ready to tell your teacher how each definition relates to the meaning of the Greek word.

microscope	microwave	microphone
microbe	microorganism	microfilm
micron	micrometer	microcosm

Use one or more of the Enrichment Activities (listed in Part 5 of each lesson) if your child completes assigned work and has the time or desire to learn more. These activities are flexible, so choose the one(s) that seem most interesting to your student. Allow work to be at an appropriate level, and remember that the learning process is more important than the product.

Lapbook Activity

E. History and Economics

Thinking Skills, Geography

Before the invention of the automobile, most goods and services that traveled over land were carried by the railroads. While railroads were a definite improvement over the horse and wagon, limitations still existed because products could only be taken where a railroad line existed. Though more railroads were built, this took time and a great deal of effort. With the invention of the automobile, new opportunities for travel arose. Roads could be built more easily and less expensively than railroad lines, even though they were not as permanent. Products could now be carried to smaller towns and markets by motorized vehicles.

While people first thought of automobiles only as a way to get around town, new uses became apparent over time. When the Ford Motor Company began in 1903, automobiles started to become more reasonably priced and affordable for families. With more automobiles on the roads, the demand for new and better roads started to grow. As you know from the law of supply and demand,  once a demand exists, supply will eventually follow. As the system of roads grew, people drove farther, and the opportunity to use motor vehicles in other ways increased.

In this case as in many others, one new invention created a need for many other new products and services. With the invention and development of the automobile, the need arose for many other things. That need continues even today. As new types of vehicles are developed, new types of services are needed. This is typical of the effect one great invention has in encouraging the development of related improvements, products, and services.

In your *Classroom Atlas of the United States*, find the section that highlights the region of the country where your family lives. Find the map that includes major roadways and interstate highways (which are highways that connect two or more states). Find the names of the roadways or **interstate** highways that are near your home. Have you ever traveled on these roads? Talk with your parents about the highways that they use most frequently.

What kind of car(s) do your parents drive? Talk with family members about what they drive and why. Make a list of the reasons those in your family drive the particular vehicles that they do. Then talk with them about what vehicle they would purchase if money were not a consideration. What makes a different vehicle preferable to what they have now? Think about the kind of car you want to drive when you grow up.

🐾🐾 Make a list of all the businesses that relate to your family's use of a car. Be sure to include all aspects of purchasing, maintenance, daily travel, and trips. For example, when traveling by car, a family might stay at a campground or hotel, increasing their business. Do you eat out when you are on the road? Restaurant business is increased by family travel. When your list is complete, count and see how many businesses are affected simply by your family's owning and using a vehicle.

🐾 In recent years, some companies that produce cars have experienced financial difficulty. Use the Internet or library to learn more about the company that makes your favorite car or the car that your family drives. After reading, tell what you think about the future of this company. Do you think they will continue to make cars, or do you think they will end up closing their doors as a business? Give several reasons for your beliefs.

F. Editing   *Language Skills, Thinking Skills*

In this unit you will review various parts of speech and find examples in your literature. The first parts you will review are nouns. Remember, there are two main types of nouns; look at the following explanations to see how they are used.

Proper noun: A particular person, place, thing, or idea that is capitalized.

> Bishop <u>M</u>ilton <u>W</u>right was born in <u>R</u>ush <u>C</u>ounty, <u>I</u>ndiana.

Common noun: A general kind of person, place, thing, or idea that is not capitalized.

> The <u>b</u>oys were interested in building <u>b</u>ikes, <u>s</u>tilts, and <u>a</u>irplanes.

Look at all your reading assignments for Lesson 1 to complete this assignment.

Make a list of at least ten proper nouns and ten common nouns from your readings.[1]

🐾 Add at least two additional nouns to each category.

🐾 Add at least five additional nouns to each category.

F. The Editing section in this unit involves skills that your child may already know. It is always a good idea to begin instruction with review, so please have your child complete these activities even if he already knows the concepts presented. A great way to enjoy a review with your child is to ask him to be the teacher and present the information to you, the student!

G. Music
Thinking Skills

Read and follow the directions on pages 38 and 39 in the *Basix Recorder Method* to play *middle C sharp* and learn about the *D major scale*. Write the names of notes that are not already labeled above the staffs on those pages. Then find the Finger Placement Tab in your Student Notebook and color in the circles that show which holes are covered when you play the *C* note. When you are finished, cut out the tab and paste it on an index card.

Don't forget to listen to the *Recorder Method* CD tracks shown on those pages to hear samples of the lessons and use your Finger Placement Tabs if you need to.

Be sure to spend a little time each day practicing what you have learned—20 minutes a session is plenty!

H. Independent Reading & Record Keeping
Thinking Skills

Review the Lesson 1 At A Glance chart in your Student Notebook to see if all the work you've done in this part has been checked off. Also, make sure the Student Notebook pages you worked on are dated and complete.

When you are finished, choose something to read that you will enjoy. Then find a quiet, comfortable place and read for the following length of time:

🌱🌱 🐾 30 minutes   🐾 35 minutes

Be sure to write down what you read today on the Reading Log in your Student Notebook.

Lesson 1, Part 3

A. Copywork & Dictation
Language Skills

Look carefully at your assigned passage below, and read it silently. Show your teacher any words you don't know, and practice saying them aloud. Now read the passage aloud, or ask your teacher to read it to you.

When you are finished copying or writing from dictation, compare your copy to the text and make any needed corrections.

🌱🌱 🐾 Copy or write as your teacher dictates from *The Story of Inventions*, page 264, paragraph 3 ("What had started…").

🐾 Write as your teacher dictates from *The Story of Inventions*, page 264, paragraph 3 ("What had started…"), and page 265, paragraph 1 ("In 1908, Wilbur…").

Teaching Tip

One approach to teaching your child a difficult task or concept is to break it down into small, manageable pieces. This keeps your child from feeling overwhelmed, yet allows him to access more difficult material that he probably would not attempt if presented all at once or as an independent assignment without assistance.

B. Reader
Language Skills, History

Homer Price: page 21, paragraph 4 ("Homer was very thoughtful…")
to the top of page 24
The New Way Things Work: pages 106 and 107 (Flying)

Follow the directions below to read or listen to the assigned passages
in *Homer Price* and *The New Way Things Work*.

When you are finished, make up five true-false statements about
the assignment in *The New Way Things Work* and write them in your
Student Notebook. (Be sure that at least two of your statements are
false.) Make an answer key at the bottom of the page and write each
false statement correctly. You do not need to rewrite the true statements. Then give your quiz to a family member!

🐾 Read the above assignment from *Homer Price* aloud, and then
follow along as someone else reads the assignment from *The New
Way Things Work*.

🐾 Read the above assignment from *Homer Price* silently, and then read
the assignment from *The New Way Things Work* aloud.

🐾 Read the above assignments from *Homer Price* and *The New Way
Things Work* silently.

C. Read-Aloud & Narration
History, Language Skills, Thinking Skills

The Wright Brothers: page 11 (Chapter 2) through page 17, paragraph 4

Follow the instructions below for your level. Then, in your own
words, tell what happened in the story from Orville or Wilbur's
point of view (or pretend you are one of them and tell what you
think happened). Try to remember as many details as possible. Tell
what you think is the most important event in the passage.

🐾🐾 Listen carefully to the assigned passage.

🐾 Read the assigned passage aloud.

D. Vocabulary
Language Skills, Thinking Skills

In this part, finish the vocabulary review you began in Part 1.

Use the second stack of vocabulary cards (that you set aside for this
part) and pick one card at a time. Read the word on the front and,
without looking, tell your teacher either what it means or how it was
used in the story. Give yourself a point for every word you are able to
use correctly. See how many points you can get!

D. One of the most important ways to develop comprehension is to build vocabulary. Becoming familiar with new words by reading, writing, speaking, and listening to them helps the new words become part of your student's functional vocabulary. Understanding the meaning and being able to use each word correctly is more important than merely memorizing a definition.

Lapbook Activity

E. Science

Thinking Skills

Human Body Basics, Digestive System: Absorption & Other Organs

As you read through the assigned pages, choose words that are new or unfamiliar and make vocabulary cards for them as directed. Keep your science cards separate from other vocabulary.

at least two words

at least four words

Read and discuss the information in the passage with your teacher and do the *Labwork 4-5* activities. The pages you need for writing and labeling are in your Student Notebook.

When you are finished, look at *Examine This* projects 3 and 4 at the end of the chapter and:

Choose one to complete.

Complete both.

Do as much as you can, but you don't have to finish the projects in this part. You will have other opportunities to work on them, such as during Part 5 and in occasional Study Hall sections.

F. Writing

Language Skills, Thinking Skills

In the next unit (Reach for the Stars) of *Paths of Progress*, you will have the opportunity to develop an idea into a Science Fair project of your choice. Even if you think you will never enter a science fair, this will be a good opportunity to learn about many of the steps people go through to research a topic, develop a hypothesis, create an experiment to test that hypothesis, document the results, and display the findings. At least two sections of each lesson in Unit 6 will be devoted to working on this project.

Your science project can be related to the tools and technology topics you studied in Volume 1, the human body systems you are exploring in this volume, an invention that interests you, or a subject that is completely unrelated to any of the things you've studied this year. It is totally up to you and your teacher! The most important thing is that you choose a topic that interests you.

Start thinking about possible topics you might like to develop into a project. If you need help with ideas, there are plenty of suggestions on-line or in various books at the library. Think of at least five possibilities and list them in your Student Notebook.

Discuss your thoughts with your teacher and then look for a little basic information about each of your possibilities. Then, under each topic, write a sentence or two telling what you would like to find out or why you think that particular subject might be interesting.

G. Music

History, Thinking Skills

Look back at pages 58 through 61 in *The Story of the Orchestra.*

Then, follow the directions in Appendix D to make two Orchestra Story question and answer cards about the bassoon or contrabassoon, and two about the brass section. Put the small letters *WI* (for woodwind instruments) in the upper left corners of your bassoon or contrabassoon answer cards. Label the brass section answer cards with a small *BI* (for brass instruments) in the upper left corners. Do not label the question cards—and remember to write the questions in your Student Notebook in the correct order.

Take out all the Orchestra Story cards you have made so far in Units 4 and 5, and separate the questions from the answers. Mix up both stacks well, and then place the question card stack facedown on the table. Draw one question at a time and see if you can find its correct answer in the other stack. Remember the answer keys you made in your Student Notebook. Remove the question and answer cards you get correct.

H. Independent Reading & Record Keeping

Thinking Skills

Review the Lesson 1 At A Glance chart in your Student Notebook to see if all the work you've done in this part has been checked off. Also, make sure the Student Notebook pages you worked on are dated and complete.

When you are finished, choose something to read that you will enjoy. Then find a quiet, comfortable place and read for the following length of time:

🖐🖐🐾 30 minutes   🐾 35 minutes

Be sure to write down what you read today on the Reading Log in your Student Notebook.

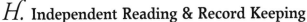

Lesson 1, Part 4

A. Copywork & Dictation

Language Skills

Look carefully at your assigned passage below, and read it silently. Show your teacher any words you don't know, and practice saying them aloud. Now read the passage aloud, or ask your teacher to read it to you.

When you are finished copying or writing from dictation, compare your copy to the text and make any needed corrections.

❦❦ Copy or write as your teacher dictates from *Homer Price*, page 28, paragraph 2 ("Well, there isn't…").

❦ Write as your teacher dictates from *The Wright Brothers*, page 14, paragraph 5 ("Our world operates…").

❦ Write as your teacher dictates from *The Wright Brothers*, page 14, paragraphs 5 and 6 ("Our world operates…").

B. **Reader**   *Language Skills, History*
Homer Price: page 24, paragraph 1 ("They were afraid…") through page 28
The New Way Things Work: pages 108 through 109 (The Airplane)

Follow the directions below to read or listen to the assigned passages in *Homer Price* and *The New Way Things Work*.

When you are finished, make up five true-false statements about the assignment in *The New Way Things Work* and write them in your Student Notebook. (Be sure that at least two of your statements are false.) Make an answer key at the bottom of the page and write each false statement correctly. (You do not need to re-write the true statements.) Then give your quiz to a family member!

❦❦ Read the above assignment from *Homer Price* aloud, and then follow along as someone else reads the assignment from *The New Way Things Work*.

❦ Read the above assignment from *Homer Price* silently, and then read the assignment from *The New Way Things Work* aloud.

❦ Read the above assignments from *Homer Price* and *The New Way Things Work* silently.

C. **Read-Aloud & Discussion**   *History, Language Skills, Thinking Skills*
The Wright Brothers: page 17, paragraph 5 ("Both Wilbur and Orville…") through page 25, paragraph 5

After reading or listening to the read-aloud assignment, talk with your teacher and try to predict what will happen in the future based on what you know of the characters and events. Write your predictions in your Student Notebook. Later you will look back and see if they were accurate. Try not to peek ahead!

❦❦ Listen carefully as your teacher reads the assigned passage. Write down two predictions.

❦ Listen carefully as your teacher reads the assigned passage. Write down three predictions.

❦ Read the assigned passage aloud; then write down at least four predictions.

Teaching Tip

If your child needs to practice reading aloud to gain fluency, but feels that it is babyish for him to have to do so, suggest that he read into a tape recorder by himself. That way, he can read, listen, and practice rereading parts that don't sound smooth. You can listen to the passage without him present to identify areas that need further practice. When you keep the tapes and your child listens to them later, they can be a proof of improvement!

D. Word Building   *Language Skills, Thinking Skills*

Earlier in this lesson you learned about the Greek word-part *micro-* or *micros-*. Read over the words you defined in Part 2 and tell your teacher what each one means.

Now add to your ability to use *micro-* or *micros-* by finding more words in the dictionary that begin with it and relate to its meaning. Write them in your Student Notebook. Be sure not to repeat any of the words you have already defined. When you are finished, pick one of your words and write a sentence that uses it correctly.

🐾 at least three words 🐾 at least six words 🐾 at least nine words

E. History and Economics   *Thinking Skills*

Another benefit that came from the invention of the car was the development of the truck. Similar to the car in basic construction, a truck is built to include more space for **cargo** (goods that are generally carried by railroad, ship, motor vehicle, or aircraft) and usually less space for passengers.

Lapbook
Activity

By 1908, approximately 4,000 trucks were in use in America, carrying goods on whatever roads were useable. By the time World

War I started, the number of trucks in use had increased dramatically. Trucks were used in every facet of life, carrying anything that would fit inside from the place where the goods were manufactured, to the place where consumers could purchase them. During World War I, trucks became an important part of the army's ability to move men, supplies, and equipment from place to place when roads were available. By the time the war ended in 1918, Americans were using approximately one million trucks. In ten short years, trucks became established as part of business in the United States.

The first trucks could hardly be called comfortable. Tires were made of solid rubber, and there was little to cushion rides over bumpy roads. But as trucks improved, so did the comfort of the drivers and passengers. Nowadays, trucks can be just as luxurious as any passenger car. For the most part, the purpose of trucks remains work-related, carrying a wide variety of cargo or driving to hard-to-reach fields or construction sites. Sometimes they might even be used as tools for pulling or pushing items like disabled vehicles.

The next time you go anywhere in your family car, make a list of the number and types of trucks you see on the road. Are there a great deal more cars than trucks on the roads near you? What type of trucks do you see most frequently? Pick-up trucks? Cargo trucks?

Large semi-trailer trucks? Tow trucks? If you need help identifying the types of trucks you are seeing, ask a family member or friend to help you. Decide what type of truck you like the best, and why.

In 1935, Congress passed the Motor Carrier Act. This act provided safety regulations for interstate freight carriers. It also gave the Interstate Commerce Commission the authority to create regulations covering trucks and drivers that traveled across state lines, approve new trucking routes, and create tariff rates. **Tariffs** are taxes, or fees, charged by a government to bring items into or out of a country or a state. The Interstate Commerce Commission (ICC) made tariff rates the same for those who carried **freight**, or cargo, and thus eliminated competition based on price.

What do you think the benefit of the ICC was? At the library or on the Internet, find out more about this Commission and some of the regulations it created. What disadvantages, if any, do you see with those regulations?

Make a list of what you think were the positives and negatives of this government agency.

Learn more about the **Motor Carrier Act of 1980**. What big changes did this law make? Talk with your parent about how you think it affected the trucking industry.

F. Spelling
Language Skills, Thinking Skills

To increase your ability to use the words you have studied in this lesson when you write, review your vocabulary and word building lists. After choosing the number of words assigned below from these lists, you and your teacher may choose words from the Challenge Spelling List in Appendix C to work on as well. You may also want to add two or three words from your own writing that you have difficulty spelling correctly. Make your spelling list on the page provided in your Student Notebook.

When you are finished, write the words you have chosen as your teacher dictates them. Then study any that you are unable to spell correctly in preparation for writing in the next lessons. Add those words to the Ongoing Spelling List in your Student Notebook. Once you can spell a word correctly in dictation, then you can cross it off. If you misspell words in your everyday writing, be sure to add them to your list. Throughout the year, you should have an ongoing list of words you are practicing.

Tips for Studying Spelling Words:

1. Read the words over. Spell each one quietly to yourself and then check to see if you were correct.

F. If you or your child would like to add a greater degree of difficulty to spelling lessons, choose more words from the Challenge Spelling List (in Appendix C) for the lesson you are on. The words on this list are taken from the literature being read.

2. Use a dry-erase board or other non-permanent surface to practice writing the words. Do this quickly until you feel more confident about their spelling.

3. When the words are called out to you, practice spelling them aloud. Picture the word in your mind as you spell it.

4. Look for any meanings or letter patterns that stand out to you. Remind yourself of these patterns or meanings as you study.

5. Remember that the most important spelling skill is to develop a sense when you look at your spelling of a word that it may not be spelled correctly. It is this sense that prompts a writer to look words up in a dictionary, and repeated exposure to a word will help you remember how to spell it.

Choose eight words from the vocabulary and word building lists, and two to four Challenge Spelling words (if you and your teacher want).

Choose ten words from the vocabulary and word building lists, and three to five Challenge Spelling words (if you and your teacher want).

Choose twelve words from your vocabulary or word building lists, and four to six Challenge Spelling words (if you and your teacher want).

G. Art
Thinking Skills

Read pages 48 and 49, "Folk Art," in *Create Anything With Clay*. Pick a couple of the projects and try them out. Remember, you don't have to copy what's done on these pages—just use the samples as inspiration to create your own things.

When you're finished, put any leftover clay back in its zip-lock bag.

H. Independent Reading & Record Keeping
Thinking Skills

Review the Lesson 1 At A Glance chart in your Student Notebook to see if all the work you've done in this part has been checked off. Also, make sure the Student Notebook pages you worked on are dated and complete.

When you are finished, choose something to read that you will enjoy. Then find a quiet, comfortable place and read for the following length of time:

30 minutes　　35 minutes

Be sure to write down what you read today on the Reading Log in your Student Notebook.

Lesson 1, Part 5

This part is set aside for completion of any work left undone from the lesson and review of concepts and content. It is also a time to expand the work of the lesson with practice and games.

- Review this lesson's Steps for Thinking, found in Part 1.

- Give the Unit 4 vocabulary cards that you reviewed in this lesson to your teacher and ask her to show you their picture sides, one at a time. Tell her what the picture or clue means and then name the word written on the other side. If you can, tell what part of speech it is. Give yourself one point for correctly naming a word and one point for knowing its part of speech. Keep track of your points and see if you beat your score from Part 3!

- Listen as your teacher reads the spelling words that you studied from Part 4, especially the ones on your Ongoing Spelling List. Write each word in your Student Notebook as she dictates it. When you are finished, look at your word list and make corrections as needed. Show your teacher how you did.

- Follow the directions in the *Human Body Basics* Instructions to play the Word Power vocabulary game, and complete the System Savvy puzzles in your Student Notebook.[2] Then work on any *Examine This* projects you have not yet completed.

- Look back at pages 38 and 39 in the *Basix Recorder Method* and practice those exercises. Then review any other lessons that may be giving you trouble. Choose several tracks on the *Recorder Method* CD and play along with them. Be sure to spend at least 20 minutes practicing—and don't forget that you can use your Finger Placement Tabs if you need to.

- Review the Lesson 1 At A Glance chart in your Student Notebook to see if all the work you've done in this part has been checked off. If you did an Enrichment activity or other extra work in this lesson, be sure to write it on the lines next to the chart.

- Complete the Success Takes Flight Word Search located in your Student Notebook.[3]

Enrichment Activities

1. One of the things that set this time period apart from others were the bursts of advancement in so many areas: transportation, communication, business, and technology. This creative time came about through inspiration and application— many people put in many hours of study, experimentation, observation, making changes, and then applying what they had learned.

   Over the next five weeks you can participate in a similar process! Talk with your parents about careers that interest you. Narrow

As you discuss the Steps for Thinking with your child, feel free to share the examples that have come to your mind during the lesson. Share the steps you went through in your thinking as well as your outcomes. Modeling is a very effective type of instruction, and your child will gain insight into connecting concepts and examples by hearing your thinking.

The goal of the spelling assignments is to improve your student's ability to spell by helping him make connections to meaning, phonics, and word patterns. Memorizing a list is not as valuable to students as increasing their ability to comfortably write words that express their understanding and opinions.

your choices down to one or two. Now begin your Career Project by learning what you can about the history of those career choices (the history of aviation if you want to be a pilot, the history of computers if you want to design video games, and so forth). After doing some research, create a timeline for the industries in which you are interested. Your timeline can show the global history of your area or just the American history.

Collect information for each part of this project and then make a presentation to your family at the end of Lesson 5. You can keep your research in a separate notebook or add it to your Student Notebook.

2. First ladies have always been an important part of the office of the Presidency. First Ladies are usually the wives of the Presidents, though there have been a few exceptions. Their duties include acting as hostess to guests in the White House, supporting charitable causes, and of course, supporting the President as wife and mother to their children. Each First Lady is as different as each President—each with her own unique characteristics. Should you choose to complete this project, you will compile information on First Lady, including:

   • Relationship to the President (wife, sister, etc.)

   • Years of service

   • Difficult issues or events during the President's term

   • Key projects initiated, or causes supported, by this First Lady

   • Main changes in culture—fashion, advancements at White House, and so forth

   • Tell what you think were the most important qualities of this First Lady

   You will research two First Ladies during each Lesson. The first two are Edith Roosevelt and Helen Taft.

   At the end of this project, present your findings to your family and highlight your favorite First Lady. Try to include a variety of presentation types, or media, in your project, like print (letters, writings, or quotes by or about the First Lady or President), pictures of culture at the time (cars, fashions, new inventions, and so forth), audio or video information, or verbal presentation by you.

3. Learn more about the mechanized vehicles of the armed forces—tanks, trucks, armored personnel carriers, or emergency vehicles (fire fighting or ambulance). You may want to learn about them as a group, or choose one specific type of vehicle to research. Make sure to include pictures of the vehicle(s) when you share what you learn with your family.

Additional Resources:

Mary Emma & Company by Ralph Moody

Orville Wright: The Flyer by Janet and Geoff Benge

Answers

1. Possible answers:

    Proper nouns: Homer, Centerburg, Tabby, Aroma, Mr. Dreggs, N.W. Blott, Mexico, Orville, Wilbur, Omaha, Cedar Rapids, Hartsville College, Euclid, Confederates, Civil War, New York City, German, Smithsonian Institute, North Carolina, and so forth.

    Common nouns: glider, motor, machine, hobby, flight, scientist, popcorn, rubber band, gravity, nuts, bolts, robbers, lotion, suitcase, and so forth.

2. Answer key is in the *Human Body Basics* Answer Key.

3. Answer key is in Appendix C.

Lesson 2, Part 1

> ### ✥ Steps for Thinking ✥
>
> 1. Many people are motivated by the challenge of solving a new problem. It takes wisdom to know when to persevere, or continue doing one type of action, and when to try something new.
>
> 2. The encouragement of those you trust is essential, or very important, in helping you to pursue something that other people think is foolish, or will not work.
>
> 3. To find out what will work, you have to put some of your ideas to the test. Once you try them out, you then have more data, or information, to adjust your ideas or to change them altogether.
>
> 4. Our economy is part of a global, or worldwide, economy. Events around the world affect the economy here, and events here affect other economies around the globe.

Make the Steps for Thinking readily accessible during the lesson. As often as possible, connect them to examples in the stories, activities, or discussion. Encourage your children to do the same.

⬥─Materials─⬥

- *The Wright Brothers*
- *Homer Price*
- *The Story of Inventions*
- *Human Body Basics*
- *The Story of the Orchestra* book & CD
- *Basix Recorder Method*
- *Create Anything With Clay*
- *Classroom Atlas of the United States*
- Polymer clay
- Recorder
- Activity (Part 1):
    Cracker
    Pen and paper
    8 different colored markers or crayons
- Activities (Part 4):
    Black & white photocopy of a design or picture
    Scissors
    Spoon

A. Copywork & Dictation
Language Skills

Look carefully at your assigned passage below, and read it silently. Show your teacher any words you don't know, and practice saying them aloud. Now read the passage aloud, or ask your teacher to read it to you.

When you are finished copying or writing from dictation, compare your copy to the text and make any needed corrections.

🐾🐾🖐 Write as your teacher dictates from *The Story of Inventions*, page 140, paragraph 3 ("The best thing…").

🖐 Write as your teacher dictates from *The Story of Inventions*, page 140, paragraphs 3 and 4 ("The best thing…").

B. Reader
Language Skills, History

Homer Price: page 34 (Chapter 2) through page 36, paragraph 9
The Story of Inventions: page 138 (Chapter 10) through the top of page 140

Follow the directions below to read or listen to the assigned passage in *Homer Price*.

B. There are many purposes in reading biographies. One is to learn about a certain individual's life, another is to read about history as it related to that individual, and a third purpose is to provide inspiration for the next generation. People are not perfect, but the individuals chosen for this text have accomplished something worthy of their consideration. Encourage your children to think about what the person accomplished and the challenge set before them. Never pass up the opportunity to inspire your children. It makes a great difference when they know others have gone before them, persevered, and been successful.

Before you begin your assignment in *The Story of Inventions*, scan it for any words you don't know and write them on a piece of scrap paper. Read over any section titles included in the passage—and then, as you read or listen to a section, think about how it relates to its title.

When you are finished, find the Comprehension Questions at the end of Chapter 10 in *The Story of Inventions*, and use a complete sentence to write the answer to Question 1 in your Student Notebook.

ᵡᵡ Read the above assignment from *Homer Price* aloud, and then follow along as someone else reads the assignment from *The Story of Inventions*.

🖐 Read the above assignment from *Homer Price* silently, and then read the assignment from *The Story of Inventions* aloud.

🐾 Read the above assignments from *Homer Price* and *The Story of Inventions* silently.

C. **Read-Aloud & Narration**   *History, Language Skills, Thinking Skills*
The Wright Brothers: page 25, paragraph 6 ("Shortly after this…") through page 33, paragraph 1

Follow the directions below to read or listen to the above passage. Then, in your own words, tell what happened in the portion you are assigned. Try to remember as many details as possible. If necessary you may reread, or listen as your teacher rereads, the part you are to retell.

ᵡᵡ Listen carefully as your teacher reads the above assignment aloud. Choose one page to retell.

🖐 Listen carefully as your teacher reads the above assignment aloud. Choose two pages to retell.

🐾 Read the above assignment aloud, and then retell the entire passage.

D. **Vocabulary**   *Language Skills, Thinking Skills*
Write each vocabulary word on the Vocabulary I.D. sheet in your Student Notebook. Then tell your teacher what you think each word means, based on the context in which you have read it. If you are not sure of a word's meaning, use a dictionary to look it up. You may have to remove any endings that have been added, such as an *s* or *ed*, to find that word in the dictionary. Write the definition on the Vocabulary Sheet.

Next, write the word's part of speech: noun, adjective, adverb, verb, and so forth. If you aren't sure, this can also be found in the dictionary.

mechanical	**drudgery**	**nevertheless**
prevalent	**standardize**	
treacherous	**distortion**	**infuriate**
contraption	**imperil**	

E. Science
Thinking Skills

Human Body Basics, Nervous System: beginning of chapter & Central Nervous System

As you read through the assigned pages, choose words that are new or unfamiliar and make vocabulary cards for them as directed. Keep your science cards separate from other vocabulary.

at least three words

at least four words

Read and discuss the information in the passage with your teacher and do the *Labwork 1-5* activities. The pages you need to complete these activities are in your Student Notebook.

When you are finished, look at *Examine This* projects 1 and 2 at the end of the chapter, and:

Choose one to complete.

Complete both.

Do as much as you can, but you don't have to finish the projects in this part. You will have other opportunities to work on them, such as during Part 5 and in occasional Study Hall sections.

F. Writing
Language Skills, Thinking Skills

Read the Labwork summaries you wrote in Section E aloud, and make sure each one either accurately describes the activity (descriptive writing), or explains exactly how to do it (expository writing).

If either of them doesn't accomplish its goal, rewrite it so that it does.

F. Writing is not a separate subject, but rather a set of skills with which to become familiar. Writing is best when it is a response to content learned, new ideas, or as a result of an activity or experience.

G. Music
History, Thinking Skills

Continue your study of brass instruments by reading pages 62 through 65 in *The Story of the Orchestra* with your teacher and discussing the information about the trumpet and the French horn. Then listen to parts of the "Concerto for Trumpet in E Flat" on Track 26 and the "Horn Concerto No. 1" on Track 27 of your CD. Were you able to discriminate between the instruments featured on each track? How did the music make you feel? What did you enjoy or dislike about it?

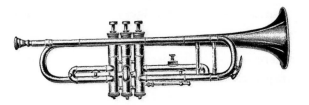

When you are finished, listen carefully to Tracks 26 and 27 again and choose your favorite. Then, draw and color a picture in your Student Notebook of the image this music brings to your mind.

H. **Independent Reading & Record Keeping**   *Thinking Skills*
Review the Lesson 2 At A Glance chart in your Student Notebook to see if all the work you've done in this part has been checked off. Also, make sure the Student Notebook pages you worked on are dated and complete.

When you are finished, choose something to read that you will enjoy. Then find a quiet, comfortable place and read for the following length of time:

ᛉᛉ ᛒ 30 minutes   ᛒ 35 minutes

Be sure to write down what you read today on the Reading Log in your Student Notebook.

Lesson 2, Part 2

A. **Copywork & Dictation**   *Language Skills*
Look carefully at the Steps for Thinking for this lesson and read them silently. Show your teacher any words you don't know, and practice saying them aloud. Then, copy or write them from dictation into your Student Notebook.

When you are finished, compare your copy to the text and make any needed corrections.

ᛉᛉ Copy the Steps for Thinking, and tell your teacher an example of each Step from your reading or your life.

ᛒ Write the Steps for Thinking as your teacher dictates them. Then, in your Student Notebook write one example of each Step from your reading or your life. Be sure to use complete sentences.

ᛒ Write the Steps for Thinking as your teacher dictates them. Then, in your Student Notebook write two examples of each Step from your reading or your life. Be sure to use complete sentences.

B. **Reader**   *Language Skills, History*

Homer Price: page 36, paragraph 10 ("At the beginning…") through page 39, paragraph 8

The Story of Inventions: page 140, paragraph 1 (A Wife for Ford) through page 142, paragraph 1

Follow the directions below to read or listen to the assigned passage in *Homer Price*.

Before you begin your assignment in *The Story of Inventions*, scan it for any words you don't know and write them on a piece of scrap paper. Read over any section titles included in the passage—and then, as you read or listen to a section, think about how it relates to its title.

Read the above assignment from *Homer Price* aloud, and then follow along as someone else reads the assignment from *The Story of Inventions*.

Read the above assignment from *Homer Price* silently, and then read the assignment from *The Story of Inventions* aloud.

Read the above assignments from *Homer Price* and *The Story of Inventions* silently.

C. **Read-Aloud & Discussion**   *History, Language Skills, Thinking Skills*

The Wright Brothers: page 33, paragraph 2 ("In the fall…") through page 40

Follow the directions below to read or listen to the above assignment. Then make up questions about the part of the story you just read or heard. Write your questions in your Student Notebook and ask your teacher to answer them. After discussing her thoughts, write down the best possible answer on the lines provided. Be sure to use complete sentences.

When you are finished, look back at the prediction or predictions you made during Lesson 1, Part 4. Were you able to predict what would happen? Be sure to mark the "Came to Pass" box for each prediction when it does happen.

Listen carefully as your teacher reads the above assignment aloud. Make up two questions.

Listen carefully as your teacher reads the above assignment aloud. Make up three questions.

Read the above assignment aloud; then make up four questions.

Connect Learning to Life

Paraphrasing is an important skill for everyday use. If someone tells you directions or gives you information, one way to make sure you understand what they have said is to paraphrase, or restate in your own words, what you understood them to say. It can be as simple as paraphrasing a conversation with a relative or telling what you understood the pastor to say in a Sunday sermon. It is also a way of communicating clearly. Show your students how checking their understanding of what another person has said can help avoid misunderstandings. Model this skill in front of your children, so that they can see its use in everyday life.

∾ Teacher Connection ∾

Continuous learning is an important part of education. Be sure to read the *Teacher Connection* note in your Parent Planner. Don't miss out on this important part of your homeschooling!

Lapbook Activity

D. Word Building   *Language Skills, Thinking Skillss*

In this section you will continue learning about Greek and Latin word-parts that help to build words in the English language. Today's word-part is ***unus-*** or ***uni-***, which is a Latin word that means one.

Look up the following words in the dictionary and write each definition in your Student Notebook. Then underline the word-part *unus-* or *uni-* in each word. Think, and be ready to tell your teacher how each definition relates to the meaning of the Latin word.

unicycle	unit	unify
unicorn	unique	universal
uniform	university	unilateral

E. History and Economics   *Thinking Skills. Geography*

The **Great Depression** was an economic crisis that began around 1929 and lasted approximately ten years. Though it started in the United States, it wasn't long before its effects were felt throughout the world. Even back then, before today's global economy, a nation's economic well-being depended on others purchasing goods from them, called **exports**. Before World War I, the United States exported many agricultural products to Europe. After the war, the U. S. continued to grow as many crops as before, but since the countries of Europe were struggling to rebuild their own economies, they had far less money to purchase exported crops. Because there were so many extra crops to sell, the prices of those crops fell.

This influenced American farmers because the costs to produce a crop were the same as before, but now the prices farmers received for their harvests were lower. They were making less profit than before. This forced many farmers to take out loans or to stop farming altogether. Eventually many farmers lost their farms and then had to find new ways to make a living. Not only did this affect farmers, but all the businesses that helped farmers such as feed stores, those who made tools for farm use, those who transported the crops, and more. As you can see, businesses are dependent on one another and when one suffers, the effects are felt by all the other businesses connected to them.

Tariffs, or taxes, were imposed by countries on their exports so that other countries would have to pay more for the goods they needed. Because of this, the amount of exported goods went down even further.

By the year 1932, world trade was down by almost half of what it had been, further reducing the amount of goods purchased by other countries. This reduced the amount of goods produced in the United States, and led to fewer jobs.

During the 1920s, many businesses made a great deal of profit, allowing them to expand. Profits seemed to be so easy to make that some businesses expanded more than they could really afford. The **stock exchange**, a place where people could invest in businesses that seemed like they would be profitable, reflected the feeling that profits would continue to flow without end. The value of some businesses rose to great heights. Many people made a great deal of money in the stock exchange at this time, betting that the level of profits would stay high. The value of many businesses became **inflated**, or exaggerated. In 1929, the real value of these businesses started to become known, causing the value of many stocks to drop. As the value of the stocks dropped, investors could take fewer profits. For three years, until 1932, stock values dropped, ruining the finances of many investors and companies. This, in turn, affected banks.

When prices of stocks began to fall and other countries were not interested or able to buy American exports, banks had trouble collecting loan payments from people who had borrowed money. When loans couldn't be repaid, many banks were unable to stay in business. As banks collapsed, this led to an even greater sense of trouble for the economy. By 1933, nearly half of all the banks in America had closed their doors. Many people had lost savings when the banks failed, causing even greater crisis for the citizens of America.

In all previous financial difficulties, the United States government had allowed the forces of the marketplace to take affect. This means that failing businesses were allowed to fail, and those that prospered were allowed to prosper. The government did not intervene to change the natural outcome of business events. This time was different, however. President Herbert Hoover believed that the proper corrections would take place in the business world, and that the government should not step in to change the natural course of events. He was up for reelection in 1932 and was opposed by Franklin D. Roosevelt. Roosevelt felt that the government should intervene by creating jobs for people, providing assistance to those who were out of work, creating programs that would provide a type of insurance for the poor and the elderly, and increase government regulations to correct problems in the business world. Roosevelt was elected President and put these changes into place. Many of these programs still exist today.

Though many programs were begun to improve the financial situation in America, the Great Depression didn't end until World War II began. When the United States entered the war after Japan bombed Pearl

Harbor (in Hawaii), a great many factories started producing the materials needed for war. As you have learned in previous lessons, when an army goes to war a great many things are needed, and businesses must provide those needs. With such a great increase in businesses, the unemployment problem in America greatly diminished. People went back to work and the economy recovered.

In your *Classroom Atlas of the United States*, look in the section about United States History and find the page about the Great Depression. Read the first two paragraphs on that page and look at the small map in the upper right corner. Fill in the chart in your Student Notebook that shows the different percentages of unemployed workers for each country in 1929 and then in 1932. Calculate the various increases in unemployment. Which country had the greatest increase in unemployment? Why do you think this was so?

Now look at the map of the United States toward the center of the page. Fill in the chart in your Student Notebook by listing each state in the column that shows the percentage of its population receiving unemployment benefits in 1934. Then compare the list of states that had the most people receiving unemployment benefits, with the list of states showing the fewest people receiving them. Tell your teacher why you think the states in those lists were in the highest and lowest unemployment benefits category.

Find your state on the above map. What was its level of unemployment benefits in 1934? Find out more about your state's unemployment rate today. What is it? Has it gone up or done in recent years? How does your state's current rate of unemployment compare to its level in 1934? Talk with your parents about the comparison.

During the Great Depression, the rate of national unemployment reached almost 30%. Using the library, Internet, or other resources, find out what the national unemployment rate is today. Talk with your family about the current rate of unemployment in the United States. What does your family believe has contributed to today's unemployment rate? Do you or your family members know anyone who is currently unemployed? Talk about why that person is unemployed.

On the "Unemployment Benefits" map, choose one or more sites of civil unrest or disobedience. Find out more about the unrest that happened at the site(s) you chose, and share what you learn with your family. There have been other movements in which people have demonstrated to bring attention to their economic beliefs. Learn more about the "Occupy Wall Street" movement of 2011. What did people involved in this movement believe? Do you agree with them? Do you agree with the way they expressed their beliefs? Talk with your parents about how the civil unrest in 1934 compares to the "Occupy Wall Street" movement.

Learn about recession. What is it? How do you know if one is taking place? After doing some research, talk with your family about what you discover. Using what you have learned, decide what factors cause a recession. Has America experienced any recessions? What relationship do recessions have to depressions?

F. Editing
Language Skills, Thinking Skills

In this section you will continue reviewing parts of speech and finding examples in your literature. The second parts you will review are adjectives. There are several types of adjectives, but for now, you will just look for the ones that describe nouns or pronouns. Look at the following examples to see how they are used.

Adjective: A word that describes, or tells about, a noun or pronoun.

> Henry Ford tried to develop <u>safe</u> and <u>reliable</u> kerosene engines.

> Wilbur and Orville built a <u>heavier-than-air</u> <u>flying</u> machine.

Note: *A, an,* and *the* are special kinds of adjectives called articles. For this assignment, don't choose that kind of adjective.

Look at all your reading assignments for Lesson 2 to complete this assignment.[1]

Make a list of at least ten adjectives from your readings.

❦ Add at least two additional adjectives to your list.

❦ Add at least five additional adjectives to your list.

G. Music
Thinking Skills

Read pages 40 and 41 in the *Basix Recorder Method* to learn about *syncopation* and *calypso*. Write the names of notes you're not sure of above the staffs on those pages and practice playing the melodies.

Don't forget to listen to the *Recorder Method* CD tracks shown on page 41 to hear samples of that lesson and use your Finger Placement Tabs if you need to. Take the quiz and show your teacher how you did.

Be sure to spend about 20 minutes a day practicing what you have learned!

H. Independent Reading & Record Keeping
Thinking Skills

Review the Lesson 2 At A Glance chart in your Student Notebook to see if all the work you've done in this part has been checked off. Also, make sure the Student Notebook pages you worked on are dated and complete.

Teaching Tip

Review sessions spaced out over several days or weeks are the best kind of review to help a child remember information. Reading words, writing words and discussing words all help a child connect the word and its meaning to long term memory. When he can relate it to something he already knows, it is even more effective.

When you are finished, choose something to read that you will enjoy. Then find a quiet, comfortable place and read for the following length of time:

ᏉᏉ Ꮗ 30 minutes   Ꮗ 35 minutes

Be sure to write down what you read today on the Reading Log in your Student Notebook.

―◦◦◦―

Lesson 2, Part 3

A. **Copywork & Dictation**   *Language Skills*
Look carefully at your assigned passage below, and read it silently. Show your teacher any words you don't know, and practice saying them aloud. Now read the passage aloud, or ask your teacher to read it to you.

When you are finished copying or writing from dictation, compare your copy to the text and make any needed corrections.

ᏉᏉ Ꮗ Copy or write as your teacher dictates from *The Story of Inventions*, page 142, paragraph 4 ("Ford's neighbors…").

Ꮗ Write as your teacher dictates from *The Story of Inventions*, page 142, paragraphs 4 and 5 ("Ford's neighbors…").

B. **Reader**   *Language Skills, History*
Homer Price: page 39, paragraph 9 ("The Super-Duper's…") through page 44, paragraph 3
The Story of Inventions: page 142, paragraph 2 (Bicycle, Tricycle, and Quadricycle) through the top of page 144

Follow the directions below to read or listen to the assigned passage in *Homer Price*.

Before you begin your assignment in *The Story of Inventions*, scan it for any words you don't know and write them on a piece of scrap paper. Read over any section titles included in the passage—and then, as you read or listen to a section, think about how it relates to its title.

When you are finished, find the Comprehension Questions at the end of Chapter 10 in *The Story of Inventions*, and use complete sentences to write the answers to Questions 2 and 3 in your Student Notebook.

ᏉᏉ Read the above assignment from *Homer Price* aloud, and then follow along as someone else reads the assignment from *The Story of Inventions*.

🐾 Read the above assignment from *Homer Price* silently, and then read the assignment from *The Story of Inventions* aloud.

🐾 Read the above assignments from *Homer Price* and *The Story of Inventions* silently.

C. Read-Aloud & Narration
History, Language Skills, Thinking Skills

The Wright Brothers: page 41 (Chapter 5) through page 49

Follow the instructions below for your level. Then, in your own words, tell what happened in the story from Orville or Wilbur's point of view. Try to remember as many details as possible. Tell what you think is the most important event in the passage.

🐾🐾 Listen carefully to the assigned passage.

🐾 Read the assigned passage aloud.

D. Vocabulary
Language Skills, Thinking Skills

Show your teacher the Vocabulary I.D. sheet that you completed in Part 1 of this lesson. Ask her to review the words with you by calling them out or writing them on a dry erase board or piece of paper. Tell her what each word means or how it was used in the story and, if you can, what part of speech it is.

Give yourself one point for each correct meaning and one point for knowing the word's part of speech. Keep track of your Vocabulary I.D. points by writing them at the bottom of the sheet, and try to beat your score when you review these words again in Part 5.

E. Science
Thinking Skills

Human Body Basics, Nervous System: Peripheral Nervous System

As you read through the assigned pages, choose words that are new or unfamiliar and make vocabulary cards for them as directed. Keep your science cards separate from other vocabulary.

🐾🐾 at least three words

🐾🐾 at least four words

Read and discuss the information in the passage with your teacher and do the *Labwork 6-9* activities. The pages you need to complete these activities are in your Student Notebook.

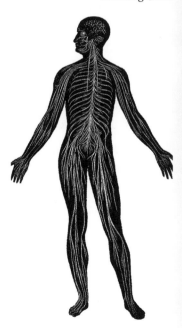

C. Point of view can seem very complex, so do a simple review. Talk about a movie you have all seen. Ask your children to tell about their favorite part of the movie and then share yours. If there are any differences in what people liked, point out that the differences come from each person's way of looking at the movie and reacting to what they saw. This is a simple definition of point of view.

Teaching Tip

It is not cheating to share your thoughts during discussions with your children, especially if they struggle getting started. By sharing your thoughts, you are modeling thinking skills for them. Once their thoughts get started, encourage them to add to what you said. Remember, teaching is not testing. Give your children the support they need to be successful. There will be plenty of time as they grow for them to experience challenges, and success!

When you are finished, look at *Examine This* projects 3 and 4 at the end of the chapter and:

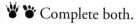 Choose one to complete.

Complete both.

Do as much as you can, but you don't have to finish the projects in this part. You will have other opportunities to work on them, such as during Part 5 and in occasional Study Hall sections.

F. Study Hall   *Thinking Skills*

This section is set aside as a "Study Hall." Use it to catch up on any work that has not yet been completed or to research extra topics that interest you.

G. Music   *History, Thinking Skills*

Look back at pages 62 through 65 in *The Story of the Orchestra*.

Then, follow the directions in Appendix D to make two Orchestra Story question and answer cards about the trumpet, and two about the French horn. Label each answer card with a small *BI* (for brass instruments) in the upper left corner. Do not label the question cards—and remember to write the questions in your Student Notebook in the correct order.

Check the directions in Lesson 1, Part 3G, and review the Orchestra Story cards you have made so far in Units 4 and 5.

H. Independent Reading & Record Keeping   *Thinking Skills*

Review the Lesson 2 At A Glance chart in your Student Notebook to see if all the work you've done in this part has been checked off. Also, make sure the Student Notebook pages you worked on are dated and complete.

When you are finished, choose something to read that you will enjoy. Then find a quiet, comfortable place and read for the following length of time:

30 minutes   35 minutes

Be sure to write down what you read today on the Reading Log in your Student Notebook.

Lapbook Activity

Lesson 2, Part 4

A. **Copywork & Dictation**   *Language Skills*

Look carefully at your assigned passage below, and read it silently. Show your teacher any words you don't know, and practice saying them aloud. Now read the passage aloud, or ask your teacher to read it to you.

When you are finished copying or writing from dictation, compare your copy to the text and make any needed corrections.

🐾 Copy or write as your teacher dictates from *Homer Price*, page 44, paragraph 10 ("Now watch!"…").

✋ Write as your teacher dictates from *The Wright Brothers*, page 34, paragraph 2 ("True, my lad…").

🐾 Write as your teacher dictates from *The Wright Brothers*, page 34, paragraph 2 ("True, my lad…"), and paragraph 8 ("Wilbur gradually began…").

B. **Reader**   *Language Skills, History*

Homer Price: page 44, paragraph 4 ("They crept a little…") through page 46
The Story of Inventions: page 144, paragraph 1 (The Assembly Line) through page 147

Follow the directions below to read or listen to the assigned passage in *Homer Price*.

Before you begin your assignment in *The Story of Inventions*, scan it for any words you don't know and write them on a piece of scrap paper. Read over any section titles included in the passage—and then, as you read or listen to a section, think about how it relates to its title.

When you are finished, find the Comprehension Questions at the end of Chapter 10 in *The Story of Inventions*, and use complete sentences to write the answers to Questions 4 and 5 in your Student Notebook.

🐾 Read the above assignment from *Homer Price* aloud, and then follow along as someone else reads the assignment from *The Story of Inventions*.

✋ Read the above assignment from *Homer Price* silently, and then read the assignment from *The Story of Inventions* aloud.

🐾 Read the above assignments from *Homer Price* and *The Story of Inventions* silently.

C. **Read-Aloud & Discussion**   *History, Language Skills, Thinking Skills*
The Wright Brothers: page 50 (Chapter 6) through page 56, paragraph 1

After reading or listening to the read-aloud assignment, talk with your teacher and try to predict what will happen in the future based

Teaching Tip

Point out to your child that chapter titles and headings are tools to identify main ideas. After your child reads a section or chapter, ask him to tell you how the title, or heading, relates to what he read.

on what you know of the characters and events. Write your predictions in your Student Notebook. Later you will look back and see if they were accurate. Try not to peek ahead!

Listen carefully as your teacher reads the assigned passage. Write down two predictions.

Listen carefully as your teacher reads the assigned passage. Write down three predictions.

Read the assigned passage aloud; then write down at least four predictions.

D. Word Building   *Language Skills, Thinking Skills*

Earlier in this lesson you learned about the Latin word-part *unus-* or *uni-*. Read over the words you defined in Part 2 and tell your teacher what each one means.

Now add to your ability to use *unus-* or *uni-* by finding more words in the dictionary that begin with it and relate to its meaning. Write them in your Student Notebook. Be sure not to repeat any of the words you have already defined. When you are finished, pick one of your words and write a sentence that uses it correctly.

at least three words   at least six words   at least nine words

E. History and Economics   *Thinking Skills, Geography*

The timing of the Dust Bowl couldn't have been worse. Following the Stock Market crash in 1929, the country did not need more economic troubles. But unfortunately, more problems were on the way.

Toward the end of the 1800s, many families moved west, some continuing on to states like Washington, Oregon, and California. Some settled in the Great Plains region which includes Texas, Oklahoma, Kansas, Nebraska, South Dakota, North Dakota, and parts of Colorado. The Great Plains region was a real testing ground for families that moved into the area. Some left quickly while others remained. This area gets very little rain, and tends to be extremely hot in the summer and cold in the winter. Grasses are the most common vegetation that grows there. Why did so many settlers come to this area? They came because there was land available for settling, at little or no cost. The only requirement was that they stay on the land for five years and settle it by building a house, growing crops, or raising animals. While this may not seem like a difficult task, without enough rain it could be very challenging indeed. With great determination, some families stayed and made a go of it.

Many farmers who lived in the Great Plains had already experienced some difficulties. After World War I, the crops grown there were abundant, but the needs for those crops were not. European coun-

E. In order to view history correctly, you have to consider the motives and understanding of the people involved. Evaluate history in the light of context, or what was happening at the time. Sometimes things done in the past are hard for us to understand. Perhaps the people would not have acted in that way if they had our perspective. Remember to evaluate people and their actions based on their knowledge and intentions.

Lapbook Activity

tries that had purchased American crops—like wheat, cotton, and corn—were struggling to rebuild, so they were not able to purchase as much from the United States. Since there was a **surplus**, or more than usual, prices for the crops went down. On the heels of this problem, **drought**, or severe shortage of rain, had begun in the Great Plains in the early 1930s. With less rain, more and more **topsoil** (the richest soil for growing plants) was blown away by dust storms, which became more common and more severe.

Some farmers tried to continue working their farms by getting loans to purchase seed and equipment, rather than relying on profit from the sale of their crops. Since they were not making profit, usually the only choices left to a farmer were to take out loans or give up farming. Many of them did both. As farmers gave up farming on the Great Plains, many moved west where there were stories of jobs. Others moved to cities and began working in factories. This had a great impact on the other businesses that depended on farmers for their **livelihoods**, or means of making a living, such as stores and even county governments that collected taxes from farmers. Many who had remained in the area for years through hard work and determination, struggled during this time.

The term Dust Bowl originated on April 14, 1935, later known as Black Sunday. After weeks of dust storms, this was the biggest yet. High winds pushed the dust everywhere, and the effects of these storms were felt all across the United States. It was during this month that the Soil Conservation Act was passed. Over time, the government sought to address the needs of the people in the Midwest by creating agencies that performed various tasks to help farmers. The Soil Conservation Service and the Farm Security Administration were two such agencies. Similar to its response during the Great Depression, the government stepped in to change the way economics worked in America. It provided supports for those who, for many reasons, struggled or failed in their business. **Subsidies**, or payments for not producing crops, were paid to farmers who agreed not to grow certain things, and help was given to those whose farms had failed. The practice of paying subsidies to farmers still continues today.

The Dust Bowl era ended in the early 1940s as rainfall increased. Also, in 1941, like at the end of the Depression, focus shifted from the Dust Bowl to preparation for war, and the country's economic situation improved.

Look again at the page that tells about the Great Depression in your *Classroom Atlas of the United States*. Read the bottom two paragraphs and examine the map on the bottom right labeled Dust Bowl. Then fill out the chart in your Student Notebook by listing the states that were a part of the Dust Bowl region. Next, list the states that were damaged by dust storms. Compare this chart to the one you made in Part 2 of this lesson, showing the states receiving the highest and lowest amounts of unemployment benefits in 1934. What conclusions, if any, can you draw by comparing these two charts?

Many farmers and businessmen relied on credit when they did not have sufficient profit to keep their farms and businesses running. Today the use of credit is very common. Some credit is considered good, such as a mortgage on a home (which should increase in value over time); other credit is considered bad when the thing purchased with credit loses its value over time. Talk with your parents about their use of credit. What guidelines do they suggest for you when it comes to using credit?

Learn more about credit cards. There are many different types advertised in print and on television and radio. Choose one type of credit card and find out what it offers and requires. What does it take to obtain one? What rate of interest is charged on the money you borrow with that credit card? What determines the amount of your payment each month? Talk with your family about what you learn.

F. Spelling
Language Skills, Thinking Skills

To increase your ability to use the words you have studied in this lesson when you write, review your vocabulary and word building lists. After choosing the number of words assigned below from these lists, you and your teacher may choose words from the Challenge Spelling List in Appendix C to work on as well. You may also want to add two or three words from your own writing that you have difficulty spelling correctly. Make your spelling list on the page provided in your Student Notebook.

When you are finished, write the words you have chosen as your teacher dictates them. Then study any that you are unable to spell correctly in preparation for writing in the next lessons. (You might want to look back at the "Tips for Studying Spelling Words" in Lesson 1, Part 4F). Add those words to the Ongoing Spelling List in your Student Notebook (Lesson 1, Part 4). Also, don't forget to add words you misspell in your everyday writing to the list. Once you can spell a word correctly in dictation, then you can cross it off. Throughout the year, you should have an ongoing list of words you are practicing.

🌱 Choose eight words from the vocabulary and word building lists, and two to four Challenge Spelling words (if you and your teacher want).

🐾 Choose ten words from the vocabulary and word building lists, and three to five Challenge Spelling words (if you and your teacher want).

🐾 Choose twelve words from your vocabulary or word building lists, and four to six Challenge Spelling words (if you and your teacher want).

G. Art   *Thinking Skills*
Read pages 50 and 51, "Clay Pictures," in *Create Anything With Clay*, and think about the many ways this technique could be used. A few are shown, but there are more—so discuss the possibilities with your teacher. Then follow the directions to imprint a design or picture that you like.

Don't forget to put any left-over clay back in its zip-lock bag.

H. Independent Reading & Record Keeping   *Thinking Skills*
Review the Lesson 2 At A Glance chart in your Student Notebook to see if all the work you've done in this part has been checked off. Also, make sure the Student Notebook pages you worked on are dated and complete.

When you are finished, choose something to read that you will enjoy. Then find a quiet, comfortable place and read for the following length of time:

🌱🐾 30 minutes   🐾 35 minutes

Be sure to write down what you read today on the Reading Log in your Student Notebook.

G. Encourage your children to see their sculpting as part of a process. After completing a model, ask them to tell you what they like about it, as well as things they might like to improve. Share with them aspects of their artwork that you enjoy. To model this process, you may want to try the activity with them and ask them to share their opinions with you!

Summary lessons and activities are very valuable. Though this may seem shorter than the other lesson parts, it is no less important. There are a variety of ways to help your children retain concepts and skills. Student presentations, review, games and activities are all effective means of helping your children solidify and remember what they have learned. Then they can take the next big step of using it in the future, so be sure to make room for Part 5!

This part is set aside for completion of any work left undone from the lesson and review of concepts and content. It is also a time to expand the work of the lesson with practice and games.

- Review this lesson's Steps for Thinking, found in Part 1.

- Use the Vocabulary I.D. sheet you completed in Part 1 of this lesson to make vocabulary cards. Write each word on an index card and try to remember what it means or how it was used in the story without looking. Check the I.D. Sheet to see if you were right. Then on the back of each card, draw a picture or write a clue to help you remember what that word means. Be sure to write a small *STF* (for Success Takes Flight) in the upper left corners.

  When you are finished, give the cards to your teacher and ask her to show you their picture sides, one at a time. Tell her what the picture or clue means and then name the word written on the other side. If you can, tell what part of speech it is. Give yourself one point for correctly naming a word and one point for knowing its part of speech. Keep track of your points and see if you beat your score from Part 3!

- Listen as your teacher reads the spelling words that you studied from Part 4, especially the ones on your Ongoing Spelling List. Write each word in your Student Notebook as she dictates it. When you are finished, look at your word list and make corrections as needed. Show your teacher how you did.

- Follow the directions in the *Human Body Basics* Instructions to play the Word Power vocabulary game, and complete the System Savvy puzzles in your Student Notebook.[2] Then work on any *Examine This* projects you have not yet completed.

- Look back at pages 38 through 41 in the *Basix Recorder Method* and review any exercises that may still be giving you trouble. Choose several tracks on the *Recorder Method* CD and play along with them. Be sure to spend at least 20 minutes practicing!

- Review the Lesson 2 At A Glance chart in your Student Notebook to see if all the work you've done in this part has been checked off. If you did an Enrichment activity or other extra work in this lesson, be sure to write it on the lines next to the chart in your Student Notebook.

- Complete the Success Takes Flight Word Scramble located in your Student Notebook.[3]

Enrichment Activities

1. Part 2 of your Career Project involves collecting information on at least two people who were key to each industry in which you are interested. What changes or advancements did they bring about? What were they like as people? What path did they take to become successful? Some examples might be Bill Gates and Steve Jobs if you are interested in computers, or Eddie Rickenbacker and Chuck Yeager if you are interested in becoming a pilot. Add the information you collect to your notebook (or Student Notebook). Use it for your presentation at the end of Lesson 5.

2. Continue finding out about First Ladies by researching Ellen Wilson and Edith Wilson. Remember to include information about the service and unique characteristics of each, such as:

    •   Relationship to the President (wife, sister, etc.)

    •   Years of service

    •   Difficult issues or events during the President's term

    •   Key projects initiated, or causes supported, by this First Lady

    •   Main changes in culture—fashion, advancements at White House, and so forth

    •   Tell what you think were the most important qualities of this First Lady

    Remember to plan a special presentation for the end of this project, highlighting your favorite First Lady. Think of interesting ways to include a variety of media.

3. Learn more about military aircraft, such as airplanes or helicopters. You may want to learn about them as a group, or choose one specific type of aircraft to research. Make sure and include pictures of the aircraft when you share what you learn with your family.

Additional Resources:

The Fields of Home by Ralph Moody

Chitty Chitty Bang Bang movie (1968 film with Dick Van Dyke, available on DVD)

Please preview any recommended movie to ensure its content is in line with your family's values, and acceptable for your children to watch.

Answers

1. Possible answers:

   electric, old, early, good, three, chromium, pretty, quavery, shiny, forty, indomitable, last, stricken, wrong, basic, peculiar, heated, first, long, mechanical, gasoline-powered, staunch-est, and so forth.

2. Answer key is in the *Human Body Basics* Answer Key.

3. Answer key is in Appendix C.

Lesson 3, Part 1

> ### ⸙ Steps for Thinking ⸙
>
> 1. When you test your ideas, recording your observations for later thought gives you the opportunity to reflect on what has worked, what hasn't worked, and why.
>
> 2. If you are to do something of value, failure must not cause you to stop trying. When you don't meet your expectations, this information helps you make adjustments so that you can be successful.
>
> 3. Inventors and scientists have to keep an open mind, willing to take unexpected results and learn from them.
>
> 4. Often the economy determines how much we spend on things that we want, as well as things that we need. How much we spend on these things affects the economy.

↬Materials↫

- *The Wright Brothers*
- *Homer Price*
- *The Story of Inventions*
- *Human Body Basics*
- *The Story of the Orchestra* book & CD
- *Create Anything With Clay*
- *Basix Recorder Method*
- *Profiles from History,* Volume 3
- Recorder
- Polymer clay
- Rummy Roots cards
- Activity (Part 1):
    Cup half full of water
- Activity (Part 3):
    Flashlight
    Lab partner
    Yardstick
    10 paper clips
    Cup
- Activity (Part 4):
    String, yarn, or leather cord

𝒜. Copywork & Dictation   *Language Skills*

Look carefully at your assigned passage below, and read it silently. Show your teacher any words you don't know, and practice saying them aloud. Now read the passage aloud, or ask your teacher to read it to you.

When you are finished copying or writing from dictation, compare your copy to the text and make any needed corrections.

🐾🐾 🐾 Copy or write as your teacher dictates from *The Story of Inventions*, page 266, paragraph 2 ("Aircraft are now…").

🐾 Write as your teacher dictates from *The Story of Inventions*, page 266, paragraphs 2 and 3 ("Aircraft are now…").

ℬ. Reader   *Language Skills, History*

Homer Price: page 50 (Chapter 3) through page 54, paragraph 4
The Story of Inventions: Review page 261 (Chapter 19) through the top of page 266

Follow the directions below to read or listen to the assigned passage in *Homer Price*.

ℬ. Sometimes children may want to read ahead in the literature, or have already read a book before. When they read for the assignment, it is a more careful type of reading than just reading to find out what happens. This time when they read, they are evaluating the story for a variety of elements. Upon closer examination, there are usually new things to learn about every story.

When you are finished, skim the review assignment from *The Story of Inventions*. Since there are no sections, divide the review pages into at least two parts, and make up a title for each. Then tell your teacher the titles you made up, and give examples of how the information in this section relates to its title.

🐾 Read the above assignment from *Homer Price* aloud, and then give one example for each section in *The Story of Inventions*.

🐾 Read the above assignment from *Homer Price*, and then give two examples for each section in *The Story of Inventions*.

🐾 Read the above assignments from *Homer Price*, and then give three examples for each section in *The Story of Inventions*.

C. Read-Aloud & Narration   *History, Language Skills, Thinking Skills*
The Wright Brothers: page 56, paragraph 2 ("They were certain…") through page 64, paragraph 1

Follow the directions below to read or listen to the above passage. Then, in your own words, tell what happened in the portion you are assigned. Try to remember as many details as possible. If necessary you may reread, or listen as your teacher rereads, the part you are to retell.

🐾 Listen carefully as your teacher reads the above assignment aloud. Choose one page to retell.

🐾 Listen carefully as your teacher reads the above assignment aloud. Choose two pages to retell.

🐾 Read the above assignment aloud, and then retell the entire passage.

D. Vocabulary   *Language Skills, Thinking Skills*

Write each vocabulary word on the Vocabulary I.D. sheet in your Student Notebook. Then tell your teacher what you think each word means, based on the context in which you have read it. If you are not sure of a word's meaning, look it up in a dictionary. Write the definition on the Vocabulary Sheet.

Next, write the word's part of speech: noun, adjective, adverb, verb, and so forth. If you aren't sure, this can also be found in the dictionary.

dispose	**fritter away**	**gadget**
caustic	**warp**	**lateral**
🐾🐾 **indomitable**	**dirigible**	**stanchion**
assurance	**sateen**	**equilibrium**

E. Science

Thinking Skills

Human Body Basics, Nervous System: Hearing

As you read through the assigned pages, choose words that are new or unfamiliar and make vocabulary cards for them as directed. Keep your science cards separate from other vocabulary.

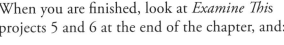 at least three words

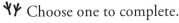 at least four words

Read and discuss the information in the passage with your teacher, and do the *Labwork 10-13* activities. The pages you need to complete these activities are in your Student Notebook.

When you are finished, look at *Examine This* projects 5 and 6 at the end of the chapter, and:

Choose one to complete.

Complete both.

Do as much as you can, but you don't have to finish the projects in this part. You will have other opportunities to work on them, such as during Part 5 and in occasional Study Hall sections.

F. Writing

Language Skills, Thinking Skills

Expository writing explains how to do something, usually step-by-step. Choose a science activity you completed in this unit and write one or two paragraphs in your Student Notebook describing how you did it. Your description should be detailed enough that anyone reading it could go through the steps and complete the same activity.

You might want to write the steps on scrap paper first, and put them in order. Then think about how you would like your paragraph(s) to read. Be sure to use words like *first, then, next,* and *finally* to connect your sentences and make the order more clear.

Choose one activity.   Choose two activities.

F. Since writing begins with thinking, once your student engages in assigned thinking activities, the way is naturally prepared. As you use this approach, your student will begin to see himself as a writer, which is the first and most important step to becoming a writer.

G. Music

History, Thinking Skills

Conclude your study of brass instruments by reading pages 66 through 69 in *The Story of the Orchestra* with your teacher and discussing the information about the trombone and the tuba. Then listen to parts of the "Symphony No. 3" on Track 28 and "Pictures at an Exhibition" on Track 29 of your CD. Were you able to discriminate between the instruments featured on each track? How did the music make you feel? What did you enjoy or dislike about it?

When you are finished, listen carefully to Tracks 28 and 29 again and choose your favorite. Then, draw and color a picture in your Student Notebook of the image this music brings to your mind.

H. Independent Reading & Record Keeping   *Thinking Skills*

Review the Lesson 3 At A Glance chart in your Student Notebook to see if all the work you've done in this part has been checked off. Also, make sure the Student Notebook pages you worked on are dated and complete.

When you are finished, choose something to read that you will enjoy. Then find a quiet, comfortable place and read for the following length of time:

    🐾🐾 🐾 30 minutes   🐾 35 minutes

Be sure to write down what you read today on the Reading Log in your Student Notebook.

Lesson 3, Part 2

A. Copywork & Dictation   *Language Skills*

Look carefully at the Steps for Thinking for this lesson and read them silently. Show your teacher any words you don't know, and practice saying them aloud. Then, copy or write them from dictation into your Student Notebook.

When you are finished, compare your copy to the text and make any needed corrections.

🐾🐾 Copy the Steps for Thinking, and tell your teacher an example of each Step from your reading or your life.

🐾 Write the Steps for Thinking as your teacher dictates them. Then, in your Student Notebook write one example of each Step from your reading or your life. Be sure to use complete sentences.

🐾 Write the Steps for Thinking as your teacher dictates them. Then, in your Student Notebook write two examples of each Step from your reading or your life. Be sure to use complete sentences.

B. Reader
Language Skills, History

Homer Price: page 54, paragraph 5 ("Just then a large…") through page 58, paragraph 3

The Story of Inventions: Review page 266, paragraph 1 ("Their next step…") through page 267

Follow the directions below to read or listen to the assigned passage in *Homer Price*.

When you are finished, skim the review assignment from *The Story of Inventions*. Since there are no sections, divide the review pages into at least two parts, and make up a title for each. Then tell your teacher the titles you made up, and give examples of how the information in each section relates to its title.

Read the above assignment from *Homer Price* aloud, and then give one example for each section in *The Story of Inventions*.

Read the above assignments from *Homer Price*, and then give two examples for each section in *The Story of Inventions*.

Read the above assignments from *Homer Price*, and then give three examples for each section in *The Story of Inventions*.

C. Read-Aloud & Discussion
History, Language Skills, Thinking Skills

The Wright Brothers: page 64, paragraph 2 ("For months the gas lamp…")) through page 70

Follow the directions below to read or listen to the above assignment. Then make up questions about the part of the story you just read or heard. Write your questions in your Student Notebook and ask your teacher to answer them. After discussing her thoughts, write down the best possible answer on the lines provided. Be sure to use complete sentences.

When you are finished, look back at the prediction or predictions you made during Lesson 2, Part 4. Were you able to predict what would happen? Be sure to mark the "Came to Pass" box for each prediction when it does happen.

Listen carefully as your teacher reads the above assignment aloud. Make up two questions.

Listen carefully as your teacher reads the above assignment aloud. Make up three questions.

Read the above assignment aloud; then make up four questions.

D. Sometimes it is helpful to take notes while your child shares his recollections of information learned. It makes what your child is saying seem important, it gives a practical example of how to use note taking, and provides a visible list for your child of all that he has accomplished.

**Lapbook
Activity**

D. Word Building
Language Skills, Thinking Skillss

Review Lessons 1 and 2 by telling your teacher about the word-parts *unus-* or *uni-* and *micro-* or *micros-*. What languages do they come from? What do they mean? Read over the words that you defined in both lessons. Then follow the directions below to make up sentences for some of the words you defined, and tell them to your teacher.

Now follow the directions in the Rummy Roots card set to play Rummy Roots II.

Make up sentences for at least three words you defined.

Make up sentences for at least four words you defined.

Make up sentences for at least five words you defined.

E. History
Thinking Skills

A Day in the Life... In this lesson, you will look at some very important firsts that took place between the years 1920 and 1945.

- Following many years of fighting for women's rights, women received the right to vote in August of 1920. The Secretary of State, Bainbridge Colby, signed the 19th Amendment to the Constitution into law.

- In 1927, Charles Lindbergh piloted the first non-stop trans-Atlantic flight. He left on the morning of May 20th from Long Island, New York, and arrived in Paris, France, late the next evening. Lindbergh, a U.S. Army reserve officer, received the Medal of Honor for his historic trip. His plane was named the Spirit of St. Louis.

- In October of 1927, the first talking picture, called "The Jazz Singer," came to theaters. Made by Warner Brothers and starring Al Jolson, one of the most famous American singers of the time, "The Jazz Singer" produced $3.5 million in profit.

- In the early 1900s you could only buy food that would be eaten within a few day's time. If you did not eat your food quickly enough, it would soon go bad. That all changed in 1930 when Clarence Birdseye started selling frozen vegetables. Now, you can purchase vegetables with the freedom to eat them within weeks instead of days.

- The F.B.I., or Federal Bureau of Investigation, was established in the year 1935. J. Edgar Hoover played a large role in the formation of the F.B.I., and was its first director. He remained in that position until his death in 1972.

- The year 1945 marked a substantial step in weaponry. For the first time in human history, an atomic bomb was unleashed by the United States over Japan, bringing about the end of World War II. The first atomic bomb was dropped on the city of Hiroshima, and the second on Nagasaki. Days following the second bombing, Japan surrendered.

After reading these firsts, choose one of them and learn more about it. Present what you learn to your family. Keep your presentation limited to between one and three minutes.

When you are finished, print and cut out the Supply and Demand Vocabulary 6 game cards from your Student Resources CD. If you want, you can glue each piece onto an index card to make the cards stronger or print them onto cardstock. Shuffle the cards, read them, and put them into sets of three—each word, its definition, and its example.[1]

Then follow the directions in Appendix D to play the Supply and Demand Concentration game.

F. Editing
Language Skills, Thinking Skills

In this section you will continue reviewing parts of speech, and finding examples in your literature. The third parts you will review are verbs. Verbs show that something is happening or has already happened. Helping verbs help the main verb by showing the time or way something took place. Helping verbs (words like may, can, is, are, was, were, had, has, did, might, could, should, and so forth) come before the main verb.

Look at the following examples to see how verbs and helping verbs are used.

Verbs: Wilbur's mother frequently <u>encouraged</u> him.
    She <u>read</u> books and <u>discussed</u> them with Wilbur.

Helping verbs: Wilbur's mother <u>was</u> sharing her love of knowledge.
    After his injury, Wilbur's dreams of Yale <u>were</u> put aside.

Look at all your reading assignments for Lesson 3 to complete this assignment.

Make a list of at least ten verbs and five helping verbs (along with the regular verbs they help) from your readings.[2]

🐾 Add at least two verbs and one helping verb (with the regular verb it helps) to your lists.

🐾 Add at least four verbs and two helping verbs (with the regular verbs they help), to your lists.

F. The activities in this section give students familiarity with the different parts of speech. The purpose of this knowledge is not to memorize them, or change the way your student writes. The purpose is to begin to recognize the words and how they're used in literature and then in their own writing. This learning paves the way for more study and focus when they are older. Remember, grammar should be a reflection, or description, of what a child reads or writes, not a prescription, or telling the child what to write. What to write comes best from a child's own thoughts.

G. Music

Read and follow the directions on pages 42 and 43 in the *Basix Recorder Method* to play *B flat* and learn about *dynamics*. Write the names of notes you're not sure of above the staffs on those pages. Then find the Finger Placement Tab in your Student Notebook and color in the circles that show which holes are covered when you play the *B flat* note. When you are finished, cut out the tab and paste it on an index card.

Don't forget to listen to the *Recorder Method* CD tracks shown on those pages to hear samples of the lessons, and use your Finger Placement Tabs if you need to.

Be sure to spend a little time each day practicing what you have learned—20 minutes a session is plenty!!

H. Independent Reading & Record Keeping

Review the Lesson 3 At A Glance chart in your Student Notebook to see if all the work you've done in this part has been checked off. Also, make sure the Student Notebook pages you worked on are dated and complete.

When you are finished, choose something to read that you will enjoy. Then find a quiet, comfortable place and read for the following length of time:

    🐾 30 minutes   🐾 35 minutes

Be sure to write down what you read today on the Reading Log in your Student Notebook.

Lesson 3, Part 3

A. Copywork & Dictation

Look carefully at your assigned passage below, and read it silently. Show your teacher any words you don't know, and practice saying them aloud. Now read the passage aloud, or ask your teacher to read it to you.

When you are finished copying or writing from dictation, compare your copy to the text and make any needed corrections.

🐾 Copy or write as your teacher dictates from *Homer Price*, page 50, paragraph 4 ("Homer's Uncle Ulysses…").

🐾 Write as your teacher dictates from *The Wright Brothers*, page 70, paragraph 3 ("Within minutes…").

🐾 Write as your teacher dictates from *The Wright Brothers*, page 70, paragraph 3 ("Within minutes…"), and page 71, paragraph 1 ("As the train…").

B. Reader   *Language Skills, History*

Homer Price: page 58, paragraph 4 ("Homer did, and the doughnuts…") through page 63, paragraph 2
The Story of Inventions: Review page 138 (Chapter 10) through page 142, paragraph 1

Follow the directions below to read or listen to the assigned passage in Homer Price. When you are finished, skim each section in the review assignment from The Story of Inventions. Then tell your teacher examples of how the information in each section relates to its title.

🐾 Read the above assignment from *Homer Price* aloud, and then give one example for each section in *The Story of Inventions*.

🐾 Read the above assignments from *Homer Price*, and then give two examples for each section in *The Story of Inventions*.

🐾 Read the above assignments from *Homer Price*, and then give three examples for each section in *The Story of Inventions*.

C. Read-Aloud & Narration   *History, Language Skills, Thinking Skills*

The Wright Brothers: page 71 (Chapter 8) through page 77, paragraph 4

Follow the instructions below for your level. Then, in your own words, tell what happened in the story from Orville or Wilbur's point of view. Try to remember as many details as possible. Tell what you think is the most important event in the passage.

🐾 Listen carefully to the assigned passage.

🐾 Read the assigned passage aloud.

D. Vocabulary   *Language Skills, Thinking Skills*

Show your teacher the Vocabulary I.D. sheet that you completed in Part 1 of this lesson. Ask her to review the words with you by calling them out or writing them on a dry erase board or piece of paper. Tell her what each word means or how it was used in the story and, if you can, what part of speech it is.

Give yourself one point for each correct meaning and one point for knowing the word's part of speech. Keep track of your Vocabulary I.D. points by writing them at the bottom of the sheet, and try to beat your score when you review these words again in Part 5.

D. The best way to learn vocabulary is in the context of meaning. It is easier to remember words as they relate to a story than it is to remember them in isolation. From time to time, ask your children to take out a stack of vocabulary cards from a past unit, play teacher, and review the words for you!

E. One of the most important skills your child can gain is the ability to do research. At the beginning levels research can include searching various locations for information such as the library and the Internet with supervision. The next step is to consider the information and decide what is useful to you or relevant to the questions you are asking.

Lapbook Activity

E. **Science**   *Thinking Skills*

Human Body Basics, Nervous System: Sight

As you read through the assigned pages, choose words that are new or unfamiliar and make vocabulary cards for them as directed. Keep your science cards separate from other vocabulary.

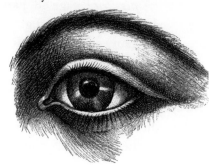

at least three words

at least four words

Read and discuss the information in the passage with your teacher and do the *Labwork 14-17* activities. The pages you need to complete these activities are in your Student Notebook.

When you are finished, look at *Examine This* projects 7 and 8 at the end of the chapter, and:

Choose one to complete.

Complete both.

Do as much as you can, but you don't have to finish the projects in this part. You will have other opportunities to work on them, such as during Part 5 and in occasional Study Hall sections.

F. **Writing**   *Language Skills, Thinking Skills*

Look back at the list of possible science projects you wrote down in Lesson 1, Part 3. Have you had any additional thoughts about those topics? Have you thought of any other subjects you'd like to add to the list?

When you're considering possible topics, take your mind out of the "oh-my-goodness-science-only" **mode** and let it wander through some other areas that might not seem related, but are interesting. For example, perhaps you enjoyed learning about organic produce or the Dust Bowl—which were studied in History and Economics sections, but could easily be adapted to science projects. Sometimes news articles, television programs, or movies can spark your curiosity about something. And what about exploring the truth of advertising claims? Sports? Hobbies? Your chores? The possibilities are unlimited.

Try to narrow your list of possible projects down to two, and write them on the page in your Student Notebook. Then do a quick search at the library or on the Internet to make sure there are resources available from which to gather information if you choose either of those topics. When you are finished, write at least five questions or thoughts about each subject you are considering.

Over the next few weeks, keep these possibilities in mind and return to this page from time to time. Make changes or additions to the list as needed and be prepared to finalize your choice of a science project when you begin Unit 6.

G. Music
History, Thinking Skills

Look back at pages 66 through 69 in *The Story of the Orchestra*.

Lapbook Activity

Then, follow the directions in Appendix D to make two Orchestra Story question and answer cards about the trombone, and two about the tuba. Label each answer card with a small *BI* (for brass instruments) in the upper left corner. Do not label the question cards—and remember to write the questions in your Student Notebook in the correct order.

Check the directions in Lesson 1, Part 3G and review the Orchestra Story cards you have made so far in Units 4 and 5.

H. Independent Reading & Record Keeping
Thinking Skills

Review the Lesson 3 At A Glance chart in your Student Notebook to see if all the work you've done in this part has been checked off. Also, make sure the Student Notebook pages you worked on are dated and complete.

When you are finished, choose something to read that you will enjoy. Then find a quiet, comfortable place and read for the following length of time:

🌱🌿🐾 30 minutes   🐾 35 minutes

Be sure to write down what you read today on the Reading Log in your Student Notebook.

Lesson 3, Part 4

A. Copywork & Dictation   *Language Skills*

Look carefully at your assigned passage below, and read it silently. Show your teacher any words you don't know, and practice saying them aloud. Now read the passage aloud, or ask your teacher to read it to you.

When you are finished copying or writing from dictation, compare your copy to the text and make any needed corrections.

Copy or write as your teacher dictates from *Homer Price*, page 62, paragraphs 7 and 8 ("Then Mr. Gabby…").

Write as your teacher dictates from *The Wright Brothers*, page 74, paragraph 6 ("By the time the boat…").

Write as your teacher dictates from *The Wright Brothers*, page 74, paragraph 6 ("By the time the boat…"), and page 75, paragraph 2 ("As the weather…").

B. Reader   *Language Skills, History*

Homer Price: page 63, paragraph 3 ("The sheriff went outside…") through page 67
The Story of Inventions: Review page 142, paragraph 2 (Bicycle, Tricycle, and Quadricycle) through the top of page 147

Follow the directions below to read or listen to the assigned passage in *Homer Price*. When you are finished, skim each section in the review assignment from *The Story of Inventions*. Then tell your teacher examples of how the information in each section relates to its title.

Read the above assignment from *Homer Price* aloud, and then give one example for each section in *The Story of Inventions*.

Read the above assignments from *Homer Price*, and then give two examples for each section in *The Story of Inventions*.

Read the above assignments from *Homer Price*, and then give three examples for each section in *The Story of Inventions*.

C. Read-Aloud & Discussion   *History, Language Skills, Thinking Skills*

The Wright Brothers: page 77, paragraph 5 ("On September 23…") to the top of page 86

After reading or listening to the read-aloud assignment, talk with your teacher and try to predict what will happen in the future based on what you know of the characters and events. Write your predictions in your Student Notebook. Later you will look back and see if they were accurate. Try not to peek ahead!

Teaching Tip

The skill of predicting what will happen in the story is an important one. It requires your child to remember what has already happened, consider the characters and events, and then come up with a reasonable idea of what may happen in the future. This process involves using critical thinking skills and can be a natural part of any reading your child is doing. Just ask, "What do you think will happen next?"

Listen carefully as your teacher reads the assigned passage. Write down two predictions.

Listen carefully as your teacher reads the assigned passage. Write down three predictions.

Read the assigned passage aloud; then write down at least four predictions.

D. Word Building   *Language Skills, Thinking Skills*

Continue reviewing Lessons 1 and 2 by telling your teacher about the word-parts *unus-* or *uni-* and *micro-* or *micros-*. What languages do they come from? What do they mean? Read over the words that you defined in both lessons. Then follow the directions below to make up sentences for some of the words you defined and tell them to your teacher.

Now follow the directions in the Rummy Roots card set to play Rummy Roots II.

Make up sentences for at least three words you defined.

Make up sentences for at least four words you defined.

Make up sentences for at least five words you defined.

E. History and Economics   *Thinking Skills, Geography*

Think about the stories of the Wright Brothers and Henry Ford you have read or listened to so far in this unit. Then complete the Invention Demand Chart 7 in your Student Notebook.

Dr. Charles Drew made a very important discovery that changed everyone's ideas about the preservation of blood. Up until he succeeded in his mission, blood could only be stored for about a week before it spoiled. This meant that people were often in need of blood but unable to receive it due to shortages. To find out what Dr. Charles Drew did to help with this, read his story in *Profiles from History, Volume 3.*

When you are finished, review the vocabulary, definitions, and examples in the Supply and Demand Vocabulary Games for Units 1, 2 and 4. Read the cards and match the words with their definitions and examples, in rows of three.

E. The study of history that focuses on dates and facts alone can be dry and hard to remember. When events in history are associated through the literature, the geography, and the relevant science concepts, it connects the learning and is much more likely to be retained.

Lapbook Activity

Then, look over the Supply and Demand Vocabulary 6 game cards you made in Part 2 of this lesson. Follow the directions in Appendix D to play the Supply and Demand Go Fish game.

F. Spelling   *Language Skills, Thinking Skills*

To increase your ability to use the words you have studied in this lesson when you write, review your vocabulary and word building lists. After choosing the number of words assigned below from these lists, you and your teacher may choose words from the Challenge Spelling List in Appendix C to work on as well. You may also want to add two or three words from your own writing that you have difficulty spelling correctly. Make your spelling list on the page provided in your Student Notebook.

When you are finished, write the words you have chosen as your teacher dictates them. Then study any that you are unable to spell correctly in preparation for writing in the next lessons. (You might want to look back at the "Tips for Studying Spelling Words" in Lesson 1, Part 4F). Add those words to the Ongoing Spelling List in your Student Notebook (Lesson 1, Part 4). Also, don't forget to add words you misspell in your everyday writing to the list. Once you can spell a word correctly in dictation, then you can cross it off. Throughout the year, you should have an ongoing list of words you are practicing.

- Choose eight words from the vocabulary and word building lists, and two to four Challenge Spelling words (if you and your teacher want).

- Choose ten words from the vocabulary and word building lists, and three to five Challenge Spelling words (if you and your teacher want).

- Choose twelve words from your vocabulary or word building lists, and four to six Challenge Spelling words (if you and your teacher want).

G. Art   *Thinking Skills*

Look over pages 52 through 55, "Jewelry" and "Mask Hysteria" in *Create Anything With Clay*. Rather than worry about finding or buying jewelry-making supplies, try creating your own candy (page 53) or bead necklace, bracelet, or keychain (page 55). You might think of other types of candy or beads not included in the samples, so feel free to experiment!

When you're finished, thread your candy or beads onto string, yarn, or leather cord. Don't forget to put any leftover clay back in its zip-lock bag.

H. Independent Reading & Record Keeping   *Thinking Skills*

Review the Lesson 3 At A Glance chart in your Student Notebook to see if all the work you've done in this part has been checked off. Also, make sure the Student Notebook pages you worked on are dated and complete.

When you are finished, choose something to read that you will enjoy. Then find a quiet, comfortable place and read for the following length of time:

    ᛉ 🐾 30 minutes   🐾 35 minutes

Be sure to write down what you read today on the Reading Log in your Student Notebook.

Lesson 3, Part 5

This part is set aside for completion of any work left undone from the lesson and review of concepts and content. It is also a time to expand the work of the lesson with practice and games.

- Review this lesson's Steps for Thinking, found in Part 1.

- Use the Vocabulary I.D. sheet you completed in Part 1 of this lesson to make vocabulary cards. Write each word on an index card, and try to remember what it means or how it was used in the story without looking. Check the I.D. Sheet to see if you were right. Then on the back of each card, draw a picture or write a clue to help you remember what that word means. Be sure to write a small *STF* (for Success Takes Flight) in the upper left corners.

  When you are finished, give the cards to your teacher and ask her to show you their picture sides, one at a time. Tell her what the picture or clue means and then name the word written on the other side. If you can, tell what part of speech it is. Give yourself one point for correctly naming a word and one point for knowing its part of speech. Keep track of your points and see if you beat your score from Part 3!

- Listen as your teacher reads the spelling words that you studied from Part 4, especially the ones on your Ongoing Spelling List. Write each word in your Student Notebook as she dictates it. When you are finished, look at your word list and make corrections as needed. Show your teacher how you did.

- Follow the directions in the *Human Body Basics* Instructions to play the Word Power vocabulary game, and complete the System Savvy puzzles in your Student Notebook.[3] Then work on any *Examine This* projects you have not yet completed.

- Look back at pages 42 and 43 in the *Basix Recorder Method* and practice those exercises. Then review any other lessons that may be giving you trouble. Choose several tracks on the *Recorder Method* CD and play along with them. Be sure to spend at least 20 minutes practicing—and don't forget that you can use your Finger Placement Tabs if you need to.

An activity like a word search, crossword, or word scramble contributes to the seeing, hearing, and understanding of a word. It provides a fun way to review learning, and gives the student another chance to encounter each word, adding to the likelihood that the child will use it again in speaking or writing. It also happens to be fun!

- Review the Lesson 3 At A Glance chart in your Student Notebook to see if all the work you've done in this part has been checked off. If you did an Enrichment activity or other extra work in this lesson, be sure to write it on the lines next to the chart in your Student Notebook.

- Complete the Success Takes Flight Crossword in your Student Notebook.[4]

Enrichment Activities

1. Part 3 of your Career Project involves collecting information on jobs that currently exist in each industry in which you are interested. These might include a computer programmer, web designer, or software engineer in the computer field; or a pilot, mechanic, or aeronautical engineer if you are interested in airplanes. Choose at least two jobs that interest you and find descriptions of each, qualifications (what education and/or training a person usually needs for this job), and average salaries earned by people in this field. You may also want to think about what ways you could prepare for this career path, such as certain training, experience, or education.

2. Add the information you collect to your notebook (or Student Notebook), and use it for your presentation at the end of Lesson 5.

3. Continue finding out about First Ladies by researching Florence Harding and Grace Anna Coolidge. Remember to include information about the service and unique characteristics of each, such as:

   - Relationship to the President (wife, sister, etc.)

   - Years of service

   - Difficult issues or events during the President's term

   - Key projects initiated, or causes supported, by this First Lady

   - Main changes in culture—fashion, advancements at White House, and so forth

   - Tell what you think were the most important qualities of this First Lady

   Remember to plan a special presentation for the end of this project, highlighting your favorite First Lady. Think of interesting ways to include a variety of media.

Additional Resources:

Shaking the Nickel by Ralph Moody

America's First Ladies Coloring Book (Dover History)

Answers

1. Answer key is in Appendix C.

2. Possible answers:

    Regular verbs: found, pulled, show, arrange, concentrated, endure, secured, withstand, soaked, blow, buck, prance, tested, allowed, released, whistled, struck, borrowed, slammed, and so forth.

    Helping verbs: had arranged, had solved, had migrated, would learn, would discover, had asked, had sought, was hinged, could fly, had misunderstood, had brought, would get, and so forth.

3. Answer key is in the *Human Body Basics* Answer Key.

4. Answer key is in Appendix C.

Lesson 4, Part 1

⚜ Steps for Thinking ⚜

1. For data collected from observation and experimentation to be useful, it must be accepted at face value, without regard to what conclusions will be drawn from the data.

2. Decisions cannot be made based only on circumstances, because they are changeable. Decisions must be based on firmly held beliefs in principles such as truth, fairness, and responsibility.

3. In business, risk is often associated with reward. For those who choose to take a risk either with money, time, or their own well-being, the rewards can be great. But the less risk that is taken financially, the less chance there is of losing money invested.

4. The element of trust is important in business. When a company loses the trust of its customers, it will be difficult for that business to continue. Not living up to promised benefits, faulty products, or poor service can lead to a lack of trust.

The Steps for Thinking section gives you the main ideas about the topics presented. Understanding these helps you to have productive discussions with your children so they, too, understand the bigger ideas. This forms more permanent learning, contrary to just learning facts, which tends to be temporary. These steps are useful prior to instruction, and they are also useful for review at the end of the week.

⚜ Materials ⚜

- *The Wright Brothers*
- *Homer Price*
- *The Story of Inventions*
- *Human Body Basics*
- *The New Way Things Work*
- *The Story of the Orchestra* book & CD
- *Basix Recorder Method*
- *Create Anything With Clay*
- *Profiles from History, Volume 3*
- Recorder
- Polymer clay
- Activity (Part 1):
    - Lab partner
    - Cotton balls
    - Small Ziploc bags
    - Blindfold
    - Variety of scents
    - Can of tuna or cat food
- Activity (Part 3):
    - Lab partner
    - Blindfold
    - Cotton ball (optional)
    - Variety of foods with similar textures
    - Q-tips
    - Salt water
    - Sugar water
    - Lemon juice
    - Strong, black coffee
    - Unsalted beef broth
- Activity (Part 4):
    - Pictures (magazine, photos, or drawings)
    - Craft glue
    - Paintbrush
    - Rolling pin or round jar

A. Copywork & Dictation

Language Skills

Look carefully at your assigned passage below, and read it silently. Show your teacher any words you don't know, and practice saying them aloud. Now read the passage aloud, or ask your teacher to read it to you.

When you are finished copying or writing from dictation, compare your copy to the text and make any needed corrections.

🐾 Write as your teacher dictates from *The Story of Inventions*, page 102, paragraph 2 ("This reaper,…").

🐾 Write as your teacher dictates from *The Story of Inventions*, page 102, paragraph 2 ("This reaper,…"), and page 103, paragraph 2 ("Although Bell's reaper…").

B. **Reader**   *Language Skills, History*

Homer Price: page 72 (Chapter 4) through page 76, paragraph 7
The Story of Inventions: page 200 (Chapter 14) through page 202, paragraph 1

Follow the directions below to read or listen to the assigned passage in *Homer Price*.

Before you begin your assignment in *The Story of Inventions*, scan it for any words you don't know and write them on a piece of scrap paper. Read over any section titles included in the passage—and then, as you read or listen to a section, think about how it relates to its title.

When you are finished, find the Comprehension Questions at the end of Chapter 14 in *The Story of Inventions*, and use complete sentences to write the answers to Questions 1 and 2 in your Student Notebook.

Read the above assignment from *Homer Price* aloud, and then follow along as someone else reads the assignment from *The Story of Inventions*.

Read the above assignment from *Homer Price* silently, and then read the assignment from *The Story of Inventions* aloud.

Read the above assignments from *Homer Price* and *The Story of Inventions* silently.

C. **Read-Aloud & Narration**   *History, Language Skills, Thinking Skills*

The Wright Brothers: page 86, paragraph 1 ("After breakfast, Orville...") through page 93, paragraph 2

Follow the directions below to read or listen to the above passage. Then, in your own words, tell what happened in the portion you are assigned. Try to remember as many details as possible. If necessary you may reread, or listen as your teacher rereads, the part you are to retell.

Listen carefully as your teacher reads the above assignment aloud. Choose one page to retell.

Listen carefully as your teacher reads the above assignment aloud. Choose two pages to retell.

Read the above assignment aloud, and then retell the entire passage.

D. **Vocabulary**   *Language Skills, Thinking Skills*

Write each vocabulary word on the Vocabulary I.D. sheet in your Student Notebook. Then tell your teacher what you think each word means, based on the context in which you have read it. If you are not sure of a word's meaning, look it up in a dictionary. Write the definition on the Vocabulary Sheet.

C. Stories about famous people in history are a wonderful way to illustrate important character qualities. Children naturally enjoy the story format and more easily connect to characters and the events surrounding their lives.

Next, write the word's part of speech: noun, adjective, adverb, verb, and so forth. If you aren't sure, this can also be found in the dictionary.

propel	**feat**	**daft**
furious	**erratic**	**decorum**
camber	**anemometer**	**surmise**
plight	**debris**	**aggregate**

E. Science   *Thinking Skills*
Human Body Basics, Nervous System: Smell

As you read through the assigned pages, choose words that are new or unfamiliar and make vocabulary cards for them as directed. Keep your science cards separate from other vocabulary.

at least three words

at least four words

Read and discuss the information in the passage with your teacher and do the *Labwork 18-21* activities. The pages you need to complete these activities are in your Student Notebook.

When you are finished, look at *Examine This* projects 9 and 10 at the end of the chapter, and:

Choose one to complete.

Complete both.

Do as much as you can, but you don't have to finish the projects in this part. You will have other opportunities to work on them, such as during Part 5 and in occasional Study Hall sections.

Lapbook Activity

F. Writing   *Language Skills, Thinking Skills*
Read the Labwork summary you wrote in Section E aloud and make sure it either accurately describes the activity (descriptive writing), or explains exactly how to do it (expository writing).

If it doesn't accomplish its goal, rewrite it so that it does.

Thinking Skills Reminder

You show what you understand by describing something to someone else.

G. Music   *History, Thinking Skills*
With your teacher, read pages 70 through 73 in *The Story of the Orchestra* and discuss the information about the percussion section and the timpani. Then listen to parts of the "Changing of the Guard" on Track 30 and "Symphony No. 7" on Track 31 of your CD. Were you able to discriminate between the instruments featured on each track? How did the music make you feel? What did you enjoy or dislike about it?

Lapbook Activity

When you are finished, listen carefully to Tracks 30 and 31 again and choose your favorite. Then, draw and color a picture in your Student Notebook of the image this music brings to your mind.

Connect Learning to Life

The most powerful influence on your children is your behavior. If you want your children to value reading, make sure they see you reading! If you read for fun, read to find information, or read as part of your spiritual life, you help make reading a natural part of your children's future.

H. **Independent Reading & Record Keeping**   *Thinking Skills*

Review the Lesson 4 At A Glance chart in your Student Notebook to see if all the work you've done in this part has been checked off. Also, make sure the Student Notebook pages you worked on are dated and complete.

When you are finished, choose something to read that you will enjoy. Then find a quiet, comfortable place and read for the following length of time:

𝑌𝑌 𝑊 30 minutes   𝑊 35 minutes

Be sure to write down what you read today on the Reading Log in your Student Notebook.

Lesson 4, Part 2

A. **Copywork & Dictation**   *Language Skills*

Look carefully at the Steps for Thinking for this lesson and read them silently. Show your teacher any words you don't know, and practice saying them aloud. Then, copy or write them from dictation into your Student Notebook.

When you are finished, compare your copy to the text and make any needed corrections.

𝑌𝑌 Copy the Steps for Thinking, and tell your teacher an example of each Step from your reading or your life.

𝑊 Write the Steps for Thinking as your teacher dictates them. Then, in your Student Notebook write one example of each Step from your reading or your life. Be sure to use complete sentences.

𝑊 Write the Steps for Thinking as your teacher dictates them. Then, in your Student Notebook write two examples of each Step from your reading or your life. Be sure to use complete sentences.

B. **Reader**   *Language Skills, History*

Homer Price: page 76, paragraph 8 ("Just as Homer…") through page 80, paragraph 5
The Story of Inventions: page 202, paragraph 2 (How Wireless Telegraphy Works) through page 204

Follow the directions below to read or listen to the assigned passage in *Homer Price*.

Before you begin your assignment in *The Story of Inventions*, scan it for any words you don't know and write them on a piece of scrap paper. Read over any section titles included in the passage—and then, as you read or listen to a section, think about how it relates to its title.

When you are finished, find the Comprehension Questions at the end of Chapter 14 in *The Story of Inventions*, and use complete sentences to write the answers to Questions 3 and 4 in your Student Notebook.

Read the above assignment from *Homer Price* aloud, and then follow along as someone else reads the assignment from *The Story of Inventions*.

Read the above assignment from *Homer Price* silently, and then read the assignment from *The Story of Inventions* aloud.

Read the above assignments from *Homer Price* and *The Story of Inventions* silently.

C. **Read-Aloud & Discussion**   *History, Language Skills, Thinking Skills*
The Wright Brothers: page 93, paragraph 3 ("The new glider…") through page 98, paragraph 7

Follow the directions below to read or listen to the above assignment. Then make up questions about the part of the story you just read or heard. Write your questions in your Student Notebook and ask your teacher to answer them. After discussing her thoughts, write down the best possible answer on the lines provided. Be sure to use complete sentences.

When you are finished, look back at the prediction or predictions you made during Lesson 3, Part 4. Were you able to predict what would happen? Be sure to mark the "Came to Pass" box for each prediction when it does happen.

Listen carefully as your teacher reads the above assignment aloud. Make up two questions.

Listen carefully as your teacher reads the above assignment aloud. Make up three questions.

Read the above assignment aloud; then make up four questions.

~ *Teacher Connection* ~

Continuous learning is an important part of education. Be sure to read the *Teacher Connection* note in your Parent Planner. Don't miss out on this important part of your homeschooling!

~ **Lapbook Activity** ~

D. Word Building   *Language Skills, Thinking Skillss*

In this section you will continue learning about Greek and Latin word-parts that help to build words in the English language. Today's word-part is **dia-**, which is a Greek word that means *across* or *through*.

Look up the following words in the dictionary and write each definition in your Student Notebook. Then underline the word-part *dia-* in each word. Think, and be ready to tell your teacher how each definition relates to the meaning of the Greek word.

diagram	diameter	diary
dialogue	diagonal	diatomic
diaphragm	diatom	diatribe

E. History, Economics & Geography   *Thinking Skills, Geography*

Advertising, or drawing attention to a product or event, is meant to grab the interest of those reading or hearing the advertisement. This desire to draw attention can lead to some pretty funny methods, such as a man walking up and down in front of a restaurant in a hotdog suit to let people know that the restaurant sells hotdogs. A special sale or giveaway might be designed to bring shoppers into a store so that more products will be sold. These are sometimes called **gimmicks**, or tricks, created to make shoppers notice something particular. It is illegal to advertise using a gimmick that includes statements that are not true. Unfortunately, over the years, people have often found that what was promised in a gimmick may not seem to live up to its claims. Today, advertising is commonly seen on television, radio, magazines, and signs, as well as the Internet. It sometimes seems it is impossible to get away from advertising, since it appears to be everywhere.

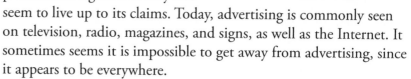

TO THE WEST!
IS THE BEST
FOR HONEST HANDS
TO TILL THE LANDS.
—
CHEAP OUTFITS
At the Sign of the
MEDITATIVE ELEPHANT.

The history of advertising in America is as old as the first sign on a shop or notice in a newspaper. By letting people know what a shopkeeper had in his shop, a service was provided to the customer. Though the first advertisements were more like announcements of stock on hand or events to take place, they grew to include attractive descriptions written with **persuasive speech**, or language convincing someone to do or believe something. In the late 1800s, more and more products were offered to consumers at stores and through printed advertisements. By the 1920s, the total amount of advertising in America had increased dramatically. Since many people no longer lived on farms where they made the majority of the things they needed, they now had to get those goods from someone else. This move away from **self-sufficiency**, or the ability to produce basic, necessary items, to dependence on others for those things increased people's desire to find the best prices.

With greater levels of communication between people through newspapers, magazines, and eventually radio and television, another aspect of advertising became important as well. With the increased communication there was also a growing awareness of what customers purchased, wore, ate, or used. Advertisers started using this awareness to encourage people to purchase the same types of products as those who were rich or famous. This is most easily seen in fashion and other products designed to increase attractiveness, such as beauty creams, hats, garments, and other **trendy**, or stylish, items.

Advertising can also be a very powerful tool in business. Most businesses devote some part of their **budget**, or estimated income and planned spending, to advertising. The advertising can be as simple as a sign in front of the store, or as complex as an advertising campaign, or organized series of events designed to reach a certain goal. During an advertising campaign, multiple types of media, or types of mass communication, may be used such as television commercials, signs, leaflets, or letters sent to previous customers. The variety of media used by a company, school, or government agency is determined by the amount of money in the advertising budget.

While the use of advertising usually has some effect, one of the oldest and most effective types is **word-of-mouth**. This means that people who use a product with favorable results tell their friends about it. **Testimonials**, or sharing personal experiences with a product or service, are a common way to attempt to convince shoppers of that product or service's effectiveness and value.

Talk with your family about advertising. What kind of advertisement does your family consider effective? What kind of advertisement makes them less likely to purchase or use a certain product? Make a list of advertisements that you and your family like. Investigate them and find out what makes them likable or trustworthy.

Then choose the number of advertisements assigned below (from any type of media), and list at least five reasons why you think each one is effective (makes you want to have the product it's promoting) or ineffective (does not make you want to have the product).

 Choose two advertisements.

Choose three advertisements.

Today many companies offer **coupons**, or vouchers to obtain an item at a special rate, to their customers. Talk with your parents about the purpose of coupons and whether or not they use them. Either on the Internet or in printed publications, find several coupons that you or members of your family think you may be interested in using. Since companies are in business to make money, why do you think they would offer discounts to purchase their items? Do you think most people would go to a store to buy only one item? What does the storeowner hope will happen once you get to the store to buy the item for which you have a coupon? Decide whether or not you think the use of coupons is a good idea for your family.

Choose four advertisements.

With your parent's permission, talk with the owner of a business. This may be someone you know personally or the owner of a business you and your family visit often. Ask this person what his or her experience has been with advertising. Does the business have an advertising budget? Has it been a good use of business resources? If so, what type of advertising has been the most effective in increasing business? Write a paragraph describing the business owner's experience with advertising. Conclude by telling whether or not you think this business will continue to advertise and what media you think will be used.

Germany invaded Holland in the year 1940. Some chose to resist Nazi tyranny and help the persecuted Jews escape capture. In doing so, they risked their lives and the lives of their loved ones. Corrie ten Boom and her family were among those who joined in the brave resistance. They opened their home as a place of refuge to many during World War II. Find out what happened next in *Profiles from History, Volume 3*.

F. There are about 150 prepositions in the English language. Some of the more common ones your child may find in prepositional phrases are: *about, across, after, against, along, among, at, before, beside, by, during, except, for, from, in, inside, instead of, like, near, next, of, on, out, outside, over, past, since, through, to, until ('til), upon, with, within* and *without*.

F. Editing

Language Skills, Thinking Skills

In this section you will continue reviewing parts of speech, and finding examples in your literature. The fourth parts you will review are prepositions. Prepositions show how nouns or pronouns relate to other words in the sentence, often showing location. A prepositional phrase starts with a preposition and ends with a noun or pronoun. Some examples of prepositional phrases are: *on the table, near the chair, inside the cup, behind the seat, to the game, without the top*, and *through the gate*.

Look at the following sentences to see how they are used:

Wilbur and Orville built a tower <u>on the dunes</u> and <u>near the water</u>.

Wilbur climbed <u>onto the glider</u> <u>with the controls</u> <u>beside him</u>.

Look at all your reading assignments for Lesson 4 to complete this assignment.[1]

Make a list of at least ten prepositional phrases from your readings.

🐾 Add at least two prepositional phrases to your list.

🐾 Add at least five prepositional phrases to your list.

G. Music   *Thinking Skills*

Read and follow the directions on pages 44 and 45 in the *Basix Recorder Method* to play the *high F* note. Write the names of notes you're not sure of above the staffs on those pages. Then find the Finger Placement Tab in your Student Notebook and color in the circles that show which holes are covered when you play the *high F* note. When you are finished, cut out the tab and paste it on an index card.

Lapbook Activity

Don't forget to listen to the *Recorder Method* CD tracks shown on those pages to hear samples of the lessons and use your Finger Placement Tabs if you need to.

Be sure to spend a little time each day practicing what you have learned—20 minutes a session is plenty!

H. Independent Reading & Record Keeping   *Thinking Skills*

Review the Lesson 4 At A Glance chart in your Student Notebook to see if all the work you've done in this part has been checked off. Also, make sure the Student Notebook pages you worked on are dated and complete.

When you are finished, choose something to read that you will enjoy. Then find a quiet, comfortable place and read for the following length of time:

🐾🐾 30 minutes   🐾 35 minutes

Be sure to write down what you read today on the Reading Log in your Student Notebook.

Lesson 4, Part 3

A. Copywork & Dictation   *Language Skills*

Look carefully at your assigned passage below, and read it silently. Show your teacher any words you don't know, and practice saying them aloud. Now read the passage aloud, or ask your teacher to read it to you.

When you are finished copying or writing from dictation, compare your copy to the text and make any needed corrections.

🐾🐾 🐾 Copy or write as your teacher dictates from *The Story of Inventions*, page 111, paragraph 1 ("The Marsh harvester…").

🐾 Write as your teacher dictates from *The Story of Inventions*, page 111, paragraphs 1 and 2 ("The Marsh harvester…").

B. Reader   *Language Skills, History*

Homer Price: page 80, paragraph 6 ("Miss Terwilliger…") through page 85
The New Way Things Work: pages 238 and 239 (Radio Transmitter)

Follow the directions below to read or listen to the assigned passages in *Homer Price* and *The New Way Things Work*.

When you are finished, make up five true-false statements about the assignment in *The New Way Things Work*, and write them in your Student Notebook. (Make sure that at least two of your statements are false.) Make an answer key at the bottom of the page, and write each false statement correctly (you do not need to re-write the true statements). Then give your quiz to a family member!

🐾🐾 Read the above assignment from *Homer Price* aloud, and then follow along as someone else reads the assignment from *TThe New Way Things Work*.

🐾 Read the above assignment from *Homer Price* silently, and then read the assignment from *The New Way Things Work* aloud.

🐾 Read the above assignments from *Homer Price* and *The New Way Things Work* silently.

C. Read-Aloud & Narration   *History, Language Skills, Thinking Skills*

The Wright Brothers: page 98, paragraph 8 ("That Saturday morning…") through page 106

Follow the instructions below for your level. Then, in your own words, tell what happened in the story from Orville or Wilbur's point of view. Try to remember as many details as possible. Tell what you think is the most important event in the passage.

🐾🐾 🐾 Listen carefully to the assigned passage.

🐾 Read the assigned passage aloud.

D. Vocabulary   *Language Skills, Thinking Skills*

Show your teacher the Vocabulary I.D. sheet that you completed in Part 1 of this lesson. Ask her to review the words with you by calling them out or writing them on a dry erase board or piece of paper. Tell her what each word means or how it was used in the story and, if you can, what part of speech it is.

Teaching Tip

When you know a subject well enough to teach it to someone else, you know it well. Asking questions for others to answer is an activity that requires students to know the subject well enough to guide others into learning about it. Not only is this a great way to enable students to consider the information as a whole and then choose what to ask about, it also requires them to evaluate the answers given to see if they meet the criteria for correctness. In addition, it emphasizes that we are all both teachers and learners!

Lapbook Activity

Give yourself one point for each correct meaning and one point for knowing the word's part of speech. Keep track of your Vocabulary I.D. points by writing them at the bottom of the sheet and try to beat your score when you review these words again in Part 5.

E. Science   *Thinking Skills*
Human Body Basics, Nervous System: Taste

As you read through the assigned pages, choose words that are new or unfamiliar and make vocabulary cards for them as directed. Keep your science cards separate from other vocabulary.

ᵠᵠ at least three words

ᵂᵂ at least four words

Read and discuss the information in the passage with your teacher and do the *Labwork 22-25* activities. The pages you need to complete these activities are in your Student Notebook.

When you are finished, look at *Examine This* projects 11 and 12 at the end of the chapter, and:

ᵠᵠ Choose one to complete.

ᵂᵂ Complete both.

Do as much as you can, but you don't have to finish the projects in this part. You will have other opportunities to work on them, such as during Part 5 and in occasional Study Hall sections.

F. Study Hall   *Thinking Skills*
This section is set aside as a "Study Hall." Use it to catch up on any work that has not yet been completed or to research extra topics that interest you.

G. Music   *History, Thinking Skills*
Look back at pages 70 through 73 in *The Story of the Orchestra*.

Then, follow the directions in Appendix D to make two Orchestra Story question and answer cards about the percussion section, and two about the timpani. Put the small letters *PI* (for percussion instruments) in the upper left corners of your answer cards. Do not label the question cards—and remember to write the questions in your Student Notebook in the correct order.

Check the directions in Lesson 1, Part 3G, and review the Orchestra Story cards you have made in Units 4 and 5.

Teaching Tip:

Independent reading gives you an opportunity to build the team mentality of your homeschool. Encourage your children to think ahead about what books they will read, while allowing them the flexibility to choose, within your guidelines. If possible, have a book on hand and join them in reading. During some non-school times, like lunch, share what you have been reading and if you have been enjoying it. This modeling is powerful.

H. Independent Reading & Record Keeping　　　*Thinking Skills*

Review the Lesson 4 At A Glance chart in your Student Notebook to see if all the work you've done in this part has been checked off. Also, make sure the Student Notebook pages you worked on are dated and complete.

When you are finished, choose something to read that you will enjoy. Then find a quiet, comfortable place and read for the following length of time:

🖐🖐 🖐 30 minutes　　　　　　🐾 35 minutes

Be sure to write down what you read today on the Reading Log in your Student Notebook.

—⚬⚬⚬—

Lesson 4, Part 4

A. Copywork & Dictation　　　*Language Skills*

Look carefully at your assigned passage below, and read it silently. Show your teacher any words you don't know, and practice saying them aloud. Now read the passage aloud, or ask your teacher to read it to you.

When you are finished copying or writing from dictation, compare your copy to the text and make any needed corrections.

🖐🖐 Copy or write as your teacher dictates from *Homer Price*, page 74, paragraph 4 ("By 'carryings on'…").

🖐 Write as your teacher dictates from *The Wright Brothers*, page 106, paragraph 2 ("After being introduced…").

🐾 Write as your teacher dictates from *The Wright Brothers*, page 106, paragraph 2 ("After being introduced…"), and paragraph 4 ("From this introduction…").

B. Reader　　　*Language Skills, History*

Homer Price: page 86 ("The measurements…") through page 90
The New Way Things Work: pages 240 (Radio Receiver) and 241 (Radio Signals)

Follow the directions below to read or listen to the assigned passages in *Homer Price* and *The New Way Things Work*.

When you are finished, make up five true-false statements about the assignment in *The New Way Things Work* and write them in your Student Notebook. (Make sure that at least two of your statements are false.) Make an answer key at the bottom of the page and write each false statement correctly. You do not need to re-write the true statements. Then give your quiz to a family member!

🐾 Read the above assignment from *Homer Price* aloud, and then follow along as someone else reads the assignment from *The New Way Things Work*.

🐾 Read the above assignment from *Homer Price* silently, and then read the assignment from *The New Way Things Work* aloud.

🐾 Read the above assignments from *Homer Price* and *The New Way Things Work* silently.

C. Read-Aloud & Discussion *History, Language Skills, Thinking Skills*

The Wright Brothers: page 107 ("Wilbur went into the history…") through page 114

After reading or listening to the read-aloud assignment, talk with your teacher and try to predict what will happen in the future based on what you know of the characters and events. Write your predictions in your Student Notebook. Later you will look back and see if they were accurate. Try not to peek ahead!

🐾 Listen carefully as your teacher reads the assigned passage. Write down two predictions.

🐾 Listen carefully as your teacher reads the assigned passage. Write down three predictions.

🐾 Read the assigned passage aloud; then write down at least four predictions.

D. Word Building *Language Skills, Thinking Skills*

Earlier in this lesson you learned about the Greek word-part *dia-*. Read over the words you defined in Part 2 and tell your teacher what each one means.

Lapbook Activity

Now add to your ability to use *dia-* by finding more words in the dictionary that begin with it and relate to its meaning. Write them in your Student Notebook. Be sure not to repeat any of the words you have already defined. When you are finished, pick one of your words and write a sentence that uses it correctly.

🐾 at least three words 🐾 at least six words 🐾 at least nine words

E. There are many purposes in reading biographies. One is to learn about a certain individual's life, another is to read about history as it related to that individual, and a third purpose is to provide inspiration for the next generation. People are not perfect, but the individuals chosen for this text have accomplished something worthy of their consideration. Encourage your children to think about what the person accomplished and the challenge set before them. Never pass up the opportunity to inspire your children. It makes a great difference when they know others have gone before them, persevered, and been successful.

Lapbook Activity

E. Economics & History   *Thinking Skills, Geography*

You have been learning about the Wright Brothers and their quest to develop an airplane that could carry a passenger and be propelled by an engine. As you know, airplanes continued developing beyond that and became useful for many purposes such as warfare, carrying cargo, and passenger flight. In 1925, the Air Mail Act was passed in the United States, which helped create the airline industry. The Air Commerce Act was passed in 1926. This act helped build the **fledgling**, or young, commercial aviation industry on the principle of safety first, and included requirements for licensing pilots and developing and enforcing air traffic rules.

As with all new inventions, not just one industry grew up around airplane flight. Businesses began to build airplanes. Mechanics had to service airplanes. They required fuel to fly, as well as tires and many other parts necessary to keep these complex machines in the air. Airports developed and required staff to maintain them; and airlines hired personnel to do everything from fixing and flying airplanes, to cleaning them and serving passengers while in flight. Many businesses and jobs were created while building the aviation industry.

After several high profile airline crashes in which public figures were killed, the government became involved more closely with aviation safety. President Roosevelt signed the Civil Aeronautics Act in 1938. This legislation created several agencies and led to the birth of the Federal Aviation Agency in 1958. As air traffic became more popular and affordable, the demand for improved safety procedures increased. Technology developed better methods of directing air traffic and detecting bad weather, and air safety grew. Again, business provided improved equipment for airlines—continuing the connection between the need for innovation and invention, investment, and improved services and products for customers. This interrelationship continues to address the needs of the airline industry as it faces the challenges of safe and comfortable air travel today and in the future.

Learn more about some aspect of the airline industry. Choose one of the following occupations and write at least one paragraph giving a description of the job and its responsibilities. Write a second paragraph telling how this job is essential to the airline industry. How are other parts of the industry dependent upon this job? Is this a job you would be interested in doing? Why or why not? Tell your family what you learn. How does this information affect what you think of air travel?

Pilot

Flight Attendant

Air Traffic Controller

Airplane Mechanic

Baggage Handler

Reservation Agent

Transportation Safety Agent

Meteorologist

An Author's Story by Debbie Strayer: My father became a pilot when he was in the U.S. Marines during the Korean War. He began his career by flying a plane called a Douglas AD5. This is a fighter airplane used during the 1950s. He was first trained to fly this plane by taking off and landing on an airstrip (an area, often not part of a regular airport, cleared and leveled for aircraft), and then he learned how to land and takeoff from the deck of an aircraft carrier. With each new step, he was first taught by using a **simulator**, or device that mimics flying conditions, and then he would be trained in an airplane with an instructor. After training, my father had to solo, or fly the plane up by himself to show that he could do all that was required to fly safely.

After the war, my father became a pilot for Eastern Airlines. This company began in 1928 and continued until it declared bankruptcy in 1991. My father greatly enjoyed the life of a pilot, though his first job was that of a co-pilot. As time went on he eventually became a pilot, or captain of the flights he flew. Those who flew airplanes seemed to share a sense of adventure. No two flights were ever the same and there were an endless variety of challenges, such as weather problems or passenger needs. Everyone has heard of babies being born on airplanes, as well as other types of medical emergencies. But the flight crew's training helped prepare them for nearly every possible circumstance.

My father flew many different types of aircraft over his career of more than forty years. He flew the DC-7, Martin 404, and Convair 440, which were propeller-driver aircraft. Then in later years, he flew jet-propelled aircraft such as Boeing 727s, Lockheed 1011s, and the Airbus. His job required great attention to detail, good health, constant training, and evaluation to make sure he was doing a good job. He was devoted to flying the aircraft safely. I often remember him studying to learn about new aircraft and how they worked. Learning and changing were required in his job as aircraft improved, as well as weather prediction, communication, and technology. This was not a job for someone who didn't want to change, because that was an important part of keeping up-to-date on safety procedures.

Challenges were also a part of his career as a pilot. His schedule frequently required him to be away from home for days in a row. When he first started flying with Eastern, his lack of **seniority**, the position gained by long employment with a company, often meant that he worked during weekends and holidays, as do many younger employees of companies. Once when a hurricane was approaching our home in south Florida, the airline asked him to help fly airplanes away from the path of the storm. Of course, this kept him away from our home during the storm. These trials are not uncommon for the families of pilots.

Sometimes other challenges occurred during flights. Once, on the way to Bermuda, the plane he was flying lost power in one of its three engines, causing a loss of **altitude**, the height above the earth's surface. This required my father to figure out what was wrong. He was able to restart the engine and continue flying normally. Though most problems encountered by the crew were mechanical in nature, on one flight my father did have a person who attempted to **hijack**, or illegally take control, of the plane. The hijacker was subdued and the flight returned to its starting point without incident. My father always credited the excellent training he received with preparing him for all the challenges he faced throughout his career. It was my observation that he, and those he worked with, displayed great calm in the face of challenges, and even danger.

After the Airline Deregulation Act was signed in 1978, many airlines had a difficult time surviving financially because of increased competition and a reduction in the prices charged for airline tickets. Longstanding airlines, like Eastern, had to do what they had been doing for many years with substantially less income. Increased fuel costs, and possible poor management, contributed to the airline's difficulties. There were many reasons for these problems, and after various attempts to help the airline survive, Eastern filed for bankruptcy. This was a very sad time, since the employees of Eastern Airlines considered themselves a family.

My father then worked for American Airlines for several years until he reached the age of 62, which was the mandatory retirement age for pilots. My children (his grandchildren) and I were able to fly with him on his last flight. It was a very special occasion.

Like many other employees of companies charged with the safety of their customers, my father worked hard to be as knowledgeable and prepared for each flight as possible. Over the years, many devoted airline employees have worked to make air travel as safe and enjoyable as possible, and his commitment to this standard of excellence continued until his retirement. He would say that he was no different from his fellow employees, who were similarly dedicated. This is the story of only one employee and his family.

Talk with your parents about airlines on which they have flown, or think about your own experience flying. What did you like about it? Was there anything that seemed difficult to you? Talk with your family about the costs and benefits of air travel. In what ways could you become better at air travel? What ways can air travel be improved to make a customer's flying experience a better one?

Irena Sendler was a small woman, not even five feet tall. Although she was small in size, Irena's unimaginable bravery has led to a larger than life legacy. If it were not for her courage, some 2,500 people would most likely never have lived past their childhoods. In this lesson you will take a look at one of World War II's great heroes. This one never wore a uniform or participated in a battle, but like other war heroes who did, she saved the lives of many people. Read more in *Profiles from History, Volume 3*.

F. Spelling　　　　　　　　　　*Language Skills, Thinking Skills*

To increase your ability to use the words you have studied in this lesson when you write, review your vocabulary and word building lists. After choosing the number of words assigned below from these lists, you and your teacher may choose words from the Challenge Spelling List in Appendix C to work on as well. You may also want to add two or three words from your own writing that you have difficulty spelling correctly. Make your spelling list on the page provided in your Student Notebook.

When you are finished, write the words you have chosen as your teacher dictates them. Then study any that you are unable to spell correctly in preparation for writing in the next lessons. (You might want to look back at the "Tips for Studying Spelling Words" in Lesson 1, Part 4F). Add those words to the Ongoing Spelling List in your Student Notebook (Lesson 1, Part 4). Also, don't forget to add words you misspell in your everyday writing to the list. Once you can spell a word correctly in dictation, then you can cross it off. Throughout the year, you should have an ongoing list of words you are practicing.

🐾 Choose eight words from the vocabulary and word building lists, and two to four Challenge Spelling words (if you and your teacher want).

🖐 Choose ten words from the vocabulary and word building lists, and three to five Challenge Spelling words (if you and your teacher want).

🐾 Choose twelve words from your vocabulary or word building lists, and four to six Challenge Spelling words (if you and your teacher want).

G. Art　　　　　　　　　　　　　　　　*Thinking Skills*

Practice the techniques described on pages 56 and 57, "Get Yourself Framed," in *Create Anything With Clay*. You can use them to frame photos, magazine pictures, or drawings if you want. See if you can come up with some different styles! When you are finished, put leftover clay back in its zip-lock bag.

H. **Independent Reading & Record Keeping**   *Thinking Skills*

Review the Lesson 4 At A Glance chart in your Student Notebook to see if all the work you've done in this part has been checked off. Also, make sure the Student Notebook pages you worked on are dated and complete.

When you are finished, choose something to read that you will enjoy. Then find a quiet, comfortable place and read for the following length of time:

ᵞᵞ ♟ 30 minutes   ♟ 35 minutes

Be sure to write down what you read today on the Reading Log in your Student Notebook.

Lesson 4, Part 5

This part is set aside for completion of any work left undone from the lesson and review of concepts and content. It is also a time to expand the work of the lesson with practice and games.

• Review this lesson's Steps for Thinking, found in Part 1.

• Use the Vocabulary I.D. sheet you completed in Part 1 of this lesson to make vocabulary cards. Write each word on an index card and try to remember what it means or how it was used in the story without looking. Check the I.D. Sheet to see if you were right. Then on the back of each card, draw a picture or write a clue to help you remember what that word means. Be sure to write a small *STF* (for Success Takes Flight) in the upper left corners.

When you are finished, give the cards to your teacher and ask her to show you their picture sides, one at a time. Tell her what the picture or clue means, and then name the word written on the other side. If you can, tell what part of speech it is. Give yourself one point for correctly naming a word and one point for knowing its part of speech. Keep track of your points and see if you beat your score from Part 3

• Listen as your teacher reads the spelling words that you studied from Part 4, especially the ones on your Ongoing Spelling List. Write each word in your Student Notebook as she dictates it. When you are finished, look at your word list and make corrections as needed. Show your teacher how you did.

• Follow the directions in the *Human Body Basics* Instructions to play the Word Power vocabulary game, and complete the System

Read the list of words to your child. If he would rather spell them aloud than write them, it is perfectly acceptable. As you dictate each word, put small dots beside any that are misspelled. Then be sure to include them in your next review.

Savvy puzzles in your Student Notebook.[2] Then work on any *Examine This* projects you have not yet completed.

- Look back at pages 44 and 45 in the *Basix Recorder Method* and practice those exercises. Then review any other lessons that may be giving you trouble. Choose several tracks on the *Recorder Method* CD and play along with them. Be sure to spend at least 20 minutes practicing—and don't forget that you can use your Finger Placement Tabs if you need to.

- Review the Lesson 4 At A Glance chart in your Student Notebook to see if all the work you've done in this part has been checked off. If you did an Enrichment activity or other extra work in this lesson, be sure to write it on the lines next to the chart in your Student Notebook.

- Complete the Success Takes Flight Who or What Am I? game in your Student Notebook.[3]

Enrichment Activities

1. Part 4 of your Career Project involves telling how you think the career path(s) in which you are interested fit you. Describe what you would like to accomplish if you were to follow each, and how you think your gifts and talents equip you for the requirements of these choices.

   Look over the different pieces of your project and prepare them for presentation after the next lesson. You may want to use a computer program to create a video presentation. If you do the presentation for your family in person, ask someone to make a video of it so you can see how you did.

2. Continue finding out about First Ladies by researching Lou Henry Hoover and Eleanor Roosevelt. Remember to include information about the service and unique characteristics of each, such as:

   - Relationship to the President (wife, sister, etc.)

   - Years of service

   - Difficult issues or events during the President's term

   - Key projects initiated, or causes supported, by this First Lady

   - Main changes in culture—fashion, advancements at White House, and so forth

   - Tell what you think were the most important qualities of this First Lady

Remember to plan a special presentation for the end of this project, highlighting your favorite First Lady. Think of interesting ways to include a variety of media.

3. Learn more about military communication and information-gathering technologies, such as radar, GPS devices, night-vision equipment, or drone aircraft. You may want to learn about them as a group or choose one specific type of technology to research. Make sure to include pictures of the technology when you share what you learn with your family.

Additional Resources:

The Dry Divide by Ralph Moody

The Hiding Place by Corrie ten Boom

"Old Time" radio programs available on CD

Answers

1. Possible answers: on the sewing machine, in these parts, to the tower, in a tent, on a glider, with the Tates, into the open, behind the position, beneath him, from the letter, in our sight, over the lower wing, and so forth.

2. Answer key is in the *Human Body Basics* Answer Key.

3. Answer key is in Appendix C.

Lesson 5, Part 1

ঌ Steps for Thinking ঌ

1. Times of great trial bind people together. When there is a common enemy, there is also a common purpose.

2. The best application of thinking skills takes into account as many consequences of an action as possible. While some may apply knowledge for destructive purposes, each person is responsible for what they do with the knowledge they possess.

3. The greatest acts of bravery are done by those who believe that their cause is more important than any one individual's life, even their own.

4. The economic impact of war is great, for both sides of the conflict. The winners experience an increase in employment and production of wartime goods. The losers must rebuild their economy, often from scratch. Their struggles usually become part of a global effort to assist the country in its recovery.

A. Copywork & Dictation   *Language Skills*

Look carefully at your assigned passage below, and read it silently. Show your teacher any words you don't know, and practice saying them aloud. Now read the passage aloud, or ask your teacher to read it to you.

When you are finished copying or writing from dictation, compare your copy to the text and make any needed corrections.

🖐 Copy or write as your teacher dictates from *The Story of Inventions*, page 268, paragraph 1 ("You will remember…").

🐾 Write as your teacher dictates from *The Story of Inventions*, page 268, paragraphs 1 and 2 ("You will remember…").

B. Reader   *Language Skills, History*

Homer Price: page 94 (Chapter 5) through page 101, paragraph 7
The Story of Inventions: page 268 (Chapter 20) through the top of page 270

৯৳Materials৽৲

- *The Wright Brothers*
- *Homer Price*
- *The Story of Inventions*
- *Human Body Basics*
- *The New Way Things Work*
- *The Story of the Orchestra* book & CD
- *Basix Recorder Method*
- *Create Anything With Clay*
- *Profiles from History, Volume 3*
- *Classroom Atlas of the United States*
- Recorder
- Polymer clay
- Activity (Part 1):
  - Lab partner
  - Paperclip or wire
  - Blindfold
  - Washable marker
  - Ruler
  - Bowl of warm water
  - Bowl of ice water
  - Bowl of room-temperature water
  - Soft-lead pencil
  - Clear packing tape
  - Unlined index cards
  - Magnifying glass (optional)

Follow the directions below to read or listen to the assigned passage in *Homer Price*.

Before you begin your assignment in *The Story of Inventions*, scan it for any words you don't know and write them on a piece of scrap paper. Read over any section titles included in the passage—and then, as you read or listen to a section, think about how it relates to its title.

When you are finished, find the Comprehension Questions at the end of Chapter 20 in *The Story of Inventions*, and use complete sentences to write the answers to Questions 1, 2, 3, and 4 in your Student Notebook.

Read the above assignment from *Homer Price* aloud, and then follow along as someone else reads the assignment from *The Story of Inventions*.

Read the above assignment from *Homer Price* silently, and then read the assignment from *The Story of Inventions* aloud.

Read the above assignments from *Homer Price* and *The Story of Inventions* silently.

C. **Read-Aloud & Narration**   *History, Language Skills, Thinking Skills*
   The Wright Brothers: page 115 (Chapter 12) through page 121

Follow the directions below to read or listen to the above passage. Then, in your own words, tell what happened in the portion you are assigned. Try to remember as many details as possible. If necessary you may reread, or listen as your teacher rereads, the part you are to retell.

Listen carefully as your teacher reads the above assignment aloud. Choose one page to retell.

Listen carefully as your teacher reads the above assignment aloud. Choose two pages to retell.

Read the above assignment aloud, and then retell the entire passage.

D. **Vocabulary**   *Language Skills, Thinking Skills*
   Write each vocabulary word on the Vocabulary I.D. sheet in your Student Notebook. Then tell your teacher what you think each word means, based on the context in which you have read it. If you are not sure of a word's meaning, look it up in a dictionary. Write the definition on the Vocabulary Sheet.

Next, write the word's part of speech: noun, adjective, adverb, verb, and so forth. If you aren't sure, this can also be found in the dictionary.

hilarious	**tailspin**	**gannet**
jubilant	**pathetic**	**data**
catapult	**magneto**	**baffle**
adhesive	**sprocket**	**slacken**

Thinking Skills Reminder

Your students show what they understand by paraphrasing, or putting what they have read or heard into their own words.

Connect Learning to Life

Together with your children, look through the stack of vocabulary cards they have made so far during this unit. Ask them to find their favorite words, words they have started using in conversation, and words that were the most challenging to learn. Remind them that they can use this approach to learn new words any time, and with any book or topic. As they look through the cards, they are doing a natural review and categorizing the words according to the way that they worked with them. Take these natural opportunities to show your children that they have used great thinking skills that are useful in many areas of life.

E. Science
Geography, Thinking Skills

Human Body Basics, Nervous System: Touch

As you read through the assigned pages, choose words that are new or unfamiliar and make vocabulary cards for them as directed. Keep your science cards separate from other vocabulary.

Lapbook Activity

🐾🐾 at least three words

🐾🐾 at least four words

Read and discuss the information in the passage with your teacher and do the *Labwork 26-30* activities. The pages you need to complete these activities are in your Student Notebook.

When you are finished, look at *Examine This* projects 13 and 14 at the end of the chapter and:

🐾🐾 Choose one to complete.

🐾🐾 Complete both.

Do as much as you can, but you don't have to finish the projects in this part. You will have other opportunities to work on them, such as during Part 5 and in occasional Study Hall sections.

F. Writing
Language Skills, Thinking Skills

Read the Labwork summary you wrote in Section E aloud and make sure it either accurately describes the activity (descriptive writing), or explains exactly how to do it (expository writing).

If it doesn't accomplish its goal, rewrite it so that it does.

G. Music
History, Thinking Skills

Continue your study of percussion instruments by reading pages 74 through 77 in *The Story of the Orchestra* with your teacher and discussing the information about the bass and snare drums, and the xylophone. There is no music that features these instruments on your CD, so try to find and listen to some at the library or on the Internet.

Lapbook Activity

If you are successful, choose a composition that is interesting to you. Then, draw and color a picture in your Student Notebook of the image that music brings to your mind.

H. **Independent Reading & Record Keeping**   *Thinking Skills*

Review the Lesson 5 At A Glance chart in your Student Notebook to see if all the work you've done in this part has been checked off. Also, make sure the Student Notebook pages you worked on are dated and complete.

When you are finished, choose something to read that you will enjoy. Then find a quiet, comfortable place and read for the following length of time:

ᕕᕗ 🖐 30 minutes   🐾 35 minutes

Be sure to write down what you read today on the Reading Log in your Student Notebook.

Lesson 5, Part 2

A. **Copywork & Dictation**   *Language Skills*

Look carefully at the Steps for Thinking for this lesson and read them silently. Show your teacher any words you don't know, and practice saying them aloud. Then, copy or write them from dictation into your Student Notebook.

When you are finished, compare your copy to the text and make any needed corrections.

ᕕᕗ Copy the Steps for Thinking, and tell your teacher an example of each Step from your reading or your life.

🖐 Write the Steps for Thinking as your teacher dictates them. Then, in your Student Notebook write one example of each Step from your reading or your life. Be sure to use complete sentences.

🐾 Write the Steps for Thinking as your teacher dictates them. Then, in your Student Notebook write two examples of each Step from your reading or your life. Be sure to use complete sentences.

B. **Reader**   *Language Skills, History*

Homer Price: page 101, paragraph 8 ("By mid-afternoon...") through page 105, paragraph 4
The Story of Inventions: page 270, paragraph 1 ("Within the next few years...") through page 272

Follow the directions below to read or listen to the assigned passage in *Homer Price*.

Before you begin your assignment in *The Story of Inventions*, scan it for any words you don't know and write them on a piece of scrap paper. Read over any section titles included in the passage—and then, as you read or listen to a section, think about how it relates to its title.

When you are finished, find the Comprehension Questions at the end of Chapter 20 in *The Story of Inventions*, and use complete sentences to write the answers to Questions 5, 6, 7, and 8 in your Student Notebook.

🐾 Read the above assignment from *Homer Price* aloud, and then follow along as someone else reads the assignment from *The Story of Inventions*.

🐾 Read the above assignment from *Homer Price* silently, and then read the assignment from *The Story of Inventions* aloud.

🐾 Read the above assignments from *Homer Price* and *The Story of Inventions* silently.

C. **Read-Aloud & Discussion**   *History, Language Skills, Thinking Skills*
The Wright Brothers: page 122 ("Harry Combs, in his excellent…") through page 128, paragraph 4

Follow the directions below to read or listen to the above assignment. Then make up questions about the part of the story you just read or heard. Write your questions in your Student Notebook and ask your teacher to answer them. After discussing her thoughts, write down the best possible answer on the lines provided. Be sure to use complete sentences.

When you are finished, look back at the prediction or predictions you made during Lesson 4, Part 4. Were you able to predict what would happen? Be sure to mark the "Came to Pass" box for each prediction when it does happen.

🐾 Listen carefully as your teacher reads the above assignment aloud. Make up two questions.

🐾 Listen carefully as your teacher reads the above assignment aloud. Make up three questions.

🐾 Read the above assignment aloud; then make up four questions.

D. **Word Building**   *Language Skills, Thinking Skillss*
In this section, you will continue learning about Greek and Latin word-parts that help to build words in the English language. Today's word-part is **visum-**, which is a Latin word that means *to see*.

Look up the following words in the dictionary and write each definition in your Student Notebook. Then underline the word-part *visum-* in each word. Think, and be ready to tell your teacher how each definition relates to the meaning of the Latin word.

vision   vista   visit

🐾🐾 visitor   vision   visor

🐾 visibility   visualize   visionary

E. It is important for students to be acquainted with various reference tools, such as an atlas. Since your goal is for students to be lifelong learners, use of reference tools can greatly enhance learning on any topic. Using these tools successfully requires familiarity and the opportunities to use the tools as part of learning that is connected to history, literature, science, and ultimately, life.

Lapbook Activity

E. Economics

Thinking Skills, Geography

A Day in the Life…Presidents Day, Memorial Day, and Veterans Day. Have you ever stopped to consider the meanings behind these national holidays, and how they began? They were set aside as **honorific** (showing respect or honor) holidays. Today, they are more known for being vacation days in which students get out of school and adults get a day off from work. Department stores have even caught on to the opportunity to maximize sales by offering special deals on these days. Take some time to explore the meanings behind these holidays, in hopes of recalling their importance.

Memorial Day is a day to remember military people who have died while defending our nation. It was originally called Decoration Day, created to honor those who gave their lives during the Civil War. It was named Decoration Day because people would decorate the graves of soldiers, mostly with flowers. The words, "Here Rests In Honored Glory An American Solider Known But To God" are inscribed on the Tomb of the Unknown Soldier in Arlington National Cemetery. Every Memorial Day and Veterans Day, a wreath is laid at the Tomb, honoring the great sacrifice of all unknown soldiers who have died in battle.

Presidents' Day, which always falls on the third Monday of February, used to be simply a celebration of George Washington's birth on February 22nd. In many places, Abraham Lincoln's birthday was also celebrated on February 12th, though it was never a federal holiday. In 1971, Richard Nixon combined the celebration of Washington and Lincoln's birthdays by creating Presidents' Day. We now honor all presidents of the United States on that day.

Veterans Day is a day to honor all living American veterans. Many people confuse Veterans Day and Memorial Day, or think they are the same thing. The difference is that Veterans Day honors the living men and women who served our country, and Memorial Day honors those who gave the ultimate sacrifice and died for our country. Originally, Veterans Day was known as Armistice Day. Armistice, which means truce, commemorates the Treaty of Versailles that ended World War I. Though it is not called Armistice Day anymore, it is still celebrated on November 11th, the anniversary of the Treaty of Versailles. In 1954, Congress legally changed the name to Veterans Day to include all veterans, not just those who served in World War I.

Now that you have read about the origin of each holiday, be sure to pay special **homage**, or respect, this year when celebrating these important days of remembrance.

Talk with your parents about any veterans who are related to you. Take the time to learn about the stories of their service, if you don't already know them. If they are living, you may want to contact them and express your appreciation for their service. If they have passed away, together with your family, plan some way to honor their memory.

Find the maps and description of World War II in the United States History section of your *Classroom Atlas of the United States*. Read the description and then look at the maps. Compare the amount of land that belonged to the Axis countries and their allies to the land belonging to the Allies and Allied-controlled areas. From the looks of these maps, what do you think the outcome of this war should have been? Why do you think it did not end up as the maps would suggest?

Choose one of the major battles shown on the map in your atlas entitled "World War II in Europe, 1939–1945" and learn more about it. Take notes on scrap paper and present the information to your family as a news reporter might. Remember to include the facts of who, what, when, where, why, and how the battle took place.

☼ Add a second battle to your research and reporting.

☼ Add a third battle to your research and reporting.

F. **Editing**   *Language Skills, Thinking Skills*

In this section, you will continue reviewing parts of speech and finding examples in your literature. The fifth parts you will review are adverbs. Adverbs are words that usually describe a verb, an adjective, or another adverb. Most adverbs tell how, when, why, where, and how much (such as *harder*, *sooner*, and *faster*). Many times, adverbs end with the suffix *ly* (such as *quickly*, *slowly*, *sadly*, and *briefly*).

Look at the following sentences to see how they are used:

> The brothers were <u>completely</u> discouraged when the glider failed.

> Orville <u>carefully</u> glued the last piece in place.

> They wanted to arrive <u>sooner,</u> but they were <u>greatly</u> delayed by the storm.

Note: Some other common adverbs are *not*, *never*, *very*, and *always*. Choose adverbs other than these for this assignment.

Thinking Skills Reminder

Students analyze, or think about the parts of information when they put things in different categories.

Look at all your reading assignments for Lesson 5 to complete this assignment.[1]

Make a list of at least ten adverbs from your readings.

🐾 Add at least two adverbs to your list.

🐾 Add at least five adverbs to your list.

G. Music
Thinking Skills

Read and follow the directions on pages 46 and 47 in the *Basix Recorder Method* to play *low C* and learn about the *slur*. Write the names of notes you're not sure of above the staffs on those pages. Then find the Finger Placement Tab in your Student Notebook and color in the circles that show which holes are covered when you play the *low C* note. When you are finished, cut out the tab and paste it on an index card.

Don't forget to listen to the *Recorder Method* CD tracks shown on those pages to hear samples of the lessons and use your Finger Placement Tabs if you need to.

Be sure to spend about 20 minutes a day practicing what you have learned!

H. Independent Reading & Record Keeping
Thinking Skills

Review the Lesson 5 At A Glance chart in your Student Notebook to see if all the work you've done in this part has been checked off. Also, make sure the Student Notebook pages you worked on are dated and complete.

When you are finished, choose something to read that you will enjoy. Then find a quiet, comfortable place and read for the following length of time:

🐾🐾 30 minutes   🐾 35 minutes

Be sure to write down what you read today on the Reading Log in your Student Notebook.

Lesson 5, Part 3

A. **Copywork & Dictation**   *Language Skills*

Look carefully at your assigned passage below, and read it silently. Show your teacher any words you don't know, and practice saying them aloud. Now read the passage aloud, or ask your teacher to read it to you.

When you are finished copying or writing from dictation, compare your copy to the text and make any needed corrections.

🐾☝ Copy or write as your teacher dictates from *The Story of Inventions*, page 270, paragraph 3 ("These early submarines…").

☝ Write as your teacher dictates from *The Story of Inventions*, page 270, paragraph 3 ("These early submarines…"), and page 271, paragraph 2 ("The latest submarines…").

B. **Reader**   *Language Skills, History*

Homer Price: page 105, paragraph 5 ("Bright and early…") through page 113, paragraph 2
The New Way Things Work: pages 94 and 95 (Floating)

Follow the directions below to read or listen to the assigned passages in *Homer Price* and *The New Way Things Work*.

When you are finished, make up five true-false statements about the assignment in *The New Way Things Work* and write them in your Student Notebook. (Make sure that at least two of your statements are false.) Make an answer key at the bottom of the page and write each false statement correctly. You do not need to re-write the true statements. Then give your quiz to a family member!

🐾 Read the above assignment from *Homer Price* aloud, and then follow along as someone else reads the assignment from *The Story of Inventions*.

☝ Read the above assignment from *Homer Price* silently, and then read the assignment from *The Story of Inventions* aloud.

☝ Read the above assignments from *Homer Price* and *The Story of Inventions* silently.

C. **Read-Aloud & Narration**   *History, Language Skills, Thinking Skills*

The Wright Brothers: page 128, paragraph 5 ("As Orville and Wilbur…") through page 135

Follow the instructions below for your level. Then, in your own words, tell what happened in the story from Orville or Wilbur's point of view. Try to remember as many details as possible. Tell what you think is the most important event in the passage.

🐾☝ Listen carefully to the assigned passage.

☝ Read the assigned passage aloud.

D. Vocabulary

Language Skills, Thinking Skills

Show your teacher the Vocabulary I.D. sheet that you completed in Part 1 of this lesson. Ask her to review the words with you by calling them out or writing them on a dry erase board or piece of paper. Tell her what each word means or how it was used in the story and, if you can, what part of speech it is.

Give yourself one point for each correct meaning and one point for knowing the word's part of speech. Keep track of your Vocabulary I.D. points by writing them at the bottom of the sheet, and try to beat your score when you review these words again in Part 5.

E. Science

Thinking Skills

Human Body Basics, Endocrine System: entire chapter

As you read through the assigned chapter, choose words that are new or unfamiliar and make vocabulary cards for them as directed. Keep your science cards separate from other vocabulary.

  at least three words   at least four words

Read and discuss the information in the passage with your teacher and do the *Labwork 1-2* activities. The page you need for labeling is in your Student Notebook.

When you are finished, look at the *Examine This* projects at the end of the chapter and:

Choose one to complete.

Complete both.

Do as much as you can, but you don't have to finish the projects in this part. You will have other opportunities to work on them, such as during Part 5 and in occasional Study Hall sections.

F. Writing

Language Skills, Thinking Skills

At the end of this unit you will be asked to make a Unit Presentation to your family and tell about what you have learned in the Success Takes Flight Unit. In this presentation, you will have an opportunity to share the work you've done in your Student Notebook, the crafts or special projects you have completed and anything else you care to include.

Think about the things you would like to include in your Unit Presentation and list them on a piece of scrap paper. Then number the items in the order that you would like to share them. When you are finished, copy your list in the correct order into your Student Notebook. You can use this list while you are giving your Unit Presentation, so that you won't forget anything you wanted to share.

G. Music　　　　　　　　　　　　　*History, Thinking Skills*

Look back at pages 74 through 77 in *The Story of the Orchestra*. Then, follow the directions in Appendix D to make two Orchestra Story question and answer cards about the bass drum, two about the snare drum, and two about the xylophone. Put the small letters *PI* (for percussion instruments) in the upper left corners of your answer cards. Do not label the question cards—and remember to write the questions in your Student Notebook in the correct order.

Check the directions in Lesson 2, Part 3G and review the Orchestra Story cards you have made in Units 4 and 5.

H. Independent Reading & Record Keeping　　　*Thinking Skills*

Review the Lesson 5 At A Glance chart in your Student Notebook to see if all the work you've done in this part has been checked off. Also, make sure the Student Notebook pages you worked on are dated and complete.

When you are finished, choose something to read that you will enjoy. Then find a quiet, comfortable place and read for the following length of time:

🐾🐾 30 minutes　　　　🐾 35 minutes

Be sure to write down what you read today on the Reading Log in your Student Notebook.

Lesson 5, Part 4

A. Copywork & Dictation　　　　　　　*Language Skills*

Look carefully at your assigned passage below, and read it silently. Show your teacher any words you don't know, and practice saying them aloud. Now read the passage aloud, or ask your teacher to read it to you.

When you are finished copying or writing from dictation, compare your copy to the text and make any needed corrections.

🐾🐾 Copy or write as your teacher dictates from *Homer Price*, page 109, paragraph 2 ("But he solved…").

🐾 Write as your teacher dictates from *The Wright Brothers*, page 119, paragraph 6 ("Terrified about his…").

🐾 Write as your teacher dictates from *The Wright Brothers*, page 119, paragraphs 6 and 7 ("Terrified about his…").

B. Reader   *Language Skills, History*

Homer Price: page 113, paragraph 3 ("Saturday dawned…") through page 121

The New Way Things Work: pages 96 (The Submersible) and 97 (The Submarine)

Follow the directions below to read or listen to the assigned passages in *Homer Price* and *The New Way Things Work*.

When you are finished, make up five true-false statements about the assignment in *The New Way Things Work* and write them in your Student Notebook. (Make sure that at least two of your statements are false.) Make an answer key at the bottom of the page, and write each false statement correctly. You do not need to re-write the true statements. Then give your quiz to a family member!

Read the above assignment from *Homer Price* aloud, and then follow along as someone else reads the assignment from *The New Way Things Work*.

Read the above assignment from *Homer Price* silently, and then read the assignment from *The New Way Things Work* aloud.

Read the above assignments from *Homer Price* and *The New Way Things Work* silently.

C. Read-Aloud & Discussion   *History, Language Skills, Thinking Skills*

The Wright Brothers: page 136 ("That problem, however…") through page 142, paragraph 4

After reading or listening to the read-aloud assignment, talk with your teacher and try to predict what will happen in the future based on what you know of the characters and events. Write your predictions in your Student Notebook. Later you will look back and see if they were accurate. Try not to peek ahead!

Listen carefully as your teacher reads the assigned passage. Write down two predictions.

Listen carefully as your teacher reads the assigned passage. Write down three predictions.

Read the assigned passage aloud; then write down at least four predictions.

D. Word Building   *Language Skills, Thinking Skills*

Earlier in this lesson you learned about the Latin word-part *visum-*. Read over the words you defined in Part 2 and tell your teacher what each one means.

Now add to your ability to use *visum-* by finding more words in the dictionary that begin with it and relate to its meaning. Write them in your Student Notebook. Be sure not to repeat any of the words you have already defined. When you are finished, pick one of your words and write a sentence that uses it correctly.

🌿 at least three words   🐾 at least six words   🐾 at least nine words

E. History & Geography
Thinking Skills, Geography

A Day in the Life... World War II was the most destructive time period in all of human history. Not only was it the deadliest war in history, with estimates of over 50 million deaths, but it was also the most devastating. Many places in Europe will always feel the effects of the war. More tragic and cruel than any other part of the war was Nazi Germany's attempt to **eradicate**, or destroy, all the Jews in Europe—the Holocaust.

Adolf Hitler rose to power in Germany after having been a soldier during World War I. Starting from nothing, the unknown and penniless Hitler used his cunning to steadily gain political power. In 1933, Hitler was elected Chancellor of Germany. For the next twelve years, until his suicide in 1945, Hitler did everything in his power to take over the world.

World War II officially began in 1939, with Germany's invasion of its neighboring country, Poland. Great Britain and France then declared war on Germany for conquering their ally. Following the First World War, Britain and France made the unfortunate decision to allow Germany to grow strong again. Then they refused to believe the growing threat was real until it was too late. In their denial they also let their own militaries fall behind the times, while Germany **amassed**, or assembled, the most powerful fighting force the world had ever seen. Britain, finally realizing the danger, began building up its military just before the war.

On the Pacific front, Japan had been invading parts of China well before Hitler ever made his move. It wasn't until Japan launched a surprise attack on Hawaii's Pearl Harbor in 1941, that the war in the Pacific truly began. This event also caused the United States to become a **pivotal**, or central, part of World War II. In the islands of the Pacific, many soldiers fell to **entrenched**, or well-established, Japanese troops, as well as to diseases, such as malaria, carried by mosquitoes.

E. An historical map gives information about history in picture form, making it easy to understand and use. Historical maps can give key information about battles and wars, because it is easy to see movement and change between those who are fighting. Give your children time to look at these maps and encourage them to tell you what they notice.

Lapbook Activity

Europe's climate also proved difficult during the freezing months of winter. Operation Overlord, or the invasion of Normandy, France, in 1944 proved to be a turning point in the war against Germany. Though there were many American and British **casualties** (the injuries and deaths caused by war), ultimately they could not be **suppressed**, or crushed, by the Germans. Gaining a foothold in France, the Allies kept pushing forward until they finally reached Germany itself.

May 8, 1945, was V-E Day, or Victory in Europe Day. It was one of the happiest days in history, and celebrations were held worldwide. While this part of the war had been terrible in many regards, greater use of force was yet to come in the Pacific. After requesting several times that the Japanese Army surrender, and being repeatedly disregarded, the United States unleashed the first atomic bomb ever used, on August 6, 1945, over the town of Hiroshima. When surrender by the Japanese military still did not come, a second atomic bomb was dropped over Nagasaki on August 9. Six days later, Japan surrendered. The war that had caused so much **devastation** and grief was finally over.

World War II **wreaked havoc** in the lives of many. Even those who survived carried the deep scars of a time of suffering. The United States is forever grateful to the countless people who sacrificed and served during those years.

An Author's Story by Debbie Strayer: On a personal note, my great-uncle was one of the Marines who perished on the shores of Iwo Jima. Iwo Jima was an island that was part of the war in the Pacific. I have grown up with an awareness of his sacrifice, yet I know he was one of thousands of brave soldiers who laid down their lives for the freedom of others. Thank you, Uncle Arthur.

Look again at the maps and description of World War II in the United States History section of your *Classroom Atlas of the United States*. Review the description, and then look at the maps. Compare the amount of land that belonged to Japan and Japanese controlled areas to the land belonging to the Allied countries. From the looks of this map, what do you think the outcome of this war should have been? Why do you think it did not end up as the map would suggest?

Choose one of the major battles shown on the map in your atlas entitled "World War II in the Pacific, 1941–1945" and learn more about it. Take notes on scrap paper and present the information to your family as a news reporter might. Remember to include the facts of who, what, when, where, why, and how the battle took place.

✋ Add a second battle to your research and reporting.

✋ Add a third battle to your research and reporting.

🐾🐾🐾 Adolf Hitler feared practically no one, though there was one **portly**, or plump, Englishman who caused him some concern. His name was Winston Churchill. Churchill, as Prime Minister of England during the Second World War, inspired his countrymen to "never give in" during their darkest times. He faced the trials of his day fearlessly and without retreat. Today, he is remembered as a champion of freedom. Read more about why Winston Churchill deserves this title in *Profiles from History, Volume 3*. Following the profile, answer the discussion questions and complete the activities.

F. Spelling

Language Skills, Thinking Skills

To increase your ability to use the words you have studied in this lesson when you write, review your vocabulary and word building lists. After choosing the number of words assigned below from these lists, you and your teacher may choose words from the Challenge Spelling List in Appendix A to work on as well. You may also want to add two or three words from your own writing that you have difficulty spelling correctly. Make your spelling list on the page provided in your Student Notebook.

When you are finished, write the words you have chosen as your teacher dictates them. Then study any that you are unable to spell correctly in preparation for writing in the next lessons. (You might want to look back at the "Tips for Studying Spelling Words" in Lesson 1, Part 4F). Add those words to the Ongoing Spelling List in your Student Notebook (Lesson 1, Part 4). Also, don't forget to add words you misspell in your everyday writing to the list. Once you can spell a word correctly in dictation, then you can cross it off. Throughout the year, you should have an ongoing list of words you are practicing.

🐾 Choose eight words from the vocabulary and word building lists, and two to four Challenge Spelling words (if you and your teacher want).

🐾 Choose ten words from the vocabulary and word building lists, and three to five Challenge Spelling words (if you and your teacher want).

🐾 Choose twelve words from your vocabulary or word building lists, and four to six Challenge Spelling words (if you and your teacher want).

G. Art

Thinking Skills

Look at page 58, "Credits," in *Create Anything With Clay*, and notice the pictures of the authors.

Of course, the images on this page aren't really pictures of the women who wrote the book, but they are photos of two simple sculptures that represent those women. If the authors themselves made these sculptures, they would be called sculpted self-portraits.

In this section, make a simple sculpture of yourself. You can use a picture or a mirror if you need help remembering what you look like. Remember—there is no right or wrong way to do this activity, so just relax and have fun!

When you are finished, put leftover clay back in its zip-lock bag.

H. Independent Reading & Record Keeping　　*Thinking Skills*

Review the Lesson 5 At A Glance chart in your Student Notebook to see if all the work you've done in this part has been checked off. Also, make sure the Student Notebook pages you worked on are dated and complete.

When you are finished, choose something to read that you will enjoy. Then find a quiet, comfortable place and read for the following length of time:

　　🐾 30 minutes　　　　　🐾 35 minutes

Be sure to write down what you read today on the Reading Log in your Student Notebook.

Lesson 5, Part 5

This part is set aside for completion of any work left undone from the lesson, and review of concepts and content. It is also a time to expand the work of the lesson with practice and games.

- Review this lesson's Steps for Thinking, found in Part 1.

- Use the Vocabulary I.D. sheet you completed in Part 1 of this lesson to make vocabulary cards. Write each word on an index card, and try to remember what it means or how it was used in the story without looking. Check the I.D. Sheet to see if you were right. Then on the back of each card, draw a picture or write a clue to help you remember what that word means. Be sure to write a small *STF* (for Success Takes Flight) in the upper left corners.

When you are finished, give the cards to your teacher and ask her to show you their picture sides, one at a time. Tell her what the picture or clue means and then name the word written on the other side. If you can, tell what part of speech it is. Give yourself one point for correctly naming a word and one point for knowing its part of speech. Keep track of your points and see if you beat your score from Part 3!

- Listen as your teacher reads the spelling words that you studied from Part 4, especially the ones on your Ongoing Spelling List. Write each word in your Student Notebook as she dictates it.

Ask your child to choose one of the Steps for Thinking and explain it to you. Ask him to share examples of the Step from the reading, activities, or discussion in the lesson. If you think your child is ready, also ask him to think of an example from the events of the day. Assist your child in thinking of examples, if needed.

When you are finished, look at your word list and make corrections as needed. Show your teacher how you did.

• Follow the directions in the *Human Body Basics* Instructions to play the Word Power vocabulary game, and complete the System Savvy puzzles in your Student Notebook.[2] Then work on any *Examine This* projects you have not yet completed.

• Look back at pages 42 through 47 in the *Basix Recorder Method* and review any exercises that may still be giving you trouble. Choose several tracks on the *Recorder Method* CD and play along with them. Be sure to spend at least 20 minutes practicing!

• Review the Lesson 5 At A Glance chart in your Student Notebook to see if all the work you've done in this part has been checked off. If you did an Enrichment activity or other extra work in this lesson, be sure to write it on the lines next to the chart in your Student Notebook.

• Print and cut out the Success Takes Flight Bingo cards and clues from your Student Resources CD. Then, follow the directions in Appendix B to play the game.

Enrichment Activities

1. Make your Career Project presentation to your family.

   Then, ask for feedback from family members in regard to your presentation's content (information), concepts (your ideas, like how you fit this career), and form (how well you communicated your thoughts). You may want to review this project in several years and see how you feel about your ideas at that time!

2. Continue finding out about First Ladies by researching Elizabeth (Bess) Truman and Mamie Eisenhower. Remember to include information about the service and unique characteristics of each, such as:

   • Relationship to the President (wife, sister, etc.)

   • Years of service

   • Difficult issues or events during the President's term

   • Key projects initiated, or causes supported, by this First Lady

   • Main changes in culture—fashion, advancements at White House, and so forth

   Tell what you think were the most important qualities of this First Lady. Plan to introduce your favorite First Lady as part of the Unit End Presentation. Remember to include a variety of media as you tell about her qualities and service.

3. Learn more about Naval craft and technology, such as ships, submarines, aircraft carriers, deep-sea exploration, or underwater combat techniques. You may want to learn about them as a group or choose one specific type of naval craft or technology to research. Make sure to include pictures of the craft or technology when you share what you learn with your family.

Additional Resources:

Horse of a Different Color by Ralph Moody

The Time Machine (H. G. Wells, adapted by Shirley Bogart)

Answers

4. Possible answers: disapprovingly, promptly, already, quickly, carefully, glumly, apparently, sufficiently, completely, and so forth.

5. Answer key is in the *Human Body Basics* Answer Key.

Lesson 6, Part 1

~*Materials*~

- *The Wright Brothers*
- *Homer Price*
- *The Story of Inventions*
- *The Story of the Orchestra* book & CD
- *Basix Recorder Method*
- *Profiles From History,* Volume 3
- *Create Anything With Clay*
- Recorder
- Polymer clay
- Rummy Roots cards

A. Copywork & Dictation   *Language Skills*

Choose the number of paragraphs assigned below from Chapter 14 in *The Story of Inventions*. Look carefully at the passage you chose, and read it silently. Show your teacher any words you don't know, and practice saying them aloud. Now read the passage aloud, or ask your teacher to read it to you.

Copy, or write as your teacher dictates, the paragraph(s). When you are finished, compare your copy to the text and make any needed corrections.

🦃 one paragraph   🐾 two paragraphs   🐾 three paragraphs

B. Reader   *Language Skills, History*

Homer Price: page 126 (Chapter 6) through page 130, paragraph 4
The Story of Inventions: Review Chapters 10 and 19

Follow the directions below to read or listen to the assigned passage in *Homer Price*.

When you are finished, skim each chapter in the review assignment from *The Story of Inventions*. Then think of some ways that the lives of Henry Ford and the Wright Brothers were similar, and some ways they were different. Record your ideas on the page in your Student Notebook.

🦃 Read the above assignment from *Homer Price* aloud; then think of two ways the inventors' lives were similar, and two ways they were different.

🐾 Read the above assignment from *Homer Price* silently; then think of three ways the inventors' lives were similar, and three ways they were different.

🐾 Read the above assignment from *Homer Price*; then think of four ways the inventors' lives were similar, and four ways they were different.

C. Read-Aloud & Narration   *History, Language Skills, Thinking Skills*

The Wright Brothers: page 142, paragraph 5 ("Neither Wilbur nor Orville…") through page 149, paragraph 4

Follow the directions below to read or listen to the above passage. Then, in your own words, tell what happened in the portion you are assigned. Try to remember as many details as possible. If necessary you may reread, or listen as your teacher rereads, the part you are to retell.

🦃 Listen carefully as your teacher reads the above assignment aloud. Choose one page to retell.

🐾 Listen carefully as your teacher reads the above assignment aloud. Choose two pages to retell.

🐾 Read the above assignment aloud, and then retell the entire passage.

Teaching Tip

If you are utilizing the assessment at the end of this lesson, remember to include time in your schedule for comfortable administration. You can give a few sections at a time, or all at once. Remember, this is an opportunity to familiarize your child with ways to be successful during assessments, so don't try to squeeze it in as an afterthought, increasing everyone's stress!

D. Vocabulary
Language Skills, Thinking Skills

Show your teacher all the Vocabulary I.D. sheets that you have completed in this unit. Ask her to review the words with you by calling them out or writing them on a dry erase board or piece of paper. Tell her what each word means or how it was used in the story and, if you can, what part of speech it is.

Give yourself one point for each correct meaning and one point for knowing the word's part of speech. Keep track of your Vocabulary I.D. points by writing them on a piece of scrap paper and try to beat your score when you review these words again in Part 3.

E. Study Hall
Thinking Skills

This section is set aside as a "Study Hall." Use it to catch up on any work that has not yet been completed in the science lessons studied in this unit. If all your science is finished, use this time to work on other assignments that are still undone.

F. Writing
Language Skills, Thinking Skills

It is time to make a final decision as to the science topic you will develop into a project in the next unit.

Look back at the revised list you made in Lesson 3, Part 3, and write the title of your final choice on the page in your Student Notebook. Decide which of the questions or thoughts you wrote down in Lesson 3 will be included in your project and eliminate any that no longer interest you. Add new ones you would like to consider, until you again have at least five. You may need to do a quick search to come up with good, basic questions about your topic.

G. Music
History, Thinking Skills

Review all the Orchestra Story cards you have made in Units 4 and 5 by matching the question cards with their correct answers.

When you are finished, follow the directions in Appendix D to make new category cards for Brass Instruments and Percussion Instruments, and to play Orchestra Story Question Quest with all the cards from Units 1 through 5.

H. Independent Reading & Record Keeping
Thinking Skills

Review the Lesson 6 At A Glance chart in your Student Notebook to see if all the work you've done in this part has been checked off. Also, make sure the Student Notebook pages you worked on are dated and complete.

When you are finished, choose something to read that you will enjoy. Then find a quiet, comfortable place and read for the following length of time:

ᵜᵜ ᵜ 30 minutes   ᵜ 35 minutes

Be sure to write down what you read today on the Reading Log in your Student Notebook.

Lesson 6, Part 2

A. **Copywork & Dictation**   *Language Skills*

Review your copywork or dictation assignments from Lessons 1-3 and make a list of mistakes you made more than once. Then discuss this list with your teacher. What is the main thing you need to work on to improve?

B. **Reader**   *Language Skills, History*

Homer Price: page 130, paragraph 5 ("Homer had heard…") through page 137, paragraph 3
The Story of Inventions: Review Chapters 10 and 19

Follow the directions below to read or listen to the assigned passage in *Homer Price*.

When you are finished, skim each chapter in the review assignment from *The Story of Inventions*. Then think of some ways that the inventions of Henry Ford and the Wright Brothers were similar, and some ways they were different. Record your ideas on the page in your Student Notebook.

ᵜᵜ Read the above assignment from *Homer Price* aloud; then think of two ways the inventions of Ford and the Wright Brothers were similar, and two ways they were different.

ᵜ Read the above assignment from *Homer Price* silently; then think of three ways the inventions of Ford and the Wright Brothers were similar, and three ways they were different.

ᵜ Read the above assignment from *Homer Price*; then think of four ways the inventions of Ford and the Wright Brothers were similar, and four ways they were different.

C. **Read-Aloud & Discussion**   *History, Language Skills, Thinking Skills*

The Wright Brothers: page 149, paragraph 5 ("The next day…") through page 156

Follow the directions below to read or listen to the above assignment. Then make up questions about the part of the story you just read or heard.

B. When children consider information looking for differences, they are using analytical skills. This type of thinking is more challenging that just recalling details or telling what happened. Since children can use a variety of types of thinking skills, this is one way to incorporate challenging questions in your discussions.

Write your questions in your Student Notebook and ask your teacher to answer them. After discussing her thoughts, write down the best possible answer on the lines provided. Be sure to use complete sentences.

When you are finished, look back at the prediction or predictions you made during Lesson 5, Part 4. Were you able to predict what would happen? Be sure to mark the "Came to Pass" box for each prediction when it does happen.

Listen carefully as your teacher reads the above assignment aloud. Make up two questions.

Listen carefully as your teacher reads the above assignment aloud. Make up three questions.

Read the above assignment aloud; then make up four questions.

D. Word Building   *Language Skills, Thinking Skilss*
Review Lessons 3 and 4 by telling your teacher about the word-parts *dia-* and *visum-*. What languages do they come from? What do they mean? Read over the words that you defined in both lessons. Then follow the directions below to make up sentences for some of the words you defined and tell them to your teacher.

Now follow the directions in the Rummy Roots card set to play Rummy Roots II.

Make up sentences for at least three words you defined.

Make up sentences for at least four words you defined.

Make up sentences for at least five words you defined.

E. History   *Thinking Skills, Geography*
Complete the Invention Demand Chart 8 in your Student Notebook by adding Guglielmo Marconi and John Holland. When you are finished, combine today's chart with Invention Demand Chart 7 from Lesson 3. Review both charts and find three things that are similar about all four inventors, and three things that are different. Make a list of these qualities on the page provided. Be sure to include this information in your presentation at the end of this lesson.

Then review the vocabulary, definitions, and examples in the Supply and Demand Vocabulary Games for Units 1, 2 and 4. Read the cards and match the words with their definitions and examples, in rows of three.

When you are finished, print and cut out the Supply and Demand Vocabulary 7 game cards from your Student Resources CD. If you want, you can glue each piece onto an index card to make the cards stronger or print them onto cardstock. Shuffle the cards, read them, and put them into sets of three—each word, its definition, and its example.[1]

Follow the directions in Appendix D to play either the Supply and Demand Concentration or Go Fish game.

F. Editing   *Language Skills, Thinking Skills*

You have reviewed several parts of speech during this unit. Now follow the directions below to go over what you have learned.

Find the following parts of speech in your lessons and review their definitions:

- nouns
- proper nouns
- common nouns
- adjectives
- articles
- verbs
- helping verbs
- prepositions
- adverbs

Look at the lists you made in Lessons 1 through 5 and make an index card for each word. Write a word's part of speech in the upper left corner of its card.

When you are finished, sort the word cards according to type: proper nouns, common nouns, adjectives, verbs, helping verbs, prepositions, and adverbs. Place each stack of words face down. Now choose the top card from each of the seven stacks, and write a sentence using all the words you drew. You may add more words, but you must include all the ones you chose. See how inventive you can be! (Funny sentences are allowed!) Not all your sentences will have all the parts, since you listed fewer helping verbs.

G. Music   *Thinking Skills*

Scan the pages you have studied so far in the *Basix Recorder Method* and review any exercises or melodies that are difficult for you. Choose several tracks on the *Recorder Method* CD to play along with. Be sure to spend at least 20 minutes practicing!

H. Independent Reading & Record Keeping   *Thinking Skills*

Review the Lesson 6 At A Glance chart in your Student Notebook to see if all the work you've done in this part has been checked off. Also, make sure the Student Notebook pages you worked on are dated and complete.

When you are finished, choose something to read that you will enjoy. Then find a quiet, comfortable place and read for the following length of time:

 30 minutes   35 minutes

Be sure to write down what you read today on the Reading Log in your Student Notebook.

Lesson 6, Part 3

A. The goal of copywork and dictation is for your children to become familiar with the language they hear and write. As your children become more familiar with the process, you can use a more natural delivery of dictation with fewer repetitions. Be careful to continue providing what your children need to be successful; but you can let them know when they are successful, you will add a little challenge by speaking at a more natural rate.

A. **Copywork & Dictation**   *Language Skills*

Choose the number of paragraphs assigned below from Chapter 20 in *The Story of Inventions*. Look carefully at the passage you chose, and read it silently. Show your teacher any words you don't know, and practice saying them aloud. Now read the passage aloud, or ask your teacher to read it to you.

Copy, or write as your teacher dictates, the paragraph(s). When you are finished, compare your copy to the text and make any needed corrections.

🐾 one paragraph   🐾 two paragraphs   🐾 three paragraphs

B. **Reader**   *Language Skills, History*

Homer Price: page 137, paragraph 4 ("Dulcey turned around…") through page 142, paragraph 1
The Story of Inventions: Review Chapters 14 and 20

Follow the directions below to read or listen to the assigned passage in *Homer Price*.

When you are finished, skim each chapter in the review assignment from *The Story of Inventions*. Then think of some ways that the lives of Guglielmo Marconi and John Holland were similar, and some ways they were different. Record your ideas on the page in your Student Notebook.

🐾 Read the above assignment from *Homer Price* aloud; then think of two ways the inventors' lives were similar, and two ways they were different.

🐾 Read the above assignment from *Homer Price* silently; then think of three ways the inventors' lives were similar, and three ways they were different.

🐾 Read the above assignment from Homer Price; then think of four ways the inventors' lives were similar, and four ways they were different.

C. **Read-Aloud & Narration**   *History, Language Skills, Thinking Skills*

The Wright Brothers: page 157 (Chapter 16) through page 164, paragraph 5

Follow the instructions below for your level. Then, in your own words, tell what happened in the story from Orville or Wilbur's point of view. Try to remember as many details as possible. Tell what you think is the most important event in the passage.

🐾🐾 Listen carefully to the assigned passage.

🐾 Read the assigned passage aloud; then write down at least four predictions.

D. Vocabulary   *Language Skills, Thinking Skills*

Gather the vocabulary cards you've made in this unit, and give them to your teacher. Ask her to show you their picture sides, one at a time. Tell her what the picture or clue means, and then name the word written on the other side. If you can, tell what part of speech it is. Give yourself one point for correctly naming a word, and one point for knowing its part of speech. Keep track of your points because you will play again in Part 5!

~ Lapbook ~
Activity

E. Science   *Thinking Skills*

Complete the Human Body Matching game in your Student Notebook.[2] When you are finished, tell your teacher what you remember about the things named in the activity. If you want help remembering, you can look back at the pages in the unit where you learned about each thing.

F. Writing   *Language Skills, Thinking Skills*

Now that you have almost completed *Homer Price* and *The Wright Brothers*, make a book review card for one of them. The purpose of a book review card is to give a brief description of what you read or heard, and then to tell what you thought of the book. It should not include as much information as a book report. The goal is to give someone who has not read the book enough information to decide whether or not they might like to read it. In a sense, it is like an advertisement for a book. Give information about the good points without retelling the story.

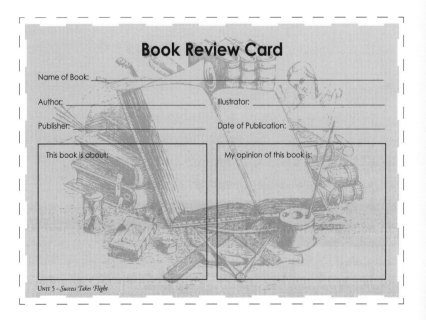

Book Review Card

Name of Book:

Author: Illustrator:

Publisher: Date of Publication:

This book is about: My opinion of this book is:

Unit 5 - *Success Takes Flight*

G. Music
History, Thinking Skills

Follow the directions in Appendix D to play Orchestra Story Question Quest with all the cards you have made in Units 1 through 5.

When you are finished, play Name-That-Instrument with your teacher and other family members. Have someone play different tracks that you have studied in Units 4 and 5 from *The Story of the Orchestra* CD. Players should take turns trying to identify the instrument featured in each piece. Name the composition for an extra point!

H. Independent Reading & Record Keeping
Thinking Skills

Review the Lesson 6 At A Glance chart in your Student Notebook to see if all the work you've done in this part has been checked off. Also, make sure the Student Notebook pages you worked on are dated and complete.

When you are finished, choose something to read that you will enjoy. Then find a quiet, comfortable place and read for the following length of time:

    30 minutes   35 minutes

Be sure to write down what you read today on the Reading Log in your Student Notebook.

Lesson 6, Part 4

A. Copywork & Dictation
Language Skills

Review your copywork or dictation assignments from Lessons 4-6 and make a list of mistakes you made more than once. Then discuss this list with your teacher. What is the main thing you need to work on to improve?

B. Reader
Language Skills, History

Homer Price: page 142, paragraph 2 ("The Judge was…") through page 149
The Story of Inventions: Review Chapters 14 and 20

Follow the directions below to read or listen to the assigned passage in *Homer Price*.

When you are finished, skim each chapter in the review assignment from *The Story of Inventions*. Then think of some ways that the inventions of Guglielmo Marconi and John Holland were similar,

B. What makes a person memorable? Many history books give only facts and dates, but that doesn't make historical figures seem real. Learning about their hearts—their thoughts and motives, struggles and successes, and ultimately how others remember them—makes them memorable. The purpose of learning about them is for their lives to make an impact on our lives.

and some ways they were different. Record your ideas on the page in your Student Notebook.

Read the above assignment from *Homer Price* aloud; then think of two ways the inventions of Marconi and Holland were similar, and two ways they were different.

Read the above assignment from *Homer Price* silently; then think of three ways the inventions of Marconi and Holland were similar, and three ways they were different.

Read the above assignment from *Homer Price*; then think of four ways the inventions of Marconi and Holland were similar, and four ways they were different.

Lapbook Activity

C. **Read-Aloud & Discussion**   *History, Language Skills, Thinking Skills*
The Wright Brothers: page 164, paragraph 6 ("On August 8…") through page 173

Look over all the predictions you made about the read-aloud story in this unit (Part 4, Section C of Lessons 1-5). Were most of them accurate? Has your ability to predict a story's events become better as you have practiced? Have you started including more details? Talk with your teacher and identify one way you have become better at making predictions. Then tell one way you need to improve in this ability.

Do you feel as though you became familiar with the motivations, the reasons a person behaves the way he or she does, and the attitudes of the book's characters? Did understanding these things help you predict the actions they would take? Talk with your teacher, and think of at least one more way you can improve in your ability to predict a character's behavior and thoughts.

D. **Word Building**   *Language Skills, Thinking Skills*
Review Lessons 1, 2, 3, and 4 by telling your teacher about the word-parts *micro-* or *micros*, *unus-* or *uni-*, *dia-*, and *visum-*. What languages do they come from? What do they mean? Read over the words that you defined in the lessons. Then follow the directions below to make up sentences for some of the words you defined and tell them to your teacher.

Now follow the directions in the Rummy Roots card set to play either Rummy Roots II or III.

Make up sentences for at least one word from each word-part studied.

Make up sentences for at least two words from each word-part studied.

Make up sentences for at least three words from each word-part studied.

Connect Learning to Life

"Why should I learn this?" What home-schooling parent hasn't heard that question? A good answer is, "Because it will help you learn about other things." The connection between science, history, and economics is such a natural one. Each teaches important ideas that build understanding in the other.

E. History　　　　　　　　　　　　*Thinking Skills*

Prepare for your Unit End Presentation by completing the following activities:

Review your Supply and Demand Vocabulary cards by shuffling the deck of cards and matching each vocabulary word to its definition and example. Next, reread your Invention Demand Charts as you prepare for your presentation. Be prepared to share this information with your family.

Review the stories you read about Dr. Charles Drew, Corrie ten Boom, Irena Sendler, and Winston Churchill in *Profiles from History, Volume 3*. Choose your two favorite profiles and plan to tell at least two key points about those people during your presentation.

Make up four questions about each of the following inventors and write them on separate index cards. Be sure to write the inventor's name in the upper left corner of his cards.

- Wright Brothers
- Nikola Tesla
- John Holland
- Henry Ford
- Guglielmo Marconi

Then find a partner and follow the directions in Appendix D to play Inventors Twenty Questions.

Increase the difficulty of this game by adding cards about other inventors you have studied this year:

- at least three inventors
- at least four inventors
- at least five inventors

F. Spelling　　　　　　*Language Skills, Thinking Skills*

Look at the words that are left on your Ongoing Spelling List. Practice spelling each one by covering it with your hand, spelling it silently, and then checking to see if you were correct. Do this several times, until you feel comfortable spelling these words.

G. Art　　　　　　　　　　　　*Thinking Skills*

In the last lesson you made a sculpted self-portrait, similar to the ones on page 58 of *Create Anything With Clay*.

In this section, make several of the same kind of sculptures for friends or members of your family. Use your imagination, have fun, and do the best job you can to make your sculptures resemble the people they represent. When you are finished, see if others can guess who is who.

Be sure to put leftover clay back in its zip-lock bag.

H. Independent Reading & Record Keeping   *Thinking Skills*

Review the Lesson 6 At A Glance chart in your Student Notebook to see if all the work you've done in this part has been checked off. Also, make sure the Student Notebook pages you worked on are dated and complete.

When you are finished, choose something to read that you will enjoy. Then find a quiet, comfortable place and read for the following length of time:

ᵛᵛ ❦ 30 minutes   ❦ 35 minutes

Be sure to write down what you read today on the Reading Log in your Student Notebook.

Lesson 6, Part 5

This part is set aside for completion of any work left undone from the lesson and review of concepts and content. It is also a time to expand the work of the lesson with practice and games.

- Listen as your teacher reviews the Steps for Thinking from the Success Takes Flight Unit that you have just completed. Talk about how you can apply the Steps to what you have read or discussed, and see if you can think of any examples in this unit.

- Gather the vocabulary cards you've made in this unit and give them to your teacher. Ask her to show you their picture sides, one at a time. Tell her what the picture or clue means and then name the word written on the other side. If you can, tell what part of speech it is. Give yourself one point for correctly naming a word and one point for knowing its part of speech. Keep track of your points and see if you can beat the score you earned in Part 3.

- Listen as your teacher reads the spelling words that you studied from Part 4, especially the ones on your Ongoing Spelling List. Write each word in your Student Notebook as she dictates it. When you are finished, look at your word list and make corrections as needed. Show your teacher how you did.

- Play Name-That-Classic with your teacher and other family members. Have someone play different tracks that you have studied so far from *The Story of the Orchestra* CD. Players should take turns trying to guess the names of the compositions. Award one point each time a player is correct and one bonus point each if the player can name either the composer or the instrument featured.

Self-evaluation is an important part of gaining new skills and knowledge. By considering the successfulness of a lesson, you are helping your child gain needed skill for future improvement. While you will have good insights as an adult, his observations can become personal revelation about the best ways to become successful.

Lapbook Activity

- Review the Lesson 6 At A Glance chart in your Student Notebook to see if all the work you've done in this part has been checked off. If you did an Enrichment activity or other extra work in this lesson, be sure to write it on the lines next to the chart.

- Make a Unit Presentation to your family that tells about what you have learned in the Success Takes Flight Unit. Share your Student Notebook, and things you made or accomplished this unit such your science projects, clay sculpture, or progress on the recorder. Don't forget to stand still and speak clearly. After your presentation, be sure to ask if anyone has questions.

- Make a Unit Presentation to your family that tells about what you have learned in the Making Connections Unit. Share your Student Notebook and things you made or accomplished in this unit, such as your play, clay sculpture, or progress on the recorder. Don't forget to stand still and speak clearly. After your presentation, be sure to ask if anyone has questions.

- Follow the directions in Appendix D to play Success Takes Flight Bingo.

Congratulations on completing Unit Five in *Paths of Progress*!

———

Answers

1. Answer key is in Appendix C.

2. Answer key is in Appendix C.

Lesson 1, Part 1

> ### ✎ Steps for Thinking Review ✎
>
> (Great Leaps Unit, Lesson 1)
>
> 1. Many young inventors and scientists focused intensely on learning about things of interest to them, making them different from others their age.
>
> 2. A first kind of thinking involves knowing basic facts about something and sharing those facts with others.
>
> 3. A first step in thinking like a scientist is to find out about something through research or observation.
>
> 4. The way goods and services are created, distributed, and consumed affects history.

As you review the Steps for Thinking with your child, feel free to share the examples that perhaps came to your mind during the lesson. Share the steps you went through in your thinking as well as your outcomes. Modeling is a very effective type of instruction, and your child will gain insight into connecting concepts and examples by hearing your thinking.

Read the Steps for Thinking that you are reviewing today. Tell your teacher what you think each step means, and:

🐾🐾 Choose two of the steps and give an example of how each one was true for any of the units.

🐾🐾 Give an example of how each step was true for any of the units.

🐾 Can you think of a time when one of the above Steps for Thinking applied to your life or to the life of someone else in your family? Share it with your teacher.

A. Copywork & Dictation
Language Skills

Together with your teacher, follow the directions below and choose a passage from today's reading assignment in either *The Story of Inventions* or *Alan Shepard*. Read the passage silently and show your teacher any words you don't know. Practice saying those words aloud until you are familiar with them. Then copy or write the passage while your teacher dictates it.

🐾🐾 at least five sentences

🐾🐾 at least seven sentences

B. Reader
Language Skills, History

The Story of Inventions: page 39 (Chapter 4) through page 41, paragraph 2

Scan the assigned passage for any words you don't know, and write them on a piece of scrap paper. Read over any section titles included

⁓ Materials ⁓

- Alan Shepard ✓
- The Story of Inventions ✓
- The Story of the Orchestra book & CD ✓
- Basix Recorder Method ✓
- Recorder
- Polymer clay
- Activity (Part 3):
  Thick hand lotion
  Glitter

in the passage—and then, as you read or listen to a section, think about how it relates to its title.

When you are finished reading, select a section title and write one or two sentences in your Student Notebook telling how the section illustrates, or tells about, it. Don't worry about the Comprehension Questions from the end of the chapter; you will work on them later in this lesson.

Read the assigned passage aloud.

Read the assigned passage silently.

C. Read-Aloud & Narration *History, Language Skills, Thinking Skills*
Alan Shepard: page 9 (Chapter 1) to the top of page 19

Follow the directions below to read or listen to the above passage. Then, in your own words, tell what happened in the portion you are assigned. Try to remember as many details as possible. If necessary you may re-read, or listen as your teacher rereads, the part you are to retell.

Listen carefully as your teacher reads the above assignment aloud. Choose two pages to retell.

Read the above assignment aloud, and then retell the entire passage.

D. Great Leaps Vocabulary Review *Thinking Skills*
Look back at the vocabulary cards you made in Unit 1. You can tell which ones they are because you wrote *GL* in their upper left corners. Go through them and see if you can remember any of the definitions. Then try using each one correctly in a sentence.

When you are finished reviewing, choose five cards and try to act out each word so that others can guess what it is. Have other players choose five words and take turns acting them out and guessing. You get a point for guessing a word or having a word guessed. See who can get the most points.

E. Great Leaps Science Review *Thinking Skills*
Complete the Tools and Technology Matching review in your Student Notebook.[1] When you are finished, tell your teacher what you remember about each thing named in the activity. If you need help remembering and your teacher agrees, you can look back at the chapters covered during Unit 1 in *The World of Tools and Technology*, and the work you did in your Student Notebook.

Teaching Tip

Paraphrasing is an important thinking skill that leads to a writing skill. When you take the words of another and put them into your own words, you go through several steps. First, you must understand what the words mean. You can gain meaning by discussion or looking up a definition. Then you think through that meaning and combine it with other words in the sentence to come up with the ideas spoken about. Once you do this, you restate, or put what you understood into words that are meaningful for you. Often this will come out in a shorter or simpler form.

F. Science Fair Project

Language Skills, Thinking Skills

In this unit you will focus attention on developing a science project. In case you're a little worried, don't be! Even if you don't especially like science, this type of project can be fun—if you choose a topic that interests you!

Hopefully you chose such a topic in Lesson 6 of the last unit. But if you weren't able to do that, time is up now and you need to settle on a choice. Deciding what you want to do is probably the hardest part of the whole project. Remember that there are many books and websites that offer a wide variety of ideas for science projects. Write down the topic you have chosen and five thoughts or questions about it.

Although you may never enter a science fair, it is a good idea to use accepted science fair guidelines as you create your project in case you ever want to enter. If you aren't associated with a school system or support group that has its own rules, with your parent's permission you can check out the ones published by the organization that sponsors the International Science and Engineering Fair, at http://www.societyforscience.org/page.aspx?pid=312.

Once you decide on a topic, settle down to do a little research. Of course, the most available resources are the library and the Internet, so plan to use both of them if your parent agrees. If you can speak to someone who's an expert in whatever area you're exploring, that adds a great **perspective**, or point of view, to your project. (Be sure you have a list of questions before you set up an interview with an expert!) Your goal is to gather basic, background information on the general topic you chose, and to increase your knowledge about the subject. You will be able to continue your research in Part 3.

In order to give proper credit to other people's work when you present your information, there is a Bibliography page in your Student Notebook. A **bibliography** is simply a list of all the resources used when writing a report or research paper. Some projects will naturally require more research than others, but it's always good to know if there is information available on your subject, and what others have found out about it. If you just look at a resource but don't find anything useful, you don't have to list it.

You can usually get all the bibliographic information you need from the title page of a book, the "About" or "Contact" page of a website, or the heading of an article. If you have trouble finding any parts of the information requested—don't worry too much about it in this activity, just do your best. Although there are several different ways to list resources in a bibliography, you will use the following forms:

F. Science project activities are suggested as ways your child can learn to prepare a science presentation within local, state, or national guidelines. Several will also help him or her to gain or improve research and writing skills. Please feel free to use these activities as suggested, or amended to better fit your student's particular abilities, needs, or interests.

<u>Book</u>:

Author's last name, first name. (followed by a period)

Title of the book, (underlined, followed by a comma)

Where it was published: (followed by a colon)

Name of publisher, (followed by a comma)

Copyright Date. (followed by a period)

Example: Wiggers, Ashley. <u>Profiles from History, Volume 3</u>, Nancy, Kentucky: Geography Matters, 2011.

<u>Encyclopedia</u>:

"Article title," (in quotation marks, followed by a comma)

Title of Encyclopedia, (underlined, followed by a comma)

Edition. (followed by a period)

Example: "Dolphins," <u>The Learning Encyclopedia</u>, First edition.

<u>Web Site</u>:

Title of the site, (followed by a comma)

Date that you got on (no punctuation)

Complete web address. (followed by a period)

Example: Trail Guide to Learning, 2/11/2007 www.trailguidetolearning.com

<u>Magazine or Other Publication</u>:

"Title of magazine," (in quotation marks followed by a comma)

Publisher, (followed by a comma)

Place of publication, (followed by a comma)

Date of publication. (followed by a period)

Example: "Home School Enrichment," Home School Enrichment, Inc., Pekin, Illinois, February 2011

<u>Video or Other Media</u>:

<u>Title</u>. (underlined, followed by a period)

Format. (Motion picture, DVD, video, etc.; followed by a period)

Director. (followed by a period)

Date of original release; (followed by a semi-colon)

Publisher/distributor, (followed by a comma)

Date of publication/distribution. (followed by a period)

Example: Drive Thru History: Discovering America's Founders.
        DVD. James Fitzgerald Jr. 2008; Coldwater Media, 2008.

Although the information on the Bibliography page is recorded in a column so it is less confusing, you will normally write it in a straight line, like the examples, when you actually add the information to the end of your report.

If possible, find at least three good resources now and record your research on the Notes Pages in your Student Notebook. To do this, list the name of each useful source you find and write a brief summary of what each one says or offers. Don't concentrate only on books—be sure to explore other things as well, like newspapers, magazines, government publications, scientific journals, videos, and so forth.

Be sure to come back to the Bibliography page and add to it whenever you find useful information in a new resource. And **use the Internet only with your parent's permission and supervision!**

G. Music
History, Thinking Skills

Continue your study of percussion instruments by reading pages 78 through 80 in *The Story of the Orchestra* with your teacher, and discussing the information about cymbals, gongs, tam-tams, and the triangle. Then listen to parts of "Symphony No. 4" on Track 32 and "Peer Gynt" on Track 33 of your CD. Were you able to discriminate between the instruments featured on each track? How did the music make you feel? What did you enjoy or dislike about it?

When you are finished, listen carefully to Tracks 32 and 33 again and choose your favorite. Then, draw and color a picture in your Student Notebook of the image this music brings to your mind.

H. Independent Reading & Record Keeping
Thinking Skills

Review the Lesson 1 At A Glance chart in your Student Notebook to see if all the work you've done in this part has been checked off. Also, make sure the Student Notebook pages you worked on are dated and complete.

When you are finished, choose something to read that you will enjoy. Then find a quiet, comfortable place and read for the following length of time:

     ✿✿ ✿ 30 minutes   ✿ 35 minutes

Be sure to write down what you read today on the Reading Log in your Student Notebook.

◦ Teacher Connection ◦

Continuous learning is an important part of education. Be sure to read the *Teacher Connection* note in your Parent Planner. Don't miss out on this important part of your homeschooling!

Lesson 1, Part 2

> ### ♪ Steps for Thinking Review ♪
>
> (Great Leaps Unit, Lesson 2)
>
> 1. Scientists and inventors are determined to solve unanswered questions and problems, even when they suffer because of it.
>
> 2. A second kind of thinking allows you to show what you know by taking information and putting it into your own words.
>
> 3. A second step in thinking like a scientist is to ask questions and try to come up with answers based on what you know.
>
> 4. Families make decisions about purchasing goods and services based on their income and their needs and wants.

Read the Steps for Thinking that you are reviewing today. Tell your teacher what you think each step means, and:

🐾 Choose two of the steps and give an example of how each one was true for any of the units.

🐾🐾 Give an example of how each step was true for any of the units.

🐾 Can you think of a time when one of the above Steps for Thinking applied to your life, or to the life of someone else in your family? Share it with your teacher.

A. **Copywork & Dictation** 　　　　　　　　　　*Language Skills*

Look carefully at your assigned passage below, and read it silently. Show your teacher any words you don't know, and practice saying them aloud. Now read the passage aloud, or ask your teacher to read it to you.

When you are finished copying or writing from dictation, compare your copy to the text and make any needed corrections.

🐾🐾 Copy or write as your teacher dictates from *The Story of Inventions*, page 39, paragraph 2 ("When he was fourteen…").

🐾 Write as your teacher dictates from *The Story of Inventions*, page 39, paragraphs 2 and 3 ("When he was fourteen…").

B. Reader

Language Skills, History

The Story of Inventions: page 41, paragraph 3 (The Lizards of Florence) through page 43, paragraph 1

Scan the assigned passage for any words you don't know, and write them on a piece of scrap paper. Read over any section titles included in the passage—and then, as you read or listen to a section, think about how it relates to its title.

When you are finished reading, select a section title and write one or two sentences in your Student Notebook telling how the section illustrates (or tells about) it.

Read the assigned passage aloud.

Read the assigned passage silently.

C. Read-Aloud & Discussion

History, Language Skills, Thinking Skills

Alan Shepard: page 19, paragraph 1 ("As the DC-3…") to the top of page 29

Follow the directions below to read or listen to the above assignment. Then make up the assigned number of questions about the part of the story you just read or heard. Write down your questions and ask your teacher to answer them. After discussing her thoughts, write down the best possible answer in your Student Notebook. Be sure to use complete sentences.

Listen carefully as your teacher reads the above assignment aloud. Make up three questions.

Read the above assignment aloud; then make up four questions.

D. Word Building

Language Skills, Thinking Skillss

Throughout *Paths of Progress* you have learned about words that have their roots in the Latin and Greek languages. Now, continue your study of word-parts by looking at the Rummy Roots Word List and choosing one that has not yet been covered.

Find the word-part you chose in the dictionary. Then write the language from which it comes, and list words that begin with it in your Student Notebook.

Underline the word-part in each of your words, and write their definitions. Think, and be ready to tell your teacher how each definition relates to the meaning of the word-part.

When you are finished, pick one of your words and write a sentence that uses it correctly.

List at least three words.

List at least six words.

B. Remember to adjust reading assignments to your children's individual needs. If they read fluently, with expression, and can retell what they have read, you may allow them to read more of the assignments silently. Occasionally ask what is happening in their story, just to get a sense of what your children are taking away from it. If your children are struggling with fluency, reading expressively, or remembering what they have read, you can increase the amount of read-aloud time.

E. **Great Leaps History Review**　　　　*Thinking Skills*

In Unit 1 you had an opportunity to learn about several important inventors, scientists, and events. Find the Great Leaps Who or What Am I review in your Student Notebook and answer the questions.[2] Then make up additional "Who or What Am I?" questions for the topics listed at the bottom of the page.

People and events listed in the Word Bank will be used to answer more than one question. When you are finished, discuss your answers with your teacher.

F. **Great Leaps Spelling Review**　　*Language Skills, Thinking Skills*

Look back at the spelling lists you made in Unit 1 and ask your teacher to choose the number of words assigned below. Then, write those words in your Student Notebook as your teacher dictates them. When you are finished, check your work and show your teacher how you did.

Add any words you had trouble spelling to the Unit 6 Ongoing Spelling List in your Student Notebook. Also, if you misspell words in your everyday writing, be sure to add them to that list as well. Remember to practice spelling the words on your ongoing list from time to time during this unit.

🌱 Choose 12 words.

🐾 Choose 16 words.

🐾 Choose 18 words.

G. **Music**　　　　　　　　　　　　　*Thinking Skills*

Read pages 48 and 49 in the *Basix Recorder Method* to learn more about, and practice, *articulation*. Write the names of notes you're not sure of above the staffs on those pages and practice playing the melodies.

Don't forget to listen to the *Recorder Method CD* tracks shown on those pages to hear samples of the lesson and use your Finger Placement Tabs if you need to.

Be sure to spend about 20 minutes a day practicing what you have learned!

H. **Independent Reading & Record Keeping**　　*Thinking Skills*

Review the Lesson 1 At A Glance chart in your Student Notebook to see if all the work you've done in this part has been checked off. Also, make sure the Student Notebook pages you worked on are dated and complete.

Teaching Tip

If you have a perfectionist child who doesn't want to practice because his music doesn't sound exactly the way he wants, encourage him to think like an inventor. Many attempts create a better product!

When you are finished, choose something to read that you will enjoy. Then find a quiet, comfortable place and read for the following length of time:

✋✋ 🐾 30 minutes   🐾 35 minutes

Be sure to write down what you read today on the Reading Log in your Student Notebook.

———— ✣ ————

Lesson 1, Part 3

> ### ✥ Steps for Thinking Review ✣
>
> (Great Leaps Unit, Lesson 3)
>
> 1. The family and friends of scientists and inventors had to try to understand and accept their ways of thinking and working.
>
> 2. A third kind of thinking happens when you take what you know and use it to solve problems and answer questions in everyday life.
>
> 3. A third step in thinking like a scientist is to think about the questions you asked and tell what you think the answers will be.
>
> 4. After looking at need, producers predict the demand for goods and services, then make supplies of those goods and services available.

Read the Steps for Thinking that you are reviewing today. Tell your teacher what you think each step means, and:

✋✋ Choose two of the steps and give an example of how each one was true for any of the units.

🐾🐾 Give an example of how each step was true for any of the units.

🐾 Can you think of a time when one of the above Steps for Thinking applied to your life or to the life of someone else in your family? Share it with your teacher.

𝒜. Copywork & Dictation   *Language Skills*
Together with your teacher, follow the directions below and choose a passage from today's reading assignment in either *The Story of*

Inventions or *Alan Shepard*. Read the passage silently and show your teacher any words you don't know. Practice saying those words aloud until you are familiar with them. Then copy or write the passage while your teacher dictates it.

🐾 at least five sentences   🐾🐾 at least seven sentences

B. Reader
Language Skills, History

The Story of Inventions: page 43, paragraph 2 (The Nobel Prize Escape) through the top of page 45

Scan the assigned passage for any words you don't know, and write them on a piece of scrap paper. Read over any section titles included in the passage—and then, as you read or listen to a section, think about how it relates to its title.

When you are finished reading, select a section title and write one or two sentences in your Student Notebook telling how the section illustrates, or tells about. it.

🐾 Read the assigned passage aloud.

🐾🐾 Read the assigned passage silently.

C. Read-Aloud & Narration
History, Language Skills, Thinking Skills

Alan Shepard: page 29, paragraph 1 ("Alan and his classmates…") through page 37

Follow the instructions below for your level. Then, in your own words, tell what happened in the story from Alan's point of view. Try to remember as many details as possible. Tell what you think is the most important event in the passage.

🐾 Listen carefully to the assigned passage.

🐾🐾 Read the assigned passage aloud.

D. Great Leaps Vocabulary Review
Language Skills, Thinking Skills

Once again, look over the vocabulary cards you made in Unit 1 (*GL*). Then give them to your teacher and ask her to show you their picture sides, one at a time. Tell her what the picture or clue means and then name the word written on the other side. If you can, tell what part of speech it is. Give yourself one point for correctly naming a word and one point for knowing its part of speech. Keep track of your points because you will play again in Part 5!

E. Science   *Thinking Skills*

Human Body Basics, Immune System: beginning of chapter &
Foreign Invaders

Lapbook Activity

As you read through the assigned pages, choose words that are new
or unfamiliar and make vocabulary cards for them as directed. Keep
your science cards separate from other vocabulary.

🐾🐾 at least three words   🐾🐾 at least four words

Read and discuss the information in the passage with your teacher
and do the *Labwork 1* and *2* activities. The pages you need to complete these activities are in your Student Notebook.

When you are finished, begin work on *Examine This* projects 1 and 2
at the end of the chapter.

Do as much as you can, but you don't have to finish the projects in
this part. You will have other opportunities to work on them, such as
during Part 5 and in your spare time.

F. Science Fair Project   *Language Skills, Thinking Skills*

Lapbook Activity

In this section, continue working on your science project by completing basic research on its topic. Find two or three additional resources and summarize each one on the Notes Pages in your Student
Notebook. Don't forget to record the new Bibliographic information.

As you look for information, keep your eyes open for good questions
you can focus on in your project—or experiments you can use to find
answers to those questions. Since you are somewhat limited by the
length of this unit, if you know your project will require growing or
observing something over a period of time, you might want to begin
doing that as soon as possible. Look ahead to Lesson 3, Part 3F to find
out how to record your observations and other **data**.

Even if you begin gathering data ahead of time, you can still follow the
lesson schedule for the other parts of your project. In Part 1 of the next
lesson you will begin writing your background research paper.

G. Music & Review   *History, Thinking Skills*

Look back at pages 78 through 80 in *The Story of the Orchestra*.

Then, follow the directions in Appendix D to make four
Orchestra Story question and answer cards from the section
about cymbals, gongs, and tam-tams, and two about the triangle.
Label each answer card with the name of instrument it is about
in the upper left corner. Do not label the question cards—and
remember to write the questions in your Student Notebook in
the correct order.

Gather the Orchestra Story cards you made in Unit 1, Great Leaps, and separate the questions from the answers. Mix up both stacks well and then place the question card stack facedown on the table. Draw one question at a time and see if you can find its correct answer in the other stack. Remember the answer keys you made in your Student Notebook. Remove the question and answer cards you get correct.

Follow the same directions to review your Orchestra Story cards from Units 4 and 5, and those you have made so far in Unit 6.

H. Independent reading provides regular practice for word study and reading skills, as well as time for practice of thinking skills. Quiet time to consider ideas and tie new information with old is essential in building new understandings.

H. **Independent Reading & Record Keeping**   *Thinking Skills*

Review the Lesson 1 At A Glance chart in your Student Notebook to see if all the work you've done in this part has been checked off. Also, make sure the Student Notebook pages you worked on are dated and complete.

When you are finished, choose something to read that you will enjoy. Then find a quiet, comfortable place and read for the following length of time:

🐾 30 minutes   🐾 35 minutes

Be sure to write down what you read today on the Reading Log in your Student Notebook.

Lesson 1, Part 4

❧ Steps for Thinking Review ❧

(Great Leaps Unit, Lesson 4)

1. Scientists and inventors try many different ways of doing something and use everything that happens to help them learn.

2. A fourth kind of thinking helps you find the parts of one piece of information and then put them in some order.

3. A fourth step in thinking like a scientist is to find out if your ideas are correct by testing them out.

4. Investing in innovation is an important, but risky way to encourage finding new solutions for problems.

Read the Steps for Thinking that you are reviewing today. Tell your teacher what you think each step means, and:

🌵 Choose two of the steps and give an example of how each one was true for any of the units.

🐾 Give an example of how each step was true for any of the units.

🐾 Can you think of a time when one of the above Steps for Thinking applied to your life or to the life of someone else in your family? Share it with your teacher.

A. **Copywork & Dictation**　　　　　*Language Skills*

Look back at the Steps for Thinking from Unit 1 that you have reviewed so far in this lesson. Pick several as directed below, and either copy or write them from dictation into your Student Notebook.

🌵 Pick four steps.

🐾 Pick five steps.

B. **Reader**　　　　　*Language Skills, History*

The Story of Inventions: page 45, paragraph 1 (An Arms Race and an Energy Race) through page 48

Scan the assigned passage for any words you don't know, and write them on a piece of scrap paper. Read over any section titles included in the passage—and then, as you read or listen to a section, think about how it relates to its title.

When you are finished reading, select a section title and write one or two sentences in your Student Notebook telling how the section illustrates, or tells about, it.

Read the assigned passage aloud.

Read the assigned passage silently.

C. **Read-Aloud & Discussion**   *History, Language Skills, Thinking Skills*
Alan Shepard: page 39 (Chapter 4) through page 47, paragraph 2

After reading or listening to the read-aloud assignment, talk with your teacher and try to predict what will happen in the future based on what you know of the characters and events. Write your predictions in your Student Notebook. Later you will look back and see if they were accurate. Try not to peek ahead!

Listen carefully as your teacher reads the assigned passage. Write down three predictions.

Read the assigned passage aloud; then write down at least four predictions.

D. **Great Leaps Word Building Review**   *Language Skills, Thinking Skills*
Print the Word Builder Review 1 cards (for your level) from the Student Resources CD and cut them out. Mix them up and place them face down in a stack. Then take turns drawing cards, one at a time, with at least one other player. When a player draws a card, he or she must tell what word-part is in that word (one point), what language it comes from (one point), and the meaning of the word (one point). See how many points you can get!

For the answers, look back at the Word Building pages for Unit 1 in your Student Notebook.

E. **Great Leaps History/Economics Review**   *Thinking Skills*
Gather or reprint the Supply and Demand 1 and 2 game cards that you made in Unit 1. Reread them, and match the words with their definitions and examples in rows of three. Then play either Supply and Demand Concentration or Go Fish Matching.

Look at the Unit Review Graphic Organizer in your Student Notebook (Lesson 1, Part 4E), and discuss the questions it asks with your teacher. Then fill in the boxes in the Great Leaps column as best you can.

When you are finished, discuss what you wrote with your teacher, and explain why you answered as you did.

D. Are games truly a valid part of school time? Absolutely! As your child revisits content, vocabulary, and concepts, an effective review of learning takes place. The game format makes review more inviting and hopefully, more frequent.

Lapbook Activity

F. Writing
Language Skills, Thinking Skills

After every chapter in *The Story of Inventions*, there is a list of Comprehension Questions. Their purpose is to determine if you understand what you have read, and are able to draw certain conclusions based on your understanding. The questions focus on main ideas expressed in the sections.

Read over the Comprehension Questions at the end of Chapter 4. Then refer back to the story to find their answers and use complete sentences to write them in your Student Notebook. (If you need help remembering how to answer questions, look back at the Writing lessons in Unit 1.)

When you are finished, check your answers with *The Story of Inventions Answer Key*. Are they in agreement? Were there things you left out? Evaluate your answers and tell your teacher if you were on target.

Create two more questions for Chapter 4; make sure they target main ideas, not just details. After writing your questions, create an Answer Key.

G. Art
Thinking Skills

In this unit, you will have an opportunity to create a Claymation video or flipbook to illustrate, highlight, or explain some part of your science project. If you don't know what a Claymation video is (or even if you do!) a sample is posted on the *Trail Guide to Learning* Yahoo group site: http://tech.groups.yahoo.com/group/LearningSeries/, in the Files section (toolbar on the left side of the page). If your parent agrees, take a look at it.

Even though it is possible to make a Claymation video with a video camera, it is actually much easier to produce with a regular still camera—either film or digital. The video does, however, require film-editing software on your computer. That's not necessarily a problem, because PC has a free download available (called Windows Movie Maker), and iMovie is standard on most Mac computers (sometimes located in a file called iDVD). You will have to spend some time getting to know the software if you choose this option.

On the other hand, if video is not a good choice for you and your family, you can make a flipbook. To do that, you go through the same processes as you would for a video. The difference is, at the end you can simply print the pictures, staple them together, and then "flip" the pages to see the animation come to life.

Talk with your parent and decide whether you would like to make a Claymation video or a flipbook. Then begin thinking about some part of your science topic you might enjoy illustrating, highlighting, or explaining with this interesting art form. It can be just about anything and involve characters that represent people doing things (like you

F. Answers to the questions from *The Story of Inventions* are located in the Answer Key for that book.

G. We are grateful to Cathryn Fowler, an award-winning videographer from Tampa, FL, for sharing her Claymation expertise with *Paths of Progress* families.

planting a seed and measuring its growth), or objects that represent various stages of your project (like a plant growing from a seed). List some ideas in your Student Notebook.

If you intend to make a video, download or open the film-editing software (**only with your parent's permission**!) and begin going through the tutorial. Take your time and discuss the program's various stages and options with your teacher. You have until Part 4 of the next lesson before you will again work on this assignment, so experiment by using the editing software with other pictures (if your parent agrees). Don't be discouraged if things don't go perfectly the first time! This is a valuable skill you are learning, and it will take a bit of practice.

H. Independent Reading & Record Keeping   *Thinking Skills*

Review the Lesson 1 At A Glance chart in your Student Notebook to see if all the work you've done in this part has been checked off. Also, make sure the Student Notebook pages you worked on are dated and complete.

When you are finished, choose something to read that you will enjoy. Then find a quiet, comfortable place and read for the following length of time:

    🐾 30 minutes   🐾 35 minutes

Be sure to write down what you read today on the Reading Log in your Student Notebook.

Lesson 1, Part 5

> ### ❧ Steps for Thinking Review ❧
>
> (Great Leaps Unit, Lesson 5)
>
> 1. Scientists and inventors often had to use old things in new ways and then convince others that what they made or discovered was important.
>
> 2. A fifth kind of thinking helps you use what you have learned in a new way and make decisions about what you think.
>
> 3. A fifth step in thinking like a scientist is to share the results of your tests honestly and tell if they showed what you thought they would.
>
> 4. The goal of a free enterprise or government-run enterprise is to benefit the people. Honestly determining effectiveness through competition (free enterprise) and informing voters (government-run) is required to assure those benefits.

Read the Steps for Thinking that you are reviewing today. Tell your teacher what you think each step means, and:

🌵 Choose two of the steps and give an example of how each one was true for any of the units.

🖐🐾 Give an example of how each step was true for any of the units.

🐾 Can you think of a time when one of the above Steps for Thinking applied to your life or to the life of someone else in your family? Share it with your teacher.

This part is set aside for completion of any work left undone from the lesson and review of concepts and content. It is also a time to expand the work of the lesson with practice and games.

- Give your teacher your stack of vocabulary cards for Unit 1, Great Leaps. Ask her to show you each word, and then tell her the meaning of the word and see if you can use it correctly in a sentence.

When you are finished reviewing, choose five cards and try to act out each word so that others can guess what it is. Have other players choose five words and take turns acting them out and guessing. You get a point for guessing a word, or having a word guessed. See who can get the most points.

An activity like a word search, crossword, or word scramble contributes to the seeing, hearing, and understanding of a word. It provides a fun way to review learning, and gives the student another chance to encounter each word, adding to the likelihood that the child will use it again in speaking or writing. It also happens to be fun!

- Review your Great Leaps spelling words. Then ask your teacher to choose the number of words indicated below for your level. Write each word in your Student Notebook as she dictates it. When you are finished, look at your word list and make corrections as needed. Show your teacher how you did.

  ✸✸16 words   ✸ ✸ 20 words

- Follow the directions in the *Human Body Basics* Instructions to play the Word Power vocabulary game, and complete the System Savvy puzzles in your Student Notebook.[3] Then work on any *Examine This* projects you have not yet completed, or on your science project.

- Look back at pages 48 and 49 in the *Basix Recorder Method* and practice those exercises. Then review any other lessons that may be giving you trouble. Choose several tracks on the *Recorder Method* CD and play along with them. Be sure to spend at least 20 minutes practicing—and don't forget that you can use your Finger Placement Tabs if you need to.

- Review the Lesson 1 At A Glance chart in your Student Notebook to see if all the work you've done in this part has been checked off. If you did an Enrichment activity or other extra work in this lesson, be sure to write it on the lines next to the chart.

- Follow the directions in Appendix D and play Great Leaps Bingo.

- Complete the Reach for the Stars Word Search located in your Student Notebook.[4]

Enrichment Activities:

Create a Medical Breakthroughs Timeline book similar to the one you made in Unit 1, Part 5 for recording progress in tools and technology.

Then briefly research the following people, places, and/or events and add them to your timeline. You can do this by simply writing their names in the correct places; or you can draw or trace pictures and symbols that you find during your research, and then color, cut, and paste them to the timeline. If you think of other medical advances you would like to include, feel free to do so!

Some of these people may be famous for other things, but you should concentrate only on their medical contribution(s). At the bottom of each timeline page, write one or two sentences describing the contributions or significance of the individuals, places, or events on that page.

- Diocles
- Hippocrates
- Salerno
- Rhazus
- Roger Bacon
- Sanctorius
- Zacharius Janssen

Additional Resources:

The Rocketeer movie

A+ Science Fair Projects by Janice VanCleave

      or other books about science fair projects

How to Make Clay Characters by Maureen Carlson

Please preview any recommended movie to ensure its content is in line with your family's values and acceptable for your children to watch.

Answers

1. Answer key is in Appendix C.

2. Answer key is in Appendix C.

3. Answer key is in the *Human Body Basics* Answer Key.

4. Answer key is in Appendix C.

Lesson 2, Part 1

> ### ♪ Steps for Thinking Review ♪
>
> (Making Connections Unit, Lesson 1)
>
> 1. An idea for an invention can often come to someone through an accident that sparks a new thought.
>
> 2. Personal determination and a desire to learn are key parts to a person's success.
>
> 3. Bravery is personal. What is brave for one person may be easy for another person. Don't compare your bravery to someone else's.
>
> 4. Learning a skill or trade from others has been an important way of continuing the production of goods and services for hundreds of years.

Materials

- *Alan Shepard*
- *The Story of Inventions*
- *The Story of the Orchestra* book & CD
- *Basix Recorder Method*
- Recorder
- Report cover with prong fasteners
- Activity (Part 3):
    - Small Styrofoam or paper plates
    - A potato
    - Ziploc bags (to hold plates)
    - Q-tips
    - Alcohol
    - Tongs
    - Timer
    - Boiling water
- Activity (Part 4G)
    - Plain, unlined paper

Read the Steps for Thinking that you are reviewing today. Tell your teacher what you think each step means, and:

🌵🌵 Choose two of the steps and give an example of how each one was true for any of the units.

🐾🐾 Give an example of how each step was true for any of the units.

🐾 Can you think of a time when one of the above Steps for Thinking applied to your life or to the life of someone else in your family? Share it with your teacher.

𝒜. Dictation   *Language Skills*

Together with your teacher, follow the directions below and choose a passage from today's reading assignment in either *The Story of Inventions* or *Alan Shepard*. Read the passage silently and show your teacher any words you don't know. Practice saying those words aloud until you are familiar with them. Then copy or write the passage while your teacher dictates it.

🌵🌵 at least five sentences   🐾🐾 at least seven sentences

ℬ. Reader   *Language Skills, History*

The Story of Inventions: page 205 (Chapter 15) through page 206

Scan the assigned passage for any words you don't know, and write them on a piece of scrap paper. Read over any section titles included in the passage—and then, as you read or listen to a section, think about how it relates to its title.

When you are finished reading, select a section title and write one or two sentences in your Student Notebook telling how the section illustrates (or tells about) it.

✌ Read the assigned passage aloud.

🐾 Read the assigned passage silently.

C. **Read-Aloud & Narration** *History, Language Skills, Thinking Skills*
Alan Shepard: page 47, paragraph 3 ("Things during Alan's…") through page 56, paragraph 1

Follow the directions below to read or listen to the above passage. Then, in your own words, tell what happened in the portion you are assigned. Try to remember as many details as possible. If necessary you may reread, or listen as your teacher rereads, the part you are to retell.

✌ Listen carefully as your teacher reads the above assignment aloud. Choose two pages to retell.

🐾 Read the above assignment aloud, and then retell the entire passage.

D. **Making Connections Vocabulary Review** *Language Skills*
Look back at the vocabulary cards you made in Unit 2. You can tell which ones they are because you wrote *MC* in their upper left corners. Go through them and see if you can remember any of the definitions. Then try using each one correctly in a sentence.

When you are finished reviewing, choose five cards and try to act out each word so that others can guess what it is. Have other players choose five words and take turns acting them out and guessing. You get a point for guessing a word, or having a word guessed. See who can get the most points.

E. **Making Connections Science Review** *Thinking Skills*
Complete the Tools and Technology Matching review in your Student Notebook.[1] When you are finished, tell your teacher what you remember about each thing named in the activity. If you need help remembering and your teacher agrees, you can look back at the chapters covered during Unit 2 in *The World of Tools and Technology*, and the work you did in your Student Notebook.

F. **Science Fair Project** *Language Skills, Thinking Skills*
It's time to start writing your background research paper! In this section you will make a **rough draft**, or first try, on regular notebook paper or (if your parent agrees) on the computer. Plan for your report to be at least the number of paragraphs assigned below, or

---

C. What makes a person memorable? Many history books give only facts and dates, but that doesn't make historical figures seem real. Learning about their hearts—their thoughts and motives, struggles and successes, and ultimately how others remember them—makes them memorable. The purpose of learning about them is for their lives to make an impact on our lives.

Connect Learning to Life
Writing skills are preparation for real life, not just a school time activity. Whenever you do an activity that equips your children for life, such as learning how to write a report or directions that others can follow, point it out to them. Take time to think about the connections you see between what you are teaching your children and the way they might actually use the knowledge or skills in their daily life. Doing this regularly will help you answer that age-old question, "Will I ever use what I'm learning?"

longer if your teacher wishes. If you need help remembering how to write a paper, look back at Unit 4, Lesson 3, Part 1F.

Generally speaking, a good rule of thumb (or practical approach) for a paper like this includes:

1. the introduction, where you tell your readers what you plan to tell them;

2. the body, where you actually tell them;

3. and the conclusion, where you tell them what you told them.

In other words, your first paragraph should introduce the topic, and summarize what the paper is going to say. The final paragraph should close your paper by using different words to summarize what you learned, and what conclusions you came to through your research. (You learned about writing conclusions in Unit 4, Lesson 3, Part 3F.) And the paragraphs in between those two should contain the information from your research.

To help recall what you found out in your research, begin your paper by using the Notes Pages in your Student Notebook to organize your notes into a simple outline. To do this, list main points you would like to include in the paper (one main point for each middle paragraph). Then under each main point, list two or three facts or pieces of information about it. This way you know exactly what to write about in each paragraph.

Be sure never to copy a resource word for word! Always put things in your own words. You will have an opportunity to revise and finalize your paper in Part 3 of this lesson.

🐾 Write at least four paragraphs.

🐾 Write at least five paragraphs.

🐾 Write at least six paragraphs.

G. Music
History, Thinking Skills

Conclude your study of percussion instruments by reading pages 81 through 83 in *The Story of the Orchestra* with your teacher, and discussing the information about the glockenspiel, celesta, and tubular bells. Then listen to part of the "Nutcracker Suite" on Track 34. Were you able to hear the instrument featured on the track? How did the music make you feel? What did you enjoy or dislike about it?

When you are finished, listen carefully to Track 34 again. Then, draw and color a picture in your Student Notebook of the image this music brings to your mind.

H. **Independent Reading & Record Keeping**　　*Thinking Skills*

Review the Lesson 2 At A Glance chart in your Student Notebook to see if all the work you've done in this part has been checked off. Also, make sure the Student Notebook pages you worked on are dated and complete.

When you are finished, choose something to read that you will enjoy. Then find a quiet, comfortable place and read for the following length of time:

　　　　🌱🌱✋ 30 minutes　　　　　✋ 35 minutes

Be sure to write down what you read today on the Reading Log in your Student Notebook.

Lesson 2, Part 2

❧ Steps for Thinking Review ❧

(Making Connections Unit, Lesson 2)

1. Often an invention would upset people because they feared it would cause them to lose their own value as workers.

2. Part of wisdom is knowing when and how to tell people about new ideas.

3. When you do what is best for others, sometimes you have to give up keeping something to yourself.

4. Improvements in methods of transportation helped people move more quickly and safely and helped business by moving products more efficiently.

Read the Steps for Thinking that you are reviewing today. Tell your teacher what you think each step means, and:

🌱🌱 Choose two of the steps and give an example of how each one was true for any of the units.

✋✋ Give an example of how each step was true for any of the units.

✋ Can you think of a time when one of the above Steps for Thinking applied to your life or to the life of someone else in your family? Share it with your teacher.

Teaching Tip

One way to solidify learning is to teach someone else what you know. When your child reviews what he has learned by telling someone else about it, the student has taken instruction and put it into his own words. This increases the likelihood that he will use the information on his own.

𝒜. Copywork & Dictation   *Language Skills*

Look carefully at your assigned passage below, and read it silently. Show your teacher any words you don't know, and practice saying them aloud. Now read the passage aloud, or ask your teacher to read it to you.

When you are finished copying or writing from dictation, compare your copy to the text and make any needed corrections.

🐾🐾 Copy or write as your teacher dictates from *The Story of Inventions*, page 206, paragraph 1 ("As a result…").

🐾 Write as your teacher dictates from *The Story of Inventions*, page 206, paragraphs 1 and 2 ("As a result…").

ℬ. Reader   *Language Skills, History*

The Story of Inventions: page 207-208

Scan the assigned passage for any words you don't know, and write them on a piece of scrap paper. Read over any section titles included in the passage—and then, as you read or listen to a section, think about how it relates to its title.

When you are finished reading, select a section title and write one or two sentences in your Student Notebook telling how the section illustrates (or tells about) it.

🐾🐾 Read the assigned passage aloud.

🐾🐾 Read the assigned passage silently.

𝒞. Read-Aloud & Discussion   *History, Language Skills, Thinking Skills*

Alan Shepard: page 56, paragraph 2 ("Alan had had his first…") through page 65, paragraph 1

Follow the directions below to read or listen to the above assignment. Then make up the assigned number of questions about the part of the story you just read or heard. Write down your questions and ask your teacher to answer them. After discussing her thoughts, write down the best possible answer in your Student Notebook. Be sure to use complete sentences.

When you are finished, look back at the predictions you made during Lesson 1, Part 4. Were you able to predict what would happen? Be sure to mark the "Came to Pass" box for each prediction when it does happen.

🐾🐾 Listen carefully as your teacher reads the above assignment aloud. Make up three questions.

🐾🐾 Read the above assignment aloud; then make up four questions.

Lapbook Activity

D. Word Building   *Language Skills, Thinking Skillss*

Throughout *Paths of Progress* you have learned about words that have their roots in the Latin and Greek languages. Now, continue your study of word-parts by looking at the Rummy Roots Word List and choosing one that has not yet been covered.

Find the word-part you chose in the dictionary. Then write the language from which it comes, and list words that begin with it in your Student Notebook.

Underline the word-part in each of your words and write their definitions. Think, and be ready to tell your teacher how each definition relates to the meaning of the word-part.

When you are finished, pick one of your words and write a sentence that uses it correctly.

🌿 Use at least three words.

🐾 Use at least six words.

E. Making Connections Geography Review   *Thinking Skills*

In Unit 2 you had an opportunity to learn about several important inventors, scientists, and events. Find the Making Connections Who or What Am I review in your Student Notebook and answer the questions.[2] Then make up additional "Who or What Am I?" questions for the topics listed at the bottom of the page.

People and events listed in the Word Bank will be used to answer more than one question. When you are finished, discuss your answers with your teacher.

F. Making Connections Spelling Review *Language Skills, Thinking Skills*

Look back at the spelling lists you made in Unit 2 and ask your teacher to choose the number of words assigned below. Then, write those words in your Student Notebook as your teacher dictates them. When you are finished, check your work and show your teacher how you did.

Add any words you had trouble spelling to the Unit 6 Ongoing Spelling List in your Student Notebook. Also, if you misspell words in your everyday writing, be sure to add them to that list as well. Remember to practice spelling the words on your ongoing list from time to time during this unit.

🌿 Choose 12 words.

🐾 Choose 16 words.

🐾 Choose 18 words.

G. Music
Thinking Skills

Read pages 50 and 51 in the *Basix Recorder Method* to learn more about, and practice, *time signatures*. Write the names of notes you're not sure of above the staffs on those pages and practice playing the melodies.

Don't forget to listen to the *Recorder Method* CD tracks shown on page 51 to hear samples of the lesson and use your Finger Placement Tabs if you need to.

Be sure to spend about 20 minutes a day practicing what you have learned!

H. Independent Reading & Record Keeping
Thinking Skills

Review the Lesson 2 At A Glance chart in your Student Notebook to see if all the work you've done in this part has been checked off. Also, make sure the Student Notebook pages you worked on are dated and complete.

When you are finished, choose something to read that you will enjoy. Then find a quiet, comfortable place and read for the following length of time:

🖐🖐 🐾 30 minutes   🐾 35 minutes

Be sure to write down what you read today on the Reading Log in your Student Notebook.

Lesson 2, Part 3

> ### ♪ Steps for Thinking Review ♪
>
> (Making Connections Unit, Lesson 3)
>
> 1. Inventors often had to endure unpleasant or trying circumstances to have the opportunity to accomplish their goals.
>
> 2. The mistakes of others give us opportunities to put our own beliefs to the test. They are not an excuse for making mistakes ourselves.
>
> 3. Choosing to stand by someone going through a hard time and have faith in them is a way of being brave yourself.
>
> 4. Continuous, or lifelong, learning is necessary for continued development in business.

Read the Steps for Thinking that you are reviewing today. Tell your teacher what you think each step means, and:

🐾 Choose two of the steps and give an example of how each one was true for any of the units.

🐾 Give an example of how each step was true for any of the units.

🐾 Can you think of a time when one of the above Steps for Thinking applied to your life or to the life of someone else in your family? Share it with your teacher.

A. **Copywork & Dictation**   *Language Skills*
Together with your teacher, follow the directions below and choose a passage from today's reading assignment in either *The Story of Inventions* or *Alan Shepard*. Read the passage silently and show your teacher any words you don't know. Practice saying those words aloud until you are familiar with them. Then copy or write the passage while your teacher dictates it.

🐾 at least five sentences

🐾 at least seven sentences

B. **Reader**   *Language Skills, History*
The Story of Inventions: page 209 through the top of page 210

Scan the assigned passage for any words you don't know, and write them on a piece of scrap paper. Read over any section titles included in the passage—and then, as you read or listen to a section, think about how it relates to its title.

When you are finished reading, select a section title and write one or two sentences in your Student Notebook telling how the section illustrates (or tells about) it.

🌵 Read the assigned passage aloud.

🐾🐾 Read the assigned passage silently.

C. **Read-Aloud & Narration**   *History, Language Skills, Thinking Skills*
Alan Shepard: page 65, paragraph 2 ("Alan and Louise enjoyed…") through page 73, paragraph 1

Follow the instructions below for your level. Then, in your own words, tell what happened in the story from Alan's point of view. Try to remember as many details as possible. Tell what you think is the most important event in the passage.

🌵 Listen carefully to the assigned passage.

🐾🐾 Read the assigned passage aloud.

D. **Making Connections Vocabulary Review**   *Language Skills*
Once again, look over the vocabulary cards you made in Unit 2 (*MC*). Then give them to your teacher and ask her to show you their picture sides, one at a time. Tell her what the picture or clue means and then name the word written on the other side. If you can, tell what part of speech it is. Give yourself one point for correctly naming a word and one point for knowing its part of speech. Keep track of your points because you will play again in Part 5!

E. **Science**   *Thinking Skills*
Human Body Basics, Immune System: Lymphatic System

As you read through the assigned pages, choose words that are new or unfamiliar and make vocabulary cards for them as directed. Keep your science cards separate from other vocabulary.

🌵 at least three words   🐾🐾 at least four words

Read and discuss the information in the passage with your teacher, and do the *Labwork 3-4* activities. The pages you need to complete these activities are in your Student Notebook.

When you are finished, look at *Examine This* projects 3 and 4 at the end of the chapter, and:

🌵 Choose one to complete.

🐾🐾 Complete both.

Do as much as you can, but you don't have to finish the projects in this part. You will have other opportunities to work on them, such as during Part 5 and in your spare time.

F. Science Fair Project

Language Skills, Thinking Skills

In this part, continue working on the background research paper that you began in Part 1. Finish your rough draft if you haven't done so already.

Then, take some time to review your paper sentence by sentence. Check to make sure:

- it says what you would like it to say;

- the information in it is as accurate as you know how to make it;

- it uses a variety of words (not the same ones over and over—use a dictionary and thesaurus if you think they would be helpful!);

- and its spelling, grammar, and punctuation are as correct as you know how to make them.

Make corrections and rewrite portions that are not as you want them to be. When you are finished, quietly read the report aloud to yourself and listen to the words. If everything sounds good to you, neatly re-write, or type and print, your background research report. Then, on another piece of paper, write, or type and print, the bibliographic information for the sources you actually used in your report.

While creating your science project, use a report cover with prong fasteners to keep your papers together. Place your background research report and its bibliography in this Project Notebook.

G. Music & Review

History, Thinking Skills

Look back at pages 81 through 83 in *The Story of the Orchestra*.

Then, follow the directions in Appendix D to make two Orchestra Story question and answer cards about the glockenspiel, two about the celesta, and two about the tubular bells. Label each answer card with the name of instrument it is about (in the upper left corner). Do not label the question cards—and remember to write the questions in your Student Notebook in the correct order.

Check the directions in Lesson 1, Part 3G and review the Orchestra Story cards you made in Unit 2, Making Connections.

Then follow the same directions to review your Orchestra Story cards from Units 4 and 5, and those you have made so far in Unit 6.

H. **Independent Reading & Record Keeping**   *Thinking Skills*

Review the Lesson 2 At A Glance chart in your Student Notebook to see if all the work you've done in this part has been checked off. Also, make sure the Student Notebook pages you worked on are dated and complete.

When you are finished, choose something to read that you will enjoy. Then find a quiet, comfortable place and read for the following length of time:

ꝩꝨ ꝩ 30 minutes   ꝩ 35 minutes

Be sure to write down what you read today on the Reading Log in your Student Notebook.

H. Completing the reading log and At A Glance each day gives your student a sense of accomplishment, as well as the opportunity to work independently.

Lesson 2, Part 4

> ## ꝩ Steps for Thinking Review ꝩ
>
> ### (Making Connections Unit, Lesson 4)
>
> 1. If you want to become your most successful, you will have to evaluate your abilities honestly.
>
> 2. Just because you are not good at something to begin with doesn't mean you shouldn't practice and become better at it.
>
> 3. Small beginnings lead to doing bigger things. Start by doing what you think is right, even if it is a small thing.
>
> 4. Most events in history have a direct affect on the economy of the people and place where the events occurs.

Read the Steps for Thinking that you are reviewing today. Tell your teacher what you think each step means, and:

ꝩꝨ Choose two of the steps and give an example of how each one was true for any of the units.

ꝩꝨ ꝩ Give an example of how each step was true for any of the units.

ꝩ Can you think of a time when one of the above Steps for Thinking applied to your life, or to the life of someone else in your family? Share it with your teacher.

A. **Copywork & Dictation**   *Language Skills*

Look back at the Steps for Thinking from Unit 2 that you have reviewed so far in this lesson. Pick several as directed below, and either copy or write them from dictation into your Student Notebook.

Pick four steps.

Pick five steps.

B. **Reader**   *Language Skills, History*

The Story of Inventions: page 210, paragraph 1 through page 211

Scan the assigned passage for any words you don't know, and write them on a piece of scrap paper. Read over any section titles included in the passage—and then, as you read or listen to a section, think about how it relates to its title.

When you are finished reading, select a section title and write one or two sentences in your Student Notebook telling how the section illustrates (or tells about) it.

Read the assigned passage aloud.

Read the assigned passage silently.

C. **Read-Aloud & Discussion**   *History, Language Skills, Thinking Skills*

Alan Shepard: page 73, paragraph 2 ("Before long Alan…") to the top of page 83

After reading or listening to the read-aloud assignment, talk with your teacher and try to predict what will happen in the future based on what you know of the characters and events. Write your predictions in your Student Notebook. Later you will look back and see if they were accurate. Try not to peek ahead!

Listen carefully as your teacher reads the assigned passage; then write down three predictions.

Read the assigned passage aloud; then write down at least four predictions.

C. Encourage your children to consider how accurate their predictions have been about the stories. Have they been mostly right? Then it may be time to step it up. Challenge them to go a little further out on the limb and give their predictions about which they may have less information or confidence. Model this step by making some predictions of your own about the story. Check and see how accurate these more adventurous predictions turn out to be!

D. **Making Connections Word Building Review**   *Language Skills*

Print the Word Builder Review 2 cards (for your level) from the Student Resources CD and cut them out. Mix them up and place them face down in a stack. Then take turns drawing cards, one at a time, with at least one other player. When a player draws a card, he or she must tell what word-part is in that word (one point), what language it comes from (one point), and the meaning of the word (one point). See how many points you can get!

For the answers, look back at the Word Building pages for Unit 2 in your Student Notebook.

E. Making Connections History/Economics Review *Thinking Skills*

Gather or reprint the Supply and Demand 3 game cards that you made in Unit 2. Reread them and match the words with their definitions and examples in rows of three. Then play either Supply and Demand Concentration or Go Fish Matching.

Look at the Unit Review Graphic Organizer in your Student Notebook (Lesson 1, Part 4E), and discuss the questions it asks with your teacher. Then fill in the boxes in the Making Connections column as best you can.

When you are finished, discuss what you wrote with your teacher and explain why you answered as you did.

F. Writing *Language Skills, Thinking Skills*

After every chapter in *The Story of Inventions*, there is a list of Comprehension Questions. Their purpose is to determine if you understand what you have read, and are able to draw certain conclusions based on your understanding. The questions focus on main ideas expressed in the sections.

Read over the Comprehension Questions at the end of Chapter 15. Then refer back to the story to find their answers and use complete sentences to write them in your Student Notebook. (If you need help remembering how to answer questions, look back at the Writing lessons in Unit 1.)

When you are finished, check your answers with *The Story of Inventions Answer Key*. Are they in agreement? Were there things you left out? Evaluate your answers and tell your teacher if you were on target.

🐾 Create two more questions for Chapter 15; make sure they target main ideas, not just details. After writing your questions, create an Answer Key.

G. Art *Thinking Skills*

By now your science topic is finalized, and you have finished gathering basic information on it and writing the background research paper. No doubt you have learned a good bit about the subject you chose and have an idea what your project will involve.

In this section, as you begin work on your Claymation video or flipbook, concentrate on the events that will take place in it to illustrate, highlight, or explain some part of your project. You wrote a few ideas in your Student Notebook during the last lesson, so look back at those and see if you still like them. Is there one that seems much better than the others? Or perhaps you have a better idea now! To get started, follow the directions in Appendix D to learn how to make a storyboard.

G. When your student undertakes an activity such as this, there are many wonderful thinking skills taking place. The student is imagining, recording, and categorizing information, and then interpreting that information. All accomplished while doing something fun!

Lapbook Activity

H. **Independent Reading & Record Keeping**   *Thinking Skills*

Review the Lesson 2 At A Glance chart in your Student Notebook to see if all the work you've done in this part has been checked off. Also, make sure the Student Notebook pages you worked on are dated and complete.

When you are finished, choose something to read that you will enjoy. Then find a quiet, comfortable place and read for the following length of time:

ᵛᵞ ᵛ 30 minutes   ᵛ 35 minutes

Be sure to write down what you read today on the Reading Log in your Student Notebook.

Lesson 2, Part 5

۞ Steps for Thinking Review ۞

(Making Connections Unit, Lesson 5)

1. It is important to listen to others who are wise. There is also a time to decide what you believe for yourself.

2. Those who risk public failure have a special feeling of gratefulness to those who stay true friends no matter what.

3. The measure of someone's life is not just personal success. Service to others, no matter how small or great, is just as important as great riches or fame.

4. National events, both happy and sad, require families and communities to make decisions about how money is spent.

Read the Steps for Thinking that you are reviewing today. Tell your teacher what you think each step means, and:

ᵛᵞ Choose two of the steps and give an example of how each one was true for any of the units.

ᵛ ᵛ Give an example of how each step was true for any of the units.

ᵛ Can you think of a time when one of the above Steps for Thinking applied to your life, or to the life of someone else in your family? Share it with your teacher.

This part is set aside for completion of any work left undone from the lesson, and review of concepts and content. It is also a time to expand the work of the lesson with practice and games.

- Give your teacher your stack of vocabulary cards for Unit 2, Making Connections. Ask her to show you each word and then tell her its meaning and see if you can use it correctly in a sentence. When you are finished reviewing, choose five cards and try to act out each word so that others can guess what it is. Have other players choose five words and take turns acting them out and guessing. You get a point for guessing a word or having a word guessed. See who can get the most points.

- Review your Making Connections spelling words. Then ask your teacher to choose the number of words indicated below for your level. Write each word in your Student Notebook as she dictates it. When you are finished, look at your word list and make corrections as needed. Show your teacher how you did.

        16 words   20 words

- Follow the directions in the *Human Body Basics* Instuctions to play the Word Power vocabulary game, and complete the System Savvy puzzles in your Student Notebook.[3] Then work on any *Examine This* projects you have not yet completed, or on your science project.

- Look back at pages 48-51 in the *Basix Recorder Method* and review any exercises that may still be giving you trouble. Choose several tracks on the *Recorder Method* CD and play along with them. Be sure to spend at least 20 minutes practicing!

- Review the Lesson 2 At A Glance chart in your Student Notebook to see if all the work you've done in this part has been checked off. If you did an Enrichment activity or other extra work in this lesson, be sure to write it on the lines next to the chart.

- Follow the directions in Appendix D and play Making Connections Bingo.

- Complete the Reach for the Stars Word Scramble located in your Student Notebook.[4]

Enrichment Activities:

1. Add to your Medical Breakthroughs Timeline book by briefly researching the following people, places, and/or events and adding them to it. You can do this by simply writing their names in the correct places; or you can draw or trace pictures and symbols that you find during your research, and then color, cut, and paste them to the timeline. If you think of other medical advances you would like to include, feel free to do so!

Enrichment activities and additional resources are suggestions for ways your child can learn more about a topic of interest, dig deeper into a subject, or gain research skills. Please feel free to use these activities as guides for your child to complete as directed, or amended to better fit his particular abilities, needs, or interests.

Some of these people may be famous for other things, but you should concentrate only on their medical contribution(s). At the bottom of each timeline page, write one or two sentences describing the contributions or significance of the individuals, places, or events on that page.

- Robert Boyle
- William Harvey
- Sir Christopher Wren
- Robert Lower
- Anton van Leewenhoek

Additional Resources:

Alan Shepard: Higher and Faster by Janet and Geoff Benge

Charles Lindbergh: A Human Hero by James Cross Giblin

Answers

1. Answer key is in Appendix C.

2. Answer key is in Appendix C.

3. Answer key is in the *Human Body Basics* Answer Key.

4. Answer key is in Appendix C.

Lesson 3, Part 1

❧ Materials ❧

- *Alan Shepard*
- *The New Way Things Work*
- *The Story of the Orchestra* book & CD
- *Basix Recorder Method*
- *Profiles from History, Volume 3*
- Recorder
- Activity (Part 1F)
  - Various items for science project
- Activity (Part 3)
  - Highlighter
- Activity (Part 4G)
  - Oil-based modeling clay (like Claytoons, VanAken, etc.)
  - Wax paper
  - 4 pieces of foam board OR large box
  - Packing tape
  - Small styrofoam balls or foil (if characters are "people")
  - Pipe cleaners (if characters are "people")
  - Paint and/or markers

A. Copywork & Dictation   *Language Skills*

Together with your teacher, follow the directions below and choose a passage from today's reading assignment in either *Alan Shepard* or *The New Way Things Work*. Read the passage silently and show your teacher any words you don't know. Practice saying those words aloud until you are familiar with them. Then copy or write the passage while your teacher dictates it.

� at least five sentences

🐾 at least seven sentences

B. Reader   *Language Skills, History*

The New Way Things Work: Sections 3, 4, or 5

Choose the number of inventions assigned below from Sections 3, 4, or 5 in *The New Way Things Work*, and read about them. Then fill out the Flow Charts in your Student Notebook, telling how each of your selections work.

To do this, you may want to list the various steps involved in each invention's operation on scrap paper, and number them. That way you can adjust them if necessary (by combining, simplifying, or extending) so you have the correct number of steps for the Flow Charts.

� Choose one invention.

🖐 Choose two inventions.

🐾 Choose three inventions.

C. Read-Aloud & Narration   *History, Language Skills, Thinking Skills*

Alan Shepard: page 83, paragraph 1 ("Then on September 13…") to the bottom of page 92

Follow the directions below to read or listen to the above passage. Then, in your own words, tell what happened in the portion you are assigned. Try to remember as many details as possible—if necessary you may reread, or listen as your teacher rereads, the part you are to retell.

� Listen carefully as your teacher reads the above assignment aloud. Choose two pages to retell.

🖐🐾 Read the above assignment aloud, and then retell the entire passage.

D. Perseverance Pays Off Vocabulary Review   *Language Skills*

Look back at the vocabulary cards you made in Unit 3. You can tell which ones they are because you wrote *PPO* in their upper left corners. Go through them and see if you can remember any of the definitions. Then try using each one correctly in a sentence.

Connect Learning to Life

Charts provide information at a glance. It is important for your child to be able to read a chart and interpret the information given, and it is a simple step from reading a chart to making one. Once you have completed this activity, be on the lookout for other charts used in daily life and point them out to your child.

When you are finished reviewing, choose five cards and try to act out each word so that others can guess what it is. Have other players choose five words and take turns acting them out and guessing. You get a point for guessing a word or having a word guessed. See who can get the most points.

E. Educators have many different feelings about grading. For a child who struggles, grading can be very discouraging. For a child who is competitive, grading may seem like a good idea, but not if the child is overly focused on competing with others. Better to focus on personal improvement than competition with peers. Keep grading in perspective.

Lapbook Activity

E. Perseverance Pays Off Science Review   *Thinking Skills*

Complete the Tools and Technology Matching review in your Student Notebook.[1] When you are finished, tell your teacher what you remember about each thing named in the activity. If you need help remembering and your teacher agrees, you can look back at the chapters covered during Unit 3 in *The World of Tools and Technology*, and the work you did in your Student Notebook.

F. Science Fair Project — Uma I'll do this pack —sp w/ *Language Skills, Thinking Skills*

You may have many ideas as to how you can accomplish your science project, or you may have none. However, as you get down to actually planning it in this section and the next, try to be realistic. Usually two, and occasionally three, sections in each lesson of this unit are devoted to working on the project, but you can (and probably should) work on it other times as well. With that in mind, try to set goals that are reachable in terms of available time, expense, information, and safety.

In Lesson 1, Part 1 you were asked to check out rules for science projects. Take a minute now to copy or print the guidelines from either your local school system or support group, or the Society for Science, and add them to your Project Notebook. You will want to refer to these rules from time to time to make sure your project stays within the guidelines.

Once that is out of the way decide on good name for your project. Try to make it both catchy and descriptive. When you're satisfied, write the project's name on the page in your Student Notebook.

Every science project begins with a question, and involves finding or proving an answer, or hypothesis. Since you have done background research on the topic, you should have enough information to either decide on or adjust the question for your project to answer. As you consider possible questions, try to think of one that expresses something you're interested in finding out or proving. Your question should be "testable," meaning you have to be able to design some way to find the answer. In a scientific "test," the parts or processes that can be changed are called variables, and parts that stay the same are called controls. In a "fair test," only one variable is changed at a time while everything else remains the same.

In addition to making sure your question is testable, try to make it as specific, or detailed, as possible. For example, you could ask something like,

"How does room temperature affect grades?"

While this question might relate to the project, it's a bit too general. Instead, try narrowing its focus to something like,

> "How do room temperatures over 90° and under 60° affect a student's concentration while studying?"

The question's answer, or **hypothesis**, is your best guess at what the research will reveal. There is usually some reason for forming a hypothesis, like observation, personal experience, or things you learned in your background research. When you have decided on a question and hypothesis, write them in your Student Notebook.

Then spend some time thinking of a way to test your question and prove the hypothesis. Your test should be an experiment or process that will give you results that can be measured in some way. If you're stumped, discuss the problem with your teacher. Also, you might find some ideas you can adapt to your needs in science project books or on websites. If you can't think of anything, try adjusting your question or hypothesis a bit, and try again. Once you decide on a method that meets your needs, write what you plan to do in your Student Notebook.

A few things to keep in mind while planning your experiment are:

- The reliability of your results will be greater if you use more test subjects (people or things) than are strictly necessary;

- If you're making comparisons, get as much information from as many sources as possible;

- If you invent or build something, test it often enough to be positive it works;

- Repeat your experiment several times to be sure of the results.

Decide what variables (things you can change to see what happens) and controls (things that will remain the same) you will use, how many times you will conduct your test, and how long you plan to spend on this part of the project. Write those things in your Student Notebook. Then make a list of all the items you need in order to begin gathering data. If possible, try to get the necessary things before Part 3 so you can get started!

G. Music   *History, Thinking Skills*

With your teacher, read pages 85 through 87 in *The Story of the Orchestra* and discuss the information about keyboard instruments and the organ. Then listen to part of the "Toccata and Fugue in D Minor" on Track 35. Were you able to hear the instrument featured this track? How did the music make you feel? What did you enjoy or dislike about it?

When you are finished, listen carefully to Track 35 again. Then, draw and color a picture in your Student Notebook of the image this music brings to your mind.

H. Independent Reading & Record Keeping　　*Thinking Skills*

Review the Lesson 3 At A Glance chart in your Student Notebook to see if all the work you've done in this part has been checked off. Also, make sure the Student Notebook pages you worked on are dated and complete.

When you are finished, choose something to read that you will enjoy. Then find a quiet, comfortable place and read for the following length of time:

🐾🖐 30 minutes　　　　🐾 35 minutes

Be sure to write down what you read today on the Reading Log in your Student Notebook.

Lesson 3, Part 2

A. Copywork & Dictation　　*Language Skills*

Together with your teacher, follow the directions below and choose a passage from today's reading assignment in either *Alan Shepard* or *The New Way Things Work*. Read the passage silently and show your teacher any words you don't know. Practice saying those words aloud until you are familiar with them. Then copy or write the passage while your teacher dictates it.

🐾 at least five sentences　　🖐🐾 at least seven sentences

B. Reader　　*Language Skills, History*

The New Way Things Work: Sections 3, 4, or 5

Choose the number of inventions assigned below from Sections 3, 4, or 5 in *The New Way Things Work* and read about them. Then fill out the Flow Charts in your Student Notebook, telling how each of your selections work.

To do this, you may want to list the various steps involved in each invention's operation on scrap paper, and number them. That way you can adjust them if necessary (by combining, simplifying, or extending) so you have the correct number of steps for the Flow Charts.

🐾 Choose one invention.

🖐 Choose two inventions.

🐾 Choose three inventions.

A. To help your children make the transition from copying to dictation, begin gradually. Ask your children to choose a sentence and write it after you read it to them. Allow them to write on a non-permanent surface, like a chalkboard, dry erase board, or scrap of paper. This will help make the point that it is truly practice, and not something you will keep and score. They can then check what they write against the text. You can build confidence for gaining a new skill this way. Over time, they will see that they are getting better at it, and often will then be willing to make the switch to dictation.

Lapbook Activity

C. Read-Aloud & Discussion　　　*History, Language Skills, Thinking Skills*

Alan Shepard: page 92, last paragraph ("Not long after…") through page 99

Follow the directions below to read or listen to the above assignment. Then make up the assigned number of questions about the part of the story you just read or heard. Write down your questions and ask your teacher to answer them. After discussing her thoughts, write down the best possible answer in your Student Notebook. Be sure to use complete sentences.

When you are finished, look back at the predictions you made during Lesson 2, Part 4. Were you able to predict what would happen? Be sure to mark the "Came to Pass" box for each prediction when it does happen.

Listen carefully as your teacher reads the above assignment aloud. Make up three questions.

Read the above assignment aloud; then make up four questions.

D. Word Building　　　*Language Skills, Thinking Skills*

Throughout *Paths of Progress* you have learned about words that have their roots in the Latin and Greek languages. Now, continue your study of word-parts by looking at the Rummy Roots Word List and choosing one that has not yet been covered.

Find the word-part you chose in the dictionary. Then write the language from which it comes, and list words that begin with it in your Student Notebook.

Underline the word-part in each of your words and write their definitions. Think, and be ready to tell your teacher how each definition relates to the meaning of the word-part.

When you are finished, pick one of your words and write a sentence that uses it correctly.

List at least three words.

List at least six words.

Lapbook Activity

E. Perseverance Pays Off History Review　　　*Thinking Skills*

In Unit 3 you had an opportunity to learn about several important inventors, scientists, and events. Find the Perseverance Pays Off Who or What Am I review in your Student Notebook and answer the questions.[2] Then make up additional "Who or What Am I?" questions for the topics listed at the bottom of the page.

People and events listed in the Word Bank will be used to answer more than one question. When you are finished, discuss your answers with your teacher.

Jackie Robinson made history as the first black player drafted into major league baseball. He was a man of character who inspired many, and helped open the door for other black athletes. Find out more about his hard-won victories in *Profiles from History, Volume 3*.

F. There are many ways to support the brain's ability to remember words. Some fun ways are to make up associations to a funny picture or story, or pronounce the word so you hear its letters. If your children have difficulty spelling, encourage them to notice something special about the word, such as a smaller word inside it.

F. **Perseverance Pays Off Spelling Review**   *Language Skills*

Look back at the spelling lists you made in Unit 3, and ask your teacher to choose the number of words assigned below. Then, write those words in your Student Notebook as your teacher dictates them. When you are finished, check your work and show your teacher how you did.

Add any words you had trouble spelling to the Unit 6 Ongoing Spelling List in your Student Notebook. Also, if you misspell words in your everyday writing, be sure to add them to that list as well. Remember to practice spelling the words on your ongoing list from time to time during this unit.

🐾 Choose 12 words.

🐾 Choose 16 words.

🐾 Choose 18 words.

G. **Music**   *Thinking Skills*

Continue to practice *time signatures* on pages 52 and 53. Write the names of notes you're not sure of above the staffs on those pages and practice playing the melodies.

Don't forget to listen to the *Recorder Method* CD tracks shown on page 53 to hear samples of the lesson and use your Finger Placement Tabs if you need to.

Be sure to spend about 20 minutes a day practicing what you have learned!

H. **Independent Reading & Record Keeping**   *Thinking Skills*

Review the Lesson 3 At A Glance chart in your Student Notebook to see if all the work you've done in this part has been checked off. Also, make sure the Student Notebook pages you worked on are dated and complete.

When you are finished, choose something to read that you will enjoy. Then find a quiet, comfortable place and read for the following length of time:

🐾🐾 30 minutes   🐾 35 minutes

Be sure to write down what you read today on the Reading Log in your Student Notebook.

Lesson 3, Part 3

A. **Copywork & Dictation**   *Language Skills*

Together with your teacher, follow the directions below and choose a passage from today's reading assignment in either *Alan Shepard* or *The New Way Things Work* Read the passage silently and show your teacher any words you don't know. Practice saying those words aloud until you are familiar with them. Then copy or write the passage while your teacher dictates it.

🌱 at least five sentences

🐾 at least seven sentences

B. **Reader**   *Language Skills, History*

The New Way Things Work: Sections 3, 4, or 5

Choose the number of inventions assigned below from Sections 3, 4, or 5 in *The New Way Things Work*, and read about them. Then fill out the Flow Charts in your Student Notebook, telling how each of your selections work.

To do this, you may want to list the various steps involved in each invention's operation on scrap paper, and number them. That way you can adjust them if necessary (by combining, simplifying, or extending) so you have the correct number of steps for the Flow Charts.

🌱 Choose one invention.

🐾 Choose two inventions.

🐾 Choose three inventions.

C. **Read-Aloud & Narration**   *History, Language Skills, Thinking Skills*

Alan Shepard: page 101 (Chapter 9) through page 109, paragraph 1

Follow the instructions below for your level. Then, in your own words, tell what happened in the story from Alan's point of view. Try to remember as many details as possible. Tell what you think is the most important event in the passage.

🌱 Listen carefully to the assigned passage.

🐾 Read the assigned passage aloud.

C. It can be difficult for some children to identify main events. When they retell a passage as if they were a character in the story, it is easier to identify what may have been most important, or caused the greatest change. Trying to see a situation through someone else's eyes helps children to connect with those key events that would have affected them the most.

D. **Perseverance Pays Off Vocabulary Review**   *Language Skills*

Once again, look over the vocabulary cards you made in Unit 3 (*PPO*). Then give them to your teacher and ask her to show you their picture sides, one at a time. Tell her what the picture or clue means, and then name the word written on the other side. If you can, tell what part of speech it is. Give yourself one point for correctly naming a word and one point for knowing its part of speech. Keep track of your points because you will play again in Part 5!

Lapbook Activity

E. Science   *Thinking Skills*

Human Body Basics, Human Development: beginning of chapter, DNA, & Genetics

As you read through the assigned pages, choose words that are new or unfamiliar and make vocabulary cards for them as directed. Keep your science cards separate from other vocabulary.

🌿🌿 at least three words

🐾🐾 at least four words

Read and discuss the information in the passage with your teacher and do the *Labwork 1* and *2* activities. The pages you need to complete these activities are in your Student Notebook.

When you are finished, complete *Examine This* project 1 at the end of the chapter, and :

🐾🐾 Work on *Examine This* project 2.

🐾 Work on *Examine This* project 3.

Do as much as you can, but you don't have to finish the project in this part. You will have other opportunities to work on it, such as during Part 5 and in your spare time.

Lapbook Activity

F. Science Fair Project *Do with mom*   *Language Skills, Thinking Skills*

As you move into the testing stage of your science project, begin keeping a special **log**, or journal. This can be kept on regular notebook paper, and will be added to your Project Notebook.

Begin by making a "to do" list that includes everything you have to do to complete the project on the first page of your log. If you need to shop for supplies, add it to the list; if you need to build a piece of equipment, or ask friends to participate in an experimental group, add those things. Then, as you accomplish each task, check it off. There's a page in your Student Notebook for this list.

Next write a step-by-step guide to the procedure, which is the plan of action, you will use to set up and test your experiment. This is a list of every action you plan to take to achieve your goal. It should be detailed enough that another person could follow it and do your project exactly as you did. Write this Procedure Plan on plain notebook paper and add it to your Project Notebook.

For example:

1. Set up eight cups:
   a. 4 cups ½ full of potting soil
   b. 4 cups ½ full of sandy soil
   c. mark cups "P" or "S"

2. Plant three seeds in each cup and water daily

3. When seeds sprout, transfer to individual cups:
   a. 6 sprouts from "P" cups to cups ½ full of potting soil
      1. mark and number cups " 1-P-P," etc.
      2. water daily
      3. measure daily

…and so forth to the end of the experiment.

After that, just concentrate on writing down everything you do (that relates to the project) in your project log. In fact, if you want to you can go back to Lesson 1 and add all the things you have done so far. You don't have to use complete sentences, but your entries need to record your activities and be clear enough for others to tell what you were doing each step of the way. You also don't have to write something every day, but be sure to date the entry when you do log information. You can include sketches of your observations if you want, along with any measurements or other types of data you collect.

Think about how you want to present the results of your project so you can plan. This is important now, because if your display includes pictures or other media, you will need to gather those things as you go. Your presentation can include a backboard, charts, tables, graphs, posters, power point, drawings, photos, videos, and on and on. Start looking around at science project books and websites to get good ideas, and begin making your plan!

If you have not yet begun setting up your experiment and collecting data, you should do so as soon as possible.

G. Music & Review
History, Thinking Skills

Look back at pages 85 through 87 in *The Story of the Orchestra*.

Then, follow the directions in Appendix D to make two Orchestra Story question and answer cards about the keyboard instruments, and four about the organ. Put the small letter *K* (for keyboard) in the upper left corner of those answer cards. Label each of the organ answer cards with the name of that instrument (in the upper left corner). Do not label the question cards—and remember to write the questions in your Student Notebook in the correct order.

Check the directions in Lesson 1, Part 3G and review the Orchestra Story cards you made in Unit 3, Perseverance Pays Off.

Then follow the same directions to review your Orchestra Story cards from Units 4 and 5, and those you have made so far in Unit 6.

Thinking Skills Reminder
You evaluate information when you decide that one thing is more important than another.

H. **Independent Reading & Record Keeping**   *Thinking Skills*

Review the Lesson 3 At A Glance chart in your Student Notebook to see if all the work you've done in this part has been checked off. Also, make sure the Student Notebook pages you worked on are dated and complete.

When you are finished, choose something to read that you will enjoy. Then find a quiet, comfortable place and read for the following length of time:

    🖐 30 minutes   🐾 35 minutes

Be sure to write down what you read today on the Reading Log in your Student Notebook.

Lesson 3, Part 4

A. **Copywork & Dictation**   *Language Skills*

Together with your teacher, follow the directions below and choose a passage from today's reading assignment in either *Alan Shepard* or *The New Story of Inventions*. Read the passage silently and show your teacher any words you don't know. Practice saying those words aloud until you are familiar with them. Then copy or write the passage while your teacher dictates it.

🌿 at least five sentences

🐾 at least seven sentences

B. **Reader**   *Language Skills, History*

The New Way Things Work: Sections 3, 4, or 5

Choose the number of inventions assigned below from Sections 3, 4, or 5 in *The New Way Things Work* and read about them. Then fill out the Flow Charts in your Student Notebook, telling how each of your selections work.

To do this, you may want to list the various steps involved in each invention's operation on scrap paper, and number them. Adjust them if necessary (by combining, simplifying, or extending) so you have the correct number of steps for the Flow Charts.

🌿 Choose one invention.

🐾 Choose two inventions.

🐾 Choose three inventions.

C. **Read-Aloud & Discussion**　　　*History, Language Skills, Thinking Skills*
Alan Shepard: page 109, paragraph 2 ("Meanwhile, Alan kept…") to the top of page 118

After reading or listening to the read-aloud assignment, talk with your teacher and try to predict what will happen in the future, based on what you know of the characters and events. Write your predictions in your Student Notebook. Later you will look back and see if they were accurate. Try not to peek ahead!

Listen carefully as your teacher reads the assigned passage. Write down three predictions.

Read the assigned passage aloud; write down at least four predictions.

D. **Perseverance Pays Off Word Building Review**　　　*Language Skills*
Print the Word Builder Review 3 cards (for your level) from the Student Resources CD and cut them out. Mix them up and place them face down in a stack. Then take turns drawing cards, one at a time, with at least one other player. When a player draws a card, he or she must tell what word-part is in that word (one point), what language it comes from (one point), and the meaning of the word (one point). See how many points you can get!

For the answers, look back at the Word Building pages for Unit 3 in your Student Notebook.

E. **Perseverance Pays Off History/Economics Review**　*Thinking Skills*
Look at the Unit Review Graphic Organizer in your Student Notebook (Lesson 1, Part 4E) and discuss the questions it asks with your teacher. Then fill in the boxes in the Perseverance Pays Off column as best you can.

When you are finished, discuss what you wrote with your teacher, and explain why you answered as you did.

Dwight D. Eisenhower was the 34th President of the United States, from 1957 to 1961. As such, he was privileged to lead this country through the early years of the Space Program. Find out more about President Eisenhower by reading his story in *Profiles from History, Volume 3*.

F. **Grammar Review**　　　*Language Skills, Thinking Skills*
To review your editing knowledge, print and cut out the "You Can Find Me" cards from your Student Resources CD. Then follow the directions in Appendix C to play the game.

For added difficulty, choose one card at a time and have a race to see who can be first to find an example of that usage in print. The finder must read and explain the usage on his or her card.

C. There are many purposes in reading biographies. One is to learn about a certain individual's life, another is to read about history as it related to that individual, and a third purpose is to provide inspiration for the next generation. People are not perfect, but the individuals chosen for this text have accomplished something worthy of their consideration. Encourage your children to think about what the person accomplished and the challenge set before them. Never pass up the opportunity to inspire your children. It makes a great difference when they know others have gone before them, persevered, and been successful.

F. Brief, spaced review is the best kind. It keeps learning fresh and it helps your child continue to connect new learning to previous knowledge. It also builds memory skills naturally.

Lapbook Activity

G. Art

In Lesson 2 you worked on creating a storyboard for your Claymation project. If you haven't yet decided what you want your story to focus on, or how you want it to progress, do so now. Make sure your storyboard shows all the stages and changes you intend to photograph.

When you are finished, follow the directions in Appendix D to begin making the set (setting, background) for your video or flipbook, and any characters or objects you will need. It is important to complete them before Part 4 of the next lesson so that you can begin photographing.

H. Independent Reading & Record Keeping

Review the Lesson 3 At A Glance chart in your Student Notebook to see if all the work you've done in this part has been checked off. Also, make sure the Student Notebook pages you worked on are dated and complete.

When you are finished, choose something to read that you will enjoy. Then find a quiet, comfortable place and read for the following length of time:

ᵛᵧ ᵂ 30 minutes   ᵂ 35 minutes

Be sure to write down what you read today on the Reading Log in your Student Notebook.

Lesson 3, Part 5

This part is set aside for completion of any work left undone from the lesson, and review of concepts and content. It is also a time to expand the work of the lesson with practice and games.

- Give your teacher your stack of vocabulary cards for Unit 3, Perseverance Pays Off. Ask her to show you each word, and then tell her its meaning and see if you can use it correctly in a sentence.

  When you are finished reviewing, choose five cards and try to act out each word so that others can guess what it is. Have other players choose five words and take turns acting them out and guessing. You get a point for guessing a word or having a word guessed. See who can get the most points.

- Review your Perseverance Pays Off spelling words. Then ask your teacher to choose the number of words indicated below for your level. Write each word in your Student Notebook as she dictates

You may want to begin previewing ideas for the unit-end presentation with your children. This will help everyone focus on similar goals for the presentation, as well as give them time to practice and get feedback for improvement.

it. When you are finished, look at your word list and make corrections as needed. Show your teacher how you did.

🌵 16 words   🐾 🐾 20 words

- Follow the directions in the *Human Body Basics* Instructions to play the Word Power vocabulary game, and complete the System Savvy puzzles in your Student Notebook.[3] Then work on any *Examine This* projects you have not yet completed, or on your science project.

- Look back at pages 50-53 in the *Basix Recorder Method* and review any exercises that may still be giving you trouble. Choose several tracks on the *Recorder Method* CD and play along with them. Be sure to spend at least 20 minutes practicing!

- Review the Lesson 3 At A Glance chart in your Student Notebook to see if all the work you've done in this part has been checked off. If you did an Enrichment activity or other extra work in this lesson, be sure to write it on the lines next to the chart.

- Follow the directions in Appendix D and play Perseverance Pays Off Bingo.

- Complete the Reach for the Stars Crossword located in your Student Notebook.[4]

Enrichment Activities:

1. Add to your Medical Breakthroughs Timeline book by briefly researching the following people, places, and events, and/or adding them to it. You can do this by simply writing their names in the correct places; or you can draw or trace pictures and symbols that you find during your research, and then color, cut, and paste them to the timeline. If you think of other medical advances you would like to include, feel free to do so!

   Some of these people may be famous for other things, but you should concentrate only on their medical contribution(s). At the bottom of each timeline page, write one or two sentences describing the contributions or significance of the individuals, places, or events on that page.

   - James Lind
   - Pennsylvania Hospital
   - Claudius Aymand
   - William Hewson
   - Joseph Priestley
   - Edward Jenner

Please preview any recommended movie to ensure its content is in line with your family's values and acceptable for your children to watch.

Additional Resources:

The Absent-Minded Professor movie (1961 version with Fred MacMurray)

Albert Einstein by Frieda Wishinsky

Answers

1. Answer key is in Appendix C.

2. Answer key is in Appendix C.

3. Answer key is in the *Human Body Basics* Answer Key.

4. Answer key is in Appendix C.

Lesson 4, Part 1

> ## ঠ **Steps for Thinking Review** ঠ
>
> (Cultivating Greatness Unit, Lesson 1)
>
> 1. Understanding something new comes from asking questions and discussing the answers.
>
> 2. Relating new information to something you already know makes learning easier. Connect new information to what you already know to help it find a place in what you remember.
>
> 3. New ideas and ways of doing things are often hard for people to accept.

Ask your children to read over the Steps for Thinking and then briefly restate each one in their own words, or give examples that they have heard or read. Remind them of any ideas or examples they thought of in the lesson when the Steps were first presented.

ঙ Materials ঙ

- *Alan Shepard*
- *The Story of Inventions*
- *The Story of the Orchestra* book & CD
- *Basix Recorder Method*
- Recorder
- Activity (Part 3):
      Yarn (small lengths in 7 colors)
- Activity (Part 4G)
      Oil-based modeling clay
      Camera
      Tripod (optional but helpful)

Read the Steps for Thinking that you are reviewing today. Tell your teacher what you think each step means, and:

🌱🌱 Choose two of the steps and give an example of how each one was true for any of the units.

🐾🐾 Give an example of how each step was true for any of the units.

🐾 Can you think of a time when one of the above Steps for Thinking applied to your life or to the life of someone else in your family? Share it with your teacher.

A. Copywork & Dictation   *Language Skills*

Together with your teacher, follow the directions below and choose a passage from today's reading assignment in either *The Story of Inventions* or *Alan Shepard*. Read the passage silently and show your teacher any words you don't know. Practice saying those words aloud until you are familiar with them. Then copy or write the passage while your teacher dictates it.

🌱🌱 at least five sentences

🐾🐾 at least seven sentences

B. Reader   *Language Skills, History*

The Story of Inventions: page 213 (Chapter 16) through the top of page 215

Scan the assigned passage for any words you don't know, and write them on a piece of scrap paper. Read over any section titles included in the passage—and then, as you read or listen to a section, think about how it relates to its title.

When you are finished reading, select a section title and write one or two sentences in your Student Notebook telling how the section illustrates (or tells about) it.

Read the assigned passage aloud.

Read the assigned passage silently.

C. Read-Aloud & Narration
History, Language Skills, Thinking Skills

Alan Shepard: page 118, paragraph 1 ("Finally it was time…") to the top of page 127

Follow the directions below to read or listen to the above passage. Then, in your own words, tell what happened in the portion you are assigned. Try to remember as many details as possible. If necessary you may reread, or listen as your teacher rereads, the part you are to retell.

Listen carefully as your teacher reads the above assignment aloud. Choose two pages to retell.

Read the above assignment aloud, and then retell the entire passage.

D. Why not just learn the meaning of a vocabulary word? Words learned individually are separate pieces of information. Words learned in the context of meaning are easier to remember and use correctly. Connecting each word to the way it was used in the story develops a more permanent link to that word in your child's mind.

D. Cultivating Greatness Vocabulary Review
Language Skills

Look back at the vocabulary cards you made in Unit 4. You can tell which ones they are because you wrote *CG* in their upper left corners. Go through them and see if you can remember any of the definitions. Then try using each one correctly in a sentence.

When you are finished reviewing, choose five cards and try to act out each word so that others can guess what it is. Have other players choose five words and take turns acting them out and guessing. You get a point for guessing a word or having a word guessed. See who can get the most points.

E. Cultivating Greatness Science Review
Thinking Skills

Complete the Human Body Matching review in your Student Notebook.[1] When you are finished, tell your teacher what you remember about each thing named in the activity. If you need help remembering and your teacher agrees, you can look back at the chapters covered during Unit 4 in the *Human Body Basics* book, and the work you did in your Student Notebook.

Lapbook Activity

F. Science Fair Project
Language Skills, Thinking Skills

In this section, continue working on your science project. Follow the Procedure Plan you made (in your Project Notebook) carefully. Be sure to change steps in the procedure if you find they aren't effective as written. Also, don't forget to record your activities, data, and observations in the project log.

Continue thinking about how you want to organize and present your work at the end of the project!

G. Music　　　　　　　　　　　　　　　*History, Thinking Skills*

Conclude your study of keyboard instruments by reading pages 88 through 91 in *The Story of the Orchestra* with your teacher and discussing the information about the piano and the harpsichord. Then listen to parts of the "Pathetique" sonata on Track 36 and the "Concerto Champetre" on Track 37 of your CD. Were you able to discriminate between the instruments featured on each track? How did the music make you feel? What did you enjoy or dislike about it?

When you are finished, listen carefully to Tracks 36 and 37 again and choose your favorite. Then, draw and color a picture in your Student Notebook of the image this music brings to your mind.

H. Independent Reading & Record Keeping　　　*Thinking Skills*

Review the Lesson 4 At A Glance chart in your Student Notebook to see if all the work you've done in this part has been checked off. Also, make sure the Student Notebook pages you worked on are dated and complete.

When you are finished, choose something to read that you will enjoy. Then find a quiet, comfortable place and read for the following length of time:

　　🌱🖐 30 minutes　　　　🐾 35 minutes

Be sure to write down what you read today on the Reading Log in your Student Notebook.

Lesson 4, Part 2

�h� Steps for Thinking Review ⸒
(Cultivating Greatness Unit, Lesson 2)

1. You are using the information you have when you make a plan and put it into action. Scientists often decide what they think will happen before trying a new plan.

2. You cannot expect a different result when doing things in the same way as before. A different result requires doing things differently.

3. Great satisfaction, or pleasure, comes from doing what you love to do, even if it is different from everyone else.

Read the Steps for Thinking that you are reviewing today. Tell your teacher what you think each step means, and:

🐾 Choose two of the steps and give an example of how each one was true for any of the units.

🐾 Give an example of how each step was true for any of the units.

🐾 Can you think of a time when one of the above Steps for Thinking applied to your life or to the life of someone else in your family? Share it with your teacher.

A. Copywork & Dictation   *Language Skills*
Look carefully at your assigned passage below, and read it silently. Show your teacher any words you don't know, and practice saying them aloud. Now read the passage aloud, or ask your teacher to read it to you.

When you are finished copying or writing from dictation, compare your copy to the text and make any needed corrections.

🐾 Copy or write as your teacher dictates from *The Story of Inventions*, page 216, paragraph 1 ("The ENIAC computer…").

🐾 Write as your teacher dictates from *The Story of Inventions*, page 216, paragraphs 1 and 2 ("The ENIAC computer…").

B. Reader   *Language Skills, History*
The Story of Inventions: page 215, paragraph 1 (Mauchly, Eckert,…) through page 216, paragraph 3

Teaching Tip

The process of copywork and dictation gives a teacher a great deal of information. Not only does it show what your child is missing, it shows what he is getting! Reading or hearing language, and then writing it down is a multi-step process that shows understanding, processing of information, and then translating that information into writing. Many times over my years as an educator, just giving a student a passage to copy or write from dictation has provided great insight into the student's ability to read, write, and comprehend. Make sure to take notice of all your child does correctly when using this process, and encourage him accordingly!

Scan the assigned passage for any words you don't know, and write them on a piece of scrap paper. Read over any section titles included in the passage—and then, as you read or listen to a section, think about how it relates to its title.

When you are finished reading, select a section title and write one or two sentences in your Student Notebook telling how the section illustrates (or tells about) it.

ꙮ Read the assigned passage aloud.

ꙮ Read the assigned passage silently.

C. **Read-Aloud & Discussion** *History, Language Skills, Thinking Skills*
Alan Shepard: page 127, paragraph 1 ("The next day…") through page 135

Follow the directions below to read or listen to the above assignment. Then make up the assigned number of questions about the part of the story you just read or heard. Write down your questions and ask your teacher to answer them. After discussing her thoughts, write down the best possible answer in your Student Notebook. Be sure to use complete sentences.

When you are finished, look back at the predictions you made during Lesson 3, Part 4. Were you able to predict what would happen? Be sure to mark the "Came to Pass" box for each prediction when it does happen.

ꙮ Listen carefully as your teacher reads the above assignment aloud. Make up three questions.

ꙮ Read the above assignment aloud; then make up four questions.

D. **Word Building** *Language Skills, Thinking Skills*
Throughout *Paths of Progress* you have learned about words that have their roots in the Latin and Greek languages. Now, continue your study of word-parts by looking at the Rummy Roots Word List and choosing one that has not yet been covered.

Find the word-part you chose in the dictionary. Then write the language from which it comes, and list words that begin with it in your Student Notebook.

Underline the word-part in each of your words and write their definitions. Think, and be ready to tell your teacher how each definition relates to the meaning of the word-part.

When you are finished, pick one of your words and write a sentence that uses it correctly.

ꙮ Choose at least three words.

ꙮ Choose at least six words.

C. Discussion is very important in developing your child's ability to organize his thoughts. This in turn builds the ability to think and write. The goal of discussing things with your student is not just to find the answer to a particular question, but also to create a situation where thoughts are shared and considered in a detailed way. Do not rush this activity, but encourage your student to share his ideas relating to the topic or events, and any additional ideas that may come to mind. You can also share your own thoughts and questions as an example.

E. **Cultivating Greatness History Review**   *Thinking Skills*

In Unit 4 you had an opportunity to learn about several important inventors, scientists, and events. Find the Cultivating Greatness Who or What Am I review in your Student Notebook and answer the questions.[2] Then make up additional "Who or What Am I?" questions for the topics listed at the bottom of the page.

People and events listed in the Word Bank will be used to answer more than one question. When you are finished, discuss your answers with your teacher.

F. **Cultivating Greatness Spelling Review**   *Language Skills*

Look back at the spelling lists you made in Unit 4, and ask your teacher to choose the number of words assigned below. Then, write those words in your Student Notebook as your teacher dictates them. When you are finished, check your work and show your teacher how you did.

Add any words you had trouble spelling to the Unit 6 Ongoing Spelling List in your Student Notebook. Also, if you misspell words in your everyday writing, be sure to add them to that list as well. Remember to practice spelling the words on your ongoing list from time to time during this unit.

F. It helps students to know that the focus of spelling lessons is to add new words to the group of words they can read and write, not just to give them busy work. When using a pretest/post-test method, personalized spelling lists result. The practice fits the children, especially when adding a few words that give them difficulty in everyday lessons, or a few words that challenge them.

🌵🌵 Choose 12 words.

🐾 Choose 16 words.

🐾 Choose 18 words.

Lapbook Activity

G. **Music**   *Thinking Skills*

Read pages 54 and 55 in the *Basix Recorder Method* to learn about the *dotted 8th and 16th note rhythm*. Write the names of notes you're not sure of above the staffs on those pages and practice playing the melodies.

Don't forget to listen to the *Recorder Method* CD tracks shown on page 55 to hear samples of that lesson, and use your Finger Placement Tabs if you need to.

Be sure to spend about 20 minutes a day practicing what you have learned!

H. **Independent Reading & Record Keeping**   *Thinking Skills*

Review the Lesson 4 At A Glance chart in your Student Notebook to see if all the work you've done in this part has been checked off. Also, make sure the Student Notebook pages you worked on are dated and complete.

When you are finished, choose something to read that you will enjoy. Then find a quiet, comfortable place and read for the following length of time:

🐾🐾 🐾 30 minutes   🐾 35 minutes

Be sure to write down what you read today on the Reading Log in your Student Notebook.

Lesson 4, Part 3

ᔒ Steps for Thinking Review ᔒ

(Cultivating Greatness Unit, Lesson 3)

1. Learning about the way something works requires you to carefully examine, or inspect, the parts of it in detail.

2. Understanding an event means you have to analyze, or think about, the steps leading up to an event. If you want something to happen, think about the steps that will bring that event about.

3. Sometimes when you think you know what will make something happen, you can try it out to see if it works. Always think about whether or not what you do will hurt yourself or someone else.

Read the Steps for Thinking that you are reviewing today. Tell your teacher what you think each step means, and:

🐾🐾 Choose two of the steps and give an example of how each one was true for any of the units.

🐾🐾 Give an example of how each step was true for any of the units.

🐾 Can you think of a time when one of the above Steps for Thinking applied to your life, or to the life of someone else in your family? Share it with your teacher.

A. **Copywork & Dictation**   *Language Skills*
Together with your teacher, follow the directions below and choose a passage from today's reading assignment in either *The Story of Inventions* or *Alan Shepard*. Read the passage silently and show your teacher any

words you don't know. Practice saying those words aloud until you are familiar with them. Then copy or write the passage while your teacher dictates it.

When you are finished copying or writing from dictation, compare your copy to the text and make any needed corrections.

　　　🐾 at least five sentences　　　　　　🐾🐾 at least seven sentences

B. Reader　　　　　　　　　　　　　　　*Language Skills, History*
The Story of Inventions: page 216, paragraph 4 (The First Commercial…) through the top of page 218

Scan the assigned passage for any words you don't know, and write them on a piece of scrap paper. Read over any section titles included in the passage—and then, as you read or listen to a section, think about how it relates to its title.

When you are finished reading, select a section title and write one or two sentences in your Student Notebook telling how the section illustrates (or tells about) it. Don't worry about the Comprehension Questions from the end of the chapter; you will work on them later in this lesson.

🐾 Read the assigned passage aloud.

🐾🐾 Read the assigned passage silently.

C. Read-Aloud & Narration　　　*History, Language Skills, Thinking Skills*
Alan Shepard: page 137 (Chapter 12) through page 145, paragraph 4

Follow the instructions below for your level. Then, in your own words, tell what happened in the story from Alan's point of view. Try to remember as many details as possible. Tell what you think is the most important event in the passage.

🐾 Listen carefully to the assigned passage.

🐾🐾 Read the assigned passage aloud.

D. Cultivating Greatness Vocabulary Review　　　　*Language Skills*
Once again, look over the vocabulary cards you made in Unit 4 (*CG*). Then give them to your teacher and ask her to show you their picture sides, one at a time. Tell her what the picture or clue means and then name the word written on the other side. If you can, tell what part of speech it is. Give yourself one point for correctly naming a word, and one point for knowing its part of speech. Keep track of your points because you will play again in Part 5!

Teaching Tip

If your child needs help remembering specific information from the reading, take a piece of blank paper and fold it in half, and then fold it in thirds. This will create a paper with six boxes. Before reading, have your child write a word in each box, such as who, what, when, where, why, and how. After listening and choosing the event to describe, have your child fill in the boxes with brief descriptions to support retelling. You can use this tool for many types of note taking.

E. Science

Thinking Skills

Human Body Basics, Human Development: Cell Division

As you read through the assigned pages, choose words that are new or unfamiliar and make vocabulary cards for them as directed. Keep your science cards separate from other vocabulary.

🐾 at least three words   🐾🐾 at least four words

Read and discuss the information in the passage with your teacher and do the *Labwork 3-7* activities. The pages you need to complete these activities are in your Student Notebook.

When you are finished, work on any *Examine This* projects you have not completed, or on your science project.

F. Science Fair Project

Language Skills, Thinking Skills

In this section, continue working on your science project. Follow the procedures in your project log carefully and don't forget to record your activities, data, and observations.

By now, you probably have some thoughts about how you want to organize and present your work at the end of the project, so put those thoughts on paper. Make a few sketches on the pages in your Student Notebook so you can see how your ideas might work. Don't forget to include space for your Project Notebook and Claymation video or flipbook! After you do that and settle on a design you like, begin gathering any special supplies you will need for your display. You will begin putting it together in Part 3 of the next lesson.

G. Music & Review

History, Thinking Skills

Look back at pages 88 through 91 in *The Story of the Orchestra*.

Then, follow the directions in Appendix D to make two Orchestra Story question and answer cards about the piano, and two about the harpsichord. Label each answer card with the name of instrument it is about (in the upper left corner). Do not label the question cards—and remember to write the questions in your Student Notebook in the correct order.

Check the directions in Lesson 1, Part 3G and review the Orchestra Story cards you made in Unit 4, Cultivating Greatness.

Then follow the same directions to review your Orchestra Story cards from Units 4 and 5, and those you have made so far in Unit 6.

H. Independent Reading & Record Keeping

Thinking Skills

Review the Lesson 4 At A Glance chart in your Student Notebook to see if all the work you've done in this part has been checked off. Also, make sure the Student Notebook pages you worked on are dated and complete.

E. After a lesson's end (maybe when Dad comes home), ask your child to use the things he or she has made and explain what was learned to someone not present at the lesson. You can encourage your child by restating what he or she says, just to clarify it for understanding. This is an excellent way to review a lesson, and using the objects from the lesson provides additional support for memory and interest.

Lapbook
Activity

When you are finished, choose something to read that you will enjoy. Then find a quiet, comfortable place and read for the following length of time:

🌵🐾 30 minutes   🐾 35 minutes

Be sure to write down what you read today on the Reading Log in your Student Notebook.

—⁂—

Lesson 4, Part 4

> ### ❦ Steps for Thinking Review ❧
>
> (Cultivating Greatness Unit, Lesson 4)
>
> 1. Once you have tried to do something a certain way, think about how it turned out. If it didn't turn out the way you expected, make changes in what you did and try it again.
>
> 2. It is important to take the time to draw conclusions, or think about, the results of what takes place around you. Not everything that is important to learn will be obvious, or easy to understand.
>
> 3. The poor choices of others shouldn't stop you from doing what you believe is right.

As your child becomes better at connecting concepts to examples in literature and instruction, a basis is forming for doing the same thing in writing.

Read the Steps for Thinking that you are reviewing today. Tell your teacher what you think each step means, and:

🌵🌵 Choose two of the steps and give an example of how each one was true for any of the units.

🖐🐾 Give an example of how each step was true for any of the units.

🐾 Can you think of a time when one of the above Steps for Thinking applied to your life or to the life of someone else in your family? Share it with your teacher.

A. **Copywork & Dictation**   *Language Skills*
Look back at the Steps for Thinking from Unit 4 that you have reviewed so far in this lesson. Pick several as directed below, and either copy or write them from dictation into your Student Notebook.

🌵🌵 Pick four steps.   🖐🐾 Pick five steps.

B. Reader   *Language Skills, History*

The Story of Inventions: page 218, paragraph 1 ("The Transistor…") through the top of page 220

Scan the assigned passage for any words you don't know, and write them on a piece of scrap paper. Read over any section titles included in the passage—and then, as you read or listen to a section, think about how it relates to its title.

When you are finished reading, select a section title and write one or two sentences in your Student Notebook telling how the section illustrates (or tells about) it.

Read the assigned passage aloud.

Read the assigned passage silently.

C. Read-Aloud & Discussion   *History, Language Skills, Thinking Skills*

Alan Shepard: page 145, paragraph 5 ("When the sun finally…") through page 156, paragraph 3

After reading or listening to the read-aloud assignment, talk with your teacher and try to predict what will happen in the future based on what you know of the characters and events. Write your predictions in your Student Notebook. Later you will look back and see if they were accurate. Try not to peek ahead!

Listen carefully as your teacher reads the assigned passage. Write down three predictions.

Read the assigned passage aloud; then write down at least four predictions.

D. Cultivating Greatness Word Building Review   *Language Skills*

Print the Word Builder Review 4 cards (for your level) from the Student Resources CD and cut them out. Mix them up and place them face down in a stack. Then take turns drawing cards, one at a time, with at least one other player. When a player draws a card, he or she must tell what word-part is in that word (one point), what language it comes from (one point), and the meaning of the word (one point). See how many points you can get!

For the answers, look back at the Word Building pages for Unit 4 in your Student Notebook.

E. Cultivating Greatness History/Economics Review   *Thinking Skills*

Gather or reprint the Supply and Demand 4 and 5 game cards that you made in Unit 4. Reread them and match the words with their definitions and examples in rows of three. Then play either Supply and Demand Concentration or Go Fish Matching.

E. Charting information about the inventors studied can show differences between periods in America's progress by focusing on challenges, attitudes, and outcomes. The graphic organizer used in this lesson allows your children to compile their observations and thoughts in one place. Later, by noting the similarities and differences, they are using their thinking skills to analyze the information.

Look at the Unit Review Graphic Organizer in your Student Notebook (Lesson 1, Part 4E) and discuss the questions it asks with your teacher. Then fill in the boxes in the Cultivating Greatness column as best you can.

When you are finished, discuss what you wrote with your teacher, and explain why you answered as you did.

F. Writing   *Language Skills, Thinking Skills*

After every chapter in *The Story of Inventions*, there is a list of Comprehension Questions. Their purpose is to determine if you understand what you have read, and are able to draw certain conclusions based on your understanding. The questions focus on main ideas expressed in the sections.

Read over the Comprehension Questions at the end of Chapter 16. Then refer back to the story to find their answers and use complete sentences to write them in your Student Notebook. (If you need help remembering how to answer questions, look back at the Writing lessons in Unit 1.)

When you are finished, check your answers with The Story of Inventions Answer Key. Are they in agreement? Were there things you left out? Evaluate your answers and tell your teacher if you were on target.

🐾 Create two more questions for Chapter 16; make sure they target main ideas, not just details. After writing your questions, create an Answer Key.

G. Art   *Thinking Skills*

In this section you will take the photographs for your Claymation project. It will most likely take several hours, so plan to work on it from time to time before Part 4 of the next lesson! If you have a digital camera, download the pictures onto your computer when you get finished. If you have a camera that uses film, you will need to get the photos developed and be ready to finish up at the end of Lesson 5.

Follow the directions in Appendix D to get started.

H. Independent Reading & Record Keeping   *Thinking Skills*

Review the Lesson 4 At A Glance chart in your Student Notebook to see if all the work you've done in this part has been checked off. Also, make sure the Student Notebook pages you worked on are dated and complete.

When you are finished, choose something to read that you will enjoy. Then find a quiet, comfortable place and read for the following length of time:

🖐🐾 30 minutes   🐾 35 minutes

Be sure to write down what you read today on the Reading Log in your Student Notebook.

Lesson 4, Part 5

> ### ❦ Steps for Thinking Review ❦
>
> (Cultivating Greatness Unit, Lesson 5)
>
> 1. Once you have learned to think carefully about information and decisions, you can give the best answers based on what you know. Often what you learn can help others if you share it with them.
>
> 2. Careful consideration of what you observe can lead you to new understanding. Even mistakes can be a great teacher for those willing to learn from them.
>
> 3. When people behave badly you can have the greatest impact on their behavior by not treating them the way they treated you.

Read the Steps for Thinking that you are reviewing today. Tell your teacher what you think each step means, and:

🖐 Choose two of the steps and give an example of how each one was true for any of the units.

🖐🐾 Give an example of how each step was true for any of the units.

🐾 Can you think of a time when one of the above Steps for Thinking applied to your life or to the life of someone else in your family? Share it with your teacher.

This part is set aside for completion of any work left undone from the lesson and review of concepts and content. It is also a time to expand the work of the lesson with practice and games.

- Give your teacher your stack of vocabulary cards for Unit 4, Cultivating Greatness. Ask her to show you each word, and then tell her its meaning and see if you can use it correctly in a sentence.

Self-evaluation is an important part of gaining new skills and knowledge. By considering the successfulness of a lesson, you are helping your child gain needed skill for future improvement. While you will have good insights as an adult, his observations can become personal revelation about the best ways to become successful.

When you are finished reviewing, choose five cards and try to act out each word so that others can guess what it is. Have other players choose five words and take turns acting them out and guessing. You get a point for guessing a word or having a word guessed. See who can get the most points.

- Review your Cultivating Greatness spelling words. Then ask your teacher to choose the number of words indicated below for your level. Write each word in your Student Notebook as she dictates it. When you are finished, look at your word list and make corrections as needed. Show your teacher how you did.

 16 words   20 words

- Follow the directions in the *Human Body Basics* Instructions to play the Word Power vocabulary game, and complete the System Savvy puzzles in your Student Notebook.[3] Then work on any *Examine This* projects you have not yet completed, or on your science project.

- Look back at pages 52-55 in the *Basix Recorder Method* and review any exercises that may still be giving you trouble. Choose several tracks on the *Recorder Method* CD and play along with them. Be sure to spend at least 20 minutes practicing!

- Review the Lesson 4 At A Glance chart in your Student Notebook to see if all the work you've done in this part has been checked off. If you did an Enrichment activity or other extra work in this lesson, be sure to write it on the lines next to the chart.

- Follow the directions in Appendix D and play Cultivating Greatness Bingo.

- Complete the Reach for the Stars Who or What Am I? located in your Student Notebook.[4]

Enrichment Activities:

Add to your Medical Breakthroughs Timeline book by briefly researching the following people, places, and/or events, and adding them to it. You can do this by simply writing their names in the correct places; or you can draw or trace pictures and symbols that you find during your research, and then color, cut, and paste them to the timeline. If you think of other medical advances you would like to include, feel free to do so!

Some of these people may be famous for other things, but you should concentrate only on their medical contribution(s). At the bottom of each timeline page, write one or two sentences describing the contributions or significance of the individuals, places, or events on that page.

- Rene Laennec
- Elizabeth Blackwell
- Joseph Lister
- Robert Koch

- Ether
- Charles Pravaz and Alexander Wood
- Louis Pasteur
- Felix Hoffman

Additional Resources:

Douglas MacArthur: What Greater Honor by Janet and Geoff Benge

Miracles on Maple Hill by Virginia Sorensen

Answers

1. Answer key is in Appendix C.

2. Answer key is in Appendix C.

3. Answer key is in the *Human Body Basics* Answer Key.

4. Answer key is in Appendix C.

Lesson 5, Part 1

♪ Steps for Thinking Review ♪

(Success Takes Flight Unit, Lesson 1)

1. Identifying a question is the first step to answering it. Put your question or idea into words. Give yourself some time to ponder, or think about, it over a bit of time, rather than trying to answer every question immediately.

2. Consider what you already know about the problem. Talking with someone else often helps clarify, or make clear, your thoughts.

3. Learn from the work of others. Read what others have said about your question. Originality, or new thoughts or new ways of doing something, is not limited by understanding what others have already done.

4. The economy is directly connected to the work of scientists and inventors. The prosperity of both is dependent on each other.

Read the Steps for Thinking that you are reviewing today. Tell your teacher what you think each step means, and:

🐾🐾 Choose two of the steps and give an example of how each one was true for any of the units.

🐾 🐾 Give an example of how each step was true for any of the units.

🐾 Can you think of a time when one of the above Steps for Thinking applied to your life or to the life of someone else in your family? Share it with your teacher.

𝒜. Copywork & Dictation   *Language Skills*

Together with your teacher, follow the directions below and choose a passage from today's reading assignment in either *The Story of Inventions* or *Alan Shepard*. Read the passage silently and show your teacher any words you don't know. Practice saying those words aloud until you are familiar with them. Then copy or write the passage while your teacher dictates it.

🐾🐾 at least five sentences

🐾 🐾 at least seven sentences

∾Materials∽

- *Alan Shepard*
- *The Story of Inventions*
- *The Story of the Orchestra* book & CD
- *Basix Recorder Method*
- Recorder
- Activity (Part 1G)
  Short stick, wooden spoon, or dowel
- Activity (Part 4G)
  Video:
      Computer
      Film-editing software
      Music (optional, for background)
      Downloaded or scanned pictures
  OR flipbook:
      Developed or printed pictures

B. When your child reads, make a list of any troublesome words. Look for possible patterns to the mistakes, and before your next session, review those words. You may read them aloud, or ask your child to do so.

Teaching Tip

Summary lessons and activities are very valuable. Though Part 5s may seem shorter than the other lesson parts, they are no less important. There are a variety of ways to help your children retain concepts and skills. Student presentations, review, games, and activities are all effective means of helping your children solidify and remember what they have learned. Then they can take the next big step of using it in the future, so be sure to make room for Part 5!

B. **Reader**   *Language Skills, History*
The Story of Inventions: page 273 (Chapter 21) through page 274

Scan the assigned passage for any words you don't know, and write them on a piece of scrap paper. Read over any section titles included in the passage—and then, as you read or listen to a section, think about how it relates to its title.

When you are finished reading, select a section title and write one or two sentences in your Student Notebook telling how the section illustrates (or tells about) it. Don't worry about the Comprehension Questions from the end of the chapter; you will work on them later in this lesson.

Read the assigned passage aloud.

Read the assigned passage silently.

C. **Read-Aloud & Narration**   *History, Language Skills, Thinking Skills*
Alan Shepard: page 156, paragraph 4 ("For a moment Alan…") to the middle of page 166

Follow the directions below to read or listen to the above passage. Then, in your own words, tell what happened in the portion you are assigned. Try to remember as many details as possible. If necessary you may re-read, or listen as your teacher rereads, the part you are to retell.

Listen carefully as your teacher reads the above assignment aloud. Choose two pages to retell.

Read the above assignment aloud, and then retell the entire passage.

D. **Success Takes Flight Vocabulary Review**   *Thinking Skills*
Look back at the vocabulary cards you made in Unit 5. You can tell which ones they are because you wrote *STF* in their upper left corners. Go through them and see if you can remember any of the definitions. Then try using each one correctly in a sentence.

When you are finished reviewing, choose five cards and try to act out each word so that others can guess what it is. Have other players choose five words and take turns acting them out and guessing. You get a point for guessing a word, or having a word guessed. See who can get the most points.

E. **Success Takes Flight Science Review**   *Thinking Skills*
Complete the Human Body Matching review in your Student Notebook.[1] When you are finished, tell your teacher what you remember about each thing named in the activity. If you need help remembering and your teacher agrees, you can look back at the chapters covered during Unit 5 in the *Human Body Basics* book, and the work you did in your Student Notebook.

F. Science Fair Project   *Language Skills, Thinking Skills*

It is time to gather the **raw data** (information that has not yet been organized or evaluated) that you have collected through the course of your science project. This data may be notes in your project log, photos, drawings, measurements, other types of information you gathered, or the finished product if you designed and built something.

Generally speaking though, you will probably want to organize the raw data on a chart of some sort, so you can see the information all in one place. The many ways to do this vary according to the type of project you chose to do. Because of that, you should once again check a few books or websites that are devoted to science projects for ideas about organizing and analyzing your particular type of data.

When everything is in one place, you can begin **evaluating**, or analyzing, the information by comparing results and checking to see if anything unusual or unexpected happened. Then you will be ready to draw a conclusion, and write a short summary of the outcomes you achieved.

A science project conclusion is simply a comparison of the experiment's results with the hypothesis written at the beginning of the project. Don't be surprised if the results of your experimentation differ from the answer you thought you would get. Either way, look for patterns in your information, and base your conclusion on the outcomes you actually observed and recorded. Then, use the page in your Student Notebook and write one paragraph that summarizes the comparison.

If you haven't yet decided how you want your project display to look, it is time to do so. You will begin putting it together in Part 3.

G. Music   *History, Thinking Skills*

With your teacher, read pages 92 and 93 in *The Story of the Orchestra*, and discuss the information about the conductor. Then use a short stick or wooden spoon to practice the patterns shown on page 92, that the conductor uses to mark the beat for the orchestra.

Choose several tracks from your *Story of the Orchestra* CD, and try to "conduct" each one by marking its beat with the appropriate pattern. Discuss this activity with your teacher. Did you find it easy to do, or difficult?

H. Independent Reading & Record Keeping   *Thinking Skills*

Review the Lesson 5 At A Glance chart in your Student Notebook to see if all the work you've done in this part has been checked off. Also, make sure the Student Notebook pages you worked on are dated and complete.

When you are finished, choose something to read that you will enjoy. Then find a quiet, comfortable place and read for the following length of time:

🐾🖐 30 minutes   🐾 35 minutes

Be sure to write down what you read today on the Reading Log in your Student Notebook.

Lesson 5, Part 2

Connect Learning to Life

When you discuss the Steps for Thinking with your children you are showing them how to connect details to ideas, and concepts to examples. This is powerful modeling, so don't think the children are the only ones who can share what they have observed. When you share what you think, they see that you are still learning. This is a model for life-long learning, not just the academics of school years.

> ### ᕤ Steps for Thinking Review ᕤ
>
> (Success Takes Flight Unit, Lesson 2)
>
> 1. Many people are motivated by the challenge of solving a new problem. It takes wisdom to know when to persevere, or continue doing one type of action, and when to try something new.
>
> 2. The encouragement of those you trust is essential, or very important, in helping you to pursue something that other people think is foolish, or will not work.
>
> 3. To find out what will work, you have to put some of your ideas to the test. Once you try them out, you then have more data, or information, to adjust your ideas or to change them altogether.
>
> 4. Our economy is part of a global, or worldwide, economy. Events around the world affect the economy here, and events here affect other economies around the globe.

Read the Steps for Thinking that you are reviewing today. Tell your teacher what you think each step means, and:

🐾🐾 Choose two of the steps and give an example of how each one was true for any of the units.

🖐🐾 Give an example of how each step was true for any of the units.

🐾 Can you think of a time when one of the above Steps for Thinking applied to your life, or to the life of someone else in your family? Share it with your teacher.

A. **Dictation** *Language Skills*

Look carefully at your assigned passage below, and read it silently. Show your teacher any words you don't know, and practice saying them aloud. Now read the passage aloud, or ask your teacher to read it to you.

When you are finished copying or writing from dictation, compare your copy to the text and make any needed corrections.

🐾🖐 Copy or write as your teacher dictates from *The Story of Inventions*, page 275, paragraph 1 ("In the meantime…").

🐾 Write as your teacher dictates from *The Story of Inventions*, page 275, paragraphs 1–2 ("In the meantime…").

B. **Reader** *Language Skills, History*

The Story of Inventions: page 275 (Goddard Goes Ahead) through page 276, paragraph 2

Scan the assigned passage for any words you don't know, and write them on a piece of scrap paper. Read over any section titles included in the passage—and then, as you read or listen to a section, think about how it relates to its title.

When you are finished reading, select a section title and write one or two sentences in your Student Notebook telling how the section illustrates, or tells about, it. Don't worry about the Comprehension Questions from the end of the chapter; you will work on them later in this lesson.

🐾🖐 Read the assigned passage aloud.

🐾🐾 Read the assigned passage silently.

C. **Read-Aloud & Discussion** *History, Language Skills, Thinking Skills*

Alan Shepard: page 166, paragraph 1 ("The hairs on the back…") through page 174, paragraph 2

Follow the directions below to read or listen to the above assignment. Then make up the assigned number of questions about the part of the story you just read or heard. Write down your questions and ask your teacher to answer them. After discussing her thoughts, write down the best possible answer in your Student Notebook. Be sure to use complete sentences.

When you are finished, look back at the predictions you made during Lesson 4, Part 4. Were you able to predict what would happen? Be sure to mark the "Came to Pass" box for each prediction when it does happen.

🖐 Listen carefully as your teacher reads the above assignment aloud. Make up three questions.

🐾🐾 Read the above assignment aloud; then make up four questions.

D. Word Building   *Language Skills, Thinking Skillss*

Throughout *Paths of Progress* you have learned about words that have their roots in the Latin and Greek languages. Now, continue your study of word-parts by looking at the Rummy Roots Word List and choosing one that has not yet been covered.

Find the word-part you chose in the dictionary. Then write the language from which it comes, and list words that begin with it in your Student Notebook.

Underline the word-part in each of your words and write their definitions. Think, and be ready to tell your teacher how each definition relates to the meaning of the word-part.

When you are finished, pick one of your words and write a sentence that uses it correctly.

🐾 List at least three words.

🐾 List at least six words.

E. Success Takes Flight History Review   *Thinking Skills*

In Unit 5 you had an opportunity to learn about several important inventors, scientists, and events. Find the Success Takes Flight Who or What Am I review in your Student Notebook and answer the questions.[2] Then make up additional "Who or What Am I?" questions for the topics listed at the bottom of the page.

People and events listed in the Word Bank will be used to answer more than one question. When you are finished, discuss your answers with your teacher.

Connect Learning to Life

Does that look right?" This is the most important sense you can help children develop as spellers. They can place a light pencil line under any word they are unsure of and then ask for a spelling or use the dictionary to verify the spelling. When your children do this, encourage them. Much better than just memorizing random words, this is a true-life skill!

F. Success Takes Flight Spelling Review   *Language Skills*

Look back at the spelling lists you made in Unit 5, and ask your teacher to choose the number of words assigned below. Then, write those words in your Student Notebook as your teacher dictates them. When you are finished, check your work and show your teacher how you did.

Add any words you had trouble spelling to the Unit 6 Ongoing Spelling List in your Student Notebook. Also, if you misspell words in your everyday writing, be sure to add them to that list as well. Remember to practice spelling the words on your ongoing list from time to time during this unit.

🐾 Choose 12 words.

🐾 Choose 16 words.

🐾 Choose 18 words.

G. **Music**   *Thinking Skills*

Read pages 56 and 57 in the *Basix Recorder Method* to learn about *triplets*. Write the names of notes you're not sure of above the staffs on those pages and practice playing the melodies.

Don't forget to listen to the *Recorder Method* CD tracks shown on page 57 to hear samples of that lesson, and use your Finger Placement Tabs if you need to.

Be sure to spend about 20 minutes a day practicing what you have learned!

H. **Independent Reading & Record Keeping**   *Thinking Skills*

Review the Lesson 5 At A Glance chart in your Student Notebook to see if all the work you've done in this part has been checked off. Also, make sure the Student Notebook pages you worked on are dated and complete.

When you are finished, choose something to read that you will enjoy. Then find a quiet, comfortable place and read for the following length of time:

🖐🖐🐾 30 minutes   🐾 35 minutes

Be sure to write down what you read today on the Reading Log in your Student Notebook.

Lesson 5, Part 3

❧ Steps for Thinking Review ❧

(Success Takes Flight Unit, Lesson 3)

1. When you test your ideas, recording your observations for later thought gives you the opportunity to reflect on what has worked, what hasn't worked, and why.

2. If you are to do something of value, failure must not cause you to stop trying. When you don't meet your expectations, this information helps you make adjustments so that you can be successful.

3. Inventors and scientists had to keep an open mind, willing to take unexpected results and learn from them.

4. Often the economy determines how much we spend on things that we want, as well as things that we need. How much we spend on these things affects the economy.

Read the Steps for Thinking that you are reviewing today. Tell your teacher what you think each step means, and:

🐾 Choose two of the steps and give an example of how each one was true for any of the units.

🐾 Give an example of how each step was true for any of the units.

🐾 Can you think of a time when one of the above Steps for Thinking applied to your life or to the life of someone else in your family? Share it with your teacher.

A. **Copywork & Dictation**   *Language Skills*
Together with your teacher, follow the directions below and choose a passage from today's reading assignment in either *The Story of Inventions* or *Alan Shepard*. Read the passage silently and show your teacher any words you don't know. Practice saying those words aloud until you are familiar with them. Then copy or write the passage while your teacher dictates it.

🐾 at least five sentences

🐾 at least seven sentences

B. Reader
Language Skills, History

The Story of Inventions: page 276, paragraph 3 ("Finally, in 1961,…") through page 277, paragraph 1

Scan the assigned passage for any words you don't know, and write them on a piece of scrap paper. Read over any section titles included in the passage—and then, as you read or listen to a section, think about how it relates to its title.

When you are finished reading, select a section title and write one or two sentences in your Student Notebook telling how the section illustrates (or tells about) it. Don't worry about the Comprehension Questions from the end of the chapter; you will work on them later in this lesson.

Read the assigned passage aloud.

Read the assigned passage silently.

C. Read-Aloud & Narration
History, Language Skills, Thinking Skills

Alan Shepard: page 174, paragraph 3 ("Alan, along with…") through page 183, paragraph 2

Follow the instructions below for your level. Then, in your own words, tell what happened in the story from Alan's point of view. Try to remember as many details as possible. Tell what you think is the most important event in the passage.

Listen carefully to the assigned passage.

Read the assigned passage aloud.

D. Success Takes Flight Vocabulary Review
Language Skills

Once again, look over the vocabulary cards you made in Unit 5 (*SF*). Then give them to your teacher and ask her to show you their picture sides, one at a time. Tell her what the picture or clue means and then name the word written on the other side. If you can, tell what part of speech it is. Give yourself one point for correctly naming a word and one point for knowing its part of speech. Keep track of your points because you will play again in Part 5!

E. Science
Thinking Skills

Human Body Basics, Human Development: Embryo Development

As you read through the assigned pages, choose words that are new or unfamiliar and make vocabulary cards for them as directed. Keep your science cards separate from other vocabulary.

at least three words   at least four words

Read and discuss the information in the passage with your teacher and do the *Labwork 8* activity.

Teaching Tip

Take the opportunities that occur in daily life to illustrate and help your children understand point of view. For example, watch or listen to a newscast together or read a newspaper or Internet article that presents an opinion about a current event. Ask your children what their point of view is on the subject, and perhaps share yours. Include as many family members as you think appropriate in the discussion. Are your points of view the same as or different from the authors of the articles or newscasts?

Lapbook Activity

When you are finished, begin work on *Examine This* project 4 at the end of the chapter.

Do as much as you can, but you don't have to finish the project in this part. You will have other opportun

F. Science Fair Project   *Language Skills, Thinking Skills*

In this section, continue working on your science project by finishing up any assigned work that has not yet been completed.

Then begin putting your display together. You will have an opportunity to continue working on the display in Part 4 of the next lesson.

G. Music & Review   *History, Thinking Skills*

Look back at pages 92 and 93 in *The Story of the Orchestra*.

Then, follow the directions in Appendix D to make three Orchestra Story question and answer cards about the conductor. Label each answer card with that title (in the upper left corner). Do not label the question cards—and remember to write the questions in your Student Notebook in the correct order.

Check the directions in Lesson 1, Part 3G, and review the Orchestra Story cards you made in Unit 5, Success Takes Flight.

Then follow the same directions to review all the Orchestra Story cards you have made in Units 4, 5, and 6.

H. A reading log is an important part of a portfolio. It documents sequential effort and is a satisfying way for a child to see work completion. You may also want to make a list of books read for this unit, which may include bibliographical information, such as author, publisher, and copyright date. This is an easy way to build awareness of bibliographical information.

H. Independent Reading & Record Keeping   *Thinking Skills*

Review the Lesson 5 At A Glance chart in your Student Notebook to see if all the work you've done in this part has been checked off. Also, make sure the Student Notebook pages you worked on are dated and complete.

When you are finished, choose something to read that you will enjoy. Then find a quiet, comfortable place and read for the following length of time:

🌱🌱🐾 30 minutes   🐾 35 minutes

Be sure to write down what you read today on the Reading Log in your Student Notebook.

Lesson 5, Part 4

♪ Steps for Thinking Review ♪

(Success Takes Flight Unit, Lesson 4)

1. For data collected from observation and experimentation to be useful, it must be accepted at face value, without regard to what conclusions will be drawn from the data.

2. Decisions cannot be made based only on circumstances, because they are changeable. Decisions must be based on firmly held beliefs in principles such as truth, fairness, and responsibility.

3. In business, risk is often associated with reward. For those who choose to take a risk either with money, time, or their own well-being, the rewards can be great. But the less risk that is taken financially, the less chance there is of losing money invested.

4. The element of trust is important in business. When a company loses the trust of its customers, it will be difficult for that business to continue. Not living up to promised benefits, faulty products, or poor service can lead to a lack of trust.

Read the Steps for Thinking that you are reviewing today. Tell your teacher what you think each step means, and:

🐾 Choose two of the steps and give an example of how each one was true for any of the units.

🐾🐾 Give an example of how each step was true for any of the units.

🐾 Can you think of a time when one of the above Steps for Thinking applied to your life, or to the life of someone else in your family? Share it with your teacher.

A. **Copywork & Dictation**   *Language Skills*

Look back at the Steps for Thinking from Unit 5 that you have reviewed so far in this lesson. Pick several as directed below, and either copy or write them from dictation into your Student Notebook.

🐾 Pick four steps.

🐾🐾 Pick five steps.

B. Reader   *Language Skills, History*
The Story of Inventions: page 277, paragraph 2 ("No other nation…") through page 279

Scan the assigned passage for any words you don't know, and write them on a piece of scrap paper. Read over any section titles included in the passage—and then, as you read or listen to a section, think about how it relates to its title.

When you are finished reading, select a section title and write one or two sentences in your Student Notebook telling how the section illustrates (or tells about) it. Don't worry about the Comprehension Questions from the end of the chapter; you will work on them later in this lesson.

🐾 Read the assigned passage aloud.

🐾 Read the assigned passage silently.

C. Stories about famous people in history are a wonderful way to illustrate important character qualities. Children naturally enjoy the story format and more easily connect to characters and the events surrounding their lives.

C. Read-Aloud & Discussion   *History, Language Skills, Thinking Skills*
Alan Shepard: page 183, paragraph 3 ("With the end of Gemini…") through page 192, paragraph 1

After reading or listening to the read-aloud assignment, talk with your teacher and try to predict what will happen in the future based on what you know of the characters and events. Write your predictions in your Student Notebook. Later you will look back and see if they were accurate. Try not to peek ahead!

🐾 Listen carefully as your teacher reads the assigned passage. Write down three predictions.

🐾 Read the assigned passage aloud; then write down at least four predictions.

D. Success Takes Flight Word Building Review   *Thinking Skills*
Print the Word Builder Review 5 cards (for your level) from the Student Resources CD and cut them out. Mix them up and place them face down in a stack. Then take turns drawing cards, one at a time, with at least one other player. When a player draws a card, he or she must tell what word-part is in that word (one point), what language it comes from (one point), and the meaning of the word (one point). See how many points you can get!

For the answers, look back at the Word Building pages for Unit 5 in your Student Notebook.

E. Success Takes Flight History/Economics Review   *Thinking Skills*
Gather or reprint the Supply and Demand 6 and 7 game cards that you made in Unit 5. Reread them, and match the words with their

definitions and examples in rows of three. Then play either Supply and Demand Concentration or Go Fish Matching.

Look at the Unit Review Graphic Organizer in your Student Notebook (Lesson 1, Part 4E) and discuss the questions it asks with your teacher. Then fill in the boxes in the Success Takes Flight column as best you can.

When you are finished, discuss what you wrote with your teacher, and explain why you answered as you did.

F. Writing
Language Skills, Thinking Skills

After every chapter in *The Story of Inventions,* there is a list of Comprehension Questions. Their purpose is to determine if you understand what you have read, and are able to draw certain conclusions based on your understanding. The questions focus on main ideas expressed in the sections.

Read over the Comprehension Questions at the end of Chapter 21. Then refer back to the story to find their answers and use complete sentences to write them in your Student Notebook. (If you need help remembering how to answer questions, look back at the Writing lessons in Unit 1.)

When you are finished, check your answers with *The Story of Inventions Answer Key.* Are they in agreement? Were there things you left out? Evaluate your answers and tell your teacher if you were on target.

🐾 Create two more questions for Chapter 16; make sure they target main ideas, not just details. After writing the questions, create an Answer Key.

G. Art
Thinking Skills

In this section you will finish up your Claymation project. Follow the directions in Appendix D to complete your video or flipbook.

H. Independent Reading & Record Keeping
Thinking Skills

Review the Lesson 5 At A Glance chart in your Student Notebook to see if all the work you've done in this part has been checked off. Also, make sure the Student Notebook pages you worked on are dated and complete.

When you are finished, choose something to read that you will enjoy. Then find a quiet, comfortable place and read for the following length of time:

     🌱🌱 🐾 30 minutes   🐾 35 minutes

Be sure to write down what you read today on the Reading Log in your Student Notebook.

F. The writing done in this activity is meant to help your child put what he or she has learned into words. The information needed to answer these questions can be found in the reader assignments, and the length of writing is not as important as giving a clear answer. Remember to encourage your child to use words from the question as a word bank to help begin writing the answer.

Lesson 5, Part 5

❧ Steps for Thinking Review ❧

(Success Takes Flight Unit, Lesson 5)

1. Times of great trial bind people together. When there is a common enemy, there is also a common purpose.

2. The best application of thinking skills takes into account as many consequences of an action as possible. While some may apply knowledge for destructive purposes, each person is responsible for what they do with the knowledge they possess.

3. The greatest acts of bravery are done by those who believe that their cause is more important than any one individual's life, even their own.

4. The economic impact of war is great, for both sides of the conflict. The winners experience an increase in employment and production of wartime goods. The losers must rebuild their economy, often from scratch. Their struggles usually become part of a global effort to assist the country in its recovery. Not living up to promised benefits, faulty products, or poor service can lead to a lack of trust.

Read the Steps for Thinking that you are reviewing today. Tell your teacher what you think each step means, and:

❧❧ Choose two of the steps and give an example of how each one was true for any of the units.

🐾🐾 Give an example of how each step was true for any of the units.

🐾 Can you think of a time when one of the above Steps for Thinking applied to your life or to the life of someone else in your family? Share it with your teacher.

This part is set aside for completion of any work left undone from the lesson and review of concepts and content. It is also a time to expand the work of the lesson with practice and games.

• Give your teacher your stack of vocabulary cards for Unit 5, Success Takes Flight. Ask her to show you each word and then tell her its meaning and see if you can use it correctly in a sentence.

Teaching Tip

Games are fun ways to reinforce the recognition and spelling of words that are important to learn. After your children complete a game, encourage them to make their own. Ask them to share these with each other, with friends, or with you. Remember, these activities are models for you and your children to make your own as well!

When you are finished reviewing, choose five cards and try to act out each word so that others can guess what it is. Have other players choose five words and take turns acting them out and guessing. You get a point for guessing a word, or having a word guessed. See who can get the most points.

- Review your Success Takes Flight spelling words. Then ask your teacher to choose the number of words indicated below for your level. Write each word in your Student Notebook as she dictates it. When you are finished, look at your word list and make corrections as needed. Show your teacher how you did.

 16 words   20 words

- Follow the directions in the *Human Body Basics* Instructions to play the Word Power vocabulary game, and complete the System Savvy puzzles in your Student Notebook.[3] Then work on any *Examine This* projects you have not yet completed, or on your science project.

- Look back at pages 48-57 in the *Basix Recorder Method* and review any exercises that may still be giving you trouble. Choose several tracks on the *Recorder Method* CD and play along with them. Be sure to spend at least 20 minutes practicing!

- Review the Lesson 5 At A Glance chart in your Student Notebook to see if all the work you've done in this part has been checked off. If you did an Enrichment activity or other extra work in this lesson, be sure to write it on the lines next to the chart.

- Follow the directions in Appendix D and play Success Takes Flight Bingo.

- Follow the directions in Appendix D and play Reach for the Stars Bingo.

Enrichment Activities:

1. Add to your Medical Breakthroughs Timeline book by briefly researching the following people, places, and/or events and adding them to it. You can do this by simply writing their names in the correct places; or you can draw or trace pictures and symbols that you find during your research, and then color, cut, and paste them to the timeline. If you think of other medical advances you would like to include, feel free to do so!

   Some of these people may be famous for other things, but you should concentrate only on their medical contribution(s). At the bottom of each timeline page, write one or two sentences describing the contributions or significance of the individuals, places, or events on that page.

- Gregor Mendel
- Sir Frederick Hopkins
- Alexander Fleming
- James Watson and Francis Crick

- Karl Landsteiner
- Insulin
- Charles Drew

Additional Resource:

The Right Stuff movie

Please preview any recommended movie to ensure its content is in line with your family's values, and acceptable for your children to watch.

Answers

1. Answer key is in Appendix C.
2. Answer key is in Appendix C.
3. Answer key is in the *Human Body Basics* Answer Key.

Lesson 6, Part 1

A. Copywork & Dictation   *Language Skills*

Together with your teacher, follow the directions below and choose a passage from today's reading assignment in either *Alan Shepard* or *The New Way Things Work*. Read the passage silently and show your teacher any words you don't know. Practice saying those words aloud until you are familiar with them. Then copy or write the passage while your teacher dictates it.

ᴪ at least five sentences

ᴥ ᴥ at least seven sentences

B. Reader   *Language Skills, History*

The New Way Things Work: Sections 3, 4, or 5

Choose the number of inventions assigned below from Sections 3, 4, or 5 in *The New Way Things Work* and read about them. Then fill out the Flow Charts in your Student Notebook, telling how each of your selections work.

To do this, you may want to list the various steps involved in each invention's operation on scrap paper, and number them. That way you can adjust them if necessary (by combining, simplifying, or extending) so you have the correct number of steps for the Flow Charts.

ᴪ Choose one invention.

ᴥ Choose two inventions.

ᴥ Choose three inventions.

C. Read-Aloud & Narration   *History, Language Skills, Thinking Skills*

Alan Shepard: page 192, paragraph 2 ("Apollo 9, followed…") through page 200, paragraph 1

Follow the directions below to read or listen to the above passage. Then, in your own words, tell what happened in the portion you are assigned. Try to remember as many details as possible. If necessary you may reread, or listen as your teacher rereads, the part you are to retell.

ᴪ Listen carefully as your teacher reads the above assignment aloud. Choose two pages to retell.

ᴥ ᴥ Read the above assignment aloud, and then retell the entire passage.

Materials

- *Alan Shepard*
- *The New Way Things Work*
- *The Story of the Orchestra* CD
- *Basix Recorder Method*
- Recorder

Teaching Tip

If your child needs help remembering specific information from the reading, take a piece of blank paper and fold it in half, and then fold it in thirds. This will create a paper with six boxes. Before reading, have your child write a word in each box, such as who, what, when, where, why, and how. After reading or listening to the passage, have your child fill in the boxes with brief descriptions to support retelling. You can use this tool for many types of note taking.

Lapbook Activity

D. Vocabulary Review
Language Skills, Thinking Skills

Gather all the vocabulary cards you made this year and mix them up. Then divide them into two stacks. Choose one of the piles to review in this section, and set the other aside to use later in Part 3.

Begin your review by picking a card. Read the word on the front and, without looking, tell your teacher either what it means or how it was used in the story. Give yourself a point for every word you are able to use correctly—see how many points you can get!

E. Science
Thinking Skills

This section is set aside as a Study Hall. Use it to catch up on any work that has not yet been completed in the science lessons studied in this unit. If all your science is finished, use this time to work on other assignments that are still undone.

F. Science Fair Project
Language Skills, Thinking Skills

In this section, you will polish up the background research paper you wrote in Lesson 2, and complete your Project Notebook so it can be included in your display. Most of the information has been written already (in your Student Notebook or on plain notebook paper), and can just be transferred into the Project Notebook.

If you are actually entering a science fair, it is possible you will need to adapt these instructions to meet the requirements of whatever organization is sponsoring the fair.

First, look over your research paper from Lesson 2. Does it still say things the way you would like to express them? Have you come across any additional information or resources you think should be included? Make any changes needed; if you add something, be sure to update the bibliography.

Second, finalize your Project Notebook:

1. write or type and print a title page (it should include the name of the project and your name);

2. the science fair rules you copied or printed in Lesson 3, part 1;

3. your updated background research paper (including its bibliography);

4. the question and hypothesis you wrote in your Student Notebook (Lesson 3, Part 1);

5. the testing description, variables, and controls you wrote in your Student Notebook (Lesson 3, Part 1). Update this to show anything that changed as you progressed through the experimental process;

6. the list of items you needed to conduct your experiments from your Student Notebook (Lesson 3, Part 1). You may need to update this to show any additional materials you had to get, or any items it turned out you didn't need;

7. the Procedure Plan you wrote on plain notebook paper;

8. the raw data chart, display, pictures, or other explanations that show your results;

9. the story board pages you made for your Claymation video or flipbook;

10. the conclusion summary you wrote in your Student Notebook (Lesson 5, Part 1);

11. your project log that you kept on plain notebook paper.

12. Number all the pages except for the title page. Then write or type and print a Table of Contents, and place it in the notebook right after the title page.

Some organizations that sponsor science fairs ask for a project overview (sometimes called an Abstract) to be displayed with your project. This is generally a one-page summary of the project from start to finish. Check the science fair rules in your Project Notebook to see if one is required, and write it if necessary.

G. Music
History, Thinking Skills

Review the Orchestra Story cards you made in Unit 6 by matching the question cards with their correct answers.

Then review all the Orchestra Story cards you have made in Units 4, 5, and 6 the same way.

When you are finished, follow the directions in Appendix D to make new category cards for Keyboard and Conductor, and to play Orchestra Story Question Quest with all the cards from Units 1 through 6.

H. Independent Reading & Record Keeping
Thinking Skills

Review the Lesson 6 At A Glance chart in your Student Notebook to see if all the work you've done in this part has been checked off. Also, make sure the Student Notebook pages you worked on are dated and complete.

When you are finished, choose something to read that you will enjoy. Then find a quiet, comfortable place and read for the following length of time:

🖐🖐 🖐 30 minutes 🐾 35 minutes

Be sure to write down what you read today on the Reading Log in your Student Notebook.

Lesson 6, Part 2

A. **Copywork & Dictation**   *Language Skills*

Together with your teacher, follow the directions below and choose a passage from today's reading assignment in either *Alan Shepard* or *The New Way Things Work*. Read the passage silently and show your teacher any words you don't know. Practice saying those words aloud until you are familiar with them. Then copy or write the passage while your teacher dictates it.

至 at least five sentences

至至 at least seven sentences

B. **Reader**   *Language Skills, History*

The New Way Things Work: Sections 3, 4, or 5

Choose the number of inventions assigned below from Sections 3, 4, or 5 in *The New Way Things Work* and read about them. Then fill out the Flow Charts in your Student Notebook, telling how each of your selections work.

To do this, you may want to list the various steps involved in each invention's operation on scrap paper, and number them. That way you can adjust them if necessary (by combining, simplifying, or extending) so you have the correct number of steps for the Flow Charts.

至 Choose one invention.

至 Choose two inventions.

至 Choose three inventions.

C. **Read-Aloud & Discussion**   *History, Language Skills, Thinking Skills*

Alan Shepard: page 200, paragraph 2 ("Alan waited anxiously…") to the top of page 210

Follow the directions below to read or listen to the above assignment. Then make up the assigned number of questions about the part of the story you just read or heard. Write down your questions and ask your teacher to answer them. After discussing her thoughts, write down the best possible answer in your Student Notebook. Be sure to use complete sentences.

When you are finished, look back at the predictions you made during Lesson 5, Part 4. Were you able to predict what would happen? Be sure to mark the "Came to Pass" box for each prediction when it does happen.

至 Listen carefully as your teacher reads the above assignment aloud. Make up three questions.

至至 Read the above assignment aloud; then make up four questions.

D. Word Building
Language Skills, Thinking Skills

Throughout *Paths of Progress* you have learned about words that have their roots in the Latin and Greek languages. Now, continue your study of word-parts by looking at the Rummy Roots Word List and choosing one that has not yet been covered.

Find the word-part you chose in the dictionary. Then write the language from which it comes, and list words that begin with it in your Student Notebook.

Underline the word-part in each of your words and write their definitions. Think, and be ready to tell your teacher how each definition relates to the meaning of the word-part.

When you are finished, pick one of your words and write a sentence that uses it correctly.

❦ List at least three words.

❦❦ List at least six words.

E. Reach for the Stars History
Thinking Skills

In Unit 6 you had an opportunity to learn about several important inventors, scientists, and events. Find the Reach for the Stars Who or What Am I review in your Student Notebook and answer the questions.[1] Then make up additional "Who or What Am I?" questions for the topics listed at the bottom of the page.

People and events listed in the Word Bank will be used to answer more than one question. When you are finished, discuss your answers with your teacher.

F. Spelling
Language Skills, Thinking Skills

Look at the words that are left on your Ongoing Spelling List. Practice spelling each one by covering it with your hand, spelling it silently, and then checking to see if you were correct. Do this several times, until you feel comfortable spelling these words.

Then listen as your teacher reads each word, and write it in your Student Notebook as she dictates it. When you are finished, check your spelling against the Ongoing Spelling List and make corrections as needed. Show your teacher how you did.

G. Music
Thinking Skills

Look back through the pages of the *Basix Recorder Method* and see what you have accomplished this year!

You may continue through the last two lessons in the book, or review any other exercises that you would like to work on. Choose several tracks on the *Recorder Method* CD and play along with them. Use

As you near the end of *Paths of Progress*, remember that culminating activities are a key part of solidifying learning. By thinking of interesting ways to present the information he or she has learned, your child's new knowledge is reinforced. Also, sharing opinions formed and skills practiced reinforces the connection between new information and past learning. Encourage your student to be the guide to the unit, acquainting others with key concepts, events, people, and activities. Allow your children to truly express their thoughts!

your Finger Placement Tabs if you need to, and be sure to spend at least 20 minutes practicing!

Now that you have completed your scheduled study of the recorder, don't give it up. Other music is available online or at a music store so you can continue to improve your skill. You may even want to learn to play another instrument!

H. **Independent Reading & Record Keeping**   *Thinking Skills*
Review the Lesson 6 At A Glance chart in your Student Notebook to see if all the work you've done in this part has been checked off. Also, make sure the Student Notebook pages you worked on are dated and complete.

When you are finished, choose something to read that you will enjoy. Then find a quiet, comfortable place and read for the following length of time:

🌵🌵 🐾 30 minutes   🐾 35 minutes

Be sure to write down what you read today on the Reading Log in your Student Notebook.

Lesson 6, Part 3

A. **Copywork & Dictation**   *Language Skills*
Together with your teacher, follow the directions below and choose a passage from today's reading assignment in either *Alan Shepard* or *The New Way Things Work*. Read the passage silently and show your teacher any words you don't know. Practice saying those words aloud until you are familiar with them. Then copy or write the passage while your teacher dictates it.

🌵🌵 at least five sentences

🐾🐾 at least seven sentences

B. **Reader**   *Language Skills, History*
The New Way Things Work: Sections 3, 4, or 5

Choose the number of inventions assigned below from Sections 3, 4, or 5 in *The New Way Things Work* and read about them. Then fill out the Flow Charts in your Student Notebook, telling how each of your selections work.

To do this, you may want to list the various steps involved in each invention's operation on scrap paper, and number them.

That way you can adjust them if necessary (by combining, simplifying, or extending) so you have the correct number of steps for the Flow Charts.

🐾 Choose one invention.

🐾 Choose two inventions.

🐾 Choose three inventions.

C. **Read-Aloud & Narration**   *History, Language Skills, Thinking Skills*
Alan Shepard: page 210, paragraph 1 ("Donald Eyles was…")
through page 218

Follow the instructions below for your level. Then, in your own words, tell what happened in the story from Alan's point of view. Try to remember as many details as possible. Tell what you think is the most important event in the passage.

🐾 Listen carefully to the assigned passage.

🐾🐾 Read the assigned passage aloud.

D. **Vocabulary Review**   *Language Skills, Thinking Skills*
In this part, finish the vocabulary review you began in Part 1.

Use the second stack of vocabulary cards (that you set aside for this part) and pick one card at a time. Read the word on the front and, without looking, tell your teacher either what it means or how it was used in the story. Give yourself a point for every word you are able to use correctly—were you able to beat your points from part 1?

E. **Reach for the Stars Science**   *Thinking Skills*
Complete the Human Body Matching game in your Student Notebook.[2] When you are finished, tell your teacher what you remember about the things named in the activity. If you want help remembering, you can look back at the pages in the *Human Body Basics* book where you learned about each thing, and the work you did in your Student Notebook.

F. **Writing**   *Language Skills, Thinking Skills*
In this section, write a character summary about Alan Shepard's life.

Be sure to focus on the main events, or highlights, of his life, showing what a great man he was and the important contributions he made. Alan Shepard passed away in 1998 at the age of 74.

A character summary is similar to an obituary, or an announcement (usually placed in a newspaper) telling about someone's death. A short biography is usually included in an obituary.

Teaching Tip

Encourage your children to use their Student Notebooks to consider all that they have done in this unit, and this year, and come up with the things they would like to share in their Unit Presentation. If your children have difficulty deciding, encourage them to share the things that were the most fun, the most interesting, and new information they learned. If there was an area of particular skill for them, be sure to include that as well. Book review cards, Steps for Thinking and charts comparing the inventors also give a good overview of the unit's focus. They may want to make their Student Notebooks available for others to view, so now is the time to check them for neatness.

F. Writing is not a separate subject, but rather a set of skills with which to become familiar. Writing is best when it is a response to content learned, new ideas, or as a result of an activity or experience..

✿✿ Use no more than 50 words to write your summary.

✿ Use no more than 45 words to write your summary.

✿ Use no more than 40 words to write your summary.

Lapbook Activity

G. **Music** History, Thinking Skills

Follow the directions in Appendix D to play Orchestra Story Question Quest with all the cards you have made in Units 1 through 6.

When you are finished, play Name-That-Classic with your teacher and other family members. Have someone play different tracks that you have studied throughout the year from *The Story of the Orchestra* CD. Players should take turns trying to identify the composition or instrument featured in each piece. Supply additional information to earn extra points!

H. **Independent Reading & Record Keeping** *Thinking Skills*

Review the Lesson 6 At A Glance chart in your Student Notebook to see if all the work you've done in this part has been checked off. Also, make sure the Student Notebook pages you worked on are dated and complete.

When you are finished, choose something to read that you will enjoy. Then find a quiet, comfortable place and read for the following length of time:

✿✿ ✿ 30 minutes   ✿ 35 minutes

Be sure to write down what you read today on the Reading Log in your Student Notebook.

Lesson 6, Part 4

A. **Copywork & Dictation**   *Language Skills*

Look back in your Student Notebook and review the copywork or dictation assignments you have done this year. What improvements do you see? Talk with your teacher about the gains you have made through the year, including things such as increased length, moving from copywork to dictation, fewer mistakes in punctuation or spelling, increased ability to hear punctuation when a passage is read or to notice it when it is copied, or less resistance to doing this type of assignment.

Write a statement in your Student Notebook that describes the improvements you see in your copywork or dictation since the beginning of Paths of Progress. Now ask your teacher to do the same. Compare your assessments and discuss any differences.

B. **Reader**   *Language Skills, History*

The New Way Things Work: Sections 3, 4, or 5

Lapbook Activity

Choose the number of inventions assigned below from Sections 3, 4, or 5 in *The New Way Things Work* and read about them. Then fill out the Flow Charts in your Student Notebook, telling how each of your selections work. To do this, you may want to list the various steps involved in each invention's operation on scrap paper, and number them. That way you can adjust them if necessary (by combining, simplifying, or extending) so you have the correct number of steps for the Flow Charts.

🐾 Choose one invention.

🐾 Choose two inventions.

🐾 Choose three inventions.

C. **Read-Aloud & Discussion**   *History, Language Skills, Thinking Skills*

Alan Shepard: page 219 (Chapter 18) through page 228

Look over all the predictions you made about the read-aloud story in this unit (Part 4, Section C of Lessons 1-5). Were most of them accurate, or on target? Has your ability to predict a story's events become better as you have practiced? Have you started including more details? Talk with your teacher and identify one way you have become better at making predictions. Then tell one way you need to improve in this ability.

🐾🐾 Do you feel as though you became familiar with the motivations and attitudes of the book's characters? Did understanding these things help you predict the actions they would take? Talk with your teacher, and think of at least one more way you can improve in your ability to predict a character's behavior and thoughts.

D. Word Building Review   *Language Skills, Thinking Skills*

Print and cut out the blank Word Builder Review cards for your level from the Student Resources CD, and write the words you chose during this unit on them. Then mix the cards up and follow the directions in Appendix D to play the Word Builder Recap game.

E. Reach for the Stars History and Economics   *Thinking Skills*

Look at the Unit Review Graphic Organizer in your Student Notebook (Lesson 1, Part 4E), and discuss the questions it asks with your teacher. Then fill in the boxes in the Reach for the Stars column as best you can.

When you are finished, discuss what you wrote with your teacher, and explain why you answered as you did.

F. Grammar Review   *Geography, Language Skills, Thinking Skills*

To review your editing knowledge, print and cut out the "You Can Find Me 2" cards from your Student Resources CD. Then follow the directions in Appendix C to play the game.[2]

For added difficulty, choose one card at a time and have a race to see who can be first to find an example of that usage in print. The finder must read and explain the usage on his or her card.

G. Doing   *Thinking Skills*

As you complete this unit and your Paths of Progress study, finish anything left to do on your Claymation video or flipbook, any writing or organization that is not yet finished, and setting up your science project display.

Plan to include your science project in the Unit End Presentation in the next part. To do that, make a list in your Student Notebook of everything you want to say, or things you want to draw special attention to, when you invite your family and others to view your display.

H. Independent Reading & Record Keeping   *Thinking Skills*

Review the Lesson 6 At A Glance chart in your Student Notebook to see if all the work you've done in this part has been checked off. Also, make sure the Student Notebook pages you worked on are dated and complete.

When you are finished, choose something to read that you will enjoy. Then find a quiet, comfortable place and read for the following length of time:

30 minutes   35 minutes

Be sure to write down what you read today on the Reading Log in your Student Notebook.

As you and your children prepare for the end of this unit, consider using the Presentation Feedback Sheet located in Appendix C and on the Student Resource CD. If you choose to use it, be sure to review the form with your students so they know what you will be looking for as they tell about the things they have learned. Reassure them that the form is not intended for grading, but simply to help them improve their presentation skills.

Lesson 6, Part 5

This part is set aside for completion of any work left undone from the lesson and review of concepts and content. It is also a time to expand the work of the lesson with practice and games.

- Gather all the vocabulary cards you made this year and mix them up. Then have your teacher draw at least thirty cards from any-place in the stack, without looking.

  Then ask her to show you their picture sides, one at a time. Tell her what the picture or clue means and then name the word written on the other side. If you can, tell what part of speech it is. Give yourself one point for correctly naming a word and one point for knowing its part of speech. See how many points you can get!

- Gather the Ongoing Spelling Lists from Units 1–6 and look through them. You have probably mastered most of them, but if any still seem challenging to you, put a checkmark beside them and spend some time practicing their spelling.

  Then ask your teacher to choose the number of words indicated below for your level, being sure to include the ones you checked. Write each word in your Student Notebook as she dictates it. When you are finished, look at your word lists and make corrections as needed. Show your teacher how you did.

  🌱🌱 four words from each unit   🐾🐾 five words from each unit

- Play Name-That-Classic with your teacher and other family members. Have someone play different tracks that you have studied so far from The Story of the Orchestra CD. Players should take turns trying to guess the names of the compositions. Award one point each time a player is correct and one bonus point each if the player can name either the composer or the instrument featured.

- Review the Lesson 6 At A Glance chart in your Student Notebook to see if all the work you've done in this part has been checked off. If you did an Enrichment activity or other extra work in this les-son, be sure to write it on the lines next to the chart.

- Make a Unit Presentation to your family that tells about what you have learned in the Reach for the Stars Unit. Share your Student Notebook, and things you made or accomplished this unit such your progress on the recorder and your science project. Don't for-get to stand still and speak clearly. After your presentation, be sure to ask if anyone has questions.

- Follow the directions in Appendix D to play Reach for the Stars Bingo.

Congratulations on completing Unit Six in *Paths of Progress*!

Teaching Tip

Success is encouraging. Look for gains made and improvement when evaluating your child's work. Record the number of questions or words completed success-fully on student work, not the number missed. Your child understands what he missed when he looks at his paper. To encourage in a realistic manner, point to gains made as a reminder of the impor-tance of continued effort.

Answers

1. Answer key is in Appendix C.
2. Answer key is in Appendix C.

Paths of Progress

· Appendix ·

Appendix C

Lesson At A Glance

Cultivating Greatness 315

Success Takes Flight..321

Reach for the Stars...327

Skills Chart

Cultivating Greatness 333

Success Takes Flight..336

Reach for the Stars...338

Challenge Spelling List **340**

Presentation Feedback Sheet.....................................**342**

Conference Summary..**342**

Game Answer Key

Cultivating Greatness 344

Success Takes Flight..347

Reach for the Stars...350

CULTIVATING GREATNESS – Lesson 1 At A Glance

Subject	Part	Level 1	Level 2	Level 3
A. Copywork & Dictation	Part 1	☐ SOI: page 67, paragraph 2	☐ SOI: page 67, paragraph 2	☐ SOI: page 67, paragraph 2, page 70, paragraph 1
	Part 2	☐ Steps for Thinking ☐ Tell one example	☐ Steps for Thinking ☐ Write one example	☐ Steps for Thinking ☐ Write two examples
	Part 3	☐ SOI: page 78, paragraph 1	☐ SOI: page 78, paragraph 1	☐ SOI: page 78, paragraphs 1-2
	Part 4	☐ SG: page 7, paragraph 1	☐ GWC: page 18, paragraph 3	☐ GWC: page 18, paragraphs 3 & 7
B. Reader		🐾 *Strawberry Girl*	🐾🐾 *The Story of Inventions*	🐾🐾🐾 *George Washington Carver*
	Part 1	☐ Page 1-page 10, paragraph 4	☐ Page 67-top of page 71 ☐ Questions 1 & 2	☐ Pages 1-6
	Part 2	☐ Page 10, paragraphs 5-page 17, paragraph 3	☐ Pages 71-75 ☐ Questions 3-5	☐ Page 7-page 13, paragraph 1
	Part 3	☐ Page 17, paragraph 4-page 25, paragraph 1	☐ Pages 75-79 ☐ Questions 6 & 7	☐ Page 13, paragraph 2-page 18
	Part 4	☐ Page 25, paragraph 2-page 32	☐ Page 79-end of chapter ☐ Question 8	☐ Page 19-page 25, paragraph 4
C. Read Aloud		🐾🐾🐾 *George Washington Carver*		
	Part 1	☐ Pages 1-6	☐ Narration ☐ Retelling	
	Part 2	☐ Page 7-page 13, paragraph 1	☐ Discussion ☐ Make up questions	☐ Additional questions
	Part 3	☐ Page 13, paragraph 2-page 18	☐ Narration ☐ Point of view	
	Part 4	☐ Page 19-page 25, paragraph 4	☐ Discussion ☐ Predictions	☐ Additional predictions
D. Vocabulary & Word Building		🐾🐾 *Human Body Basics*		
	Part 1	☐ Unit 3 vocabulary review		
	Part 2	☐ "Chrono-" words	☐ Additional "chrono-" words	☐ Additional "chrono-" words
	Part 3	☐ Unit 3 vocabulary review		
	Part 4	☐ 3 "chrono-" words ☐ Write sentence	☐ 6 "chrono-" words ☐ Write sentence	☐ 9 "chrono-" words ☐ Write sentence
E. Economics, History & Science	Part 1	☐ Atoms ☐ Molecules ☐ Vocab ☐ Activity ☐ Elements		
	Part 2	☐ Family farms ☐ Agriculture	☐ Trends in farming ☐ Organic farmig	☐ Comparisons
	Part 3	☐ Cells ☐ Vocab ☐ 2 Activities ☐ Game Prep ☐ Project	☐ Additional projects	
	Part 4	☐ Family farm problems/solutions ☐ Alvin York profile		
F. Writing, Editing & Spelling	Part 1	☐ Expository writing	☐ Additional expository writing	☐ Additional expository writing
	Part 2	☐ Dialect: 2 sentences ☐ Subject-verb agreement: 1 sentence	☐ Additional sentences	☐ Additional sentences
	Part 3	☐ 50 word character summary	☐ 45 word character summary	☐ 40 word character summary
	Part 4	☐ Choose 8-12 words ☐ Study ☐ Spell	☐ Choose 10-15 words ☐ Study ☐ Spell	☐ Choose 12-18 words ☐ Study ☐ Spell
G. Music & Art		🐾🐾 *The Story of the Orchestra*		
	Part 1	☐ Pages 42-45 ☐ String section ☐ Violin ☐ Drawing		
	Part 2	☐ Basix Recorder Method: pages 29-30		
	Part 3	☐ Orchestra Story cards		
	Part 4	☐ Create Anything With Clay: page 41		
H. Independent Reading		🐾 30 minutes daily ☐☐☐☐	🐾🐾 30 minutes daily ☐☐☐☐	🐾🐾🐾 35 minutes daily ☐☐☐☐
Review	Part 5	☐ Steps for Thinking review ☐ Vocabulary review ☐ Spelling review	☐ Spelling review ☐ Science game ☐ Recorder practice	☐ Word Search
Materials		*Strawberry Girl* / The Story of Inventions / Basix Recorder Method / Human Body Basics / The Story of the Orchestra book & CD	*George Washington Carver* / Profiles from History, Volume 3 / Create Anything With Clay	Recorder, Polymer clay; Activity (Part 4): Rolling pin or round jar, Table knife

Cultivating Greatness Unit – *Lesson 2 At A Glance*

Section	Part	Column 1	Column 2	Column 3
A. Copywork & Dictation	Part 1	☐ *SOI*: page 82, paragraph 2	☐ *SOI*: page 82, paragraph 2	☐ *SOI*: page 82, paragraph 2, page 83, paragraph 1
	Part 2	☐ Steps for Thinking ☐ Tell one example	☐ Steps for Thinking ☐ Write one example	☐ Steps for Thinking ☐ Write two examples
	Part 3	☐ *SOI*: page 92, paragraph 1	☐ *SOI*: page 92, paragraph 1	☐ *SOI*: page 92, paragraphs 1 & 2
	Part 4	☐ *SG*: page 42, paragraph 2	☐ *GWC*: page 46, paragraph 2	☐ *GWC*: page 46, paragraphs 2 & 8
B. Reader		*Strawberry Girl*	*The Story of Inventions*	*George Washington Carver*
	Part 1	☐ Page 33-page 41, paragraph 1	☐ Pages 81-86 ☐ Question 1	☐ Page 25, paragraph 5-Page 30, paragraph 6
	Part 2	☐ Page 41, paragraph 2-page 47	☐ Pages 86-90 ☐ Question 2	☐ Page 30, paragraph 7-top of page 36
	Part 3	☐ Pages 48-55	☐ Pages 90-93 ☐ Question 3	☐ Page 36, paragraph 1-page 40
	Part 4	☐ Page 56-page 61, paragraph 3	☐ Page 93-end of chapter ☐ Questions 4 & 5	☐ Pages 41-45
C. Read Aloud		*George Washington Carver*		
	Part 1	☐ Page 25, paragraph 5-Page 30, paragraph 6	☐ Narration ☐ Retelling	
	Part 2	☐ Page 30, paragraph 7-top of page 36	☐ Discussion ☐ Make up questions	☐ Additional questions
	Part 3	☐ Page 36, paragraph 1-page 40	☐ Narration ☐ Point of view	
	Part 4	☐ Pages 41-45	☐ Discussion ☐ Predictions	☐ Additional predictions
D. Vocabulary & Word Building		*Human Body Basics*		
	Part 1	☐ Vocabulary I.D. Sheet ☐ 6 words	☐ Vocabulary I.D. Sheet ☐ 12 words	
	Part 2	☐ "Pro-" words	☐ Additional "pro-" words	☐ Additional "pro-" words
	Part 3	☐ Vocabulary review		
	Part 4	☐ 3 "pro-" words ☐ Write sentence	☐ 6 "pro-" words ☐ Write sentence	☐ 9 "pro-" words ☐ Write sentence
E. Economics, History & Science		*Human Body Basics*		
	Part 1	☐ Bones ☐ Vocab ☐ 5 Activities		
	Part 2	☐ Homestead Act ☐ Conflicts ☐ Qualities ☐ Examples	☐ Additional examples	
	Part 3	☐ Review ☐ Activity ☐ Project	☐ Additional project	
	Part 4	☐ Plains states ☐ State profile chart ☐ Questions	☐ Additional questions	☐ Product list ☐ Comparisons
F. Writing, Editing & Spelling	Part 1	☐ Expository writing	☐ Additional expository writing	☐ Additional expository writing
	Part 2	☐ Dialect: 2 sentences ☐ Subject-verb agreement: 1 sentence	☐ Additional sentences	☐ Additional sentences
	Part 3	☐ 50 word character summary	☐ 45 word character summary	☐ 40 word character summary
	Part 4	☐ Choose 8-12 words ☐ Study ☐ Spell	☐ Choose 10-15 words ☐ Study ☐ Spell	☐ Choose 12-18 words ☐ Study ☐ Spell
G. Music & Art		*The Story of the Orchestra*		
	Part 1	☐ Pages 46-47 ☐ Viola ☐ Cello ☐ Drawing		
	Part 2	☐ *Basix Recorder Method*: page 31		
	Part 3	☐ Orchestra Story cards		
	Part 4	☐ *Create Anything With Clay*: page 42		
H. Independent Reading		☐ 30 minutes daily ☐☐☐	☐ 30 minutes daily ☐☐☐	☐ 35 minutes daily ☐☐☐
Review	Part 5	☐ Steps for Thinking review ☐ Vocabulary review	☐ Spelling review ☐ Vocabulary review ☐ Science game ☐ Recorder practice	☐ Word Scramble

Materials

Column 1	Column 2	Column 3
Strawberry Girl *The Story of Inventions* *Create Anything With Clay* *The Story of the Orchestra book & CD*	*George Washington Carver* *Basix Recorder Method* *Human Body Basics*	Recorder, Polymer clay; Activity (Part 1): Masking tape, Cooked chicken leg bone, Vinegar, Jar or other container (to hold bone); Activity (Part 4): Rolling pin or round jar, Paper, Scissors, Craft glue, Table knife, Ribbon or yarn

CULTIVATING GREATNESS UNIT – Lesson 3 At A Glance

A. COPYWORK & DICTATION

Part	Column 1	Column 2	Column 3
Part 1	□ SOI: page 72, paragraph 3 □ Tell one example	□ SOI: page 72, paragraph 3	□ SOI: page 72, paragraph 3 & page 73, paragraph 1
Part 2	□ Steps for Thinking □ Write one example	□ Steps for Thinking	□ Steps for Thinking □ Write two examples
Part 3	□ SOI: page 87, paragraph 3	□ SOI: page 87, paragraph 3	□ SOI: page 87, paragraph 3 & 4
Part 4	□ SG: page 93, paragraph 3	□ GWC: page 66, paragraph 3	□ GWC: page 66, paragraph 3 & page 67, paragraph 2

B. READER

🐾🐾 *Strawberry Girl* | *The Story of Inventions* | 🐾🐾 *George Washington Carver*

Part	*Strawberry Girl*	*The Story of Inventions*	*George Washington Carver*
Part 1	□ Page 61, paragraph 4-page 71, paragraph 4	□ Review pages 67-75 □ Give examples	□ Page 46-top of page 52
Part 2	□ Page 71, paragraph 5-page 78	□ Review page 75-end of chapter □ Give examples	□ Page 52, paragraph 1-page 57, paragraph 9
Part 3	□ Page 79-page 86, paragraph 4	□ Review pages 81-90 □ Give examples	□ Page 57, paragraph 10-page 63, paragraph 6
Part 4	□ Page 86, paragraph 5-page 94, paragraph 2	□ Review page 90 □ Give examples	□ Page 63, paragraph 7-page 68

C. READ ALOUD

🐾🐾 *George Washington Carver*

Part	Column 1	Column 2	Column 3
Part 1	□ Page 46-top of page 52	□ Narration □ Retelling	🐾
Part 2	□ Page 52, paragraph 1-page 57, paragraph 9	□ Discussion □ Make up questions	□ Additional questions
Part 3	□ Page 57, paragraph 10-page 63, paragraph 6	□ Narration □ Point of view	
Part 4	□ Page 63, paragraph 7-page 68	□ Discussion □ Predictions	□ Additional predictions

D. VOCABULARY & WORD BUILDING

🐾🐾 *Human Body Basics*

Part	Column 1	Column 2	Column 3
Part 1	□ Vocabulary I.D. Sheet □ 6 words	□ Vocabulary I.D. Sheet □ 12 words	🐾
Part 2	□ Review "chrono" & "pro" □ 3 sentences □ Rummy Roots	□ 4 sentences	□ 5 sentences
Part 3	□ Vocabulary review		
Part 4	□ Review "chrono" & "pro" □ 3 sentences □ Rummy Roots	□ 4 sentences	□ 5 sentences

E. ECONOMICS, HISTORY & SCIENCE

Part	Column 1	Column 2	Column 3
Part 1	□ Muscles □ 3 vocab cards □ Activities 8-10	□ 4 vocab cards □ Project 3	🐾
Part 2	□ A Day in the Life □ Presentation □ Supply & Demand game		□ 4 vocab cards □ Extended project 3
Part 3	□ Review □ Project 4		
Part 4	□ Invention Demand Chart □ Supply & Demand game		

F. WRITING, EDITING & SPELLING

Part	Column 1	Column 2	Column 3
Part 1	□ Essay writing	□ Additional essay	🐾
Part 2	□ Dialect: 2 sentences □ Subject-verb agreement: 1 sentence	□ Additional sentences	□ Additional essay
Part 3	□ Conclusions □ Revising		□ Additional paragraph
Part 4	□ Choose 8-12 words □ Study □ Spell	□ Choose 10-15 words □ Study □ Spell	□ Choose 12-18 words □ Study □ Spell

G. MUSIC & ART

🐾🐾 *The Story of the Orchestra*

Part	Column 1	Column 2	Column 3
Part 1	□ Pages 48-49 □ Double bass □ Harp □ Drawing		🐾
Part 2	□ Basix Recorder Method: pages 32 & 33		
Part 3	□ Orchestra Story cards		
Part 4	□ Create Anything With Clay: page 43		

H. INDEPENDENT READING

🐾🐾 | 30 minutes daily □□□□ | 30 minutes daily □□□□ | 35 minutes daily □□□□

REVIEW

Part	Column 1	Column 2	Column 3
Part 5	□ Steps for Thinking review □ Vocabulary review	□ Spelling review □ Science review □ Vocabulary review	□ Recorder practice □ Crossword

MATERIALS

Strawberry Girl
The Story of Inventions
Human Body Basics
The Story of the Orchestra book & CD

George Washington Carver
Create Anything With Clay
Basix Recorder Method

Recorder, Polymer clay; Rummy Roots Word Cards; Activity (Part 1): Clothespin, Timer that can clock 30-second intervals; Activity (Part 3): Uncooked chicken leg quarter, Sharp scissors, Disposable vinyl or plastic gloves (optional); Activity (Part 4): Table knife, Toothpick; String or yarn, Scissors, Small paper punch or awl

Cultivating Greatness Unit – Lesson 4 At A Glance

		Column 1	Column 2	Column 3
A. Copywork & Dictation	Part 1	☐ *SOI:* page 102, paragraph 2	☐ *SOI:* page 102, paragraph 2	☐ *SOI:* page 102, paragraph 2 & page 103, paragraph 2
	Part 2	☐ Steps for Thinking ☐ Tell one example	☐ Steps for Thinking ☐ Write one example	☐ Steps for Thinking ☐ Write two examples
	Part 3	☐ *SOI:* page 111, paragraph 1	☐ *SOI:* page 111, paragraph 1	☐ *SOI:* page 111, paragraphs 1 & 2
	Part 4	☐ *SG:* page 123, paragraph 3	☐ *GWC:* page 89, paragraph 6	☐ *GWC:* page 89, paragraph 6-page 90, paragraph 4
B. Reader		🐾 🐾 *Strawberry Girl*	🐾 🐾 *The Story of Inventions*	🐾 🐾 *George Washington Carver*
	Part 1	☐ Page 94, paragraph 3-page 103	☐ Pages 99-103 ☐ Questions 1 & 2	☐ Page 69-page 74, paragraph 6
	Part 2	☐ Pages 104-112	☐ Pages 103-108 ☐ Question 3	☐ Page 74, paragraph 7-page 80, paragraph 6
	Part 3	☐ Page 113-page 122, paragraph 8	☐ Pages 108-114 ☐ Question 4-6	☐ Page 80, paragraph 7-page 84
	Part 4	☐ Page 122, paragraph 9-page 131, paragraph 4	☐ Pages 114-end of chapter ☐ Questions 7 & 8	☐ Page 85-page 90, paragraph 8
C. Read Aloud		🐾 🐾 *George Washington Carver*	🐾 🐾	🐾 🐾
	Part 1	☐ Page 69-page 74, paragraph 6	☐ Narration ☐ Retelling	
	Part 2	☐ Page 74, paragraph 7-page 80, paragraph 6	☐ Discussion ☐ Make up questions	☐ Additional questions
	Part 3	☐ Page 80, paragraph 7-page 84	☐ Narration ☐ Point of view	
	Part 4	☐ Page 85-page 90, paragraph 8	☐ Discussion ☐ Predictions	☐ Additional predictions
D. Vocabulary & Word Building		🐾 🐾 *Human Body Basics*	🐾 🐾	🐾 🐾
	Part 1	☐ Vocabulary I.D. Sheet ☐ 6 words	☐ Vocabulary I.D. Sheet ☐ 12 words	
	Part 2	☐ 3 "tele-" words	☐ Additional "tele-" words	☐ Additional "tele-" words
	Part 3	☐ Vocabulary review		
	Part 4	☐ 3 "tele-" words ☐ Write sentence	☐ 6 "tele-" words ☐ Write sentence	☐ 9 "tele-" words ☐ Write sentence
E. Economics, History & Science		🐾 🐾	🐾 🐾	🐾 🐾
	Part 1	☐ Heart ☐ Vocab ☐ 5 Activities		
	Part 2	☐ General stores ☐ Department stores ☐ Comparisons	☐ Family shopping patterns	☐ Family preferences
	Part 3	☐ Blood ☐ Vessels ☐ Vocab ☐ 2 activities ☐ Project	☐ Additional project	
	Part 4	☐ Supply demand ☐ Railroads ☐ Discussion ☐ Comparisons	☐ Additional comparisons	
F. Writing, Editing & Spelling		🐾 🐾	🐾 🐾	🐾 🐾
	Part 1	☐ Play writing		
	Part 2	☐ Dialect: 2 sentences ☐ Subject-verb agreement: 1 sentence	☐ Additional sentences	☐ Additional sentences
	Part 3	☐ 50 word character summary	☐ 45 word character summary	☐ 40 word character summary
	Part 4	☐ Choose 8-12 words ☐ Study ☐ Spell	☐ Choose 10-15 words ☐ Study ☐ Spell	☐ Choose 12-18 words ☐ Study ☐ Spell
G. Music & Art		🐾 🐾 *The Story of the Orchestra*	🐾 🐾	
	Part 1	☐ Pages 50-53 ☐ Woodwind ☐ Flute ☐ Piccolo ☐ Drawing		
	Part 2	☐ *Basic Recorder Method:* pages 34 & 35		
	Part 3	☐ Orchestra Story cards		
	Part 4	☐ *Create Anything With Clay,* pages 44-45		
H. Independent Reading		🐾 🐾	🐾 🐾	🐾 🐾
		30 minutes daily ☐☐☐☐	30 minutes daily ☐☐☐☐	35 minutes daily ☐☐☐
Review	Part 5	☐ Steps for Thinking ☐ Vocabulary cards/review	☐ Spelling review ☐ Science review ☐ Recorder practice	☐ Who or What Am I?
Materials		*Strawberry Girl* *Basic Recorder Method* *Human Body Basics* *The Story of the Orchestra book & CD*	*George Washington Carver* *Create Anything With Clay* *The Story of Inventions*	Recorder, Polymer clay; Activity (Part 1): Timer that measures seconds, Cardboard paper towel roll; Activity (Part 4): Stiff paper, Scissors, Craft glue, Toothpick, String or yarn

Cultivating Greatness Unit – Lesson 5 At A Glance

		Level 1	Level 2	Level 3
A. Copywork & Dictation	Part 1	☐ SOI: page 120, paragraph 1	☐ SOI: page 120, paragraphs 1 & 2 ☐ Write one example	☐ SOI: page 120, paragraphs 1 & 2 ☐ Write two examples
	Part 2	☐ Steps for Thinking ☐ Tell one example	☐ Steps for Thinking ☐ Write one example	☐ Steps for Thinking ☐ Write two examples
	Part 3	☐ SOI: page 130, paragraph 1	☐ SOI: page 130, paragraph 1	☐ SOI: page 130, paragraphs 1 & 2
	Part 4	☐ SG: page 147, paragraph 5	☐ GWC: page 107, paragraph 10	☐ GWC: page 107 paragraph 10 & page 108, paragraph 2
B. Reader		*Strawberry Girl*	*The Story of Inventions*	*George Washington Carver*
	Part 1	☐ Page 131, paragraph 5-bottom of page 138	☐ Pages 116-120 ☐ Questions 1 & 2	☐ Page 90, paragraph 9-page 95
	Part 2	☐ Page 138, last paragraph-page 145	☐ Pages 120-128 ☐ Questions 3 & 4	☐ Page 96-bottom of page 100
	Part 3	☐ Page 146-page 155, paragraph 2	☐ Pages 128-133 ☐ Questions 5 & 6	☐ Page 100, last paragraph-bottom of page 104
	Part 4	☐ Page 155, paragraph 3-page 163, paragraph 7	☐ Pages 133-end of chapter ☐ Questions 7-9	☐ Page 104, last paragraph-page 111, paragraph 2
C. Read Aloud		*George Washington Carver*		
	Part 1	☐ Page 90, paragraph 9-page 95	☐ Narration ☐ Retelling	
	Part 2	☐ Page 96-bottom of page 100	☐ Discussion ☐ Make up questions	☐ Additional questions
	Part 3	☐ Page 100, last paragraph-bottom of page 104	☐ Narration ☐ Point of view	
	Part 4	☐ Page 104, last paragraph-page 111, paragraph 2	☐ Discussion ☐ Predictions	☐ Additional predictions
D. Vocabulary & Word Building		*Human Body Basics*		
	Part 1	☐ Vocabulary I.D. Sheet ☐ 6 words	☐ Vocabulary I.D. Sheet ☐ 12 words	
	Part 2	☐ "trans-" words ☐ Definitions (3 words)	☐ Additional "trans-" words	☐ Additional "trans-" words
	Part 3	☐ Vocabulary review		
	Part 4	☐ 3 "trans-" words ☐ Write sentence	☐ 6 "trans-" words ☐ Write sentence	☐ 9 "trans-" words ☐ Write sentence
E. Economics, History & Science		*Human Body Basics*		
	Part 1	☐ Respiratory ☐ Vocab ☐ 3 Activities ☐ Project	☐ Additional project	☐ Additional project
	Part 2	☐ Mail ☐ Mail order ☐ Comparisons ☐ Christmas ☐ Discussion	☐ Additional comparisons	☐ Delivery methods
	Part 3	☐ Urinary ☐ Vocab ☐ 2 Activities ☐ Project		
	Part 4	☐ World War 1 ☐ Wartime business		
F. Writing, Editing & Spelling	Part 1	☐ Expository writing	☐ Additional expository writing	☐ Additional expository writing
	Part 2	☐ Dialect: 2 sentences ☐ Subject-verb agreement: 1 sentence	☐ Additional sentences	☐ Additional sentences
	Part 3	☐ 50 word character summary	☐ 45 word character summary	☐ 40 word character summary
	Part 4	☐ Choose 8-12 words ☐ Study ☐ Spell	☐ Choose 10-15 words ☐ Study ☐ Spell	☐ Choose 12-18 words ☐ Study ☐ Spell
G. Music & Art		*The Story of the Orchestra*		
	Part 1	☐ Pages 54-57 ☐ Oboe ☐ Clarinet ☐ Saxophone ☐ Drawing		
	Part 2	☐ *Basix Recorder Method*: pages 36-37		
	Part 3	☐ Orchestra Story cards		
	Part 4	☐ *Create Anything With Clay*: page 46		
H. Independent Reading		30 minutes daily ☐☐☐	30 minutes daily ☐☐☐☐	35 minutes daily ☐☐☐☐
Review	Part 5	☐ Steps for Thinking review ☐ Vocabulary cards/review	☐ Spelling review ☐ Science review ☐ Recorder practice	☐ Bingo

Materials

Strawberry Girl *Classroom Atlas of the U.S.* *Basix Recorder Method* *Human Body Basics* *The Story of the Orchestra book & CD*	*George Washington Carver* *The Story of Inventions* *Create Anything With Clay* *Profiles from History, Volume 3*	Recorder, Polymer clay; Activity (Part 1): Timer that measures seconds, Plastic 2-liter soda bottle, 1 small round balloon, 1 large round balloon, 2 rubber bands, Packing or masking tape, Straw, Modeling clay, Hammer and ** nail; Activity (Part 4): Cardboard or paper mache box, Table knife, Craft glue, Paintbrush

Cultivating Greatness Unit – Lesson 6 At A Glance

Section	Part	Column 1	Column 2	Column 3
A. Copywork & Dictation	Part 1	□ SOI: 1 paragraph of choice	□ SOI: 2 paragraphs of choice	□ SOI: 3 paragraphs of choice
	Part 2	□ List of mistakes □ Discussion	□ List of mistakes □ Discussion	□ List of mistakes □ Discussion
	Part 3	□ SOI: 1 paragraph of choice	□ SOI: 2 paragraphs of choice	□ SOI: 3 paragraphs of choice
	Part 4	□ List of mistakes □ Discussion	□ List of mistakes □ Discussion	□ List of mistakes □ Discussion
B. Reader		*Strawberry Girl*	*The Story of Inventions*	*George Washington Carver*
	Part 1	□ Page 163, paragraph 8-page 171, paragraph 8	□ Review chapters 6 & 7 □ Compare lives	□ Page 111, paragraph 3-top of page 117
	Part 2	□ Page 171, paragraph 9-top of page 180	□ Review chapters 6 & 7 □ Compare inventions	□ Page 117, paragraph 1-top of page 122
	Part 3	□ Page 180, paragraph 1-page 187, paragraph 3	□ Review chapters 8 & 9 □ Compare lives	□ Page 122, paragraph 1-page 127
	Part 4	□ Page 187, paragraph 4-page 194	□ Review chapters 8 & 9 □ Compare inventions	□ Pages 128-133
C. Read Aloud		*George Washington Carver*		
	Part 1	□ Page 111, paragraph 3-top of page 117	□ Narration □ Retelling	□ Character motivations
	Part 2	□ Page 117, paragraph 1-top of page 122	□ Discussion: improvements	
	Part 3	□ Page 122, paragraph 1-page 127	□ Narration □ Point of view	
	Part 4	□ Pages 128-133	□ Discussion: evaluate predictions	
D. Vocabulary & Word Building		*Human Body Basics*		
	Part 1	□ Vocabulary I.D. Sheet □ 6 words	□ Vocabulary I.D. Sheet □ 12 words	
	Part 2	□ Review "tele" & "trans" □ 3 sentences □ Rummy Roots	□ 4 sentences	□ 5 sentences
	Part 3	□ Vocabulary review		
	Part 4	□ Review words □ 1 sentence for each □ Rummy Roots	□ 2 sentences for each □ Rummy Roots	□ 3 sentences for each □ Rummy Roots
E. Economics, History & Science	Part 1	□ Finish science project □ Other work		
	Part 2	□ Invention Demand Chart □ Supply & Demand game		
	Part 3	□ Human Body Matching □ Review		
	Part 4	□ Review □ Inventors 20 Questions □ Add 3 inventors	□ Add 4 inventors	□ Add 5 inventors
F. Writing, Editing & Spelling	Part 1	□ 50 word character summary	□ 45 word character summary	□ 40 word character summary
	Part 2	□ Conclusions □ Revising		
	Part 3	□ Round/flat characters □ Changes □ Two examples	□ Three examples	□ Four examples
	Part 4	□ Ongoing spelling review		
G. Music & Art		*The Story of the Orchestra*		
	Part 1	□ Orchestra Story review □ Question Quest		
	Part 2	□ Basix Recorder Method: review □ Practice		
	Part 3	□ Question Quest □ Name That Instrument		
	Part 4	□ Create Anything With Clay: page 47		
H. Independent Reading		30 minutes daily □□□□	30 minutes daily □□□□	35 minutes daily □□□□
Review	Part 5	□ Vocabulary cards/review □ Spelling review □ Name-That-Classic	□ Name-That-Classic □ Unit Presentation □ Bingo	

Materials

Strawberry Girl / *The Story of Inventions* / *Create Anything With Clay* / *The Story of the Orchestra book & CD*

George Washington Carver / *Basix Recorder Method* / *Human Body Basics*

Recorder, polymer clay; Rummy Roots cards; Activity (Part 4): Toothpick, Old washcloth, Alphabet macaroni (optional), Rice (optional), String, yarn, or leather cord

SUCCESS TAKES FLIGHT UNIT – *Lesson 1 At A Glance*

Section	Part	Column 1	Column 2	Column 3
A. Copywork & Dictation	Part 1	☐ *SOI:* page 262, paragraph 1	☐ *SOI:* page 262, paragraph 1	☐ *SOI:* page 262, paragraphs 1–2
	Part 2	☐ Steps for Thinking ☐ Tell one example	☐ Steps for Thinking ☐ Write one example	☐ Steps for Thinking ☐ Write two examples
	Part 3	☐ *SOI:* page 264, paragraph 3	☐ *SOI:* page 264, paragraph 3	☐ *SOI:* page 264, paragraph 3 & page 265, paragraph 1
	Part 4	☐ *HP:* page 28, paragraph 2	☐ *WB:* page 14, paragraph 5	☐ *WB:* page 14, paragraphs 5 & 6
B. Reader		🐾 *Homer Price*	🐾 *The Story of Inventions*	🐾 *The Wright Brothers*
	Part 1	☐ Page 10–top of page 16	☐ Pages 261–264 ☐ Questions 1–4	☐ Preface–page 5, paragraph 5
	Part 2	☐ Page 16, paragraph 1–page 21, paragraph 3	☐ Pages 264–267 ☐ Questions 5–8	☐ Page 5, paragraph 6–page 10
	Part 3	☐ Page 21, paragraph 4–top of page 24	☐ *The New Way Things Work:* pages 106–107	☐ Page 11–page 17, paragraph 4
	Part 4	☐ Page 24, paragraph 1–page 28	☐ *The New Way Things Work:* pages 108–109	☐ Page 17, paragraph 5–page 25, paragraph 5
C. Read Aloud		🐾 🐾 *The Wright Brothers*		🐾
	Part 1	☐ Preface–page 5, paragraph 5	☐ Narration ☐ Retelling	
	Part 2	☐ Page 5, paragraph 6–page 10	☐ Discussion ☐ Make up questions	☐ Additional questions
	Part 3	☐ Page 11–page 17, paragraph 4	☐ Narration ☐ Point of view	
	Part 4	☐ Pg 17, paragraph 5–pg 25, paragraph 5	☐ Discussion ☐ Predictions	☐ Additional predictions
D. Vocabulary & Word Building		🐾 🐾		🐾
	Part 1	☐ Unit 4 vocabulary review		
	Part 2	☐ "micro-" & "micros-" words	☐ Additional "micro-" & "micros-" words	☐ Additional "micro-" & "micros-" words
	Part 3	☐ Vocabulary review		
	Part 4	☐ 3 "micro-" & "micros-" words ☐ Write sentence	☐ 6 "micro-" & "micros-" words ☐ Write sentence	☐ 9 "micro-" & "micros-" words ☐ Write sentence
E. Economics, History & Science		🐾 🐾 *Human Body Basics*		🐾
	Part 1	☐ Digestive System ☐ Vocab ☐ 3 Activities ☐ Project	☐ Additional project	
	Part 2	☐ Automobiles ☐ Discussion ☐ List	☐ Additional list	☐ Research
	Part 3	☐ Absorbtion ☐ Vocab ☐ Other organs ☐ 2 activities ☐ Project	☐ Additional project	
	Part 4	☐ Trucks ☐ Observation ☐ Discussion	☐ Research ☐ List	☐ Additional research ☐ Discussion
F. Writing, Editing & Spelling		🐾 🐾		🐾
	Part 1	☐ Expository writing	☐ Additional expository writing	☐ Additional expository writing
	Part 2	☐ Review types of nouns ☐ List 10 of each	☐ List 12 of each	☐ List 15 of each
	Part 3	☐ Research topic (science project) ☐ List		
	Part 4	☐ Choose 8–12 words ☐ Study ☐ Spell	☐ Choose 10–15 words ☐ Study ☐ Spell	☐ Choose 12–18 words ☐ Study ☐ Spell
G. Music & Art		🐾 🐾 *The Story of the Orchestra*		
	Part 1	☐ Pages 58–61 ☐ Bassoon ☐ Brass Section ☐ Track 25 ☐ Drawing		
	Part 2	☐ *Basix Recorder Method:* pages 38 & 39		
	Part 3	☐ Orchestra Story cards		
	Part 4	☐ *Create Anything With Clay:* pages 48–49		
H. Independent Reading		🐾 30 minutes daily ☐☐☐☐		🐾 35 minutes daily ☐☐☐☐
Review	Part 5	☐ Steps for Thinking review ☐ Vocabulary cards/review	☐ Spelling review ☐ Science review ☐ Recorder practice	☐ Steps for Thinking review ☐ Word Search
Materials		*The Wright Brothers* / *The Story of Inventions* / *Create Anything With Clay* / *Classroom Atlas of the U.S.* / *The Story of the Orchestra book & CD*	*Homer Price* / *The New Way Things Work* / *Basix Recorder Method*	Recorder; Polymer clay: Activity (Part 4): Various supplies (pages 48 & 49 in *Clay* book)

SUCCESS TAKES FLIGHT UNIT – *Lesson 2 At A Glance*

Section	Part	Column 1	Column 2	Column 3
A. Copywork & Dictation	Part 1	SOI: page 140, paragraph 3	SOI: page 140, paragraph 3	SOI: page 140, paragraphs 3–4
	Part 2	Steps for Thinking / Tell one example	Steps for Thinking / Write one example	Steps for Thinking / Write two examples
	Part 3	SOI: page 142, paragraph 4	SOI: page 142, paragraph 4	SOI: page 142, paragraphs 4–5
	Part 4	HP: page 44, paragraph 10	HP: page 34, paragraph 2	HP: page 34, paragraph 2 & paragraph 8
B. Reader		*Homer Price*	*The Story of Inventions*	*The Wright Brothers*
	Part 1	Page 34–page 36, paragraph 9	Pages 138–140 / Question 1	Page 25, paragraph 6–page 33, paragraph 1
	Part 2	Page 36, paragraph 10–page 39, paragraph 8	Pages 140–142	Page 33, paragraph 2–page 40
	Part 3	Page 39, paragraph 9–page 44, paragraph 3	Pages 142–144 / Questions 2 & 3	Pages 41–49
	Part 4	Page 44, paragraph 4–page 46	Pages 144–147 / Questions 4 & 5	Page 50–page 56, paragraph 1
C. Read Aloud		*The Wright Brothers*		
	Part 1	Page 25, paragraph 6–page 33, paragraph 1	Narration	
	Part 2	Page 33, paragraph 2–page 40	Discussion / Make up questions	Additional questions
	Part 3	Pages 41–49	Narration / Point of view	
	Part 4	Page 50–page 56, paragraph 1	Discussion / Predictions	Additional predictions
D. Vocabulary & Word Building	Part 1	Vocabulary I.D. Sheet / 6 words	Vocabulary I.D. Sheet / 12 words	
	Part 2	"unus-" & "uni-" words	Additional "unus-" & "uni-" words	Additional "unus-" & "uni-" words
	Part 3	Vocabulary review		
	Part 4	3 "unus-" & "uni-" words / Write sentence	6 "unus-" & "uni-" words / Write sentence	9 "unus-" & "uni-" words / Write sentence
E. Economics, History & Science		*Human Body Basics*		
	Part 1	CNS / Vocab / 5 Activities / Project	Additional project	
	Part 2	Great Depression / Unemployment chart / Benefits chart	Home state research	Civil unrest research / Comparisons
	Part 3	PNS / Vocab / 4 Activities / Project	Additional project	
	Part 4	Dust Bowl / State chart / Compare	Discussion	Research
F. Writing, Editing & Spelling	Part 1	Expository writing	Additional expository writing	Additional expository writing
	Part 2	Review adjectives / List 10	List 12	List 15
	Part 3	Complete science projects / Other work		
	Part 4	Choose 8–12 words / Study / Spell	Choose 10–15 words / Study / Spell	Choose 12–18 words / Study / Spell
G. Music & Art		*The Story of the Orchestra*		
	Part 1	Pages 62–65 / Trumpet / French horn / Tracks 26 & 27 / Drawing		
	Part 2	Basix Recorder Method: pages 40–41		
	Part 3	Orchestra Story cards		
	Part 4	Create Anything With Clay: pages 50–51 / Review		
H. Independent Reading		30 minutes daily	30 minutes daily	35 minutes daily
Review	Part 5	Steps for Thinking review / Vocabulary cards/review	Spelling review / Science review / Recorder practice	Word Scramble

Materials

The Wright Brothers
The Story of Inventions
Create Anything With Clay
The Story of the Orchestra book & CD

Homer Price
Basix Recorder Method
Classroom Atlas of the U.S.

Recorder; Polymer clay; Activity (Part 4): Black & white photocopy of a design or picture, Scissors, Spoon

SUCCESS TAKES FLIGHT UNIT – *Lesson 3 At A Glance*

		Column 1	Column 2	Column 3
A. Copywork & Dictation	Part 1	☐ SOI: page 266, paragraph 2	☐ SOI: page 266, paragraph 2	☐ SOI: page 266, paragraphs 2–3
	Part 2	☐ Steps for Thinking ☐ Tell one example	☐ Steps for Thinking ☐ Write one example	☐ Steps for Thinking ☐ Write two examples
	Part 3	☐ HP: page 50, paragraph 4	☐ WB: page 70, paragraph 3	☐ WB: page 70, paragraph 3 & page 71, paragraph 1
	Part 4	☐ HP: page 62, paragraphs 7–8	☐ WB: page 74, paragraph 6	☐ WB: page 74, paragraph 6 & page 75, paragraph 2
B. Reader		*Homer Price*	*The Story of Inventions*	*The Wright Brothers*
	Part 1	☐ Page 50–page 54, paragraph 4	☐ Review pages 261-266 ☐ Examples	☐ Page 56, paragraph 2–page 64, paragraph 1
	Part 2	☐ Page 54, paragraph 5–page 58, paragraph 3	☐ Review pages 266-267 ☐ Examples	☐ Page 64, paragraph 2–page 70
	Part 3	☐ Page 58, paragraph 4–page 63, paragraph 2	☐ Review pages 138-142 ☐ Examples	☐ Page 71–page 77, paragraph 4
	Part 4	☐ Page 63, paragraph 3–page 67	☐ Review pages 142-147 ☐ Examples	☐ Page 77, paragraph 5–top of page 86
		The Wright Brothers		
	Part 1	☐ Page 56, paragraph 2–page 64, paragraph 1		
	Part 2	☐ Page 64, paragraph 2–page 70		
	Part 3	☐ Page 71–page 77, paragraph 4		
	Part 4	☐ Page 77, paragraph 5–top of page 86		
C. Read Aloud	Part 1	☐ Narration ☐ Retelling	☐ Narration ☐ Retelling	
	Part 2	☐ Discussion ☐ Make up questions	☐ Discussion ☐ Make up questions	☐ Additional questions
	Part 3	☐ Narration ☐ Point of view	☐ Narration ☐ Point of view	
	Part 4	☐ Discussion ☐ Predictions	☐ Discussion ☐ Predictions	☐ Additional predictions
D. Vocabulary & Word Building	Part 1	☐ Vocabulary I.D. Sheet ☐ 6 words	☐ Vocabulary I.D. Sheet ☐ 12 words	
	Part 2	☐ Vocabulary review ☐ Rummy Roots ☐ 3 sentences	☐ 4 sentences	☐ 5 sentences
	Part 3	☐ Vocabulary review		
	Part 4	☐ Vocabulary review ☐ Rummy Roots ☐ 3 sentences	☐ 4 sentences	☐ 5 sentences
E. Economics, History & Science		*Human Body Basics*		
	Part 1	☐ Hearing ☐ Vocab ☐ 4 Activities ☐ Project		☐ Additional activity
	Part 2	☐ A Day In the Life ☐ Research ☐ Supply and Demand Game		
	Part 3	☐ Sight ☐ Vocab ☐ 4 Activites ☐ Project		
	Part 4	☐ Invention Demand Chart ☐ Supply and Demand Matching		
F. Writing, Editing & Spelling	Part 1	☐ Expository writing	☐ Additional expository writing	☐ Additional expository writing
	Part 2	☐ Review verbs ☐ List 10 regular verbs ☐ List 5 helping verbs	☐ List 12 regular verbs ☐ List 6 helping verbs	☐ List 14 regular verbs ☐ List 7 helping verbs
	Part 3	☐ Research topics ☐ Narrow list ☐ 5 questions/thoughts		
	Part 4	☐ Choose 8-12 words ☐ Study ☐ Spell	☐ Choose 10-15 words ☐ Study ☐ Spell	☐ Choose 12-18 words ☐ Study ☐ Spell
G. Music & Art		*The Story of the Orchestra*		
	Part 1	☐ Pages 66-69 ☐ Trombone ☐ Tuba ☐ Tracks 28 & 29 ☐ Drawing		
	Part 2	☐ Basix Recorder Method: pages 42 & 43		
	Part 3	☐ Orchestra Story cards		
	Part 4	☐ Create Anything With Clay: pages 52-55		
H. Independent Reading		30 minutes daily ☐☐☐☐	30 minutes daily ☐☐☐☐	35 minutes daily ☐☐☐☐
Review	Part 5	☐ Steps for Thinking review ☐ Vocabulary cards/review	☐ Spelling review ☐ Science review ☐ Recorder practice	☐ Crossword
Materials		*The Wright Brothers* / *The Story of Inventions* / *Basix Recorder Method* / *The Story of the Orchestra book & CD* / *Homer Price* / *Create Anything With Clay* / *Profiles from History Volume 3*	Recorder, Polymer clay; Rummy Roots cards; Activity (Part 4): String, yarn, or leather cord	

Success Takes Flight Unit – *Lesson 4 At A Glance*

		Column 1	Column 2	Column 3
A. Copywork & Dictation	Part 1	□ SOI: page 102, paragraph 2	□ SOI: page 102, paragraph 2	□ SOI: page 102, paragraph 2 & page 103, paragraph 2
	Part 2	□ Steps for Thinking □ Tell one example	□ Steps for Thinking □ Write one example	□ Steps for Thinking □ Write two examples
	Part 3	□ SOI: page 111, paragraph 1	□ SOI: page 111, paragraph 1	□ SOI: page 111, paragraphs 1–2
	Part 4	□ HB: page 74, paragraph 4	□ WB: page 106, paragraph 2	□ WB: page 106, paragraphs 2 and 4
B. Reader		*Homer Price*	*The Story of Inventions*	*The Wright Brothers*
	Part 1	□ Page 72–page 76, paragraph 7	□ Pages 200-202 □ Questions 1 & 2	□ Page 86, paragraph 1–page 93, paragraph 2
	Part 2	□ Page 76, paragraph 8–page 80, paragraph 5	□ Pages 202-204 □ Questions 3 & 4	□ Page 93, paragraph 3–page 98, paragraph 7
	Part 3	□ Page 80, paragraph 6–page 85	□ *The New Way Things Work*: Pages 238-239 □ 5 true/false	□ Page 98, paragraph 8–page 106
	Part 4	□ Page 86–page 90	□ *The New Way Things Work*: Pages 240-241 □ 5 true/false	□ Pages 107–114
C. Read Aloud		*The Wright Brothers*		
	Part 1	□ Page 86, paragraph 1–page 93, paragraph 2	□ Narration □ Retelling	□ Additional questions
	Part 2	□ Page 93, paragraph 3–page 98, paragraph 7	□ Discussion □ Make up questions	□ Additional predictions
	Part 3	□ Page 98, paragraph 8–page 106	□ Narration □ Point of view	
	Part 4	□ Pages 107–114	□ Discussion □ Predictions	
D. Vocabulary & Word Building		*Human Body Basics*		
	Part 1	□ Vocabulary I.D. Sheet □ 6 words	□ Vocabulary I.D. Sheet □ 12 words	
	Part 2	□ "dia-" words	□ Additional "dia-" words	□ Additional "dia-" words
	Part 3	□ Vocabulary review		
	Part 4	□ 3 "dia-" words □ Write sentence	□ 6 "dia-" words □ Write sentence	□ 9 "dia-" words □ Write sentence
E. Economics, History & Science				
	Part 1	□ Smell □ Vocab □ 4 Activites □ Project	□ Additional project	
	Part 2	□ Advertising □ List □ 2 adjectives □ 5 reasons each	□ Products	
	Part 3	□ Taste □ Vocab □ 4 Activites □ Project	□ Additional project	
	Part 4	□ Airlines □ Research □ 2 paragraphs □ Discussion □ Irena Sendler profile		
F. Writing, Editing & Spelling				
	Part 1	□ Expository writing	□ Additional expository writing	□ Additional expository writing
	Part 2	□ Review prepositions □ List 10 phrases	□ List 12 phrases	□ List 14 phrases
	Part 3	□ Complete science projects □ Other work		
	Part 4	□ Choose 8-12 words □ Study □ Spell	□ Choose 10-15 words □ Study □ Spell	□ Choose 12-18 words □ Study □ Spell
G. Music & Art		*The Story of the Orchestra*		
	Part 1	□ Pages 70-73 □ Percussion □ Timpani □ Tracks 30 & 31 □ Drawing		
	Part 2	□ *Basix Recorder Method*: pages 44-45		
	Part 3	□ Orchestra Story cards		
	Part 4	□ *Create Anything With Clay*: pages 56-57		
H. Independent Reading		30 minutes daily □□□□	30 minutes daily □□□□	35 minutes daily □□□□
Review	Part 5	□ Steps for Thinking review □ Vocabulary cards/review	□ Spelling review □ Science review □ Recorder practice	□ Who or What Am I?

Materials

The Wright Brothers
The Story of Inventions
Basix Recorder Method
The New Way Things Work
The Story of the Orchestra book & CD

Homer Price
Create Anything With Clay
Profiles from History Volume 3

Recorder, Polymer clay; Activity (Part 4): Pictures (magazines, photos, drawings), Craft glue, Paintbrush, Rolling pin or round jar

SUCCESS TAKES FLIGHT UNIT – *Lesson 5 At A Glance*

Section	Part	Level 1	Level 2	Level 3
A. Copywork & Dictation	Part 1	☐ SOI: page 268, paragraph 1	☐ SOI: page 268, paragraph 1	☐ SOI: page 268, paragraphs 1–2
	Part 2	☐ Steps for Thinking ☐ Tell one example	☐ Steps for Thinking ☐ Write one example	☐ Steps for Thinking ☐ Write two examples
	Part 3	☐ SOI: page 270, paragraph 3	☐ SOI: page 270, paragraph 3	☐ SOI: page 270, paragraph 3 & page 271, paragraph 2
	Part 4	☐ HP: page 109, paragraph 2	☐ WB: page 119, paragraph 6	☐ WB: page 119, paragraphs 6–7
B. Reader		🐾🐾 *Homer Price*	🐾🐾 *The Story of Inventions*	🐾🐾 *The Wright Brothers*
	Part 1	☐ Page 94–page 101, paragraph 7	☐ Pages 268–270 ☐ Questions 1–4	☐ Pages 115–121
	Part 2	☐ Page 101, paragraph 8–page 105, paragraph 4	☐ Pages 270–272 ☐ Questions 5–8	☐ Page 122–page 128, paragraph 4
	Part 3	☐ Page 105, paragraph 5–page 113, paragraph 2	☐ *The New Way Things Work*: pages 94–95 ☐ 5 true/false	☐ Page 128, paragraph 5–page 135
	Part 4	☐ Page 113, paragraph 3–page 121	☐ *The New Way Things Work*: pages 96–97 ☐ 5 true/false	☐ Page 136–page 142, paragraph 4
		🐾🐾 *The Wright Brothers*		
	Part 1	☐ Pages 115–121		
	Part 2	☐ Page 122–page 128, paragraph 4		
	Part 3	☐ Page 128, paragraph 5–page 135		
	Part 4	☐ Page 136–page 142, paragraph 4		
C. Read Aloud		🐾🐾	🐾🐾	🐾🐾
	Part 1	☐ Narration	☐ Narration ☐ Retelling	
	Part 2	☐ Discussion	☐ Discussion ☐ Make up questions	☐ Additional questions
	Part 3	☐ Narration	☐ Narration ☐ Point of view	
	Part 4	☐ Discussion	☐ Discussion ☐ Predictions	☐ Additional predictions
D. Vocabulary & Word Building		🐾🐾	🐾🐾	🐾🐾
	Part 1	☐ Vocabulary I.D. Sheet ☐ 6 words	☐ Vocabulary I.D. Sheet ☐ 12 words	
	Part 2	☐ "visum-" words	☐ Additional "visum-" words	☐ Additional "visum-" words
	Part 3	☐ Vocabulary review		
	Part 4	☐ 3 "visum-" words ☐ Write sentence	☐ 6 "visum-" words ☐ Write sentence	☐ 9 "visum-" words ☐ Write sentence
E. Economics, History & Science		🐾🐾 *Human Body Basics*	🐾🐾	🐾🐾
	Part 1	☐ Touch ☐ Vocab ☐ 4 activities ☐ Project	☐ Additional project	☐ Additional project
	Part 2	☐ Honorific holidays ☐ Discussion ☐ Research battle ☐ Report	☐ 2 battles ☐ 2 reports	☐ 3 battles ☐ 3 reports
	Part 3	☐ Endocrine system ☐ Vocab ☐ 2 activites ☐ Project	☐ Additional project	☐ Additional activity
	Part 4	☐ WWII ☐ Discussion ☐ Research battle ☐ Report ☐ Churchill profile	☐ 2 battles ☐ 2 reports	☐ 3 battles ☐ 3 reports
F. Writing, Editing & Spelling		🐾🐾	🐾🐾	🐾🐾
	Part 1	☐ Expository writing	☐ Additional expository writing	☐ Additional expository writing
	Part 2	☐ Review adverbs ☐ List 10	☐ List 12	☐ List 14
	Part 3	☐ Presentation planning		
	Part 4	☐ Choose 8-12 words ☐ Study ☐ Spell	☐ Choose 10-15 words ☐ Study ☐ Spell	☐ Choose 12-18 words ☐ Study ☐ Spell
G. Music & Art		🐾🐾 *The Story of the Orchestra*		
	Part 1	☐ Pages 74-77 ☐ Bass ☐ Snare drums ☐ Xylophone ☐ Drawing		
	Part 2	☐ *Basix Recorder Method*: pages 46-47		
	Part 3	☐ Orchestra Story cards		
	Part 4	☐ *Create Anything With Clay*: page 58		
H. Independent Reading		🐾🐾	🐾	🐾
	Part 5	30 minutes daily ☐☐☐☐	30 minutes daily ☐☐☐☐	35 minutes daily ☐☐☐☐
Review	Part 5	☐ Steps for Thinking review ☐ Vocabulary cards/review	☐ Spelling review ☐ Science review ☐ Recorder practice	☐ Bingo
Materials		*The Wright Brothers* / *The Story of Inventions* / *Basix Recorder Method* / *The New Way Things Work* / *The Story of the Orchestra book & CD*	*Homer Price* / *Create Anything With Clay* / *Profiles from History, Volume 3* / *Classroom Atlas of the U.S.*	Recorder, Polymer clay

SUCCESS TAKES FLIGHT UNIT – *Lesson 6 At A Glance*

Section	Part	Column A	Column B	Column C
A. COPYWORK & DICTATION	Part 1	☐ SOI: one paragraph of choice	☐ SOI: two paragraphs of choice	☐ SOI: three paragraphs of choice
	Part 2	☐ List of repeat mistakes	☐ List of repeat mistakes	☐ List of repeat mistakes
	Part 3	☐ SOI: one paragraph of choice	☐ SOI: two paragraphs of choice	☐ SOI: three paragraphs of choice
	Part 4	☐ List of repeat mistakes	☐ List of repeat mistakes	☐ List of repeat mistakes
B. READER		*Homer Price*	*The Story of Inventions*	*The Wright Brothers*
	Part 1	☐ Page 126–page 130, paragraph 4	☐ Review chapters 10 & 19 ☐ Compare lives	☐ Page 142, paragraph 5–page 149, paragraph 4
	Part 2	☐ Page 130, paragraph 5–page 137, paragraph 3	☐ Review chapters 10 & 19 ☐ Compare inventions	☐ Page 149, paragraph 5–page 156
	Part 3	☐ Page 137, paragraph 4–page 142, paragraph 1	☐ Review chapters 14 & 20 ☐ Compare lives	☐ Page 157–page 164, paragraph 5
	Part 4	☐ Page 142, paragraph 2–page 149	☐ Review chapters 14 & 20 ☐ Compare inventions	☐ Page 164, paragraph 6–page 173
C. READ ALOUD		*The Wright Brothers*		
	Part 1	☐ Page 142, paragraph 5–page 149, paragraph 4	☐ Narration ☐ Retelling	
	Part 2	☐ Page 149, paragraph 5–page 156	☐ Discussion ☐ Make up questions	☐ Additional questions
	Part 3	☐ Page 157–page 164, paragraph 5	☐ Narration ☐ Point of view	
	Part 4	☐ Page 164, paragraph 6–page 173	☐ Discussion: evaluate predictions	
D. VOCABULARY & WORD BUILDING	Part 1	☐ Vocabulary review		
	Part 2	☐ Vocabulary review ☐ 3 sentences ☐ Rummy Roots	☐ 4 sentences	☐ 5 sentences
	Part 3	☐ Vocabulary review		
	Part 4	☐ Vocabulary review ☐ Rummy Roots ☐ 1 sentence for each	☐ 2 sentences for each	☐ 3 sentences for each
E. ECONOMICS, HISTORY & SCIENCE		*Human Body Basics*		
	Part 1	☐ Complete science projects ☐ Other work		
	Part 2	☐ Supply and Demand Game ☐ Invention Demand Chart		
	Part 3	☐ Review ☐ Human Body Matching		
	Part 4	☐ Review ☐ Inventor's 20 Questions ☐ Add 3 inventors	☐ Add 4 inventors	☐ Add 5 inventors
F. WRITING, EDITING & SPELLING	Part 1	☐ Finalize choice ☐ Revise questions/thoughts		
	Part 2	☐ Review parts of speech, sentences		
	Part 3	☐ Book Review		
	Part 4	☐ Ongoing spelling review		
G. MUSIC & ART		*The Story of the Orchestra*		
	Part 1	☐ Orchestra Story Review ☐ Question Quest		
	Part 2	☐ Basix Recorder Method Review ☐ Practice		
	Part 3	☐ Question Quest ☐ Name-That-Instrument		
	Part 4	☐ Create Anything With Clay: sculptures		
H. INDEPENDENT READING		30 minutes daily ☐☐☐☐	30 minutes daily ☐☐☐☐	35 minutes daily ☐☐☐☐
REVIEW	Part 5	☐ Steps for Thinking review ☐ Vocabulary cards/review	☐ Spelling review ☐ Science review ☐ Recorder practice	☐ Bingo
MATERIALS		*The Wright Brothers* / *The Story of Inventions* / *Basix Recorder Method*	*Homer Price* / *Create Anything With Clay* / *Profiles from History Volume 3*	Recorder, Polymer clay; Rummy Roots cards

REACH FOR THE STARS UNIT – Lesson 1 At A Glance

A. COPYWORK & DICTATION	Part 1	☐ Passage of choice: 5 sentences	☐ Passage of choice: 7 sentences
	Part 2	☐ SOI: page 39, paragraph 2	☐ SOI: page 39, paragraphs 2–3
	Part 3	☐ Passage of choice: 5 sentences	☐ Passage of choice: 7 sentences
	Part 4	☐ 4 Steps for Thinking of choice	☐ 5 Steps for Thinking of choice
B. READER		*The Story of Inventions*	*Alan Shepard*
	Part 1	☐ Page 39–pg 41, paragraph 2 ☐ Relate: title to section	☐ Page 9–top of page 19
	Part 2	☐ Page 41, paragraph 3–page 43, paragraph 1 ☐ Relate: title to section	☐ Page 19, paragraph 1–top of page 29
	Part 3	☐ Page 43, paragraph 2–top of page 45 ☐ Relate: title to section	☐ Page 29, paragraph 1–page 37
	Part 4	☐ Page 45, paragraph 1–page 48 ☐ Relate: title to section	☐ Page 39–page 47, paragraph 2
C. READ ALOUD		*Alan Shepard*	
	Part 1	☐ Page 9–top of page 19	☐ Narration ☐ Retelling
	Part 2	☐ Page 19, paragraph 1–top of page 29	☐ Discussion ☐ Make up questions
	Part 3	☐ Page 29, paragraph 1–page 37	☐ Narration ☐ Point of view
	Part 4	☐ Page 39–page 47, paragraph 2	☐ Discussion ☐ Predictions
D. VOCABULARY & WORD BUILDING		*Human Body Basics*	
	Part 1	☐ Unit 1 Vocabulary review	
	Part 2	☐ Word-part of choice, 3 Words ☐ Sentence	
	Part 3	☐ Unit 1 Vocabulary review	
	Part 4	☐ Unit 1 Word Building review	☐ 6 words
E. ECONOMICS, HISTORY, & SCIENCE		*Human Body Basics*	
	Part 1	☐ Unit 1 Tools & Technology Matching	
	Part 2	☐ Unit 1 Who or What Am I?	
	Part 3	☐ Vocab ☐ Foreign invaders ☐ 3 activities ☐ 2 projects	
	Part 4	☐ Unit 1 Graphic Organizer	
F. WRITING, EDITING, SPELLING & SCIENCE PROJECT	Part 1	☐ Topic ☐ Bibliography ☐ Background research ☐ Notes	
	Part 2	☐ Unit 4 Spelling review, 12 words	☐ 16 words ☐ 18 words
	Part 3	☐ Background research	
	Part 4	☐ Answer SOI comprehension questions	☐ Make up additional questions
G. MUSIC & ART		*The Story of the Orchestra*	
	Part 1	☐ Pages 78–80 ☐ Percussion instruments ☐ Tracks 32, 33 ☐ Drawing	
	Part 2	☐ Basix Recorder Method: pages 48–49	
	Part 3	☐ Orchestra Story Cards	
	Part 4	☐ Claymation project intro ☐ Download ☐ Study	
H. INDEPENDENT READING		30 minutes daily ☐☐☐☐	35 minutes daily ☐☐☐
REVIEW	Part 5	☐ Spelling review ☐ Vocabulary review ☐ Spelling Review ☐ Science Review ☐ Recorder practice ☐ Unit 1 Bingo ☐ Word Search	
MATERIALS		*Alan Shepard* • *Profiles from History, Vol. 3* • *The Story of the Orchestra book & CD* • *The Story of Inventions* • *Basix Recorder Method* • Recorder; Activity (Part 4G): Oil-based modeling clay (or plasticine)	

Reach For The Stars Unit – Lesson 2 At A Glance

Section	Part	Column 1	Column 2	Column 3
A. COPYWORK & DICTATION	Part 1	☐ Passage of choice: 5 sentences	☐ Passage of choice: 7 sentences	
	Part 2	☐ SOI: page 206, paragraph 1	☐ SOI: page 206, paragraph 1	☐ SOI: page 206, paragraphs 1–2
	Part 3	☐ Passage of choice: 5 sentences	☐ Passage of choice: 7 sentences	
	Part 4	☐ 4 Steps for Thinking of choice	☐ 5 Steps for Thinking of choice	
B. READER		*The Story of Inventions*		*Alan Shepard*
	Part 1	☐ Pages 205–206 ☐ Relate: title to section		☐ Page 47, paragraph 3–page 56, paragraph 1
	Part 2	☐ Pages 207–208 ☐ Relate: title to section		☐ Page 56, paragraph 2–page 65, paragraph 1
	Part 3	☐ Page 209–top of page 210 ☐ Relate: title to section		☐ Page 65, paragraph 2–page 73, paragraph 1
	Part 4	☐ Page 210, paragraph 1–page 211 ☐ Relate: title to section		☐ Page 73, paragraph 2–top of page 83
C. READ ALOUD		*Alan Shepard*		
	Part 1	☐ Page 47, paragraph 3–page 56, paragraph 1	☐ Narration ☐ Retelling	
	Part 2	☐ Page 56, paragraph 2–page 65, paragraph 1	☐ Discussion ☐ Make up questions	☐ Additional questions
	Part 3	☐ Page 65, paragraph 2–page 73, paragraph 1	☐ Narration ☐ Point of view	
	Part 4	☐ Page 73, paragraph 2–top of page 83	☐ Discussion ☐ Predictions	☐ Additional predictions
D. VOCABULARY & WORD BUILDING	Part 1	☐ Unit 2 Vocabulary review		
	Part 2	☐ Word-part of choice ☐ 3 Words ☐ Sentence	☐ 6 words	
	Part 3	☐ Unit 2 Vocabulary review		
	Part 4	☐ Unit 2 Word Building review		
E. ECONOMICS, HISTORY & SCIENCE		*Human Body Basics*		
	Part 1	☐ Unit 2 Tools & Technology Matching		
	Part 2	☐ Unit 2 Who or What Am I?		
	Part 3	☐ Vocab ☐ Lymphatic system ☐ 2 activities ☐ Project	☐ Additional project	
	Part 4	☐ Unit 2 Graphic Organizer		
F. WRITING, EDITING & SPELLING	Part 1	☐ Outline ☐ Rough draft ☐ 4 paragraphs	☐ 5 paragraphs	☐ 6 paragraphs
	Part 2	☐ Unit 2 Spelling review, 12 words	☐ 16 words	☐ 18 words
	Part 3	☐ Revise/rewrite ☐ Proofread ☐ Bibliography		
	Part 4	☐ Answer SOI comprehension questions		☐ Make up additional questions
G. MUSIC & ART		*The Story of the Orchestra*		
	Part 1	☐ Pages 81–83 ☐ Percussion instruments ☐ Track 34 ☐ Drawing		
	Part 2	☐ Basix Recorder Method: pages 50–51		
	Part 3	☐ Orchestra Story Cards		
	Part 4	☐ Claymation project: Storyboard		
H. INDEPENDENT READING		30 minutes daily ☐☐☐☐	30 minutes daily ☐☐☐☐	35 minutes daily ☐☐☐☐
REVIEW	Part 5	☐ Vocabulary review ☐ Spelling review ☐ Science review ☐ Recorder practice ☐ Unit 2 Bingo ☐ Word Scramble		

MATERIALS

Alan Shepard
Basix Recorder Method
The Story of the Orchestra book & CD
The Story of Inventions
Profiles From History, Volume 3
Recorder; Report cover with pronged fasteners; Activity (Part 4G): Plain, unlined paper

REACH FOR THE STARS UNIT – *Lesson 3 At A Glance*

A. Copywork & Dictation

Part		
Part 1	□ Passage of choice: 5 sentences	□ Passage of choice: 7 sentences
Part 2	□ Passage of choice: 5 sentences	□ Passage of choice: 7 sentences
Part 3	□ Passage of choice: 5 sentences	□ Passage of choice: 7 sentences
Part 4	□ Passage of choice: 5 sentences	□ Passage of choice: 7 sentences

B. Reader — *The New Way Things Work* / *Alan Shepard*

Part 1	□ Section 3, 4, or 5 □ 1 invention □ Flow Chart	□ Additional inventions □ Flow Charts	□ Page 83, paragraph 1–bottom of page 92
Part 2	□ Section 3, 4, or 5 □ 1 invention □ Flow Chart	□ Additional inventions □ Flow Charts	□ Page 92, last paragraph–page 99
Part 3	□ Section 3, 4, or 5 □ 1 invention □ Flow Chart	□ Additional inventions □ Flow Charts	□ Page 101–page 109, paragraph 1
Part 4	□ Section 3, 4, or 5 □ 1 invention □ Flow Chart	□ Additional inventions □ Flow Charts	□ Page 109, paragraph 2–top of page 118

C. Read Aloud — *Alan Shepard*

Part			
Part 1	□ Page 83, paragraph 1–bottom of page 92	□ Narration □ Retelling	
Part 2	□ Page 92, last paragraph–page 99	□ Discussion □ Make up questions	□ Additional questions
Part 3	□ Page 101–page 109, paragraph 1	□ Narration □ Point of view	
Part 4	□ Page 109, paragraph 2–top of page 118	□ Discussion □ Predictions	□ Additional predictions

D. Vocabulary & Word Building — *Human Body Basics*

Part		
Part 1	□ Unit 3 Vocabulary review	
Part 2	□ Word-part of choice □ 3 Words □ Sentence	□ 6 words
Part 3	□ Unit 3 Vocabulary review	
Part 4	□ Unit 3 Word Building review	

E. Economics, History, & Science — *Human Body Basics*

Part			
Part 1	□ Tools & Technology Matching		
Part 2	□ Unit 3 Who or What Am I?		
Part 3	□ Vocab □ DNA □ Genetics □ 3 activities □ Project	□ 2 projects	□ 3 projects
Part 4	□ Unit 3 Graphic Organizer		

F. Writing, Editing, Spelling & Science Project

Part 1	□ Rules □ Name □ Question □ Hypothesis □ Design test □ List		
Part 2	□ Unit 3 Spelling review □ 12 words	□ 16 words	□ 18 words
Part 3	□ Project log □ To-do list □ Procedure □ Planning □ Experiment		
Part 4	□ You Can Find Me 1 game		

G. Music & Art — *The Story of the Orchestra*

Part	
Part 1	□ Pages 85–87 □ Keyboard instruments □ Organ □ Track 35 □ Drawing
Part 2	□ *Basix Recorder Method*: pages 52–53
Part 3	□ Orchestra Story Cards
Part 4	□ Claymation project: set and characters

H. Independent Reading

Part			
Part 5	30 minutes daily □□□□	30 minutes daily □□□□	35 minutes daily □□□□

Review

□ Vocabulary review □ Spelling review □ Science review □ Recorder practice □ Unit 3 Bingo □ Crossword

Materials

Alan Shepard · *Basix Recorder Method* · *The Story of the Orchestra* book & CD · *The New Way Things Work* · *Profiles From History, Volume 3*

Recorder; Activity (Part 1F): Various items for science project; Activity (Part 4G): Oil-based modeling clay (or plasticine), wax paper, ziplock bags (quart size), packing tape, 4 pieces of foam board OR large box (at least ** x ** x **), 1" styrofoam balls (if characters are "people"), pipe cleaners (if characters are "people"), paint and/or markers

Reach For The Stars Unit – *Lesson 4 At A Glance*

A. Copywork & Dictation
Part 1	□ Passage of choice: 5 sentences	□ Passage of choice: 7 sentences
Part 2	□ SOI: page 216, paragraph 1	□ SOI: page 216, paragraphs 1–2
Part 3	□ Passage of choice: 5 sentences	□ Passage of choice: 7 sentences
Part 4	□ 4 Steps for Thinking of choice	□ 5 Steps for Thinking of choice

B. Reader
The Story of Inventions / *Alan Shepard*
Part 1	□ Page 213–top of page 215 □ Relate: topic to section	□ Page 118, paragraph 1–top of page 127
Part 2	□ Page 215, paragraph 1–pg 216, paragraph 3 □ Relate: topic to section	□ Page 127, paragraph 1–page 135
Part 3	□ Page 216, paragraph 4–top page 218 □ Relate: topic to section	□ Page 137–page 145, paragraph 4
Part 4	□ Page 218, paragraph 1–top page 220 □ Relate: topic to section	□ Page 145, paragraph 5–page 156, paragraph 3

C. Read Aloud
Alan Shepard
Part 1	□ Page 118, paragraph 1–top of page 127	□ Narration □ Retelling
Part 2	□ Page 127, paragraph 1–page 135	□ Discussion □ Make up questions	□ Additional questions
Part 3	□ Page 137–page 145, paragraph 4	□ Narration □ Point of view
Part 4	□ Page 145, paragraph 5–page 156, paragraph 3	□ Discussion □ Predictions	□ Additional predictions

D. Vocabulary & Word Building
Part 1	□ Unit 4 Vocabulary review	
Part 2	□ Word-part of choice, 3 Words □ Sentence	□ 6 words
Part 3	□ Unit 4 Vocabulary review	
Part 4	□ Unit 4 Word Building review	

E. Economics, History & Science
Human Body Basics
Part 1	□ Unit 4 Human Body Matching
Part 2	□ Unit 4 Who or What Am I?
Part 3	□ Vocab □ Cell Division □ 4 activities
Part 4	□ Unit 4 Graphic Organizer

F. Writing, Editing & Spelling
Part 1	□ Procedure plan □ Log □ Planning	
Part 2	□ Unit 4 Spelling review □ 12 words	□ 16 words □ 18 words
Part 3	□ Procedure plan □ Display sketches	
Part 4	□ Answer SOI comprehension questions	□ Make up additional questions

G. Music & Art
The Story of the Orchestra
Part 1	□ Pages 88–91 □ Piano □ Harpsichord □ Tracks 36, 37 □ Drawing
Part 2	□ Basix Recorder Method: pages 54–55
Part 3	□ Orchestra Story Cards
Part 4	□ Claymation project: photographs

H. Independent Reading
30 minutes daily □□□□	35 minutes daily □□□□

Review
Part 5	□ Vocabulary review □ Spelling review □ Science review □ Recorder practice □ Unit 4 Bingo □ Who or What Am I?
	30 minutes daily □□□□

Materials
Alan Shepard
Basix Recorder Method
The Story of the Orchestra book & CD
The Story of Inventions
Profiles from History, Vol. 3
Recorder; Activity (Part 4G): Camera, tripod (optional but helpful)

PERSEVERANCE PAYS OFF UNIT – Lesson 5 At A Glance

Section	Part	🐾🐾	🐾
A. Copywork & Dictation	Part 1	□ Passage of choice: 5 sentences	□ Passage of choice: 7 sentences
	Part 2	□ SOI: page 275, paragraph 1	□ SOI: page 275, paragraphs 1–2
	Part 3	□ Passage of choice: 5 sentences	□ Passage of choice: 7 sentences
	Part 4	□ 4 Steps for Thinking of choice	□ 5 Steps for Thinking of choice
B. Reader		🐾🐾 🐾 *The Story of Inventions*	🐾🐾 🐾 *Alan Shepard*
	Part 1	□ Pages 273–274 □ Relate: title to section	□ Page 156, paragraph 4–middle of page 166
	Part 2	□ Page 275–page 276, paragraph 2 □ Relate title to section	□ Page 166, paragraph 1–page 174, paragraph 2
	Part 3	□ Page 276, paragraph 3–page 277, paragraph 1 □ Relate title to section	□ Page 174, paragraph 3–page 183, paragraph 2
	Part 4	□ Page 277, paragraph 2–page 279 □ Relate title to section	□ Page 183, paragraph 3–page 192, paragraph 1
C. Read Aloud		🐾🐾 🐾 *Alan Shepard*	🐾🐾 🐾
	Part 1	□ Page 156, paragraph 4–middle of page 166 □ Narration □ Retelling	
	Part 2	□ Page 166, paragraph 1–page 174, paragraph 2 □ Discussion □ Make up questions	□ Additional questions
	Part 3	□ Page 174, paragraph 3–page 183, paragraph 2 □ Narration □ Point of view	
	Part 4	□ Page 183, paragraph 3–page 192, paragraph 1 □ Discussion □ Predictions	□ Additional predictions
D. Vocabulary & Word Building		🐾🐾 🐾 *Human Body Basics*	🐾🐾 🐾
	Part 1	□ Unit 5 Vocabulary review	
	Part 2	□ Word-part of choice □ 3 Words □ Sentence	□ 6 words
	Part 3	□ Unit 5 Vocabulary review	
	Part 4	□ Unit 5 Word Building review	
E. Economics, History, & Science		🐾🐾 🐾 *Human Body Basics*	🐾🐾 🐾
	Part 1	□ Unit 5 Human Body Matching	
	Part 2	□ Unit 5 Who or What Am I?	
	Part 3	□ Vocab □ Fetal development □ 2 activities □ Project	
	Part 4	□ Unit 5 Graphic Organizer	
F. Writing, Editing, Spelling & Science Project		🐾🐾 🐾 *The Story of the Orchestra*	🐾🐾 🐾
	Part 1	□ Gather raw data □ Chart □ Write conclusion	
	Part 2	□ Unit 5 Spelling review □ 12 words	□ 15 words □ 18 words
	Part 3	□ Begin display	
	Part 4	□ Answer *SOI* comprehension questions	□ Make up additional questions
G. Music & Art		🐾🐾 🐾 *The Story of the Orchestra*	🐾🐾 🐾
	Part 1	□ Pages 92–93 □ Conductor □ Try conducting	
	Part 2	□ Basix Recorder Method: pages 56–57	
	Part 3	□ Orchestra Story Cards	
	Part 4	□ Claymation project: Complete video or flipbook	
H. Independent Reading		🐾 30 minutes daily □□□□	🐾 35 minutes daily □□□□
Review	Part 5	□ Vocabulary review □ Spelling review □ Science review □ Recorder practice □ Unit 5 Bingo	□ Unit 6 Bingo
Materials		*Alan Shepard* / *Basix Recorder Method* / *The Story of the Orchestra* book & CD / *The Story of Inventions* / *Profiles from History, Vol. 3*	Recorder: Activity (Part 1G): Short stick, wooden spoon, or dowel; Activity (Part 4G): Video: Computer, film-editing software, music (optional, for background), downloaded or scanned pictures OR Flipbook: Developed or printed pictures

REACH FOR THE STARS UNIT – *Lesson 6 At A Glance*

Section	Part	Column 1	Column 2	Column 3
A. COPYWORK & DICTATION	Part 1	☐ Passage of choice: 5 sentences	☐ Passage of choice: 7 sentences	
	Part 2	☐ Passage of choice: 5 sentences	☐ Passage of choice: 7 sentences	
	Part 3	☐ Passage of choice: 5 sentences	☐ Passage of choice: 7 sentences	
	Part 4	☐ Evaluation of work ☐ Ways to improve ☐ Discussion	☐ Passage of choice: 7 sentences	
B. READER		*The New Way Things Work*		*Alan Shepard*
	Part 1	☐ Sections 3, 4, or 5 ☐ 1 invention ☐ Flow Chart	☐ Additional inventions ☐ Flow Charts	☐ Page 192, paragraph 2–page 200, paragraph 1
	Part 2	☐ Sections 3, 4, or 5 ☐ 1 invention ☐ Flow Chart	☐ Additional inventions ☐ Flow Charts	☐ Page 200, paragraph 2–top of page 210
	Part 3	☐ Sections 3, 4, or 5 ☐ 1 invention ☐ Flow Chart	☐ Additional inventions ☐ Flow Charts	☐ Page 210, paragraph 1–page 218
	Part 4	☐ Sections 3, 4, or 5 ☐ 1 invention ☐ Flow Chart	☐ Additional inventions ☐ Flow Charts	☐ Pages 219–228
C. READ ALOUD		*Alan Shepard*		
	Part 1	☐ Page 192, paragraph 2–page 200, paragraph 1	☐ Narration ☐ Retelling	
	Part 2	☐ Page 200, paragraph 2–top of page 210	☐ Discussion ☐ Make up questions	☐ Additional questions
	Part 3	☐ Page 210, paragraph 1–page 218	☐ Narration ☐ Point of view	
	Part 4	☐ Pages 219–228	☐ Discussion	
D. VOCABULARY & WORD BUILDING	Part 1	☐ Vocabulary review		
	Part 2	☐ Word-part of choice ☐ 3 words ☐ Sentence	☐ 6 words	
	Part 3	☐ Vocabulary review		
	Part 4	☐ Unit 6 Word Building review		
E. ECONOMICS, HISTORY & SCIENCE		*Human Body Basics*		
	Part 1	☐ Finish science projects ☐ Other work		
	Part 2	☐ Unit 6 Who or What Am I?		
	Part 3	☐ Unit 6 Human Body Matching		
	Part 4	☐ Unit 6 Graphic Organizer		
F. WRITING, EDITING & SPELLING	Part 1	☐ Revise background report ☐ Project Notebook		
	Part 2	☐ On-going spelling review		
	Part 3	☐ Character summary ☐ 50 words	☐ 45 words	☐ 40 words
	Part 4	☐ You Can Find Me 2		
G. MUSIC & ART		*The Story of the Orchestra*		
	Part 1	☐ Orchestra Story review ☐ Question Quest		
	Part 2	☐ Recorder review		
	Part 3	☐ Question Quest ☐ Name-That-Classic		
	Part 4	☐ Finish science project ☐ List		
H. INDEPENDENT READING		30 minutes daily ☐☐☐☐	30 minutes daily ☐☐☐☐	35 minutes daily ☐☐☐☐
REVIEW	Part 5	☐ Vocabulary review ☐ Spelling review ☐ Name-That-Classic	☐ Unit Presentation	☐ Bingo
MATERIALS		*Alan Shepard* *Basic Recorder Method* *The Story of the Orchestra* book & CD	*The New Way Things Work* *Profiles From History, Volume 3*	Recorder

CULTIVATING GREATNESS UNIT

LANGUAGE SKILLS

Skills & Topics	✱	✱	✱
Answering questions	•	•	•
Antecedent-pronoun agreement	•	•	•
Charts:			
Making	•	•	•
Reading	•	•	•
Decoding	•	•	•
Dictionary skills	•	•	•
Dialogue	•	•	•
Discussion	•	•	•
Editing	•	•	•
Flat Characters	•	•	•
Grammar	•	•	•
Graphic organizers	•	•	•
Graphs:			
Reading	•	•	•
Interpretation	•	•	•
Identifying key words	•	•	•
Main ideas	•	•	•
Narration	•	•	•
Parts of Speech	•	•	•
Presentation skills	•	•	•
Prompts	•	•	•
Reading for enjoyment	•	•	•
Reading for understanding	•	•	•
Research/reference skills	•	•	•
Round characters	•	•	•
Sentence skills	•	•	•
Skimming	•	•	•
Spelling	•	•	•
Subject-verb agreement	•	•	•
Vocabulary	•	•	•
Word Roots:			
Greek: *chrono-, chronos-, tele-*	•	•	•
Latin: *pro-, trans-*	•	•	•
Writing from dictation	•	•	•
Writing or drawing clues	•	•	•
Extension of applications		•	•

WRITING

Skills & Topics	✱	✱	✱
Character summaries	•	•	•
Conclusions	•	•	•
Descriptive writing	•	•	•
Dialogue	•	•	•
Essay writing	•	•	•
Expository writing	•	•	•
Lab reports	•	•	•
List making	•	•	•
Narrative writing	•	•	•
Paragraph writing	•	•	•
Play writing	•	•	•
Revising	•	•	•
Elaboration on topics		•	•

THINKING SKILLS

Skills & Topics	✱	✱	✱
Analyzing information	•	•	•
Application of principles	•	•	•
Categorizing information	•	•	•
Compare and contrast	•	•	•
Context clues	•	•	•
Deductive reasoning	•	•	•
Defending a position	•	•	•
Design	•	•	•
Discussion	•	•	•
Drawing conclusions	•	•	•
Estimating	•	•	•
Evaluating answers	•	•	•
Evaluating outcomes	•	•	•
Following directions	•	•	•
Gathering data	•	•	•
Identifying a position	•	•	•
Identifying examples	•	•	•
Identifying main points	•	•	•
Imagery	•	•	•
Inductive reasoning	•	•	•
Inference	•	•	•
Interpreting data	•	•	•
Listening comprehension	•	•	•
Listening skills	•	•	•
Narration	•	•	•
Organization skills	•	•	•
Point of view	•	•	•
Predicting	•	•	•
Questioning skills	•	•	•
Reading comprehension	•	•	•
Relating concepts	•	•	•
Spelling strategies	•	•	•
Study skills:			
Graphic organizers	•	•	•
Recording progress	•	•	•
Self-monitoring	•	•	•
Self-assessment	•	•	•
Summarizing	•	•	•
Synthesizing information	•	•	•
Writing or drawing clues	•	•	•
Extended concepts		•	•

HISTORICAL FIGURES

Skills & Topics	✱	✱	✱
Henry Bessemer	•	•	•
George Washington Carver	•	•	•
Elias Howe	•	•	•
Cyrus McCormick	•	•	•
James C. Penney	•	•	•
Alvah C. Roebuck	•	•	•
Richard Sears	•	•	•
Eli Whitney	•	•	•
Sgt. Alvin C. York	•	•	•

Cultivating Greatness Unit, Con't

HISTORY/ECONOMICS

Skills & Topics	🌱	👐	🐾
American milestones	•	•	•
Christmas	•	•	•
Cotton gin	•	•	•
Farms:			
Developments	•	•	•
Economics	•	•	•
Manpower	•	•	•
Subsidies	•	•	•
Corporate-owned	•	•	•
Family-owned	•	•	•
Great Plains states:			
Average precipitation	•	•	•
Average temperatures	•	•	•
Climate regions	•	•	•
Land use	•	•	•
Vegetation	•	•	•
Homestead Act:			
Benefits	•	•	•
Characteristics	•	•	•
Conflicts	•	•	•
Other problems	•	•	•
Map study	•	•	•
Markets:			
Artificial support	•	•	•
General Stores	•	•	•
Growth and development	•	•	•
Supply and demand	•	•	•
Trading posts	•	•	•
Department stores	•	•	•
Catalog sales:			
Mock orders	•	•	•
Comparisons	•	•	•
Organic produce	•	•	•
Postal service	•	•	•
Railroads:			
Building	•	•	•
Evaluation of routes	•	•	•
Reaper	•	•	•
Sewing machine	•	•	•
Steel-making	•	•	•
Trends in farming		•	•
World War I:			
Alliances	•	•	•
Army necessities	•	•	•
Catalysts	•	•	•
Economics	•	•	•
Statistics	•	•	•
Treaty of Versailles	•	•	•
Extension of topics		•	•
Additional research		•	•

SCIENCE/ANATOMY/PHYSIOLOGY

Skills & Topics	🌱	👐	🐾
Atoms	•	•	•
Cells	•	•	•
Circulatory System:			
Blood	•	•	•
Circulation	•	•	•
Heart	•	•	•
Vessels	•	•	•
Molecules	•	•	•
Musculoskeletal System:			
Bones	•	•	•
Joints	•	•	•
Muscles	•	•	•
Organ Systems	•	•	•
Respiratory System:			
Bronchi	•	•	•
Diaphragm	•	•	•
Larynx	•	•	•
Lungs	•	•	•
Pharynx	•	•	•
Trachea	•	•	•
Urinary System:			
Bladder	•	•	•
Kidneys	•	•	•
Nephrons	•	•	•
Ureters/urethra	•	•	•
Additional research		•	•
Extension of topics		•	•

CULTIVATING GREATNESS UNIT, CON'T

Skills & Topics	ѰѰ	♛	🐾
Design	•	•	•
Illustrating	•	•	•
Instruments:			
Cello	•	•	•
Clarinet	•	•	•
Double bass	•	•	•
Flute	•	•	•
Harp	•	•	•
Oboe	•	•	•
Piccolo	•	•	•
Saxophone	•	•	•
Viola	•	•	•
Violin	•	•	•
Music:			
Bolero	•	•	•
Carnival of Animals	•	•	•
Concerto for Clarinet and Orchestra	•	•	•
Concerto for Viola and Orchestra	•	•	•
Dance of the Blessed Spirits	•	•	•
Sinfonia in G Major for Two Oboes	•	•	•
Sonata for Violin and Piano in A Major	•	•	•
Suite No. 2 for Flute, Strings, and Basso Continuo	•	•	•
Symphony No. 4	•	•	•
Symphony No. 4	•	•	•
William Tell Overture	•	•	•
Orchestra sections:			
String section	•	•	•
Woodwind section	•	•	•
Performance	•	•	•
Recorder:			
Dotted quarter notes	•	•	•
Eighth rest	•	•	•
Fermata	•	•	•
High E	•	•	•
Key signatures	•	•	•
Repeat signs	•	•	•
Staccato dot	•	•	•
Ties	•	•	•
1st and 2nd endings	•	•	•
Sculpting techniques	•	•	•

HUMANITIES

Skills Chart

Language Skills

Skills & Topics	🐾	🐾	🐾
Answering questions	•	•	•
Charts:			
Making	•	•	•
Reading	•	•	•
Decoding	•	•	•
Dictionary skills	•	•	•
Discussion	•	•	•
Editing	•	•	•
Grammar	•	•	•
Graphic organizers	•	•	•
Identifying cause and effect	•	•	•
Identifying key words	•	•	•
Main ideas	•	•	•
Narration	•	•	•
Parts of speech:			
Adjectives	•	•	•
Adverbs	•	•	•
Common nouns	•	•	•
Helping verbs	•	•	•
Prepositions	•	•	•
Proper nouns	•	•	•
Verbs	•	•	•
Presentation skills	•	•	•
Reading for enjoyment	•	•	•
Reading for understanding	•	•	•
Research/reference skills	•	•	•
Sentence skills	•	•	•
Skimming	•	•	•
Spelling	•	•	•
Vocabulary	•	•	•
Word Roots:			
Greek: *micro-, micros-, dia-*	•	•	•
Latin: *unus-, uni-, visum-*	•	•	•
Writing from dictation	•	•	•
Writing or drawing clues	•	•	
Extension of applications			•

Science/Anatomy/Physiology

Skills & Topics	🐾	🐾	🐾
Digestive system:			
Digestion:			
Mouth	•	•	•
Esophagus	•	•	•
Stomach	•	•	•
Absorption:			
Intestines	•	•	•
Other organs:			
Liver	•	•	•
Gallbladder	•	•	•
Pancreas	•	•	•
Endocrine system:			
Glands	•	•	•
Hormones	•	•	•
Nervous system:			
CNS	•	•	•
PNS	•	•	•
Five Sense	•	•	•
Research science topic	•	•	•

Writing

Skills & Topics	🐾	🐾	🐾
Book review	•	•	•
Character summary	•	•	•
Expository writing	•	•	•
Lab reports	•	•	•
List making	•	•	•
Narrative writing	•	•	•
Paragraph writing	•	•	•
Summaries	•	•	•
Elaboration on topics			•

Thinking Skills

Skills & Topics	🐾	🐾	🐾
Analyzing information	•	•	•
Application of principles	•	•	•
Categorizing information	•	•	•
Cause and effect	•	•	•
Compare and contrast	•	•	•
Context clues	•	•	•
Deductive reasoning	•	•	•
Design	•	•	•
Discussion	•	•	•
Drawing conclusions	•	•	•
Evaluating answers	•	•	•
Evaluating outcomes	•	•	•
Following directions	•	•	•
Gathering data	•	•	•
Identifying examples	•	•	•
Identifying main points	•	•	•
Imagery	•	•	•
Inductive reasoning	•	•	•
Inference	•	•	•
Interpreting data	•	•	•
Listening comprehension	•	•	•
Listening skills	•	•	•
Narration	•	•	•
Organization skills	•	•	•
Point of view	•	•	•
Predicting	•	•	•
Questioning skills	•	•	•
Reading comprehension	•	•	•
Relating concepts	•	•	•
Spelling strategies	•	•	•
Study skills:			
Graphic organizers	•	•	•
Recording progress	•	•	•
Self-monitoring	•	•	•
Self-assessment	•	•	•
Summarizing	•	•	•
Synthesizing information	•	•	•
Writing or drawing clues	•	•	•
Extended concepts		•	•

Success Takes Flight Unit, Con't

HISTORICAL FIGURES — Skills & Topics			
Corrie ten Boom	•	•	•
Winston Churchill	•	•	•
Dr. Charles Drew	•	•	•
Henry Ford	•	•	•
John Holland	•	•	•
Guglielmo Marconi	•	•	•
Franklin D. Roosevelt	•	•	•
Irena Sendler	•	•	•
Nikola Tesla	•	•	•
Wright Brothers	•	•	•

HISTORY/ECONOMICS/GEOGRAPHY

Skills & Topics			
Advertising:			
Campaigns	•	•	•
Gimmicks	•	•	•
Word of mouth	•	•	•
Airline industry:			
Acts and agencies	•	•	
Personal story	•	•	
Airplane	•	•	
American milestones	•	•	
Automobiles	•	•	
Civil unrest/disobedience		•	
Credit			•
Credit cards			•
Coupons		•	
Dust Bowl:			
Causes	•	•	•
Economic effects	•	•	•
Great Depression:			
Causes	•	•	•
Economic effects	•	•	•
Interview of business owner			•
Map study	•	•	
Major roadways	•	•	
Memorial Day	•	•	
Presidents Day	•	•	
Radio			•
Recession			•
Stock exchange	•	•	
Submarine	•	•	
Trucks/trucking:			
Motor Carrier Act	•	•	•
Interstate Commerce	•	•	•
Commission	•	•	•
Unemployment		•	•
Veterans Day	•	•	•
Wireless telegraphy	•	•	•
World War II:			
Alliances	•	•	•
Events	•	•	•
V-E Day	•	•	•
Extension of topics		•	•
Additional research		•	•

HUMANITIES

Skills & Topics			
Design	•	•	•
Illustrating	•	•	•
Instruments:			
Bass drum	•	•	•
Bassoon	•	•	•
Contrabassoon	•	•	•
French Horn	•	•	•
Snare drums	•	•	•
Timpani	•	•	•
Trombone	•	•	•
Trumpet	•	•	•
Tuba	•	•	•
Xylophone	•	•	•
Music:			
Changing of the Guard	•	•	•
Concerto for Trumpet in E Flat	•	•	•
Horn Concerto No. 1	•	•	•
Mother Goose Suite	•	•	•
Pictures at an Exhibition	•	•	•
Symphony No. 3	•	•	•
Symphony No. 7	•	•	•
Orchestra sections:			
Brass section	•	•	•
Percussion section	•	•	•
Woodwind section (cont.)	•	•	•
Performance	•	•	•
Recorder:			
Calypso	•	•	•
D major scale	•	•	•
Dynamics	•	•	•
Notes:			
Middle C sharp		•	•
B flat		•	•
High F		•	•
Low C	•	•	•
Slur		•	•
Syncopation		•	•
Sculpting techniques	•	•	•

Reach for the Stars Unit

Language Skills

Skills & Topics	✸	✸	✸
---	:-::	:-:	:-:
Answering questions	•	•	•
Charts:			
Making	•	•	•
Reading	•	•	•
Decoding	•	•	•
Dictionary skills	•	•	•
Discussion	•	•	•
Editing	•	•	•
Grammar review	•	•	•
Graphic organizers	•	•	•
Identifying key words	•	•	•
Main ideas	•	•	•
Narration	•	•	•
Parts of speech review	•	•	•
Presentation skills	•	•	•
Reading for enjoyment	•	•	•
Reading for understanding	•	•	•
Research/reference skills	•	•	•
Sentence skills	•	•	•
Skimming	•	•	•
Spelling review	•	•	•
Vocabulary review	•	•	•
Word Root review	•	•	•
Writing or drawing clues	•	•	•
Extension of applications		•	•

Historical Figures

Skills & Topics	✸	✸	✸
Unit 1 review	•	•	•
Unit 2 review	•	•	•
Unit 3 review	•	•	•
Unit 4 review	•	•	•
Unit 5 review	•	•	•
Unit 6:			
John Baird	•	•	•
Dwight Eisenhower	•	•	•
Enrico Fermi	•	•	•
Gregor Mendel	•	•	•
Jackie Robinson	•	•	•
Alan Shepard		•	•

History/Economics/Geography

Skills & Topics	✸	✸	✸
Unit 1 review	•	•	•
Unit 2 review	•	•	•
Unit 3 review	•	•	•
Unit 4 review	•	•	•
Unit 5 review	•	•	•

Writing

Skills & Topics	✸	✸	✸
Bibliography	•	•	•
Character summary	•	•	•
Descriptive writing	•	•	•
Expository writing	•	•	•
Lab Reports	•	•	•
List making	•	•	•
Paragraph writing	•	•	•
Research paper	•	•	•
Rough drafts	•	•	•
Table of Contents	•	•	•
Elaboration on topics		•	•

Thinking Skills

Skills & Topics	✸	✸	✸
Analyzing information	•	•	•
Application of principles	•	•	•
Categorizing information	•	•	•
Compare and contrast	•	•	•
Context clues	•	•	•
Deductive reasoning	•	•	•
Design		•	•
Discussion	•	•	•
Drawing conclusions	•	•	•
Evaluating answers	•	•	•
Evaluating outcomes	•	•	•
Following directions	•	•	•
Gathering data	•	•	•
Identifying examples	•	•	•
Identifying main points	•	•	•
Imagery	•	•	•
Inductive reasoning	•	•	•
Inference	•	•	•
Interpreting data	•	•	•
Listening comprehension	•	•	•
Listening skills	•	•	•
Narration	•	•	•
Organization skills	•	•	•
Point of view	•	•	•
Predicting	•	•	•
Questioning skills	•	•	•
Reading comprehension	•	•	•
Relating concepts	•	•	•
Reporting events	•	•	•
Sequencing	•	•	•
Spelling strategies	•	•	•
Study skills:			
Graphic organizers	•	•	•
Recording progress	•	•	•
Self-monitoring	•	•	•
Self-assessment	•	•	•
Summarizing	•	•	•
Synthesizing information	•	•	•
Writing or drawing clues	•	•	•
Extended concepts		•	•

Reach for the Stars Unit, Con't

Skills & Topics	🌿	🐾	🐾
Human development:			
Cell division:			
Meiosis	•	•	•
Mitosis	•	•	•
DNA	•	•	•
Embryo development	•	•	•
Genetics:			
Chromosomes	•	•	•
Genes	•	•	•
Inheritance	•	•	•
Immune system:			
Foreign invaders	•	•	•
Lymphatic system	•	•	•
Science project:			
1. Formulate a question	•	•	•
2. Conduct background research	•	•	•
3. Construct a hypothesis	•	•	•
4. Test through experimentation	•	•	•
5. Analyze data	•	•	•
6. Draw conclusion	•	•	•
7. Communicate results	•	•	•
Unit 1 review	•	•	•
Unit 2 review	•	•	•
Unit 3 review	•	•	• •
Unit 4 review	•	•	•
Unit 5 review	•		
Additional research		•	•
Extension of topics		•	•

(Left sidebar label: SCIENCE/ANATOMY/PHYSIOLOGY)

Skills & Topics	🌿	🐾	🐾
Claymation:			
Flipbook	•	•	•
Video	•	•	•
Design	•	•	•
Illustrating	•	•	•
Instruments:			
Celesta		•	•
Cymbals		•	•
Glockenspiel		•	•
Gongs		•	•
Harpsichord		•	•
Organ		•	•
Piano		•	•
Tam-tams	•	•	•
Triangle	•	•	•
Tubular bells	•	•	•
Music:			
Concerto Champetre	•	•	•
Nutcracker Suite	•	•	•
Pathetique	•	•	•
Peer Gynt	•	•	•
Symphony No. 4	•	•	•
Orchestra sections:			
Conductor	•	•	•
Keyboard instruments	•	•	•
Percussion section	•	•	•
Performance	•	•	•
Recorder:			
Articulation	•	•	•
Dotted 8th and 16th note rhythm	•	•	•
Time signatures		•	•
Triplets	•	•	•

(Left sidebar label: HUMANITIES)

Unit 4 – Cultivating Greatness Challenge Spelling

If your child masters the majority of the words presented during Part 1, you may want to choose some words from the next higher level in the lesson or choose words from the Challenge Spelling List for that lesson. You may choose as many or as few words as you would like to add to the current list. The words on this list come from the literature assigned in each lesson. Remember that success and use of the words in discussion and writing are the goal, not just memorizing spelling.

Unit 4 Lesson 1

Missouri	handkerchief	palmetto	superstitions
Psalms	authentic	geranium	alligator
sultry	regional	merciless	hominy
trellis	descendants	currycomb	complexion

Unit 4 Lesson 2

mongrel	eerie	biscuit	horrified
appetite	defiance	delicious	commotion
scholarship	punctuated	razorbacks	paraffin
whippoorwill	melodious	peaceable	millinery

Unit 4 Lesson 3

rejection	drabness	toothache	indifference
haughty	graphite	pummel	pliers
specimen	institute	frolic	accompaniment
laboratories	beckoning	fermented	mysteriously

Unit 4 Lesson 4

Tuskegee	nutrients	uncomfortably	bream
appetite	sarcasm	anxiously	strenuous
agricultural	suspicious	foliage	lustily
Gethsemane	squabble	inquiringly	lassoing

Unit 4 Lesson 5

separator	vicious	heifer	billowy
muscled	nutritional	scuttling	vigorously
womenfolk	luncheon	Osceola	drawling
weevil	calmness	turpentine	furiously

Unit 5 – Success Takes Flight Challenge Spelling

If your child masters the majority of the words presented during Part 1, you may want to choose some words from the next higher level in the lesson or choose words from the Challenge Spelling List for that lesson. You may choose as many or as few words as you would like to add to the current list. The words on this list come from the literature assigned in each lesson. Remember that success and use of the words in discussion and writing are the goal, not just memorizing spelling.

Unit 5 Lesson 1

aerial	inefficient	specialized	methodically
professor	simplicity	exaggerate	propellers
scientific	transmission	invigorating	mysterious
kerosene	conveyance	environment	mischievously

Unit 5 Lesson 2

villain	pince-nez	guaranteed	standardization
colossal	delirium	opponents	annihilation
notorious	psychological	differential	immaculately
chromium	monosyllable	rejuvenation	insurmountable

Unit 5 Lesson 3

doughnut	chauffeur	inadequacy	instinctively
Ulysses	filament	horrified	notoriety
marvelous	binoculars	drastically	commercial
pinochle	moustache	mathematician	Smithsonian

Unit 5 Lesson 4

oscillator	combustion	fractious	frequency
theorize	aeronautics	antenna	kilohertz
radiotelegraphy	mosquitoes	modulation	megahertz
transatlantic	cautiously	electromagnetic	amplitude

Unit 5 Lesson 5

torpedoes	carburetor	revolutions	buoyancy
aluminum	irritating	occupants	hydroplane
superiority	recalculated	submersible	manipulators
submergence	simultaneously	characteristically	maneuverable

✑ *Presentation Feedback Sheet* ✑

This sheet is a guide to giving your children feedback on their presentations. Grading is not its purpose, but rather to assist them in making progress. Review this page with your children before they begin, so they know what you will be looking for. Be sure to wait until they are finished to record your feedback, and give full attention to your children as they are speaking. After each presentation, give your children self-evaluation forms to complete.

At an appropriate time, hold a conference with each child. For some children, this will be immediately following their presentations; for others, it may be at another time. Be sensitive to your child's ability to gain the most benefit from this process. Conferences should be done in a private setting, so that your children are encouraged to share their difficulties freely as well as to hear suggestions for improvement. End the conferences by asking your students to set at least one goal for improvement in presentation, content, or organization. They may set more than one goal.

Presentation Feedback Form

Elements	Yes	No	Unsure
Organization:			
Child had a plan for presentation.			
Child shared notebook or visual aids.			
Presentation lasted a reasonable length of time (not too short, not too long).			
Presentation:			
Child spoke loudly enough and clearly.			
Child stood calmly before the audience.			
Child did not distract the audience with too much movement, or lack of focus.			
Child spoke with enthusiasm.			
Content:			
Child stated purpose of presentation.			
Child stated concepts or facts learned.			
Child shared connections between concepts, facts, or principles learned.			
Child shared information about people and books included in study.			
Evaluation:			
Child shared favorite activities.			
Child shared key principles or concepts learned.			
Child presented information for others to learn about the topic.			

Conference Summary

Strengths of presentation:

_____

_____

_____

_____

_____

_____

_____

Suggestions for improvement:

_____

_____

_____

_____

_____

_____

_____

Goal(s) set following conference:

1. _____

_____

_____

2. _____

_____

_____

Unit # _____   Date of conference: _____

Conference Participants: _____

_____

～ *Game Answer Key* ～

Word Search - Lesson 1, Part 5

```
R E V R A C N O T G N I H S A W E G R O E G L
F Q F K H E R O T S T N E M T R A P E D P T E
I X G D X O Z B P H J M D Y G Q S Q S X E V L
B Q E Q J Q T A G E M R Q W F Y T J F T L T J
W N N F Q H M J H H A Y Z B A U C L Q U I Z W
X O E E H X L R W E O N Y Q S W Q M G S A K H
C I R B X O C T A Q N M U K S N A J K D S N I
O N A L L I K R S F U R E T J U S D O A H O T
T T D L D V E A V V Y G S S G M S R O O T N N
T D S R R W E W L E L B B T L L E C R W E E Y
O X T U E R A H U E Y L I V E B B O L E L L M
N S O S D P N R I A O Z J M I S A V P I K E M
G C R R C J A N U O U X A W A R S D C A J K V
I W E V F N S E D V M M F W Y F O E A R F S T
N L V M S T A G R I C U L T U R E N M C U D Z
U O W R I S A A C S I N G E R W Q K O E T N J
B Q D T V V X T T Q H L Y Q P P W O X R R C K
C G U S K C I M R O C C M S U R Y C C M E G D
Q T R H X N U V S M C A T A L O G G M F J D J
E R L W F U C M Q D J T E O J B U O F H G L K
```

Word Scramble - Lesson 2, Part 5

1. joint
2. heart
3. Eli Whitney
4. Homestead Act
5. department store
6. railroad
7. Tuskegee Institute
8. reaper
9. Elias Howe
10. general store
11. catalog
12. family farm
13. Isaac Singer
14. iron ore
15. Henry Bessemer
16. Cyrus McCormick
17. World War I
18. cotton gin
19. skeleton
20. blood
21. cell
22. peanuts
23. George W Carver
24. agriculture

Supply and Demand Game 4 - Lesson 3, Part 2

farm - a business that produces and sells crops and/or livestock to others
    Example: raising strawberries and citrus fruit for sale

family farm - a farm, usually small, where the owners live and work
    Example: A place like the one where George Carver grew up.

agriculture - the business of growing crops and raising livestock
    Example: family farms, corporate-owned farms, feed stores, fertilizer companies

irrigation - ways to water plants, like crops grown on a farm
    Example: systems of sprinklers, culverts with water, rain

acre - land equal to approximately 5,000 square yards
    Example: An average farm in America is about 450 acres.

profit margin - the amount by which the selling price is greater than cost of production
    Example: A farm without a profit margin goes into debt or stops functioning.

viable - capable of being successful
    Example: The Boyers' neighbors didn't think raising cattle was viable.

subsidies - grants from the government to help a farm continue to function
    Example: payments made to farmers to help grow, or not grow, certain crops

reinvest - put money or profit back into a business
    Example: The Boyers used money from the sale of strawberries to buy a new mule.

open range - the ability of livestock to roam freely to find places to graze
    Example: The Slater family let their cows follow this policy.

barbed wire - an invention that made fencing easier and more affordable
    Example: The Slater family used metal cutters to get rid of this.

crop - a group of plants grown by people for food or some other use, usually on a large scale at a farm
    Example: wheat, cotton, corn, oranges, timber.

Crossword - Lesson 3, Part 5

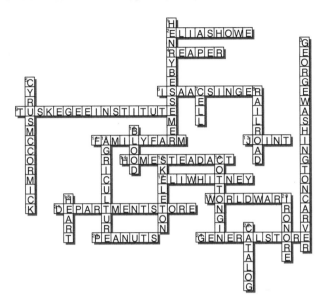

Who or What Am I - Lesson 4, Part 5

1. skeleton	13. Eli Whitney
2. Henry Bessemer	14. catalog
3. general store	15. agriculture
4. cotton gin	16. Elias Howe
5. peanuts	17. heart
6. blood	18. iron ore
7. reaper	19. Homestead Act
8. railroad	20. Tuskegee Institute
9. family farm	21. Cyrus McCormick
10. George Washington Carver	22. cell
11. World War I	23. Isaac Singer
12. joint	24. department store

Supply and Demand Game 5 - Lesson 6, Part 2

rural - related to living in the country
　Example: more open spaces, farms and gardens, dirt roads

general store - a store providing a variety of goods, mail service, and community connections
　Example: A store that may have begun as a trading post.

trading post - store in a remote area with basic supplies for sale or barter
　Example: Explorers, pioneers, and frontiersmen often got supplies here.

bartering - trading goods or services for needed supplies
　Example: exchanging animal pelts for flour, eggs for sugar, or corn for farming tools

blacksmith - someone who makes or repairs things made of iron or metal
　Example: made shoes for horses, tools, rims for wagon wheels

livery stable - a place where horses are cared for, rented, or sold
　Example: a place to provide food and shelter for your horses while on a trip

artificial support - man-made support that is contrary to the principles of business
　Example: bank bail-outs, paying a farmer not to grow certain crops

dry goods - merchandise like fabric, clothing, or books
　Example: dresses, hats, decorations, toys, textbooks, blankets

department store - a large store with many sections that sell different kinds of goods
　Example: Penney's, Sears

suburb - residential areas on the edge of a town or city
　Example: Shopping malls, subdivisions, or clusters of houses on lots of varying sizes are often located here.

post roads - routes used regularly to deliver mail
　Example: wagon trails, waterways, railroad tracks, and roads

mail-order catalogs - source of goods purchased from a company that delivered the goods by post roads
　Example: first used by Sears to sell watches, then used to sell other goods

Human Body Matching - Lesson 6, Part 3

1. ventricles - lower chambers of the heart
2. joint - an area where bone meets bone
3. urinary system - removes toxins and waste from the body
4. marrow - produces blood cells
5. bronchi - small tubes that carry air deep into the lungs
6. diaphragm - main muscle that controls breathing
7. circulatory system - made up of the heart, blood, and vessels
8. nephrons - filter over one quart of blood a minute
9. molecules - formed when two or more atoms join
10. atria - upper chambers of the heart
11. cells - the smallest living unit in the body
12. skeleton - gives your body shape and structure
13. respiratory system - exchanges oxygen for carbon dioxide
14. atoms - made of protons, neutrons, and electrons
15. skeletal muscles - provide the power needed for movement
16. ligaments - help join bones and hold them in place
17. trachea - another name for the windpipe
18. nucleic acids - store genetic information
19. cartilage - flexible tissue that cushions bones
20. epiglottis - flap that keeps food out of the lungs

Word Search - Lesson 1, Part 5

```
V E K M B G R E A T D E P R E S S I O N W U V
D J N G H Q Q P W H A J H W S C U E L G D R O
X X D Q U Y M M O G C I D I H C K Y N Y I N V
B Q E E U V Q A N I S B D N C W Z A G S G D A
N C T H O M E R P R I C E E A R Q D H M E J C
P X H Z E Q E C J W P O F H M U F S H D S S O
X D G S H D N O H E N R Y F O R D N N Y T O O
L U I Q D R A N D L G T Y F Q B X A E A I N J
J O R H W T N U N T A R I F F L R R N V A A H
K C W M O D E L T I L X V K M L H E V L E B R
S T R C R T L X K V K V K W Q O R E T O J S Z X
M P U R L Z V I Z R P W G H N L R E U X Y W J
Q M B X D U S T B O W L N O L S C V S Y S R Z
X J L R W E R O B R A H L R A E P V S Y T N A
M C I U A C G N I K O L A T E S L A Y R E Y A
D Z W X R C D D B J U R R X Z V V E S V M K P
Q Q L Z I F E N D O C R I N E S Y S T E M I N
Q A W J U I C H A R L E S L I N D B E R G Q V
D T Q N X T N E M E S I T R E V D A M I O B O
R M I X Y A D L A I R O M E M N J F H B V K K
```

Word Scramble - Lesson 2, Part 5

1. Memorial Day
2. Great Depression
3. Homer Price
4. digestive system
5. Wilbur Wright
6. Marconi
7. endocrine system
8. Nikola Tesla
9. advertisement
10. nervous system
11. World War II
12. Model T
13. Dust Bowl
14. sonar
15. Henry Ford
16. senses
17. Charles Lindberg
18. tariff
19. Veterans Day
20. media
21. John Holland
22. Kitty Hawk
23. Pearl Harbor
24. Orville Wright

Supply and Demand Game 6 - Lesson 3, Part 2

cargo - goods carried as freight by truck, train, ship or airplane
   Example: produce grown on a farm that is taken to a store for sale

Great Depression - economic crisis beginning around 1929
   Example: Many people lost their jobs during this time.

exports - goods produced in one nation and sold to other nations
   Example: wheat, cotton, or corn grown in the United States and sold to China

profit - amount of money received for a product that is greater than its cost
   Example: income to reinvest in a business or farm, or to take as benefit

tariff - tax imposed on exported goods or services
   Example: People in Japan pay more for American wheat than we do.

stock exchange - a place where individuals can invest in businesses
   Example: Shares of airline stock can be bought and sold.

inflated - worth is exaggerated
   Example: the value of many businesses before the Great Depression

subsidies - grants from the government to help a farm continue to function
   Example: payments made to farmers to help grow, or not grow, certain crops

surplus - more than usual
   Example: supplies of wheat, corn, and cotton after World War I

drought - severe shortage of water, usually because of a lack of rain
   Example: absence of water needed for crops and livestock

loan - money borrowed, usually from a bank, to pay bills or make investments
   Example: Many farmers needed these to keep going during drought.

livelihood - means of making a living
   Example: farming, factory work, cattle ranching, teaching

Crossword - Lesson 3, Part 5

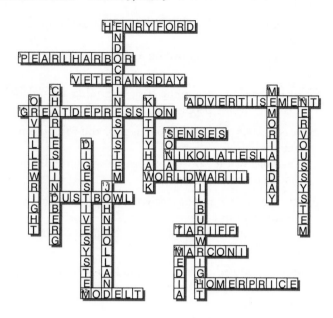

Who or What Am I - Lesson 4, Part 5

1. Memorial Day
2. Great Depression
3. nervous system
4. Orville or Wilbur Wright
5. Orville or Wilbur Wright
6. Nikola Tesla
7. Charles Lindberg
8. Pearl Harbor
9. advertisement
10. Homer Price
11. Veterans Day
12. Model T
13. media
14. John Holland
15. senses
16. Dust Bowl
17. endocrine system
18. Kitty Hawk
19. World War II
20. digestive system
21. sonar
22. Henry Ford
23. tariff
24. Marconi

Supply and Demand Game - Lesson 6, Part 2

advertising - drawing attention to a product or service
Example: a person wearing a sign that says, "Eat at Joe's!"

advertisement - the use of media to draw attention to a product or service
Example: a picture in a newspaper of a car available for sale

gimmick - tricks designed to bring shoppers to see a particular product
Example: The first fifty people to come to a store get a special prize.

persuasive speech - convincing arguments used to sell products or services
Example: Joe's Market sells the best fruit in our town!

self-sufficiency - the ability to produce the basic items needed for survival
Example: individuals who produce or make all the items needed to live

trendy - clothing, vehicles, and decorations that are up-to-date in style
Example: the most recently obtained items of clothing

budget - estimated income and planned spending
Example: $100 for food, $50 for gas weekly

advertising campaign - an organized series of events to promote a product or service
Example: commercials, signs, or leaflets promoting a new restaurant

media - a variety of types of mass communication
Example: television, radio, newspapers, Internet, magazines

word-of-mouth advertising - when people tell others about a product they like
Example: You find a new restaurant you really like, so you tell your friend about it.

testimonial - when someone's personal experience with a product is used in advertising
Example: "I have been having Joe fix my car for many years, and he does a great job. You should go to Joe's Garage, too."

coupon - voucher to obtain an item at a special rate
Example: $1.00 off of Gary's Soup when you buy three cans

Human Body Matching - Lesson 6, Part 3

1. motor neurons - in charge of voluntary actions
2. brain - control-center for all body systems and organs
3. nutrients - vitamins, minerals, proteins, fats, and carbohydrates
4. skin - organ responsible for the sense of touch
5. taste buds - recognize flavors
6. mucous membrane - traps particles and moistens air you breathe
7. rods and cones - nerve cells that respond to light
8. chemical digestion - enzymes and acids break food down
9. pupil - opening in the eye where light enters
10. nervous system - the brain, spinal cord, and nerves
11. middle ear - where sound waves are converted to vibrations
12. dermis - layer of skin that holds touch receptors
13. mechanical digestion - stomach and teeth break up large pieces
14. endocrine system - balances body chemicals and processes
15. cerebrum - the largest portion of the brain
16. ossicles - transfer vibrations to the inner ear
17. hormones - chemicals that tell cells and organs what to do
18. olfactory - relates to the sense of smell
19. papillae - bumps on the tongue
20. small intestine - where most absorption of nutrients takes place

Unit 1: Science Review - Lesson 1, Part 1

1. work - when a force moves an object or load

2. zipper - a fastener that uses wedges to open and close

3. friction - a force created when rough surfaces are rubbed together

4. tools - items that help to complete work by changing the amount or direction of force

5. inclined plane - slanted surface that decreases the force needed to raise an object

6. weight - one thing that affects the amount of friction created when an object is moved

7. wedge - a moveable inclined plane

8. force - a push or a pull

9. lubrication - putting certain liquids on a surface to reduce friction

10. stairs - one example of an inclined plane

11. plow - a machine that uses several wedges to prepare soil for planting

12. movement - what is necessary in order for work to take place

13. brake - something that uses friction to stop or slow movement

14. effort - the amount of force used to move an object

15. axe - one simple use of a wedge

16. output force - the force exerted by a tool or machine on a load

17. physics - the study of the properties of matter and energy

18. input force - the force exerted on a tool or machine

19. mechanical advantage - the amount of effort saved by using a tool or machine

20. complex machine - anything that uses two or more basic tools

Unit 1: History/Economics Review - Lesson 1, Part 2

1. Amos Fortune
2. George Washington
3. Benjamin Franklin
4. Robert Fulton
5. John Gutenberg
6. Alexander Hamilton
7. Samuel Morse
8. Samuel Morse
9. James Watt
10. Alexander Hamilton
11. Robert Fulton
12. John Gutenberg
13. James Watt
14. George Washington
15. Amos Fortune
16. Benjamin Franklin

Word Search - Lesson 1, Part 5

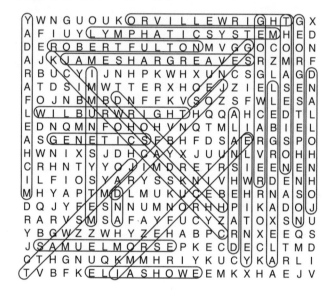

Unit 2: Science Review - Lesson 1, Part 5

1. threads - the spirals around a screw
2. fulcrum - the part of a lever that does not move
3. effort arm - part of a class one lever to which force is applied
4. wheelbarrow - one example of a class two lever
5. lever - tool that uses a fulcrum to move loads
6. screw - an inclined plane wrapped around a cylinder
7. scissors - one example of a class one lever
8. rake - one example of a class three lever
9. screwdriver - one example of a wheel and axle
10. bar or rod - the part of a class one lever that moves
11. axle - the shaft on which a wheel turns when it is used as a tool
12. class one lever - tool that has a load at one end, a fulcrum in the middle, and the force at the other end
13. class two lever - tool that has a fulcrum at one end, the load in the middle, and the force at the other end
14. class three lever - tool that has a fulcrum at one end, the force in the middle, and the load at the other end
15. pitch - the distance between the threads of a screw
16. pivot-point - what a fulcrum is called when the lever can rotate
17. Archimedes' screw - a large screw inside a cylinder, first used to move water
18. dragging force - another name for friction
19. water wheel - machine that helped the Industrial Revolution succeed
20. foundry - a place where metal is molded

Unit 2: History/Economics Review - Lesson 2, Part 2

1. George Stephenson
2. Noah Webster
3. Michael Faraday
4. Samuel Crompton
5. William McGuffey
6. Harriet Beecher Stowe
7. James Hargreaves
8. Abraham Lincoln
9. Michael Faraday
10. Harriet Beecher Stowe
11. Noah Webster
12. Samuel Crompton
13. Abraham Lincoln
14. James Hargreaves
15. William McGuffey
16. George Stephenson

Word Scramble - Lesson 2, Part 5

1. Orville Wright
2. Enrico Fermi
3. Alexander G Bell
4. Alan Shepard
5. Robert Fulton
6. Elias Howe
7. Thomas Edison
8. Eli Whitney
9. John Holland
10. immune system
11. genes
12. George Stephenson
13. genetics
14. Wilbur Wright
15. James Hargreaves
16. Michael Faraday
17. DNA
18. Cyrus McCormick
19. James Watt
20. lymphatic system
21. John Baird
22. Henry Ford
23. Samuel Morse
24. George W Carver

Unit 3: Science Review - Lesson 3, Part 1

1. pulley - a tool that uses a wheel and a rope
2. load - weight of an object being lifted
3. sewing machine - one example of cams and cranks
4. basic tools - inclined plane, screw, wheel and axle, wedge, lever, and pulley
5. moveable pulley - the wheel moves with the load
6. complex machine - two or more basic tools used in one machine
7. gears - wheels with teeth in the outer edge
8. raising blinds - one example of a fixed pulley
9. fixed pulley - changes the direction of input force
10. cam - a wheel and axle with an extension attached to the wheel
11. compound pulley - a fixed and a moveable pulley used together
12. spring - used to weigh loads
13. clocks - one example of gears
14. cogs - the teeth on gears
15. crane - one example of a moveable pulley
16. effort distance – how far the rope is moved when using a pulley
17. crankshaft - used to create a rotating movement in engines
18. internal combustion - type of engine that replaced the steam engine
19. rack and pinion - gears that move back and forth instead of circling
20. elevator - one example of a compound pulley

Unit 3: History/Economics Review - Lesson 3, Part 2

1. Thomas H. Gallaudet
2. Thomas Edison
3. Henry Ford
4. Thomas H. Gallaudet
5. Alexander Graham Bell
6. Helen Keller
7. Thomas Edison
8. Henry Ford
9. Helen Keller
10. Alexander Graham Bell
11. Helen Keller
12. Thomas H. Gallaudet
13. Thomas Edison
14. Alexander Graham Bell
15. Henry Ford

You Can Find Me Review 1 - Lesson 3, Part 4

capital letter - beginning of a sentence

capital letter - beginning of a proper noun, like Steve

capital letter - beginning of an abbreviation

capital letter - beginning of a proper noun, like Texas

capital letter - beginning of a quotation

lower case letter - beginning of a common noun

pronoun - takes the place of one or more nouns

question mark - end of an asking sentence

period - end of a telling sentence

period - end of an abbreviation

quotation marks - around words spoken or thought

comma - before a quotation

comma - to separate a quote from the sentence

comma - to separate two equal describing words

comma - to separate an appositive

italics - slanted type used for a title

italics - slanted type used for special words

apostrophe - used to show missing letters from a word

colon - draws attention to important information

ellipsis - shows words left out or pause in dialogue

parenthesis - sets information apart to make clearer

dash - shows change or interruption in words

Crossword - Lesson 3, Part 5

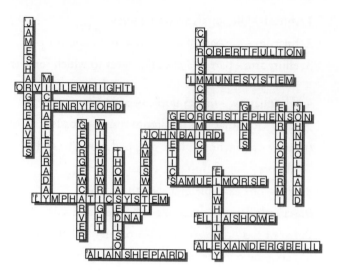

Unit 4: History/Economics Review - Lesson 4, Part 2

1. family farm
2. Elias Howe
3. Sgt. Alvin C. York
4. Cyrus McCormick
5. Eli Whitney
6. George Washington Carver
7. Henry Bessemer
8. World War I
9. George Washington Carver
10. Cyrus McCormick
11. Sgt. Alvin C. York
12. Elias Howe
13. Henry Bessemer
14. World War I
15. Eli Whitney
16. family farm

Who or What Am I - Lesson 4, Part 5

1. John Baird
2. Alan Shepard
3. genes
4. Wilbur Wright
5. Elias Howe
6. Robert Fulton
7. Enrico Fermi
8. Michael Faraday
9. immune system
10. George Washington Carver
11. Thomas Edison
12. John Holland
13. lymphatic system
14. James Watt
15. George Stephenson
16. Henry Ford
17. James Hargreaves
18. Orville Wright
19. DNA
20. Alexander Graham Bell
21. Cyrus McCormick
22. Samuel Morse
23. genetics
24. Eli Whitney

Unit 5: History/Economics Review - Lesson 5, Part 2

1. Nikola Tesla
2. Wright Brothers
3. Dr. Charles Drew
4. Irena Sendler
5. John Holland
6. Corrie ten Boom
7. Winston Churchill
8. Guglielmo Marconi
9. Guglielmo Marconi
10. Wright Brothers
11. John Holland
12. Dr. Charles Drew
13. Irena Sendler
14. Nikola Tesla
15. Winston Churchill
16. Corrie ten Boom

Unit 6: History/Economics Review - Lesson 6, Part 2

1. Alan Shepard
2. Dwight Eisenhower
3. John Baird
4. Enrico Fermi
5. Jackie Robinson
6. John Baird
7. Alan Shepard
8. Dwight Eisenhower
9. Jackie Robinson
10. Enrico Fermi
11. Enrico Fermi
12. Dwight Eisenhower
13. John Baird
14. Jackie Robinson
15. Alan Shepard

You Can Find Me Review 2 - Lesson 6, Part 4

singular subject-verb agreement - <u>Dad</u> **eats** steak.

plural subject-verb agreement - <u>Mom and Dad</u> **eat** steak.

singular antecedent-pronoun agreement - <u>She</u> likes to **eat** her pizza.

plural antecedent-pronoun agreement - <u>They</u> like to eat **their** pizza.

dialect - language particular to a region or group

proper noun - the name of a particular person, place, thing, or idea

common noun - a general kind of person, place, thing, or idea

adjective - a word that describes a noun or pronoun

verb - shows something is happening or happened

helping verb - comes before a verb, and helps it express meaning

preposition - shows how nouns or pronouns relate to other words in a sentence

prepositional phrase - starts with a preposition and ends with a noun or pronoun

adverb - tells how, when, why, where, and how much

pronoun: takes the place of a noun

Human Body Matching - Lesson 6, Part 3

1. homologous pair - two chromosomes alike in size, shape, and types of genes
2. immune system - protects your body from invaders
3. fetus - an unborn baby from eight weeks to birth
4. replication - when DNA is copied before cell division
5. meiosis - cell division resulting in four daughter cells that are not alike
6. chromosome - two strands of DNA bonded together
7. foreign invaders - bacteria, parasites, fungi, viruses, and allergens
8. skin - largest organ in the body
9. lymphocytes - develop into B-cells or T-cells
10. mucous - traps foreign particles and moistens air you breathe
11. lymphatic system - destroys things that cause disease
12. double helix - the shape of a chromosome
13. genes - determine physical traits
14. lymph nodes - produce white blood cells
15. mitosis - cell division resulting in two identical daughter cells
16. recombination - chromosome pairs exchange some genes
17. antibodies - recognize germs that have attacked you before
18. phagocytes - eat foreign, dead, and infected cells
19. allele - part of a gene coded for a specific trait
20. antigens - identify invaders for the immune system to destroy

Appendix D

Word Search... 357

Word Scramble 360

Crossword.. 363

Instructions

Game Instructions...366

Question Quest Game Board 369

Claymation Instructions....................................370

Bingo

Cultivating Greatness 375

Success Takes Flight.......................................383

Reach for the Stars......................................391

~ *Cultivating Greatness Word Search* ~

```
R E V R A C N O T G N I H S A W E G R O E G L
F Q F K H E R O T S T N E M T R A P E D P T E
I X G D X O Z B P H J M D Y G Q S Q S X E V L
B Q E Q J Q T A G E M R Q W F Y T J F T L T I
W J N F Q H M J H H A Y Z B A U C L Q U I Z W
X O E E H X L R W E O N Y Q S W Q M G S A K H
C I R B X O C T A Q N M U K S N A J K D S N I
O N A L L I K R S F U R E T J U S D O A H O T
T T L D D V E A V V Y G Y S S G M S R O O T N
T D S R R W I E W L E L B B T L L E C R W E E
O X T U E R A H U E Y L I V E E B B O L E L Y
N S O S D P N R I A O Z J M I S A V P I K E M
G C R R C J A N I O U X A W A R S D C A J K V
I W E V F N S E D V M M F W Y F O E A R F S T
N L V M S T A G R I C U L T U R E N M C U D Z
U O W R I S A A C S I N G E R W Q K O E T N J
B Q D T V V X T T Q H L Y Q P P W O X R R C K
C G U S K C I M R O C C M S U R Y C C M E G D
Q T R H X N U V S M C A T A L O G G M F J D J
E R L W F U C M Q D J T E O J B U O F H G L K
```

agriculture

blood

catalog

cell

cotton gin

Cyrus McCormick

department store

Eli Whitney

Elias Howe

family farm

general store

George Washington Carver

heart

Henry Bessemer

Homestead Act

iron ore

Isaac Singer

joint

peanuts

railroad

reaper

skeleton

Tuskegee Institute

World War I

~ *Success Takes Flight Word Search* ~

```
V E K M B G R E A T D E P R E S S I O N W U V
D J N G H Q Q P W H A J H W S C U E L G D R O
X X D Q U Y M M O G C I D I H C K Y N Y I N V
B Q E E U V Q A N I S B D N C W Z A G S G D A
N C T H O M E R P R I C E E A R Q D H M E J C
P X H Z E Q E C J W P O E H M U F S H D S S W
X D G S H D N O H E N R Y F O R D N N Y T O O
L U I Q D R A N D L G T Y F Q B X A E A I N J
J O R H W T N I N L T A R I F F L R R N V A H
K C W M O D E L T I L X V K M L H E V L E R R
S T R C R T L X K V V K W O O R E T O J S Z X
M P U R L Z V I Z R P W G H N L R E U X Y W J
Q M B X D U S T B O W L N O L S C V S Y S R Z
X J L R W E R O B R A H L R A E P V S Y T N N
M C I U A C G N I K O L A T E S L A Y R E Y A
D Z W X R C D D B J U R R X Z V V E S V M K P
Q Q L Z I F E N D O C R I N E S Y S T E M I N
Q A W J I I C H A R L E S L I N D B E R G Q V
D T Q N X T N E M E S I T R E V D A M I O B O
R M I X Y A D L A I R O M E M N J F H B V K K
```

advertisement	John Holland	Orville Wright
Charles Lindberg	Kitty Hawk	Pearl Harbor
digestive system	Marconi	senses
Dust Bowl	media	sonar
endocrine system	Memorial Day	tariff
Great Depression	Model T	Veterans Day
Henry Ford	nervous system	Wilbur Wright
Homer Price	Nikola Tesla	World War II

✑ *Reach for the Stars Word Search* ✑

```
Y W N G U O U K O R V I L L E W R I G H T G X
A F I U Y L Y M P H A T I C S Y S T E M H E D
D E R O B E R T F U L T O N M V G G O C O O N
A J K J A M E S H A R G R E A V E S R Z M R F
R B U C Y I J N H P K W H X U N C S G L A G D
A T D S I M W T T E R X H O E J Z I E L S E N
F O J N B M B D N F F K V S O Z S F W L E S A
L W I L B U R W R I G H T Q Q A H C E D T L L
E D N Q M N F O H O H V N Q T M L I A B I E L
A S G E N E T I C S F B H F D S A E R G S P O
H W N I X S J D H C A Y X J U U N L V R O H H
C R H N T Y Y O J I M D R E T R S I E E N E N
I L F I O S Y A R Y S S K N I V H W R D E N H
M H Y A P T M D L M U K U C E B E H R N A S O
D Q J Y F E S N N U M N O R H H P I K A D O J
R A R V S M S A F A Y F U C Y Z A T O X S N U
Y B G W Z Z W H Y Z E H A B P C R N X E E Q S
J S A M U E L M O R S E P K E C D E C L T M D
C T H G N U Q K M M H R I Y K U C Y K A R L I
T V B F K E L I A S H O W E E M K X H A E J V
```

Alan Shepard
Alexander G Bell
Cyrus McCormick
DNA
Eli Whitney
Elias Howe
Enrico Fermi
genes

genetics
George Stephenson
George W Carver
Henry Ford
immune system
James Hargreaves
James Watt
John Baird

John Holland
lymphatic system
Michael Faraday
Orville Wright
Robert Fulton
Samuel Morse
Thomas Edison
Wilbur Wright

～ *Cultivating Greatness Word Scramble* ～

agriculture	department store	heart	peanuts
blood	Eli Whitney	Henry Bessemer	railroad
catalog	Elias Howe	Homestead Act	reaper
cell	family farm	iron ore	skeleton
cotton gin	general store	Isaac Singer	Tuskegee Institute
Cyrus McCormick	George W Carver	joint	World War I

Unscramble these words and write them correctly on the line.

1. jotin _____

2. arhte _____

3. iitWlhEney _____

4. cemAattHeosd_____

5. tontadeetsmrper _____

6. aaroirld _____

7. etstustlTeeuegkni _____

8. perare _____

9. weEHalsio _____

10. eenosrarlegt _____

11. lgaacot _____

12. mfaayifrlm _____

13. rlaiSgcneas _____

14. iorenro _____

15. BemHsesrerney _____

16. crmrusCiCyMcko _____

17. oldarWlrW _____

18. ngtniocto _____

19. elsoktne _____

20. bdloo _____

21. lelc _____

22. tauensp _____

23. GrearerWeCgvo _____

24. irratulceug _____

☙ *Success Takes Flight Word Scramble* ☜

advertisement	Henry Ford	Memorial Day	senses
Charles Lindberg	Homer Price	Model T	sonar
digestive system	John Holland	nervous system	tariff
Dust Bowl	Kitty Hawk	Nikola Tesla	Veterans Day
endocrine system	Marconi	Orville Wright	Wilbur Wright
Great Depression	media	Pearl Harbor	World War II

Unscramble these words and write them correctly on the line.

1. ayroemlMDai _____

2. atisoeerprDGens _____

3. reHmPciore _____

4. metvessyesdigti _____

5. WurrgWbitihl _____

6. aocMrni _____

7. srodcyeeintenms _____

8. kaNlelTsioa _____

9. teaeresvdmnit _____

10. tnomrueeysvss _____

11. rarllWdloW _____

12. elMdoT _____

13. wolDtsBu _____

14. orans _____

15. yrFenrdHo _____

16. nseses _____

17. LdeCnsilbrregah _____

18. arfitf _____

19. atyaenVerDs _____

20. aidme _____

21. ndlJloHnhoa _____

22. aKkHittyw _____

23. HorabrerPla _____

24. glirhvtlieOWr _____

✦ *Reach For the Stars Word Scramble* ✦

Alan Shepard	Enrico Fermi	immune system	Michael Faraday
Alexander G Bell	genes	James Hargreaves	Orville Wright
Cyrus McCormick	genetics	James Watt	Robert Fulton
DNA	George Stephenson	John Baird	Samuel Morse
Eli Whitney	George W Carver	John Holland	Thomas Edison
Elias Howe	Henry Ford	lymphatic system	Wilbur Wright

Unscramble these words and write them correctly on the line.

1. vrhOglreiWtli _____

2. cnmeEioiFrr _____

3. nlelABeerxGdal _____

4. nrdalApahSe _____

5. rFotnbetlouR _____

6. iaelEowsH _____

7. EaooTsdnshmi _____

8. niyEleWhti _____

9. aohonIndJHl _____

10. ystnmeisumme _____

11. egesn _____

12. eregteonseGhpSno _____

13. stngeiec _____

14. WihurrgWbtil _____

15. raJsrHaeegvsmea _____

16. iaraMycdlaFeah _____

17. NDA _____

18. CsmMcCcyokurir _____

19. eatJtsaWm _____

20. spmcamytyiesthl _____

21. BaoJnhidr _____

22. FeydrHron _____

23. eSIMrosmeua _____

24. erWrergoaGCev _____

∽ Cultivating Greatness Crossword ∽

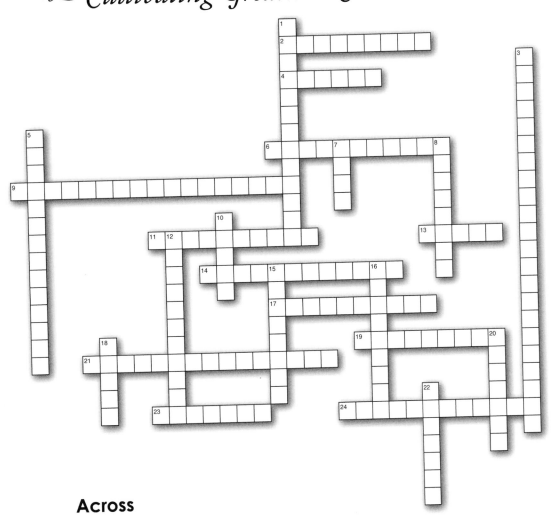

Across

2. inventor of the sewing machine
4. machine used to harvest grain
6. inventor who improved Howe's machine, and successfully marketed his creation
9. school in Alabama where George Washington Carver taught
11. farm that is owned by, and produces enough for, one family
13. place where bones come together, which enables movement
14. law that gave citizens the right to claim 160 acres of undeveloped land
17. inventor of the cotton gin that works with green seed cotton
19. first war to use airplanes, tanks, and machine guns
21. a large store with many sections that sell different kinds of goods
23. southern crop that greatly interested George Washington Carver
24. a rural store that provided a variety of necessities

Down

1. invented a process to make steel inexpensively
3. American educator and scientist who was born a slave
5. inventor of the first reaping machine
7. the smallest living unit in the human body
8. transportation system that greatly improved the delivery of mail and goods
10. liquid that delivers nutrients to body organs, and removes waste
12. business and science of growing crops and raising livestock
15. all the bones in your body together
16. machine that removes seeds from cotton
18. organ that pumps blood through the body
20. iron in its natural state, mixed with clay, rock, or other things
22. book with a list of goods that can be ordered and delivered by mail

❧ Success Takes Flight Crossword ❧

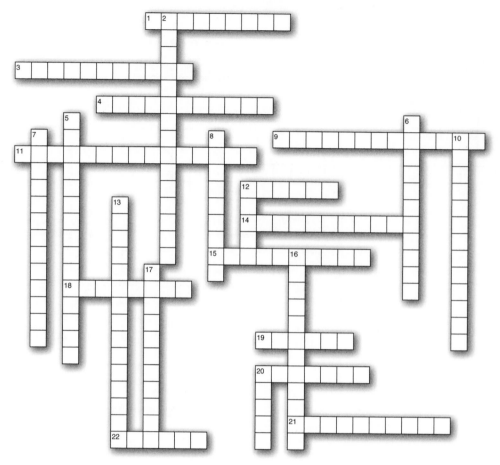

Across

1. introduced assembly line for mass production of automobiles

3. place in Hawaii that was bombed by Japan during World War II

4. holiday to honor American veterans who are living

9. something designed to draw attention to a product or service

11. global economic crisis beginning in 1929

12. hearing, sight, smell, taste, and touch

14. developed wireless telegraphy

15. worldwide conflict that took place in Europe and the Pacific

18. drought and dust storms in the Great Plains in the 1930s

19. tax charged by the government to import or export items

20. helped develop long distance radiotelegraphy

21. inventive young resident of Centerburg

22. successful Ford automobile known as the "Tin Lizzie"

Down

2. network that maintains the balance of chemicals and processes in the body

5. pilot who made the first solo flight across the Atlantic Ocean

6. holiday to remember people who died defending the U.S.

7. one of the brothers who invented the airplane

8. site of the Wright Brothers first flight

10. network that controls all the parts and functions of your body

12. undersea listening device of submarines

13. network that provides the energy your body needs to function

16. one of the brothers who invented the airplane

17. developed and built successful submarines

20. different types of mass communication

～ Reach For the Stars Crossword ～

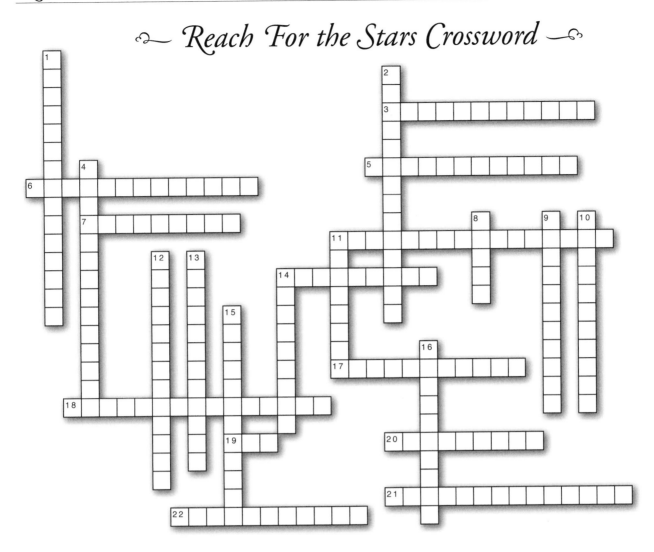

Across

3. developer of the steamboat for work and travel
5. network that protects your body from invaders
6. one of the inventors of the first successful airplane
7. introduced the assembly line for mass production of automobiles
11. inventor of the first steam locomotive
14. developed technology that would become the television
17. inventor of the electric telegraph
18. part of the immune system that destroys things that cause disease
19. chemical code that stores the design for how your body looks and functions
20. inventor of the sewing machine
21. inventor of the telephone
22. first American astronaut to go into space

Down

1. inventor of the spinning jenny
2. inventor of the first reaping machine
4. scientist and inventor of the electric motor
8. sections of DNA coded to produce specific proteins
9. helped develop nuclear energy and the world's first atomic bomb
10. developed and built successful submarines
11. the study of genes, chromosomes, and inheritance
12. American educator and scientist who was born a slave
13. inventor, brother, and partner to Orville Wright
14. inventor of the steam engine
15. inventor of the phonograph, motion picture camera, and a practical electric light bulb
16. inventor of the cotton gin that works with green seed cotton

❧ Game Instructions ❧

Word Search (All Units – Lesson 1, Part 5s)

Circle or highlight the words from the list provided. Mark off each word as you find it.

Word Scramble (All Units – Lesson 2, Part 5s)

Unscramble the words and write them on the lines provided.

Crosswords (All Units – Lesson 3, Part 5s)

Use the clues provided and write the answers in the correct places across or down.

Who or What Am I? (All Units – Lesson 4, Part 5s)

The object of this game is to match each name or term to its description or definition. To begin, place all cards face down, in rows. The first player turns up two cards. If they match, the player removes them and turns up two more cards. Each time the cards match, the player takes another turn. If the cards do not match, turn them back down for the next player. When no cards are left, the game is over and the player with the most cards wins.

Question Quest (All Units – Lesson 6)

Begin by sorting your Orchestra Story answer cards into groups according to the small letters you placed in the upper left corners.

If you have not yet made category cards for the music topics studied so far, do so by cutting index cards in half horizontally. Then write the name of each topic on one of the card-strips. Select four category cards for the first round, and tape each one to the top of a column on the game board.

Now find the Orchestra Story answer cards for each category you selected, and place them in the envelopes. Do this by putting the card you numbered "5" (on its bottom right corner) in the "500" envelope under its category, the one numbered "4" in the "400" envelope, and so forth. You may use the answer keys you prepared in your Student Notebook to determine if a player has provided a correct question.

Players take turns choosing a category and a point value. Each then reads the answer card he has selected aloud, and supplies the correct question in a complete sentence—it does not need to be word for word with the question written down, but should contain the same idea. If the player is correct, he is awarded the number of points on the envelope he chose, and play passes to the next person. If he is incorrect, another player (the first to raise his hand) can supply the question and receive the points.

Variation: Since you have been using the Orchestra Story cards for review, they may become too familiar. Therefore, you or your teacher might want to make up additional questions and answers for the existing topics, or choose new topics from any other subject you study in *Paths of Progress*. Question Quest is an excellent way to help remember things you have learned!

Unit Bingo (Units 5 & 6)

Give each player at least one Bingo game board and a number of tokens such as buttons, pennies, or dried beans. Listen as someone reads the Bingo clues. Place tokens in the squares that provide the correct answers to the clues. The first player to place tokens on all boxes in a row that runs across, down, or diagonally says, "Bingo!" and wins that round. Play as many rounds as you wish.

Word-Part Concentration (Unit 4, Lesson 3, Parts 2 and 4; Lesson 6, Parts 2 and 4)

Place the black cards face up in two equal rows. Then shuffle the remaining cards and place them in a stack face down. To play, each person draws a card from the stack, checks the Rummy Roots Word List, and picks an English word that matches its meaning. After playing this way one or two times, you can either:

- shuffle the two groups of cards separately and place the black word cards face down in one section, and the rest of the cards face down in another section;
- or shuffle all the cards together and place them face down in rows

The first player then turns over two cards, and tries to match a black word card (the English meaning) with one of the other cards (its Greek or Latin word-part). If a match is made, the player gets another turn. If not, the next player takes a turn. Continue until all pairs are made.

Supply and Demand Concentration (All Units – Lesson 3, Part 2)

Print and cut out the Supply and Demand game cards from the Student Resources CD. Make a deck of the cards and shuffle them. Then read each card and match it with the correct definition and example, in rows of three.

One example of a set includes the cards that say "goods," "items made for others to use or consume," and "Example: cookies, cakes, and muffins."

Once you have reviewed the sets, reshuffle the cards and lay them all face down in rows of five. Each player then turns over three cards, attempting to make a set. When a set is made, the cards are removed and that person gets another turn. Play ends when all sets are made. The player with the most sets wins.

Supply and Demand Go Fish Matching (Units 4 – Lesson 3, Part 4, Lesson 6, Part 2)

Print and cut out the Supply and Demand game cards from the Student Resources CD. Make a deck of the cards and shuffle them. Then read each card and match it with the correct definition and example, in rows of three.

One example of a set includes the cards that say "goods," "items made for others to use or consume," and "Example: cookies, cakes, and muffins."

Inventors Twenty Questions (Units 4 and 5, Lesson 6, Part 4)

Place all four questions about an inventor face down in one stack (so you have four stacks). The first person then chooses a stack, and another player reads the questions to him or her. Every time a player cannot answer the question on a card, he or she is given a point. When an inventor's name is guessed correctly, or all the questions have been asked, the next person gets to try with a new stack. The object of the game is to guess the name of an inventor with the fewest number of questions asked—so the lowest score wins.

You Can Find Me (Unit 6 – Lesson 6, Part 2)

This is a concentration-type game in which you shuffle all the cards together and lay them face-down in rows. Each player takes a turn flipping two cards over, trying to match the name of an edit with an example of where you would use it. Even if a player makes a match, he only gets one turn. The goal is to use the fewest turns possible to win, so remember where each card is after it is revealed!

Word Builder Recap (Unit 6 – Lessons 6, Part 2)

This is a concentration-type game in which you mix all the cards up, and then lay them face down in rows of five. Each player then turns over three cards at a time, trying to make a set of any three words with the same word-part. If no set is made, turn the cards face down again and play passes to the right.

When a set of three is made, the player must tell what word-part is on the cards (one point), what language it comes from (one point), and the meaning of at least one of the words before he or she removes the set from the game. If the player knows more than one definition, extra points can be awarded.

Orchestra Story Cards

Make up at least five questions about the musical era, composer(s), or instrument(s) you just read about, and write them on separate index cards. Arrange the question cards for each topic in a stack so that the simplest one is on top, a harder question is next, and so forth—with the most difficult on the bottom. Then, in that order, copy your questions onto the page provided in your Student Notebook. This will be an answer key for a game you will play later.

Next, use complete sentences to write the answers to your questions on separate index cards. Number the cards from one to five in the bottom right corner, in the same order as the questions in your Student Notebook. Do not number the question cards!

Question Quest Game Board

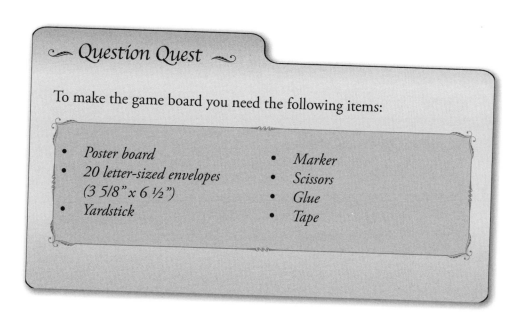

Instructions

1. Begin by using the yardstick to draw a grid on your poster board, with rectangles 4-inches high by 7-inches long. When you finish, you will have 20 rectangles of that size, and four at the top that are 2-inches by 7-inches—perfect for labeling the categories!

   NOTE: To draw the grid, place your yardstick next to one long side of the poster board, being careful that the ends of the yardstick and poster are even. Then make pencil dots every seven inches. Do the same to the other long side. When you are finished, lay the yardstick across the poster from first-dot to first-dot, and draw a line to connect them. (This can be done in pencil, crayon, or marker.) Connect the rest of the dots in the same way.

2. Next, place the yardstick beside one of the short sides, with its end even with the poster, and make dots that are four inches apart. Your marks will not come out even, and you will have two inches left over at one end. This will be the top of your game board. Make the same measurements on the other short side, and be careful that the leftover two inches on that side are also at the top of the board. Connect the dots with straight lines.

3. Cut the flaps off all your envelopes. Then, use a marker to write $100 on four envelopes, $200 on the next four, $300 on four, and so forth.

4. Glue the $500 envelopes in the rectangles along the bottom of your game board, the $400 envelopes in the row above, and so forth.

5. Now prepare category headings by cutting several index cards in half horizontally. Carefully write the name of each topic you have studied in a unit on one card-strip. For example, for Unit 1 you would write "Baroque Period," "Classical Era," "Bach," "Vivaldi," and so forth. Set the category headings aside. Later, you will choose four at a time to play Question Quest. They can be attached to the top of the columns on the game board with a rolled piece of tape on the back. That way you can easily change them as needed.

Claymation Instructions

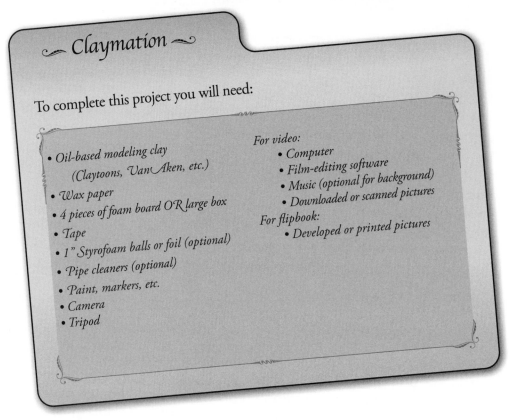

~ Claymation ~

To complete this project you will need:

- *Oil-based modeling clay*
    (Claytoons, Van Aken, etc.)
- *Wax paper*
- *4 pieces of foam board OR large box*
- *Tape*
- *1" Styrofoam balls or foil (optional)*
- *Pipe cleaners (optional)*
- *Paint, markers, etc.*
- *Camera*
- *Tripod*

For video:
- *Computer*
- *Film-editing software*
- *Music (optional for background)*
- *Downloaded or scanned pictures*

For flipbook:
- *Developed or printed pictures*

Lesson 2, Part 4

It is important to start your Claymation project with an idea, and some questions. Who or what are the characters of your story going to be? Where and when does it take place? What is your plot (what the story is about)? How are you going to make your story come to life—how are you going to create your Claymation project?

Once you have answered your questions, you can begin your storyboard. A storyboard is a plan of action for your project, and is basically an outline of the story you want to tell, done as a series of drawings. It is a very necessary part of Claymation, because you need to know your characters' movements throughout the duration of the project, in as much detail as possible. I usually put six to nine drawings on a page, but you can set up your storyboard any way you wish. One simple way is to fold a plain piece of paper in half length-wise, and then in thirds width-wise. When you unfold it,

the paper will be divided into six sections; each section is a place for one of your storybook sketches. You will probably need quite a few of these pages.

Keep in mind that if you are creating a flipbook, a shorter story is generally better. You will be taking a lot of pictures, and you want to be able to easily flip through your finished project.

For a video or flipbook, however, you should draw a few frames/pictures from each scene (part). For each scene you can capture a different perspective (view, angle) with your camera—get a close up for one scene, or have your camera placed at an angle for another scene. For instance, if your characters will be walking across a room, you may want to draw a picture of your figures on one side of the room, a picture of them in the middle, and a picture of them on the other side of the room. A storyboard makes it easy to remember what you want to show your characters doing, and how you will handle your camera throughout the project. It is surprising how many scenes it will take to make your character move smoothly!

Lesson 3, Part 4

After your storyboard is complete, you then need to create the stars of the show—your clay figures. For this, you need an oil-based modeling clay. This is because regular clay will dry out quickly under the lights (while you are taking the many photographs necessary), and then become brittle and fall apart. That can be very frustrating!

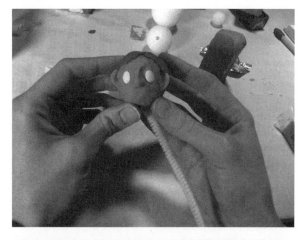

To make working with clay a little easier, here are some helpful tips:

- Create your figures on wax paper. This will help to keep your work area clean.

- If the clay is too firm and hard to work with, try rolling it around in your hands. The heat your hands generate while working with the clay will help to soften it.

- During the creation process, refer back to your storyboard and think about what movements your characters will be making. If they

will be walking around, make sure they are not too top-heavy and make sure their legs can support them while moving. If you are worried about a characters' heaviness, you can create an inside structure out of Styrofoam and pipe cleaners. For example, you can create a person's head out of a Styrofoam ball. Join the Styrofoam head to the clay body using a pipe cleaner. Then you can cover the head and the neck with clay. This will make your characters much lighter—and you can use the same method for their bodies as well.

Take another look at your storyboard and ask yourself if there are any props that you might also need to make from clay.

Store all your figures and props in a small box when you are finished, just in case you decide to add more shots and need them.

After creating your clay characters and props, you will need to make the place where your story will come to life—your set.

There are many different ways to make your set, and you can get as creative as you want. An easy place to start is with a cardboard box, or four pieces of foam board that you tape together. To give you a general idea, my set is 28" long, 22" wide, and 22" high. You will have to use your judgment to decide how much room your story needs. If your figures stay in one place, then you can have a smaller set. If you have several characters that move around a lot, a larger set will be better. Create your own background using paint, markers, or any other materials that you like.

You need a floor and three walls. This will allow you to photograph from the front opening, and it leaves the top open to let the light in.

Lesson 4, Part 4

After your characters, props, and set are completed, you are ready to start filming! Try these helpful hints whether you're shooting (photographing) a video or a flipbook:

Shoot your Claymation in a place where you can leave it up for an extended period of time. Also, make sure your set is located in a place where it is easy to shoot and maneuver your characters.

It's best to use a tripod, because your camera needs to stay in one position to avoid changing its perspective when you don't want to. If you don't have a tripod, you can just set the camera on a chair or some other level surface—just be careful not to move it unless you are ready to change its viewpoint. The more the camera moves between frames/shots, the more inconsistent and choppy your final project will look.

Lighting is another important aspect of shooting your project. You should take into consideration how different lighting will affect your shots. Since you may not know the exact time you will be photographing, it is probably best to use lamps instead of relying on natural light. Position the lamps close around your set in a way that will eliminate as many shadows as possible. This way it won't matter when you are working, your set will always look the same.

As you begin, remember that you will be taking a lot of pictures and your characters will be making very small movements. If you're making a video, you can expect to take at least five to seven photos (or different frames of footage) for each second of the story. With that in mind, make very small adjustments when moving your character. As a matter of fact, the smaller the movements and the more pictures you take, the smoother your project will be. For example, if the character is raising his hand to his face, take several shots of small movements gradually showing his hand getting closer to his face.

It's action time! Following your storyboard, place all of your characters and props in their starting positions. Once they are set, you're ready to take your first shot. Then make a slight adjustment to your figures, and take another shot. Keep your camera as still as possible. Repeat, repeat, repeat, and repeat. Remember that you need about five to seven different frames of footage for one second of your final project. Once you've completed a scene, re-set your stage for the next scene, make adjustments on your camera (zoom in, zoom out, or move to another angle according to your storyboard), and start the process over again. More advanced techniques involve slightly panning (moving from one side to the other), tilting, or zooming (moving in or out) your camera while at the same time moving your characters, and taking a shot for every slight movement until a complete pan, tilt, or zoom is made. This difficult technique creates a very unique perspective. If you stop working on your project in the middle of a scene, be sure to mark your figure and its location as accurately as possible. This way when you start again you will be able to avoid having a jumpy spot in the middle of your scene.

Have fun with your shooting!

Lesson 5, Part 4

If you haven't finished photographing your project, do so now.

The best moment is when you see your story spring to life at the end.

You can easily create a flipbook of your story by first either having your film developed and printed (if your camera uses film), or downloading your pictures onto the computer and printing them yourself (if your camera is digital).

Either way, when you have all your pictures, carefully trim their white edges off. Then put them in order from the first (on top) to the last (on the bottom). Cut index cards into one-inch strips (one strip for each photo).

Place a strip of cardstock next to the left edge of a picture so that the two edges are touching, but not overlapping. Carefully tape them together.

If you have a very large stack of pictures, it is probably a good idea to make more than one booklet by separating the photos by scenes. Check once more to make sure your pictures are in order, and then fasten the index cards together with staples, brads, or large clips.

To make a video, either download your digital pictures or scan developed photos onto your computer.

Hopefully you have taken time to become familiar with one of the film-editing programs by now, and have an idea where to go from here. Generally speaking, you will just need to drop your pictures into the timeline in the order that they were taken. Then press "play" and see how it looks. You can shorten the amount of time each picture is given on screen by dragging their edges in the timeline. This will help your movie run more smoothly.

Play around and have fun! Don't forget to follow the instructions in your editing software to add a soundtrack or printed screens to your project. You have now made your very own handcrafted movie—burn a DVD to add to your portfolio!!

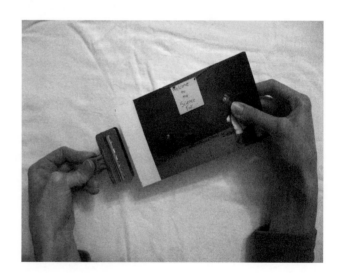

inventor of the cotton gin that works with green seed cotton Eli Whitney	machine that removes seeds from cotton cotton gin	farm that is owned by, and produces enough for, one family family farm
inventor of the sewing machine Elias Howe	inventor who improved Howe's machine, and successfully marketed his creation Isaac Singer	business and science of growing crops and raising livestock agriculture
school in Alabama where George Washington Carver taught Tuskegee Institute	American educator and scientist who was born a slave George Washington Carver	a large store with many sections that sell different kinds of goods department store
southern crop that greatly interested George Washington Carver peanuts	inventor of the first reaping machine Cyrus McCormick	machine used to harvest grain reaper

book with a list of goods that can be ordered and delivered by mail catalog	invented a process to make steel inexpensively Henry Bessemer	iron in its natural state, mixed with clay, rock, or other things iron ore
organ that pumps blood through the body heart	transportation system that greatly improved the delivery of mail and goods railroad	law that gave citizens the right to claim 160 acres of undeveloped land Homestead Act
a rural store that provided a variety of necessities general store	first war to use airplanes, tanks, and machine guns World War I	the smallest living unit in the human body cell
all the bones in your body together skeleton	place where bones come together, which enables movement joint	liquid that delivers nutrients to body organs, and removes waste blood

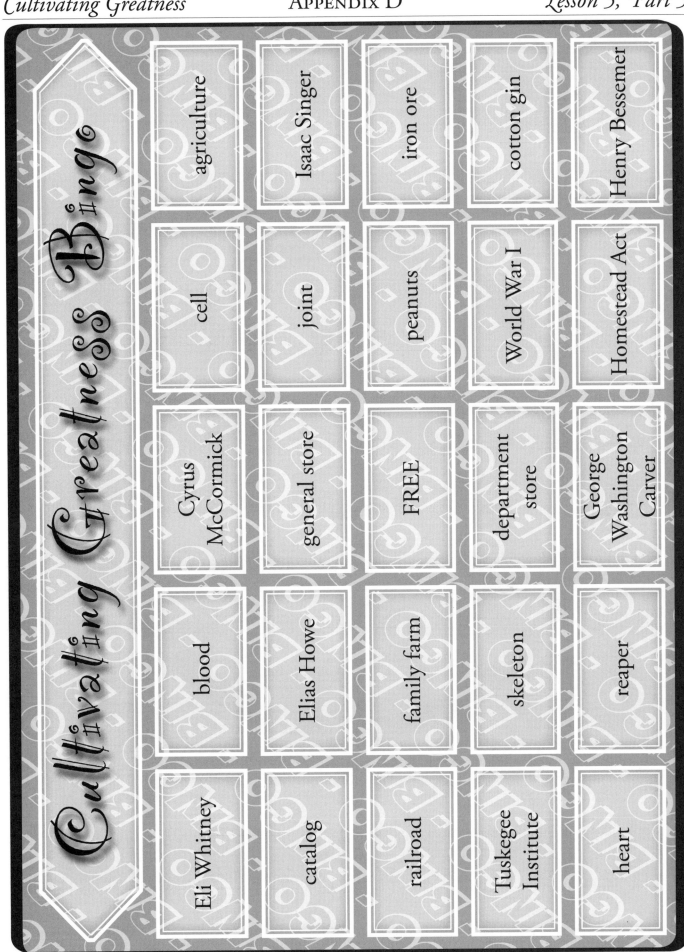

Cultivating Greatness Bingo

agriculture	Isaac Singer	iron ore	cotton gin	Henry Bessemer
cell	joint	peanuts	World War I	Homestead Act
Cyrus McCormick	general store	FREE	department store	George Washington Carver
blood	Elias Howe	family farm	skeleton	reaper
Eli Whitney	catalog	railroad	Tuskegee Institute	heart

Cultivating Greatness Bingo

Henry Bessemer	heart	Elias Howe	Tuskegee Institute	Homestead Act
World War I	agriculture	peanuts	blood	Isaac Singer
railroad	George Washington Carver	FREE	family farm	Eli Whitney
joint	reaper	general store	iron ore	department store
skeleton	cell	cotton gin	catalog	Cyrus McCormick

one of the brothers who invented the airplane **Orville Wright**	one of the brothers who invented the airplane **Wilbur Wright**	site of the Wright Brothers first flight **Kitty Hawk**
holiday to honor American veterans who are living **Veterans Day**	pilot who made the first solo flight across the Atlantic Ocean **Charles Lindberg**	inventive young resident of Centerburg **Homer Price**
introduced assembly line for mass production of automobiles **Henry Ford**	successful Ford automobile known as the "Tin Lizzie" **Model T**	developed wireless telegraphy **Nikola Tesla**
helped develop long distance radiotelegraphy **Marconi**	developed and built successful submarines **John Holland**	undersea listening device of submarines **sonar**

global economic crisis beginning in 1929 **Great Depression**	drought and dust storms in the Great Plains in the 1930s **Dust Bowl**	something designed to draw attention to a product or service **advertisement**
worldwide conflict that took place in Europe and the Pacific **World War II**	tax charged by the government to import or export items **tariff**	place in Hawaii that was bombed by Japan during World War II **Pearl Harbor**
different types of mass communication **media**	holiday to remember people who died defending the U.S. **Memorial Day**	network that provides the energy your body needs to function **digestive system**
network that controls all the parts and functions of your body **nervous system**	network that maintains the balance of chemicals and processes in the body **endocrine system**	hearing, sight, smell, taste, and touch **senses**

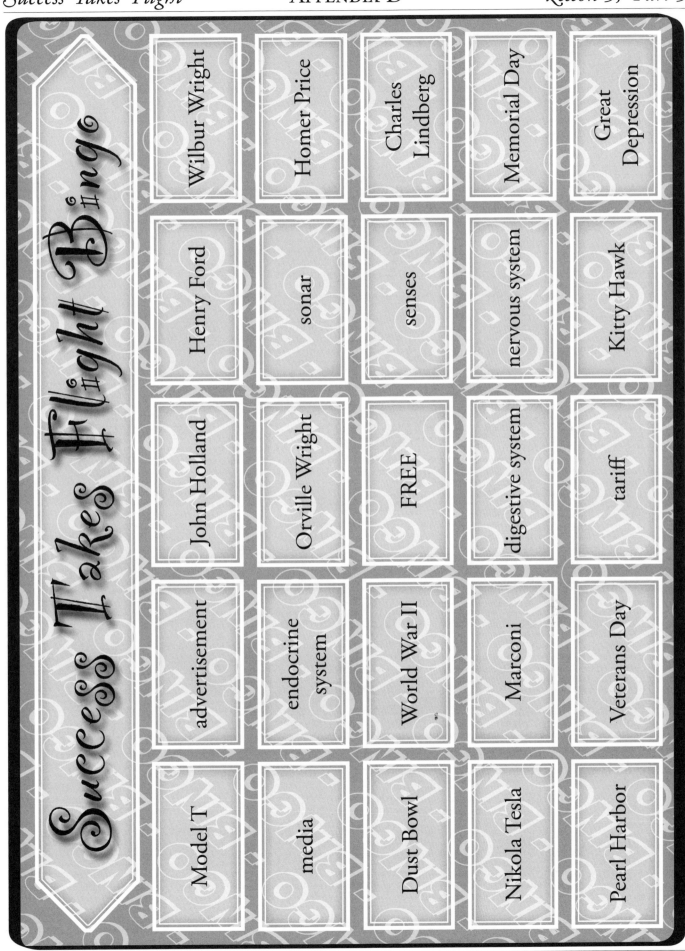

Success Takes Flight Bingo

Wilbur Wright	Homer Price	Charles Lindberg	Memorial Day	Great Depression
Henry Ford	sonar	senses	nervous system	Kitty Hawk
John Holland	Orville Wright	FREE	digestive system	tariff
advertisement	endocrine system	World War II	Marconi	Veterans Day
Model T	media	Dust Bowl	Nikola Tesla	Pearl Harbor

Success Takes Flight Bingo

BINGO GAME BOARD - BACK

Success Takes Flight Bingo

sonar	Great Depression	Memorial Day	senses	Dust Bowl
Model T	Homer Price	media	World War II	Wilbur Wright
tariff	nervous system	FREE	Orville Wright	Pearl Harbor
Veterans Day	digestive system	John Holland	Kitty Hawk	Nikola Tesla
Charles Lindberg	Marconi	endocrine system	advertisement	Henry Ford

inventor of the electric telegraph **Samuel Morse**	developer of the steamboat for work and travel **Robert Fulton**	first American astronaut to go into space **Alan Shepard**
inventor of the steam engine **James Watt**	scientist and inventor of the electric motor **Michael Faraday**	inventor of the spinning jenny **James Hargreaves**
inventor of the telephone **Alexander Graham Bell**	inventor of the first steam locomotive **George Stephenson**	inventor of the phonograph, motion picture camera, and a practical electric light bulb **Thomas Edison**
the study of genes, chromosomes, and inheritance **genetics**	developed technology that would become the television **John Baird**	helped develop nuclear energy and the world's first atomic bomb **Enrico Fermi**

inventor of the cotton gin that works with green seed cotton

Eli Whitney

inventor of the sewing machine

Elias Howe

American educator and scientist who was born a slave

George Washington Carver

inventor of the first reaping machine

Cyrus McCormick

one of the inventors of the first successful airplane

Orville Wright

inventor, brother, and partner to Orville Wright

Wilbur Wright

introduced the assembly line for mass production of automobiles

Henry Ford

developed and built successful submarines

John Holland

network that protects your body from invaders

immune system

part of the immune system that destroys things that cause disease

lymphatic system

chemical code that stores the design for how your body looks and functions

DNA

sections of DNA coded to produce specific proteins

genes

Reach For the Stars Bingo

Thomas Edison	DNA	James Watt	Alan Shepard	lymphatic system
Eli Whitney	immune system	James Hargreaves	George Stephenson	genes
Cyrus McCormick	Samuel Morse	FREE	Elias Howe	John Holland
Henry Ford	Alexander Graham Bell	Robert Fulton	Wilbur Wright	John Baird
Enrico Fermi	Michael Faraday	genetics	George Washington Carver	Orville Wright

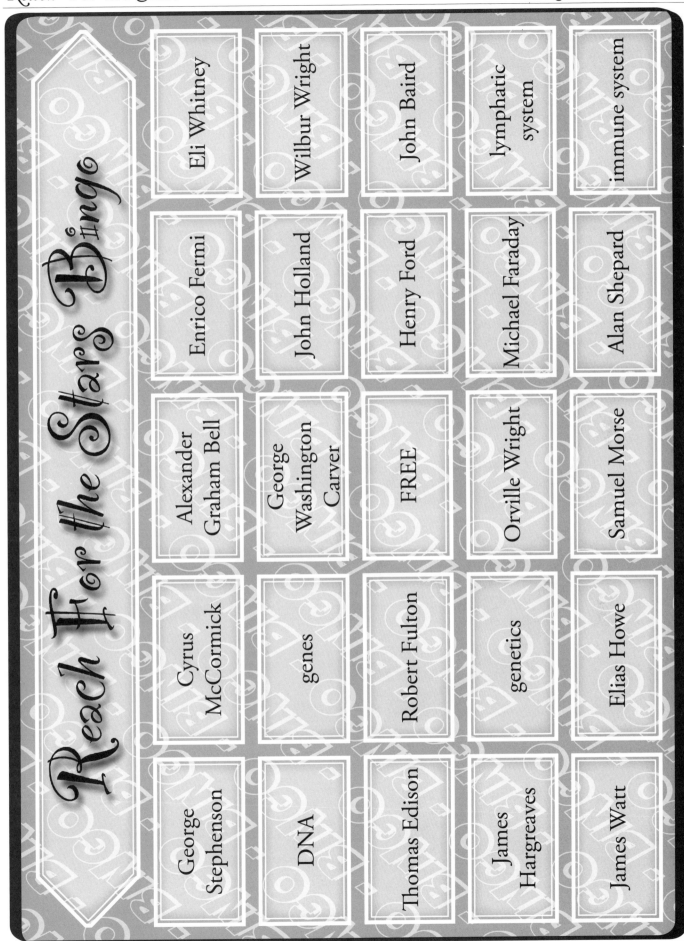

Reach For the Stars Bingo

Eli Whitney	Enrico Fermi	Alexander Graham Bell	Cyrus McCormick	George Stephenson
Wilbur Wright	John Holland	George Washington Carver	genes	DNA
John Baird	Henry Ford	FREE	Robert Fulton	Thomas Edison
lymphatic system	Michael Faraday	Orville Wright	genetics	James Hargreaves
immune system	Alan Shepard	Samuel Morse	Elias Howe	James Watt

Reach For the Stars Bingo

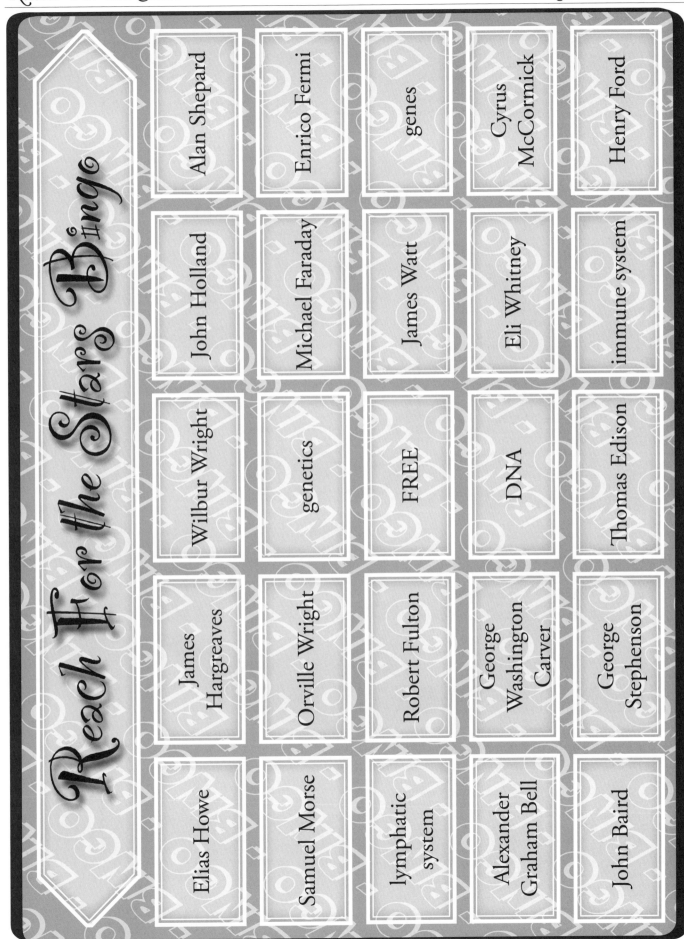

Trail Guide to Geography Series
by Cindy Wiggers

The *Trail Guide to Geography* series is a multi-level geography curriculum guide for elementary grades through High School. Three books in the *Trail Guide to ...Geography* series include U.S., World, and Bible geography. Each book provides clear directions and assignment choices to encourage self-directed learning as students create their own personal geography notebooks. Daily atlas drills, mapping activities, and various weekly assignment choices address learning styles in a way that has kids asking for more!

Trail Guide features:
• Weekly lesson plans – for 36 weeks
• 5-minute daily atlas drills (2 questions/day, four days/week)
• 3 levels of difficulty – all ages participate together
• Weekly mapping assignments
• A variety of weekly research and hands-on activity choices

Student Notebooks are available on CD-ROM

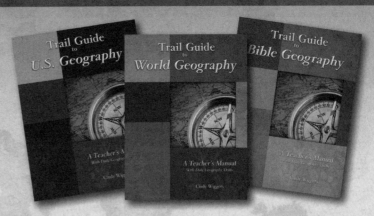

Trail Guide Levels
The *Trail Guide* Levels are just a guide. Select a level according to student ability, and match level with the appropriate atlas or student notebook.

• Primary: grades 2– 4
• Intermediate: grades 5–7
• Secondary: grades 8– 12
All 3 levels in each book!

Note: Primary is ideal for independent 4th graders. Second and third graders will need plenty of guidance. If your oldest is 2nd–3rd grade range, please consider *Galloping the Globe* or *Cantering the Country* first.

Trail Guide to U.S. Geography
Grades **2 - 12**

"The *Trail Guide to U.S. Geography* provides lots of guidance while allowing for (and encouraging) flexibility and this is just the balance most homeschool moms need! The manual is easy to navigate and I am very impressed with how thoroughly material is covered. This resource is destined to be a favorite with homeschool families for years to come!"
–Cindy Prechtel, homeschoolingfromtheheart.com
Paperback, 144 pages, $18.95

Trail Guide to World Geography
Grades **2 - 12**

"We have the *Trail Guide to World Geography* and **love** it!! We are using it again this year just for the questions... I will never sell this guide!! I am looking forward to doing the U.S. one next year."
–Shannon, OK
Paperback, 128 pages, $18.95

Trail Guide to Bible Geography
Grades **2 - 12**

"Here is another winner from Geography Matters! *Trail Guide to Bible Geography* is multi-faceted, user-friendly, and suited to a wide range of ages and abilities."
–Jean Hall, Eclectic Homeschool Association
Paperback, 128 pages, $18.95

Galloping the Globe
by Loreé Pettit and Dari Mullins
Grades **K - 4**

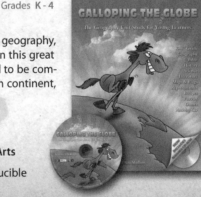

"If you've got kindergarten through fourth grade students, and are looking for unit study material for geography, hold on to your hat and get ready for *Galloping the Globe*! Loreé Pettit and Dari Mullins have written this great resource to introduce children to the continents and some of their countries. This book is designed to be completed in one to three years, depending on how much time you spend on each topic. And for each continent, there are suggestions and topics galore." –Leslie Wyatt, www.homeschoolenrichment.com

Organized by continent, incorporates student notebooking, and covers these topics:
• **Basic Geography** • **History and Biographies** • **Literature** • **Science**
• **Bible** • **Activities** • **Internet Sources** • **Language Arts**

The 2010 edition of *Galloping the Globe* includes an Activity CD-ROM jam-packed with all the reproducible activity sheets found in the book plus added bonus pages. Paperback with CD-ROM, 272 pages, $29.95

Cantering the Country
by Loreé Pettit and Dari Mullins
Grades **1–5**

Saddle up your horses and strap on your thinking caps. Learning geography is an adventure. From the authors who brought you *Galloping the Globe,* you'll love its U.S. counterpart, *Cantering the Country.* This unit study teaches a wide range of academic and spiritual disciplines using the geography of the U.S. as a starting point. With this course, you won't have to put aside one subject to make time for another. They're all connected! This comprehensive unit study takes up to three years to complete and includes all subjects except math and spelling. Incorporates student notebooking and covers these topics:

• **U.S. Geography** • **Character** • **Science** • **Language Arts**
• **Activities** • **Literature** • **Civics** • **History and Biographies**
• **Internet Sources**

In addition to the 250+ page book, you will receive a CD-ROM packed full of reproducible outline maps and activities. Dust off your atlas and get ready to explore America! Paperback with CD-ROM, 272 pages, $29.95

Adventures of Munford Series
by Jamie Aramini

Although he's just two parts hydrogen and one part oxygen, Munford is all adventure. He can be rain, snow, sleet, or steam. He has traveled the world in search of excitement. Throughout history, he has been present at some of the most important and world-changing events.

Fun and educational, Munford will inspire your children to learn more about many of history's greatest events. These readers make a great addition to your learning experience in areas such as history, geography, and science. This book series was written on an elementary reading level, but provides plenty of read-aloud entertainment for the entire family! Paperback, $8.95.

The American Revolution

In this adventure, Munford travels to colonial America and experiences first–hand the events leading to the American Revolution. He meets famed American Founding Fathers, such as Samuel Adams, Thomas Jefferson, and George Washington. He joins the Sons of Liberty under cover of night to dump tea into Boston Harbor. He tags along for Paul Revere's most famous ride, and even becomes a part of the Declaration of Independence in a way that you might not expect!

The Klondike Gold Rush

In this adventure, Munford finds himself slap into the middle of the Klondike Gold Rush. He catches gold fever on this dangerous, yet thrilling, adventure. Meet some of the Gold Rush's most famous characters, like gold baron Alex McDonald or the tricky villain named Soapy Smith. Take a ride on the Whitehorse Rapids, and help Munford as he pans for gold. This is an adventure you won't soon forget!

Munford Meets Lewis & Clark

Join Munford on an epic adventure with Meriwether Lewis and William Clark, as they make their perilous journey in search of the Northwest Passage to the Pacific Ocean.

Munford Meets Robert Fulton

Join Munford— the world's most daring water molecule in his latest adventure! Munford joins forces with Robert Fulton, inventor of the world's first practical steam boat!

Eat Your Way Through the USA
by Loreé Pettit

Taste your way around the U.S.A. without leaving your own dining room table! Each state has its unique geographical features, culinary specialities, and agricultural products. These influence both the ingredients that go into a recipe and the way food is prepared. Compliment your geography lesson and tantalize your tastebuds at the same time with this outstanding cookbook.

This cookbook includes a full meal of easy to follow recipes from each state. Though they aren't written at a child's level, it's easy to include your students in the preparation of these dishes. Cooking together provides life skills and is a source of bonding and pride. More than just a cookbook, it is a taste buds-on approach to geography. Spiral bound, 118 pages, $14.95

Eat Your Way Around the World
by Jamie Aramini

Get out the sombrero for your Mexican fiesta! Chinese egg rolls… corn pancakes from Venezuela… fried plantains from Nigeria. All this, and more, is yours when you take your family on a whirlwind tour of over thirty countries in this unique international cookbook. Includes a full meal of recipes from each country. Recipes are easy to follow, and ingredients are readily available. Jam-packed with delicious dinners, divine drinks, and delectable desserts, this book is sure to please.

The entire family will be fascinated with tidbits of culture provided for each country including: Etiquette Hints, Food Profiles, and Culture a la Carté. For more zest, add an activity and violà, create a memorable learning experience that will last for years to come. Some activities include: Food Journal, Passport, and World Travel Night. Spiral bound, 120 pages, $14.95

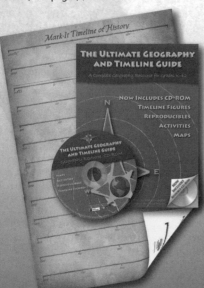

The Ultimate Geography and Timeline Guide
by Maggie Hogan and Cindy Wiggers

Parent 2005

Cathy Duffy's 100 TOP PICKS

Grades K - 12

Learn how to construct timelines, establish student notebooks, teach geography through literature, and integrate science with activities on volcanoes, archaeology, and other subjects. Use the complete multi-level geography course for middle and high school students. Now includes CD-ROM of all reproducible activity and planning pages. Use for all students kindergarden through high school. Paperback with CD-ROM, 353 pages, $39.95

- 18 Reproducible Outline Maps
- Teaching Tips
- Planning Charts
- Over 150 Reproducible Pages
- Over 300 Timeline Figures
- Lesson Plans
- Scope and Sequence
- Flash Cards
- Games

Mark-It Timeline of History

There's hardly no better way to keep history in perspective than creating a timeline in tandem with your history studies. This poster is just the tool to do so. Write or draw images of events as they are studied, or attach timeline figures to aid student understanding and comprehension of the topic at hand. 23" x 34". Laminated, $10.95, Paper (folded), $5.95

 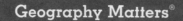

Lewis & Clark - Hands On
Art and English Activities
by Sharon Jeffus

Follow the experiences of Meriwether Lewis and William Clark with hands-on art and writing projects associated with journal entries made during the Corps of Discovery Expedition. Ideal for adding interest to any Lewis and Clark study or to teach drawing and journaling. Includes profiles of American artists, step by step drawing instructions, actual journal entries, and background information about this famous adventure.
Paperback, 80 pages, $12.95

Geography Through Art
by Sharon Jeffus and Jamie Aramini

Geography Through Art is the ultimate book of international art projects. Join your children on an artistic journey to more than twenty-five countries spanning six continents (includes over a dozen United States projects). Previously published by Visual Manna as *Teaching Geography Through Art*, Geography Matters has added a number of enhancements and practical changes to this fascinating art book. Use this book as an exciting way to supplement any study of geography, history, or social studies. You'll find yourself reaching for this indispensable guide again and again to delight and engage students in learning about geography through the culture and art of peoples around the world.
Paperback, 190 pages, $19.95

Profiles from History
by Ashley (Strayer) Wiggers

When studying history, a human connection is the most important connection that we can make. In *Profiles from History*, your student will not only learn about twenty famous people – but also why each one is worthy of remembrance. Everyone knows that Benjamin Franklin was a great inventor, but how many realize he was also a great man? He valued helping people more than making money or becoming famous. He refused to patent his popular Franklin stove, so more families could keep their homes warm during the cold, winter months. *Profiles from History* tells stories like this one, stories of greatness and inspiration. Each profile includes fun activities such as crosswords, word search, & timeline usage. Paperback, $16.95

Also Available:
Profiles from History - Volume 2   *Profiles from History - Volume 3*

Timeline Figures on CD-ROM

Kids love the look of their timelines when they add color and variety. Students can draw on their timeline, write events and dates, and add timeline figures. We've created two different sets of color timeline figures that are ready to print from any computer. There are over 350 figures in each set plus templates to create your own. Our figures are appealing in style, simple to use, and include color-coding and icons to aid memory. Available with biblical events and general world events. CD-ROM (Mac & Windows Compatible), $19.95

- Reproducible Outline Maps -

Reproducible outline maps have a myriad of uses in the home, school, and office. Uncle Josh's quality digital maps provide opportunities for creative learning at all ages. His maps feature rivers and grid lines where possible, and countries are shown in context with their surroundings. (No map of Germany "floating" in the center of the page, here!) When students use outline maps and see the places they are studying in context they gain a deeper understanding of the subject at hand.

Uncle Josh's Outline Map Book

Take advantage of those spontaneous teaching moments when you have this set of outline maps handy. They are:

• Over 100 reproducible maps
• 15 world regions
• Continents with and without borders

• 25 countries
• Each of the 50 United States
• 8 U.S. regions

Useful for all grades and topics, this is by far one of the best book of reproducible outline maps you'll find. Paperback, 128 pages, $19.95

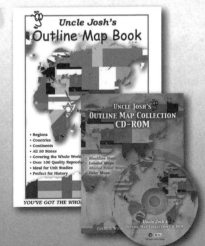

Uncle Josh's Outline Map Collection CD-ROM

In addition to all maps in *Uncle Josh's Outline Map Book* the CD-Rom includes color, shaded-relief, and labeled maps. Over 260 printable maps plus bonus activities. CD-ROM (Mac & Windows), $26.95

- Large-scale Maps -

Large-scale maps are great for detail labeling and for family or classroom use. Laminated Mark-It maps can be reused for a variety of lessons. Quality digital map art is used for each of the map titles published and laminated by Geography Matters. Choose from large scale continents, regions, United States, and world maps. US and World available in both outline version and with state, country, and capitals labeled. Ask about our ever expanding library of full, color shaded-relief maps. Paper and laminated, each title available separately or in discounted sets.

  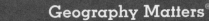

Trail Guide to Learning Series

Paths of Progress

A Complete Curriculum
by Debbie Strayer and Linda Fowler

Volume 1   *Volume 2*

Optional Support Resources

Assessments
Coupled with daily observations and interactive discussions and games this disk provides ample material upon which to base an accurate evaluation of student progress. Answer keys included.

Light for the Trail Bible Study Supplement
Optional Bible study curriculum that coincides with the six units in *Paths of Progress*. Easy-to-use guide provides daily assignments and helps students make the most important connection of all - the one between their faith and their view of the world around them. Includes an enrichment level of Bible study for older students.

Student Notebook Pages
Printing the student notebook pages from the Student Resources CD-ROM included in the curriculum is easy enough, but many folks requested we have them already printed and ready-to-use. Each set includes all notebook pages for that level and volume, three hole-punched for placing in a 3-ring binder.

Game Cards
Although these games are in the textbook and Student Notebook Resources CD, this package saves you the time and preparation of printing or cutting out of the book. Includes instructions, game boards, and game cards used in both volumes of *Paths of Progress*. Printed on cardstock for durability, 50 cards, 8.5 x 11.

Lapbooks
Lapbooks provide interactive, hands-on visual learning. Their biggest benefit is that they dramatically increase your student's memory retention. Great for all ages, using the Lapbooks makes it even easier to teach younger students. Each unit has a separate lapbook with multiple activities for learning fun. These are available as digital downloads (eBook), printed and ready to use, or on CD for you to print. For your convenience, file folders are already included in the printed versions!

Middle School Supplement
A Middle School Supplement is available to provide guidance for older students. It includes the same content plus adds interesting and challenging activities on a higher level along with additional assignments from new readers.

Required Resources

Volume 1
Samuel F. B. Morse	$7.99
Munford Meets Robert Fulton	$8.95
Ben and Me	$6.99
Michael Faraday	$10.99
Caddie Woodlawn	$6.99
Thomas Edison	$8.99
The World of Tools and Technology	$24.00

Volume 2
George Washington Carver	$7.99
Strawberry Girl	$5.99
Wright Brothers	$7.99
Homer Price	$5.99
Alan Shepard	$8.99
Human Body Basics	$15.95

Core
Profiles from History: Volume 3	$16.95
The Story of Inventions (2nd edition)	$9.99
The Story of Inventions Answer Key	$2.99
The Story of the Orchestra with CD	$19.95
Recorder	$5.95
Basix Recorder book with CD	$10.99
Create Anything With Clay	$19.95
Classroom Atlas of US	$12.95
The New Way Things Work	$35.00
Rummy Roots	$15.95

Optional Resources

Assessments CD	$24.95
Light for the Trail CD	$12.95
Student Notebook Pages (price per volume)	$32.00
Game Cards	$18.95
Lapbook Set (price per volume)	$50.00
Lapbook Set CD (includes all 6 units)	$60.00
Middle School Supplement CD	$24.95

 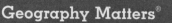

Geography Matters

- Order Form -

Core:	Price	Qty	Total
Profiles from History, Volume 3			
The Story of Inventions (2nd edition)			
The Story of Inventions Answer Key			
The Story of the Orchestra with CD			
Basix Recorder book with CD			
Create Anything With Clay			
Classroom Atlas of US			
The New Way Things Work			
Rummy Roots			

Volume 1:	Price	Qty	Total
Samuel F. B. Morse	7.99		
Munford Meets Robert Fulton	8.95		
Ben and Me	6.99		
The Wright Brothers	10.99		
Caddie Woodlawn	6.99		
Thomas Edison	8.99		
The World of Tools and Technology	24.00		

Other:	Price	Qty	Total
Paths of Progress	160.00		
Assessments CD	24.95		
Student Notebook Pages (price per volume)			
Grade 5 Volume 1 ☐ Volume 2 ☐	32.00		
Grade 6 Volume 1 ☐ Volume 2 ☐	32.00		
Grade 7 Volume 1 ☐ Volume 2 ☐	32.00		
Lapbook Set Volume 1	50.00		
Lapbook Set Volume 2	50.00		
Lapbook CD	60.00		
Game Cards	18.95		
Light for the Trail CD	12.95		
Middle School Supplement CD	24.95		

Volume 2:	Price	Qty	Total
George Washington Carver	7.99		
Strawberry Girl	5.99		
Wright Brothers	7.99		
Homer Price	5.99		
Alan Shepard	8.99		
Human Body Basics	15.95		

Subtotal _____

S & H (12% of Subtotal $6 min) _____

Tax: KY residents add 6% _____

Total _____

Visa ☐   Mastercard ☐   Discover ☐   Check ☐

Payment Type (Check One)

—   —   —

Card Number

/

All prices and availability are subject to change. Call or check online for current information.

800-426-4650   **orders@geomatters.com**   **www.geomatters.com**

About the Authors

Debbie Strayer is uniquely suited to write this curriculum. The *Trail Guide to Learning* Series is a culmination of years of education—experience teaching, training and consulting in the public schools, home schooling her own children through high school, and being mentored by Dr. Ruth Beechick. She holds both a bachelor's and master's degree in education, has been an advisor to homeschool families, and student evaluator for more than twenty years. She is the former editor and co-founder of *Homeschooling Today* magazine, the author of numerous books including co-author of the *Learning Language Arts Through Literature* Series and the editor of *The Homeschool Answer Book* by Dr. Ruth Beechick. Her twenty-year friendship with Dr. Beechick has contributed to her clear understanding about how children think and learn and how to make the important connections necessary to teaching all subjects together in a unified, effective, and memorable way—all while inspiring children to delight in learning.

Linda Fowler is a gifted writer, a creative force making hands-on activities come to life, and the organization behind making all of the various parts of the *Trail Guide to Learning* Series flow together seamlessly. She holds a bachelor's degree in Visual Communications, homeschooled her four children for 17 years through high school, and has developed an unshakeable appreciation for the power of encouragement and the importance of teaching thinking on every level. She now has two married children and is looking forward to sharing her love of life with grandchildren.